TEEJAY PUBLISHERS

Level D Textbook

Produced by members of the TeeJay Writing Group

T. Strang (P.T. Mathematics - Clydebank High School)

J. Geddes (P.T. Mathematics - Renfrew High School)

TeeJay Publishers

P.O. Box 1375
Barrhead
Glasgow
G78 1JJ

Tel: 0141 880 6839

Fax: 0870 124 9189

e-mail: teejaypublishers@ntlworld.com

web page: www.teejaypublishers.co.ok

© TeeJay Publishers 2004
 First Edition published by TeeJay Publishers - January 2004

All rights in this book are reserved. No part of this book may be copied or reproduced in any format, including electronic, without the express permission of the authors in accordance with the Copyright, Design and Patents Act of 1988.

Any person or organisation who makes unauthorised copies of any part of this book may be liable to prosecution and possible civil claims for damages.

Level D Textbook

The book can be used in both Primary and Secondary with pupils who have gained a Level C.

® In secondary schools it can be used to condense the S1/2 Level D course into a **ONE** year course for those pupils who had already gained a National Test level C in Primary or early Secondary.

- It should prepare pupils to sit maths level D national test, **or equivalent**, by the end of Primary 6, 7 or by the end of Secondary 1.

- There are no A and B exercises. It basically covers the **entire Level D course** without the teacher having to pick and choose which questions to leave out and which exercises are important. They all are !

- Unlike other commercial resources out at present or in production, it will cover the important work of level D in ONE textbook.

- It should prove to be an invaluable aid to the "fast tracking" of pupils in S1/2 and allow them to begin their Standard Grade General course (or Credit course - after level E), at some stage throughout S2.

- It contains a 7 page "**Chapter Zero**" which primarily revises every topic at level C and can be used as a diagnostic tool. This could be followed by a diagnostic assessment * of the work of Level C.

- Non-calculator skills will be emphasised and encouraged throughout the book

- Each topic will have a "**Topic in a Nutshell**" exercise as a summary.

- Homework will be available as a photocopiable pack along with an Assessment pack which can be used topic by topic or combined to form a series of level D cumulative Tests.

Pupils should then be able to complete their Standard Grade (or National Qualifications Course) course leisurely by the end of S3 or early in S4.

We make no apologies for the multiplicity of colours used throughout the book, both for text and in diagrams - we feel it helps brighten up the pages !!

Tom Strang and Jim Geddes

(January 2004)

* Diagnostic Assessments for levels B to E included in Homework Pack.

Contents

page

Chapter 0	Quick Revision/Diagnosis of all Level C work	1 - 8
Ch 1 Whole Numbers	Place values and reading scales	9 - 10
	Add/subtract whole numbers	11 - 13
	Multiply/divide decimals by 10, 100	14 - 16
	Multiply/divide by a single digit	17 - 19
	Multiply by 20, 50, 300, 600 etc (E*)	20
	Round to nearest 10, 100	21
	Estimate answers using rounding	22
	Using a calculator	23
	Topic in a Nutshell	24 - 25
Ch 2 Symmetry	Lines of symmetry	26 - 28
	Creating symmetry	29 - 31
	Topic in a Nutshell	32
Ch 3 Decimal Numbers	Working with decimals	33 - 35
	Reading decimal scales	36 - 38
	Rounding to nearest whole number	39 - 40
	Add/subtract decimals	41 - 43
	Topic in a Nutshell	44
Ch 4 Time	12 hour and 24 hour notations	45 - 46
	Small time intervals	47 - 48
	Minutes and seconds	49
	Stopwatches (E*)	50
	Topic in a Nutshell	51
Ch 5 Statistics	Organising/interpreting information	52 - 55
	Line graphs	56 - 58
	Pie charts	59 - 60
	Interpreting tables/databases/spreadsheets	61 - 62
	Topic in a Nutshell	63 - 65
	(Conducting a survey)	65
Ch 6 Decimals 2	Multiply/divide decimals by 10, 100	66 - 67
	Multiply decimals by single digit whole number	68 - 69
	Divide decimals by single digit whole number	70 - 71
	Mixed problems	72 - 73
	Topic in a Nutshell	74
Ch 7 Algebra	Basic "equations"	75 - 77
	Algebraic "equations"	78 - 79
	Function machines	80 - 84
	Topic in a Nutshell	85 - 86
Ch 8 Angles	Types of angles	87 - 88
	Naming angles using 3 letters	88 - 89
	Measuring with a protractor	90 - 91
	Drawing angles	92 - 93
	Calculating missing angles	93 - 94
	Vertically opposite angles	95
	Corresponding/alternate angles (E*)	96 - 97
	Compass points	98 - 99
	3 figure bearings	100-102
	Topic in a Nutshell	103 - 105

Ch 9	Money	The value of money	106
		Adding/subtracting money	107 - 108
		Mixed money problems	110-113
		Topic in a Nutshell	114
Ch 10	2 - Dimensions	2D work	115 - 117
		Triangles and angles	118 - 121
		Tilings using 2-dimensional shapes	122 - 123
		The circle	124 - 125
		Rotating shapes using a template	126
		Topic in a Nutshell	127
Ch 11	Fractions	Identifying fractions	128 - 129
		Equivalent fractions	130 - 131
		Fractions of a quantity	132 - 134
		Topic in a Nutshell	135
Ch 12	Coordinates	Coordinates of a point	136 - 137
		The x and y axes	138 - 140
		Coordinates for fun	140 - 141
		Topic in a Nutshell	142
Ch 13	Percentages	Equivalences - percentages/decimals/fractions	143 - 145
		Simple percentages of quantities (E*)	146
		Topic in a Nutshell	147
Ch 14	Length and Area	Measuring and drawing lengths	148 - 150
		Units of length - converting	151 - 152
		Problems involving lengths	153
		Perimeters	154 - 155
		Areas of rectangles and squares	156-159
		Areas of right angled triangles	160 - 162
		Topic in a Nutshell	163
Ch 15	Patterns	Revision of basic patterns	164 - 166
		Describing number patterns	167 - 168
		Fibonacci and other simple patterns	169 - 170
		Topic in a Nutshell	171
Ch 16	3 - Dimensions	3 dimensional shapes and their properties	172 - 174
		Working with skeletons	175 - 176
		Nets of cubes and cuboids	177 - 178
		Topic in a Nutshell	179
Ch 17	Volume	What is volume ?	180 - 181
		Litres and millilitres	182 - 183
		Volumes by counting cubes	184
		Topic in a Nutshell	185
Ch 18	Revision	Revision of all Level D work	186 - 192
		Answers	

The following questions (pages 1 - 7) cover every topic set at Level C.
(No calculator unless stated)

1. Write the following in words :-

   a 6820   b 9082   c 5007   d 9898.

2. Write the following in figures :-

   a seven thousand two hundred and sixty five

   b nine thousand eight hundred and seven

   c six thousand and fifty.

3. Put the following numbers in order starting with the **largest** :-

   6010,   5995,   5898,   6001,   5989,   6100,   5099.

4. What does the **7** stand for in each of the following :-

   a 60**7**2   b 5**7**91   c **7**508   d 591**7** ?

5. a What is the number that is 50 **up from** 6370 ?

   b What number is 200 **down from** 5150 ?

6. Copy and complete this sentence using the diagram to help.

   $\frac{1}{2} = \frac{?}{4}$

   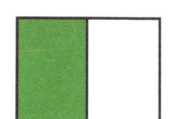 =

7. Find the missing values here :-

   a $\frac{3}{4} = \frac{?}{8}$ b $\frac{8}{10} = \frac{4}{?}$ c $\frac{4}{6} = \frac{?}{3}$.

8. Write $3 + \frac{2}{10} + \frac{7}{100}$ as a decimal.

9. When Alex did a **MONEY** sum on his calculator, the answer 16·8 appeared on the display.

   How much, in money terms, did this really stand for ?

   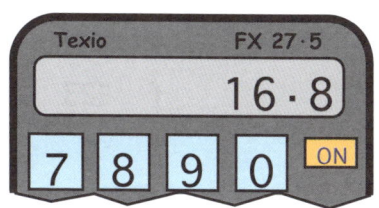

this is Chapter Zero   page 1   REVISION of LEVEL C

10. Write the following in pounds using the £ symbol :-

   a 4 pounds and 18 pence.　　　b 6 pounds and 8 pence.

11. a I bought a magazine for £1·75 and a newspaper for 68p.

   How much change did I receive from a £5 note ?

   b If my change was all in coins, what is the fewest number of coins I could receive ? (*List the coins*).

12. Do the following mentally (**just write down your answers**) :-

   a 7 + 7　　b 38 + 5　　c 99 + 8　　d 139 + 9
   e 250 + 30　f 70 + 340　g 25 − 9　　h 51 − 6
   i 130 − 7　　j 350 − 20　k 410 − 50　l 900 − 70.

13. Copy down the following and find :-

   a 397
      + 64

   b 512
      − 70

   c 600
      − 48

   d 721 − 87.

14. Find the following :- (**you must know your tables by now**).

   a 3 × 7　　b 4 × 8　　c 7 × 6　　d 2 × 9
   e 6 × 6　　f 9 × 8　　g 7 × 8　　h 8 × 6
   i 5 × 7　　j 9 × 7　　k 6 × 9　　l 10 × 7.

15. Do the following mentally (**just write down your answers**) :-

   a 10 × 7　　b 9 × 10　　c 18 × 10　　d 10 × 71
   e 120 × 10　f 10 × 317　g 500 × 10　h 10 × 709.

16. Copy down the following and find :-

   a 17
      × 5

   b 28
      × 7

   c 92
      × 6

   d 39
      × 8

17. Round the following numbers to the nearest 10 :-

   a 63　　b 287　　c 794　　d 498
   e 76　　f 123　　g 166　　h 43.

18. Copy and complete the following by ESTIMATING :-

    "327 + 147"
    is about 330 + ...
    = ...

19. Find :-
    a $\frac{1}{2}$ of 42   b $\frac{1}{3}$ of 24   c $\frac{1}{5}$ of 75   d $\frac{1}{10}$ of 320.

20. Write down the next **3 numbers** in each of the following patterns :-
    a 3, 6, 9, 12, ...   b 5, 10, 15, 20, ...
    c 64, 56, 48, 40, ...   d 3, 7, 11, 15, ...
    e 8, 14, 20, 26, ...   f 50, 47, 44, 41, ...

21. Copy the following function machines and calculate the values of the missing numbers.

    a    b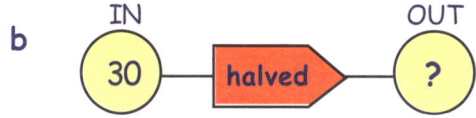

    c    d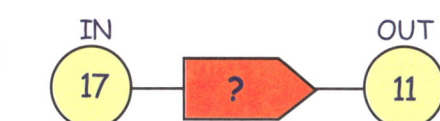

22. How many grams are in :-
    a 1 kg   b 3 kg   c $\frac{1}{4}$ kg   d $1\frac{1}{2}$ kg ?

23. Estimate the volume of liquid in this jug (**in litres**).

24. Write down the areas of these 2 shapes (**in cm²**).

    a 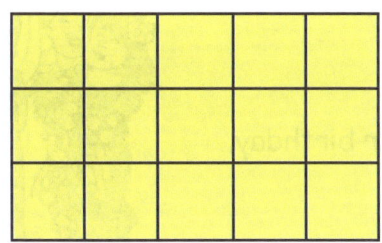   b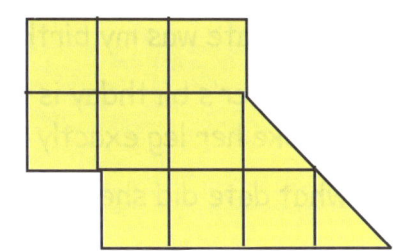

this is Chapter Zero   page 3   REVISION of LEVEL C

25. The height of the classroom door is about :–

$\frac{1}{2}$ m,   1 m,   2 m,   5 m,   10 m   — **Which one ?**

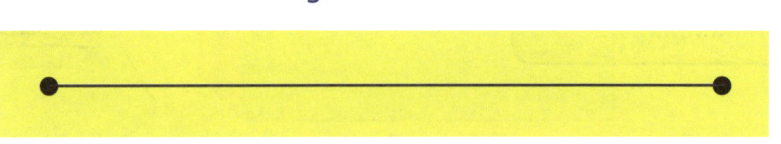

26. A good estimate for the length of this line is :–

2 cm,   5 cm,   10 cm,   20 cm — **Which one ?**

27. What numbers are represented by the arrows shown below ?

a 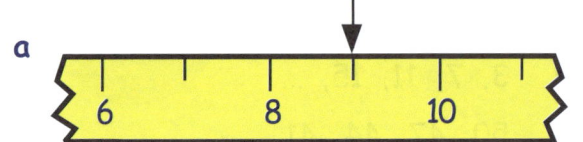   b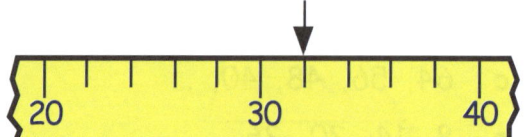

c 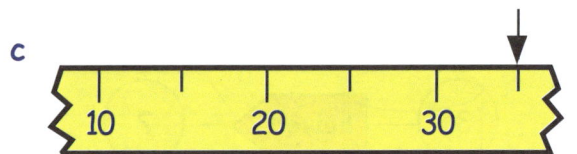   d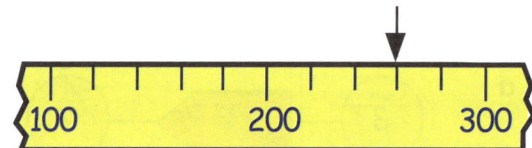

28. 2·50 pm means **10 to 3 in the afternoon**.
Write the following times in a similar way :–

   a   3·35 am   b   8·40 pm   c   12·45 am.

29. How long is it from :–

   a   7 am till 9 am   b   6·25 pm till 6·45 pm

   c   10 to 5 till 20 past 5   d   11·40 am till 12·25 pm ?

30. 2nd May 1987 can be written as 02.05.87.
Write down the following in the same way :–

   a   15th January 1968   b   22nd November 1999   c   7th August 2002.

31. a   My wedding anniversary was on the 25th June.
My birthday was 10 days later.

On what date was my birthday ?

   b   My daughter's birthday is on 3rd December.
She broke her leg exactly 1 week before her birthday.

On what date did she break her leg ?

this is Chapter Zero   REVISION of LEVEL C

32. Name the following mathematical shapes :-

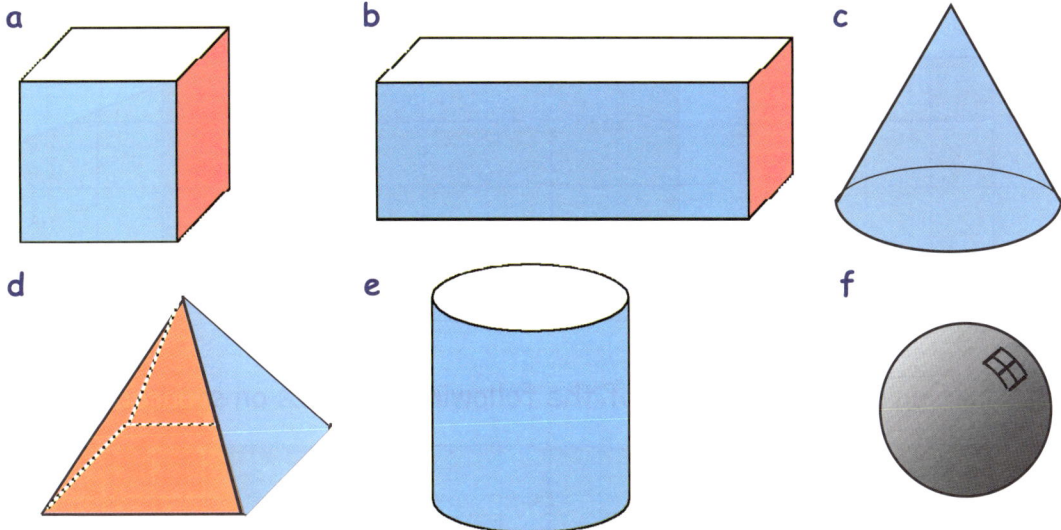

33. Name the blue shape in each of the following :-

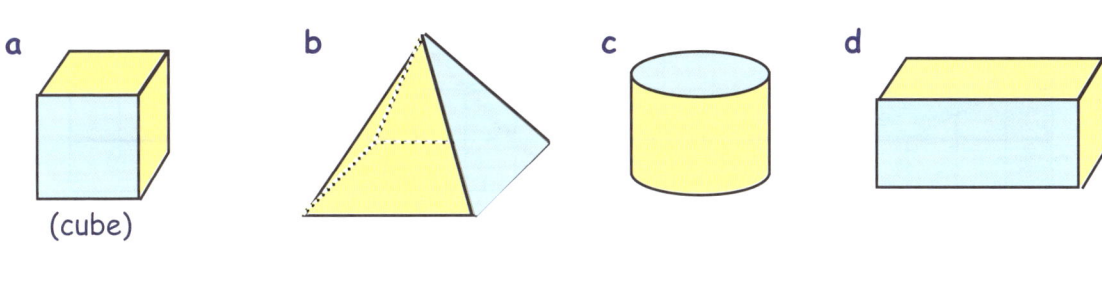

(cube)

34. Use a pair of compasses to draw a full size circle which has a radius of 4 cm.

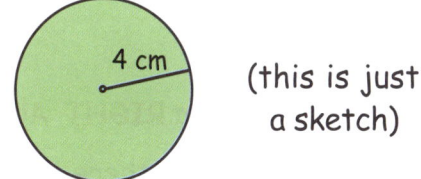

4 cm   (this is just a sketch)

35. You meet a man when you are in the bank.

He asks directions to the Post Office.

Describe clearly what directions you would give him.
(from inside the bank)

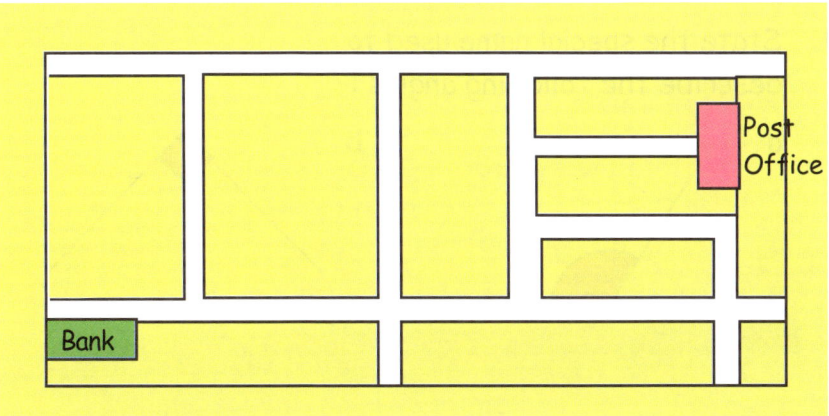

this is Chapter Zero   page 5   REVISION of LEVEL C

36. Make a neat copy of these shapes.
    Mark, in colour or as a dotted line, the lines of symmetry.

    a 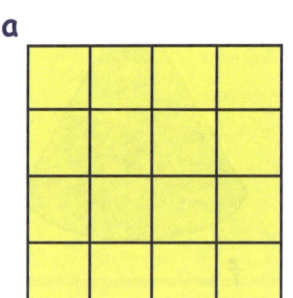   b    c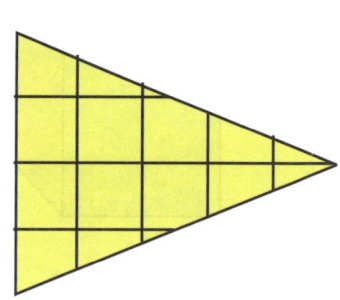

37. a   Make an accurate drawing of the following 2 shapes on squared paper.

    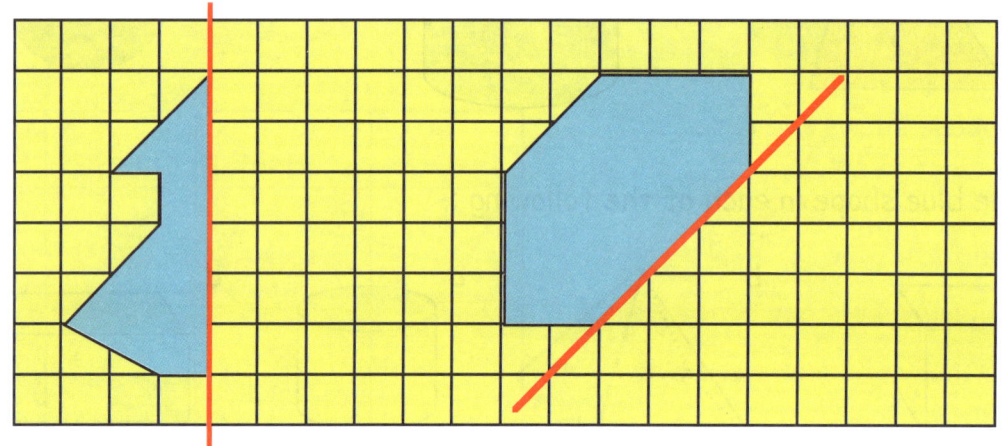

    b   Complete the missing half of each shape so that the red lines
        are lines of symmetry.

38. This diagram shows a RIGHT ANGLE.

    How many degrees are there in a right angle ?

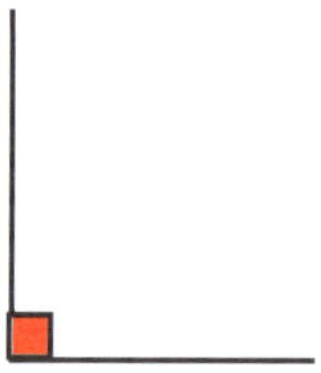

39. State the special name used to
    describe the following angles :-

    a 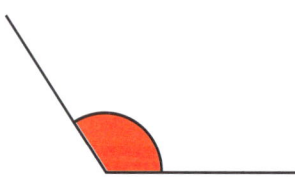   b 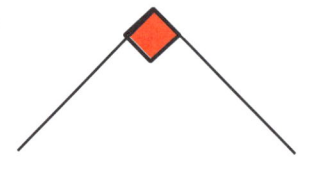   c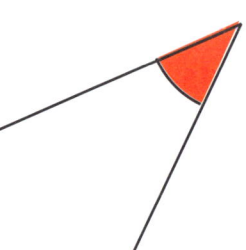

40. Calculate the size of the red shaded
    angle in this figure.
    (Do NOT measure it)

    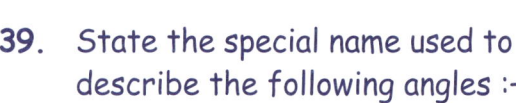

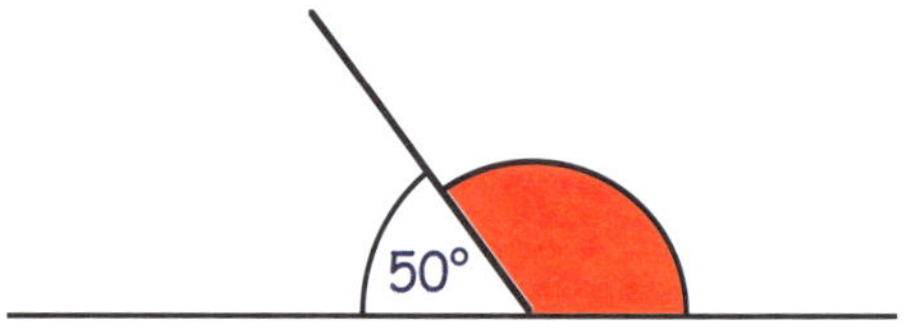

this is Chapter Zero   page 6   REVISION of LEVEL C

41. A group of people were asked to name their favourite fruit.

apple	banana	banana	orange	orange
orange	apple	banana	pear	banana
grapes	pear	banana	orange	apple
apple	banana	apple	banana	pear
grapes	orange	banana	apple	banana

Fruit	Tally Marks	Number
apple		
orange	COPY	
banana		
pear		
grapes		

a Copy the table and use tally marks to fill in the 2nd column

b Complete the table by filling in the 3rd column in your table.

42. The database shows the results of a survey of the name, hair colour, eye colour and height of seven children.

Name	Hair	Eyes	Height
Tom	brown	blue	1·45 m
Lucy	brown	blue	1·38 m
Jane	blonde	brown	1·51 m
Steve	red	blue	1·61 m
Nick	black	grey	1·54 m
Alan	brown	green	1·57 m
Brian	blonde	grey	1·49 m

a How many boys had brown hair ?

b How many children were over 1·5 metres tall ?

c How tall was the boy with brown hair and green eyes ?

d How would you describe Lucy in words ?

43. Children were asked to name their favourite breakfast cereal.

Cereal	Corn Flakes	Frosties	Sugar Puffs	Weetabix	Rice Crispies
Number	12	20	16	6	10

Use a ruler to draw a (**VERY NEAT**) bar graph using the scale shown below and **label** your diagram.

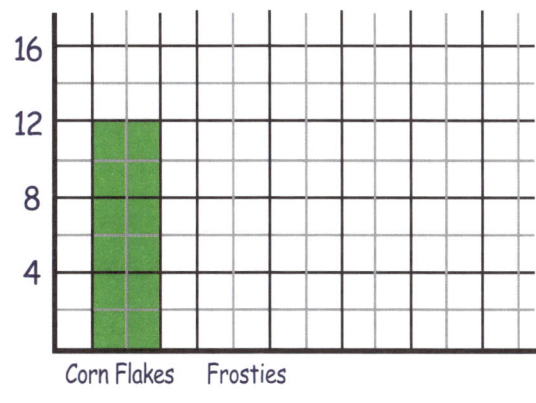

this is Chapter Zero   page 7   REVISION of LEVEL C

Chapter 1

Place Values

Calculators should NOT be used anywhere in this chapter except in the final exercise.

Whole Numbers

Example :-

In the number 2436,

the 2 stands for two thousand   2000
the 4 stands for four hundred   400
the 3 stands for three tens   30
the 6 stands for six units   6
                               2436

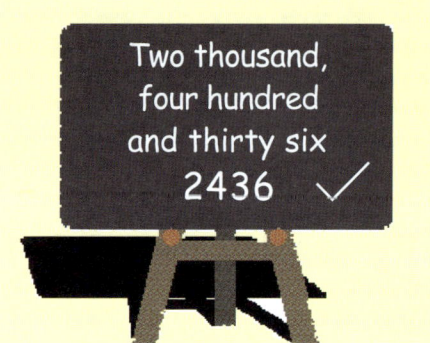

Two thousand, four hundred and thirty six
2436 ✓

Exercise 1

1. What do the following **digits** stand for in the number 3471 :-

   a 3   b 4   c 7   d 1 ?

2. What does the **5** stand for in each of these numbers :-

   a 5741   b 8750   c 9875   d 1599 ?

3. Write the following numbers out fully **in words** :-

   a 3870   b 9051   c 12 045   d 20 040
   e 120 427   f 800 350   g 702 050   h 909 090.

4. Write the following numbers **using digits** :-

   a nine hundred and ten.
   b twenty thousand and fifty.
   c sixty thousand and six.
   d one hundred thousand and one.
   e nine hundred and nine thousand.
   f one hundred and eleven thousand and eleven.
   g one million.

5. Put the following sets of numbers in order, **smallest first** :-

   a 460, 406, 399, 501, 451, 510, 401, 603, 499.
   b 8045, 8100, 7999, 8054, 8109, 8200, 8199, 9001.

this is Chapter One   page 8   WHOLE NUMBERS

6. Write down the number that is :-
   a 10 after 760
   b 200 after 880
   c 70 before 950
   d 300 before 5390
   e 2000 after 7999
   f 1000 before 8700
   g 4500 after 3500
   h 4000 before 5250.
   i 8700 before 9900.
   j four hundred and thirty after three thousand nine hundred.
   k two thousand five hundred before five thousand six hundred.
   l two thousand nine hundred before nine thousand.

7. Look at the following scales. What numbers are represented by the letters A, B, C, …

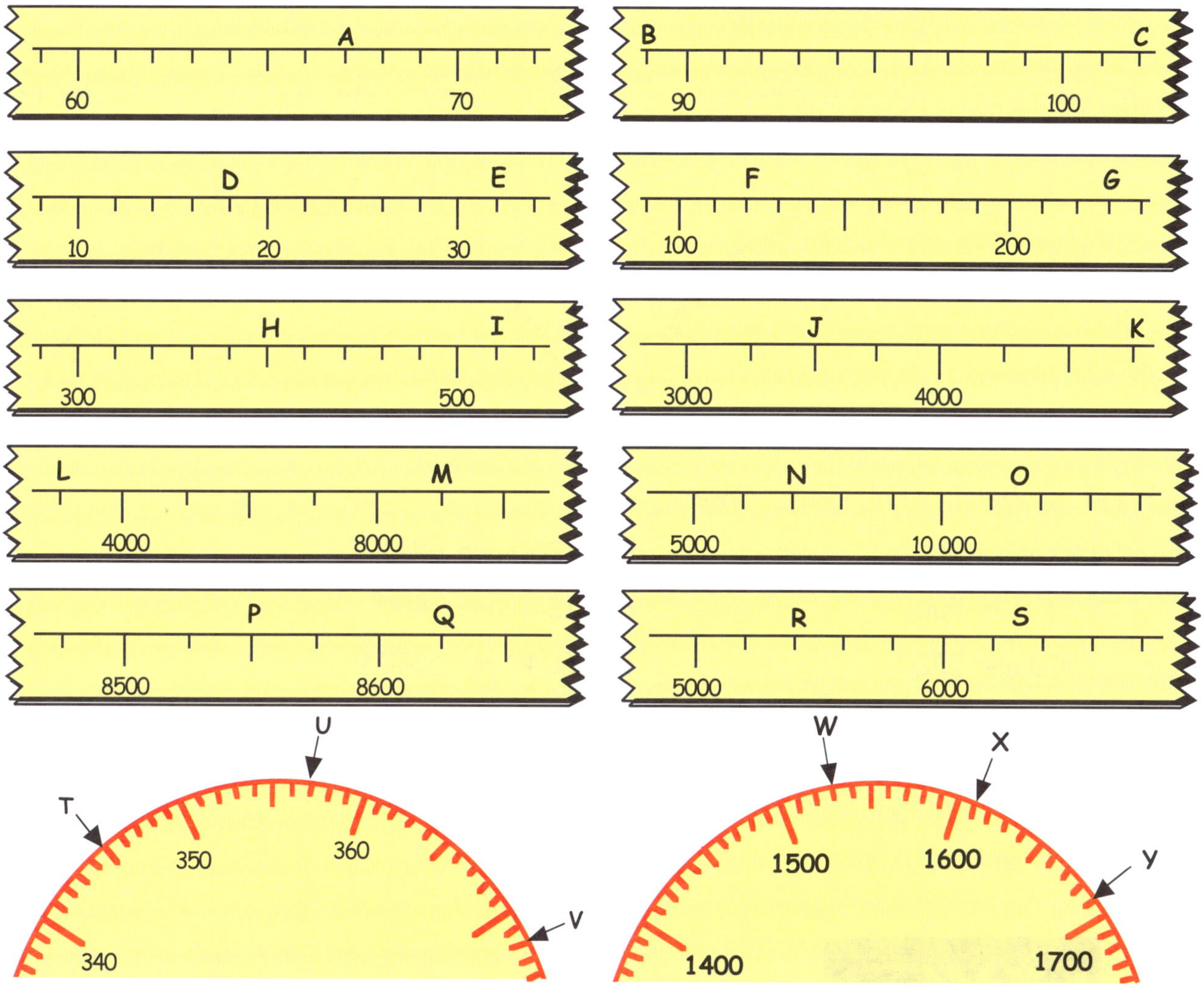

8. What are the readings on these thermometers :-

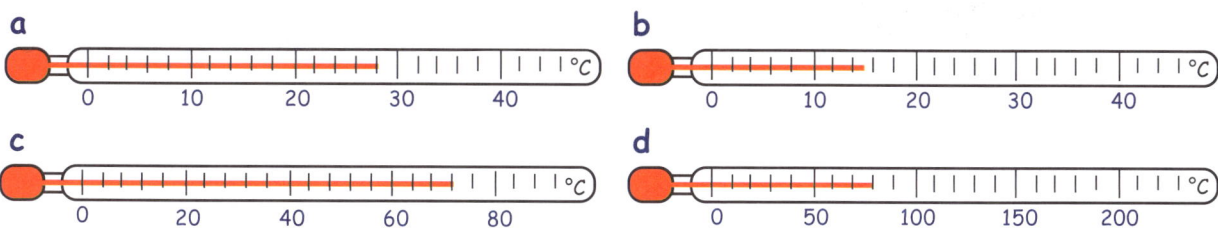

9. **(Harder)** - Write down the numbers that are represented by each letter :-

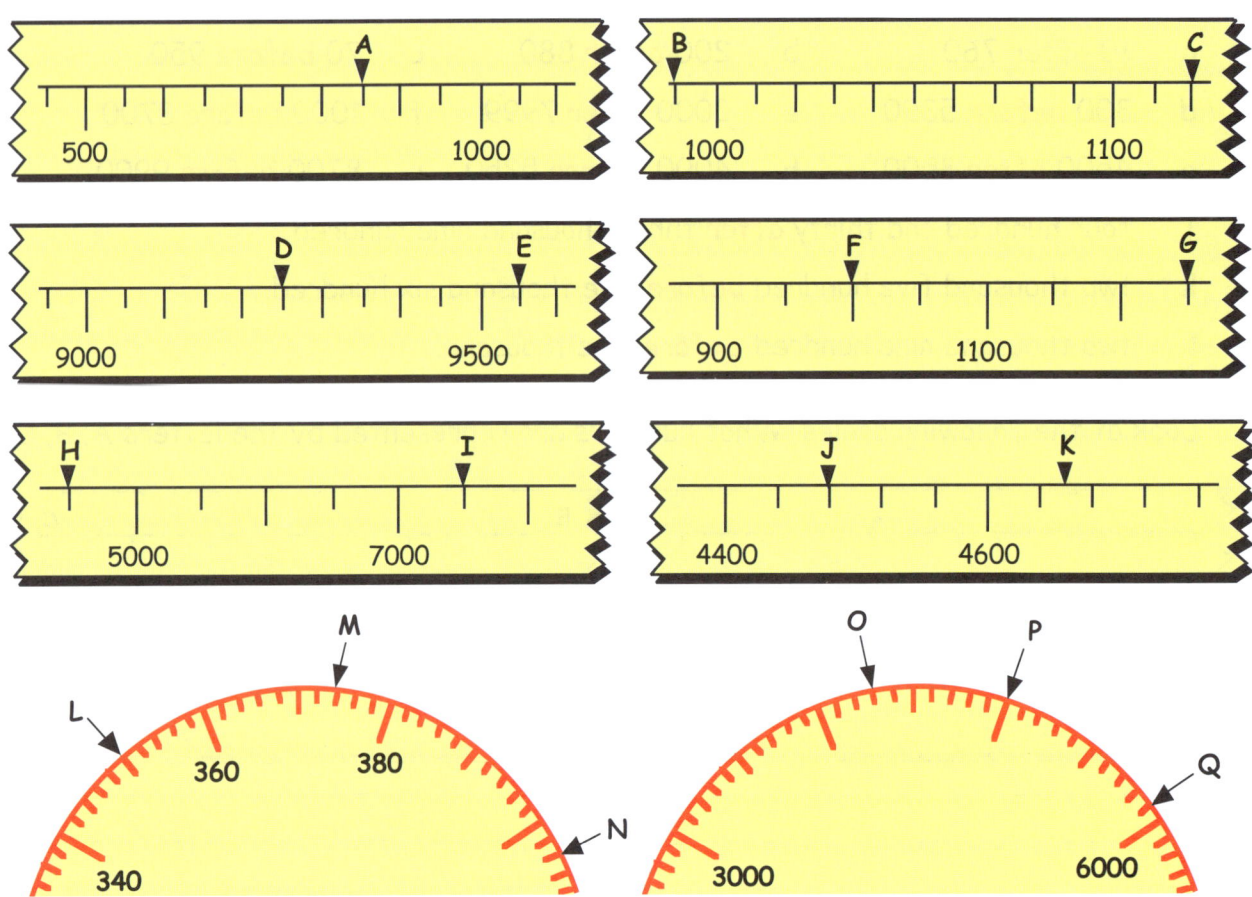

10. What number lies **half-way** between :-
    a   140 and 150
    b   1200 and 1400
    c   5200 and 5600
    d   1800 and 2400
    e   4300 and 5300
    f   6040 and 6140 ?

11. The average **(mean)** of 2 numbers always lies **half-way** between the 2 numbers.
    What is the average of :-
    a   1200 and 1500
    b   180 and 220 ?

12.  Space Probe A travelled 8600 km.
    Space Probe B travelled 9200 km.
    Space Probe C ended up halfway between A and B.

    What distance was travelled by Space Probe C ?

13. A rich businessman donates half a million dollars to charity.
    Write out this amount in full.

this is Chapter One   page 10   WHOLE NUMBERS

Add/Subtract Whole Numbers

There are **quick ways** of adding and subtracting numbers.

Example :-   To add 390 and 540,

Discuss these and other methods.

you could add
390 + 500 = 890
then add   40
                930

OR

you could add
400 + 540 = 940,
then subtract   10
                930.

Exercise 2

Try to do this exercise mentally.

1. Write down the answers to :-

   a 39 + 54   b 62 + 49   c 39 + 25   d 57 + 38
   e 75 + 45   f 69 + 64   g 125 + 77   h 90 + 49
   i 260 + 190   j 390 + 520   k 270 + 630   l 720 + 990
   m 3400 + 4300   n 2600 + 2400   o 3900 + 1700   p 7450 + 1950.

2. Write down the answers to :-

   a 67 – 54   b 54 – 29   c 77 – 58   d 31 – 18
   e 70 – 35   f 74 – 55   g 100 – 37   h 190 – 39
   i 260 – 190   j 490 – 220   k 370 – 190   l 620 – 490
   m 1900 – 650   n 3700 – 1100   o 7700 – 4900   p 10 000 – 2900.

3. Find :-

   a 470 + 750   b 1720 – 580   c 4350 + 2900   d 5840 – 3110
   e 4320 + 4580   f 9990 – 1190   g 1860 + 3240   h 8760 – 1650.

4. a A train with 87 passengers stops at a station.
      At the station 44 people get on the train.

      How many are there now on the train ?

   b The garage charged Mr Benson £145 for parts and £88 for labour.
      How much was Mr. Benson's **total** garage bill ?

   c Jamie earned £960 per month and Josie earned £790.

      (i) How much did they earn **altogether** ?

      (ii) How much **more** did Jamie earn than Josie ?

d Of the 3100 miles from London to New York, a plane had flown 1900 miles.

How much **further** had it to travel ?

e  Patrick won £2000 in the pub lottery. He bought a new laptop for £1390.

How much had Patrick left ?

f Stacy has 4200 stamps in her collection. Two thousand four hundred of them are foreign.

How many stamps in her collection are **not** foreign ?

g Last year, Marie sent 2450 text messages. This year she sent 3140 messages.

(i) How many text messages has Marie sent **in total** ?

(ii) How many **more** messages did she send this year ?

Exercise 3

Show all your working for this exercise.

1. Copy the following and find the answers :-

	a	362 + 177	b	579 + 247	c	296 + 466	d	789 + 321
	e	836 − 176	f	4009 + 2678	g	2345 + 4678	h	5762 − 4876
	i	1000 − 763	j	7777 + 1333	k	9067 − 4568	l	10000 − 7209

m 6479 + 372   n 1234 + 7777   o 8519 − 6621   p 6000 − 296

q 4902 + 2199   r 5002 − 2893   s 9617 + 295   t 10 000 − 7891

2. **a** There were 4372 Hibs Supporters and 3986 Hearts supporters at the local derby match.

(i) How many supporters were there **altogether** ?

(ii) How many **more** Hibs than Hearts supporters were there ?

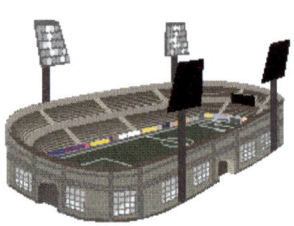

b From 6 a.m. to 6 p.m. a train travels 748 kilometres.
From 6 p.m. to midnight it travels 269 kilometres.

How far has the train travelled **in total**?

c  A secretary earned £9240 last year.
This year her pay **dropped** by £1360.

What was her salary this year?

d The local newspaper prints 10 000 copies per week.
The paper sold 8768 copies last week.

How many copies were **not** sold?

e  A judge fines a man £1750 for breach
of the peace **plus** £2350 damages.

How much in total did the man have to pay?

f Davie bought 3500 bricks to build a wall.
When he had finished, he found he had 976
bricks **left over**.

How many bricks had he used to build the wall?

Puzzle 1

Any line of three numbers on each diagram below must total 15.
Copy and complete each diagram using the numbers 1 to 9.

a 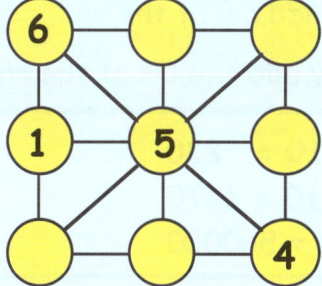 **b**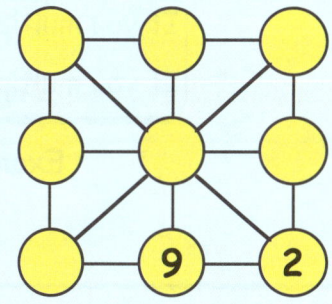

Puzzle 2

Using a 4 litre and a 5 litre jug and no
other measuring device, explain how it is
possible to measure out exactly 3 litres
of water from a well.

this is Chapter One   page 13   WHOLE NUMBERS

Multiply and Divide Whole Numbers

For this, you **really must know your tables**.
Learn them NOW - **they are a must !!**

2 x 2 = 4	3 x 2 = 6	4 x 2 = 8	5 x 2 = 10
2 x 3 = 6	3 x 3 = 9	4 x 3 = 12	5 x 3 = 15
2 x 4 = 8	3 x 4 = 12	4 x 4 = 16	5 x 4 = 20
2 x 5 = 10	3 x 5 = 15	4 x 5 = 20	5 x 5 = 25
2 x 6 = 12	3 x 6 = 18	4 x 6 = 24	5 x 6 = 30
2 x 7 = 14	3 x 7 = 21	4 x 7 = 28	5 x 7 = 35
2 x 8 = 16	3 x 8 = 24	4 x 8 = 32	5 x 8 = 40
2 x 9 = 18	3 x 9 = 27	4 x 9 = 36	5 x 9 = 45
6 x 2 = 12	7 x 2 = 14	8 x 2 = 16	9 x 2 = 18
6 x 3 = 18	7 x 3 = 21	8 x 3 = 24	9 x 3 = 27
6 x 4 = 24	7 x 4 = 28	8 x 4 = 32	9 x 4 = 36
6 x 5 = 30	7 x 5 = 35	8 x 5 = 40	9 x 5 = 45
6 x 6 = 36	7 x 6 = 42	8 x 6 = 48	9 x 6 = 54
6 x 7 = 42	7 x 7 = 49	8 x 7 = 56	9 x 7 = 63
6 x 8 = 48	7 x 8 = 56	8 x 8 = 64	9 x 8 = 72
6 x 9 = 54	7 x 9 = 63	8 x 9 = 72	9 x 9 = 81

Multiplication by 10 and 100

Learn these rules :

Simple rules for whole numbers :-

If you multiply by 10, simply add a 0 at the end.
If you multiply by 100, simply add two 0's at the end.

Examples   23 x 10 =   23**0**
147 x 10 = 147**0**
5600 x 100 = 5600**00**

Exercise 4

1. Write down the answers to the following :-

a 22 x 10	b 12 x 10	c 17 x 10	d 10 x 34
e 10 x 176	f 406 x 10	g 10 x 755	h 10 x 130
i 450 x 10	j 101 x 10	k 10 x 140	l 1472 x 10
m 1507 x 10	n 2300 x 10	o 4500 x 10	p 10 x 6000

this is Chapter One   page 14   WHOLE NUMBERS

2. Write down the answers to the following :-
   a 23 × 100   b 76 × 100   c 100 × 137   d 100 × 140
   e 290 × 100   f 100 × 706   g 100 × 309   h 340 × 100
   i 700 × 100   j 100 × 450   k 100 × 5010   l 8000 × 100

3. Write down the answers to these :-
   a 1700 × 10   b 210 × 100   c 360 × 10   d 100 × 310
   e 10 × 800   f 4500 × 100   g 1000 × 10   h 2000 × 100

4. A crate holds 100 bottles.
   How many bottles are there in :-
   a 16 crates   b 40 crates
   c 165 crates   d 800 crates ?

5. There are 100 centimetres in 1 metre. How many centimetres are there in :-
   a 3 m   b 72 m   c 107 m   d 200 m ?

6. There are 10 millimetres in 1 centimetre. How many millimetres are there in :-
   a 7 cm   b 50 cm   c 301 cm   d 7000 cm ?

Division by 10 and 100

Learn these rules

Simple rules for whole numbers :-

If you divide by 10, simply remove last 0

If you divide by 100, simply remove last **two** 0's

Examples   790 ÷ 10 = 79
           8700 ÷ 100 = 87
           43000 ÷ 100 = 430

Exercise 5

1. Write down the answers to the following :-
   a 240 ÷ 10   b 920 ÷ 10   c 770 ÷ 10   d 3210 ÷ 10
   e 1400 ÷ 10   f 3800 ÷ 10   g 4000 ÷ 10   h 2200 ÷ 10
   i 60 000 ÷ 10   j 99 000 ÷ 10   k 10 000 ÷ 10   l 105 500 ÷ 10
   m 88 500 ÷ 10   n 65 000 ÷ 10   o 70 000 ÷ 10   p 120 000 ÷ 10

2. Write down the answers to the following :-
   a 400 ÷ 100   b 2500 ÷ 100   c 7100 ÷ 100   d 39 000 ÷ 100
   e 90 000 ÷ 100 f 35 500 ÷ 100 g 205 000 ÷ 100 h 1 000 000 ÷ 100

3. Write down the answers to these :-
   a 7000 ÷ 100   b 2000 ÷ 10   c 54 000 ÷ 100   d 3500 ÷ 10
   e 3500 ÷ 100   f 1000 ÷ 10   g 1000 ÷ 100   h 100 ÷ 100

4. A ship's cargo hold can carry 100 cars.
   How many similar ships are needed to carry :-
   a 700 cars   b 9000 cars
   c 12 000 cars d 100 000 cars ?

5. There are **100 centimetres** in **1 metre**. How many **metres** are there in :-
   a 7000 cm   b 12 000 cm   c 160 000 cm   d 1 000 000 cm ?

6. There are **10 millimetres** in **1 centimetre** and **100 centimetres** in **1 metre**.
   How many **metres** are equivalent to :-
   a 700 cm   b 600 000 cm   c 5000 mm   d 80 000 mm ?

Puzzle 3

There are 10 millimetres in one centimetre, 100 centimetres in one metre and 1000 metres in one kilometre.

How many millimetres are there in one kilometre ?

Puzzle 4

A truck can carry 4 tonnes of waste.

a How many trips will the truck need to make to carry 67 tonnes of waste ?

b How many tonnes will it be carrying on its last trip ?

Puzzle 5

From base   Tank A travelled 360 km West.
            Tank B travelled 150 km East.
            Tank C moved to a position exactly halfway between Tank A and Tank B.

            How far and in what direction did Tank C travel ?

Multiplication by a Single Digit

This is where knowing your tables really pays off !

Examples :-

Find   a   26 × 7   b   387 × 4   c   3276 × 8

a
```
  26
×  7
---
 182
  4
```

b
```
 387
×  4
---
1548
 3 2
```

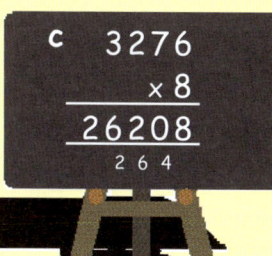
c
```
 3276
×   8
----
26208
 2 6 4
```

Exercise 6

1. Copy the following and complete the calculations :-

   a 34 × 3   b 27 × 4   c 63 × 7   d 44 × 4

   e 126 × 8   f 245 × 6   g 208 × 5   h 192 × 9

   i 1252 × 4   j 3619 × 7   k 8004 × 9   l 9138 × 8

2. Rewrite each of these in the above form and complete the calculations :-

   a 67 × 8   b 84 × 7   c 6 × 93   d 29 × 5
   e 8 × 123   f 7 × 222   g 709 × 8   h 3 × 986
   i 4 × 2462   j 5 × 2222   k 1967 × 7   l 9 × 9067

3. Show your working in answering the following questions :-

   a Madge pays £24 **each month** for her mobile phone.
      How much will she have paid after **6 months** ?

   b Shona pays £18 **each week** to reduce her catalogue account ?
      How much had she paid after **8 weeks** ?

   c If there are **sixty minutes** in **one hour**, how many minutes are there in **9 hours** ?

d Chaz has filled 6 photograph albums. **Each** album contains 217 photographs. How many photographs does Chaz have?

e A Teejay maths book contains 256 pages. How many pages would be needed for
  (i) 3 books   (ii) 9 books?

f Find the value of
  (i) 2 × 5 × 34
  (ii) 3 × 46 × 4
  (iii) 6 × 7 × 43.

Division by a Single Digit

Again, knowing your tables is a must!

Examples :-

Find   a 36 ÷ 4   b 168 ÷ 7   c 5856 ÷ 8

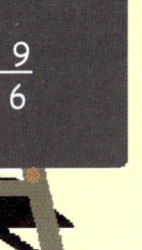

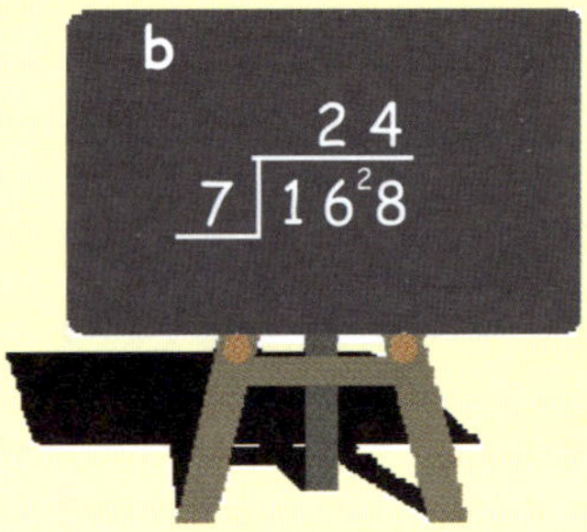

Exercise 7

1. Copy the following and complete each calculation :-

   a 7)35   b 5)925   c 6)744   d 8)520

   e 6)6486   f 4)9008   g 7)8764   h 9)8964

2. Set the following down in the same way as above and complete each calculation :-

   a 72 ÷ 6   b 472 ÷ 2   c 465 ÷ 3   d 801 ÷ 9

   e 728 ÷ 7   f 6315 ÷ 5   g 8708 ÷ 4   h 6561 ÷ 3

   i 1197 ÷ 9   j $\dfrac{6035}{5}$ k $\dfrac{1821}{3}$ l 4134 ÷ 6

   m $\dfrac{9072}{8}$ n 2219 ÷ 7   o $\dfrac{8892}{9}$ p $\dfrac{8806}{7}$

this is Chapter One   page 18   WHOLE NUMBERS

3. Show **all** your working in solving the following :-

   a   A bar of chocolate has 9 squares.

       How many bars are there if there are 702 squares ?

   b   A packet contains 8 biscuits.

       How many packets are needed for 3384 biscuits ?

   c   Six people share equally a prize of £2274.

       How much will each receive ?

   d   A freezer container holds 6 ice cubes.

       How many containers are needed for 774 cubes ?

   e   Find the answer to   (i)   9436 ÷ 4 ÷ 7

                            (ii) 6 × 845 ÷ 5.

Not all divisions work out exactly !!
6 is called the remainder.

$$\begin{array}{r} 823 \text{ r } 6 \\ 9\overline{)7\,4^{2}1^{3}3} \end{array}$$

---

4. Find the remainder each time here :-

   a   2)7135   b   5)2314   c   7)4062   d   4)3143

   e   513 ÷ 8   f   2715 ÷ 6   g   4317 ÷ 9   h   6134 ÷ 10

   i $\dfrac{4444}{6}$ j $\dfrac{1827}{8}$ k $\dfrac{3143}{5}$ l $\dfrac{6172}{3}$

5. A bag containing 135 pennies is **shared equally** amongst 8 children.

   a   How many pennies will each child receive ?

   b   How many coins are left over ?

6.

    The 627 **five** pence pieces contained in a large piggy-bank are **shared equally** amongst 6 people.

    a   How many coins will each person receive ?

    b   How many coins are left over ?

        One person changes his money into one pence pieces.

    c   How many coins does this person have now ?

Multiplication by Multiples of 10 or 100.

Multiplication by 20, 300, etc.

To multiply by 20, or 300, do so using two steps.

        Step 1   =>   multiply by the 10 or 100 first

        Step 2   =>   then multiply by the 2, 3, 4 etc.

Examples :-

To multiply 763 x 20
Step 1   Find 763 x 10 = 7630
Step 2   Now find
$$\begin{array}{r}7630\\ \times\ 2\\ \hline 15\,260\end{array}$$

To multiply 315 x 400
Step 1   Find 315 x 100 = 31 500
Step 2   Now find
$$\begin{array}{r}31\,500\\ \times\ 4\\ \hline 126\,000\end{array}$$

Exercise 8

1. Try to do the following **mentally** :-   (*use the 2-step approach*)

    a 21 x 20   b 31 x 30   c 12 x 40   d 32 x 60

    e 20 x 25   f 30 x 103   g 50 x 60   h 60 x 40

    i 80 x 70   j 30 x 203   k 20 x 613   l 90 x 410

2. Calculate each of the following (*not necessarily mentally*) :-

    a 341 x 40   [Find 10 x 341 first = 341**0** and then find 3410 x 4]

    b 723 x 60   c 509 x 90   d 278 x 70   e 480 x 30

    f 923 x 70   g 498 x 20   h 316 x 80   i 278 x 90

3. Calculate each of the following :-

    a 254 x 200   [Find 254 x 100 first = 254**00** and then find 25 400 x 2]

    b 269 x 300   c 208 x 400   d 836 x 500

    e 410 x 900   f 869 x 600   g 927 x 700

    h 987 x 800   i 567 x 900   j 999 x 900

Rounding to nearest 10 and 100

To round to the nearest 10 look at the **units** digit :-

12<u>7</u> —> **130**
- if it is a 0, 1, 2, 3 or 4 - leave the 10's digit as it is.
- if it is a 5, 6, 7, 8 or 9 - round the 10's digit up by one.

To round to the nearest 100 look at the **tens** digit :-

13<u>3</u>8 —> **1300**
- if it is a 0, 1, 2, 3 or 4 - leave the 100's digit as it is.
- if it is a 5, 6, 7, 8 or 9 - round the 100's digit up by one.

Exercise 9

1. Round to the **nearest 10** :-
   - a   79
   - b   32
   - c   86
   - d   55
   - e   9
   - f   212
   - g   374
   - h   781
   - i   19
   - j   405
   - k   847
   - l   599
   - m   1871
   - n   2605
   - o   8729
   - p   3999.

2. Round to the **nearest 100** :-
   - a   571
   - b   963
   - c   417
   - d   349
   - e   251
   - f   549
   - g   1629
   - h   3071
   - i   8809
   - j   6491
   - k   6055
   - l   8981
   - m   12 240
   - n   16 872
   - o   19 895
   - p   9988.

3. A Junior Football Cup Final between Arthurlie and Pollock had an attendance of 8754.

   Round this figure to the nearest :-
   - a   10
   - b   100

4.

   The local paper sold 9957 copies.

   Round this figure to the nearest :-
   - a   10
   - b   100.

5. A survey showed that in one day, twenty nine thousand nine hundred and fifty three vehicles passed over a busy road bridge.

   Round this figure to the nearest :-
   - a   10
   - b   100.

Using Rounding to Estimate Answers

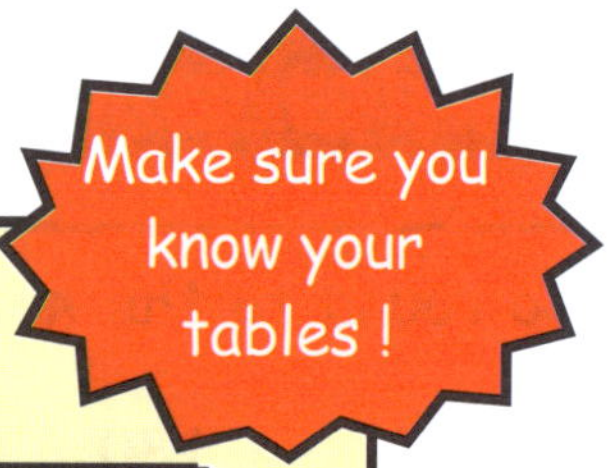

Make sure you know your tables !

It is possible to "**MENTALLY**" estimate the answer to a question by rounding the numbers to "**1 figure**" accuracy first.

Examples :-

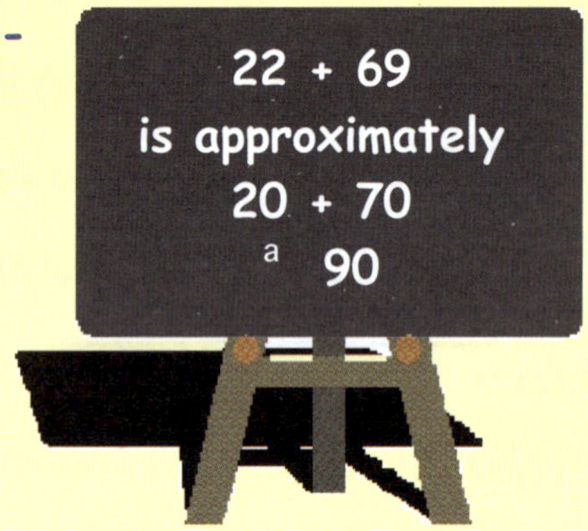

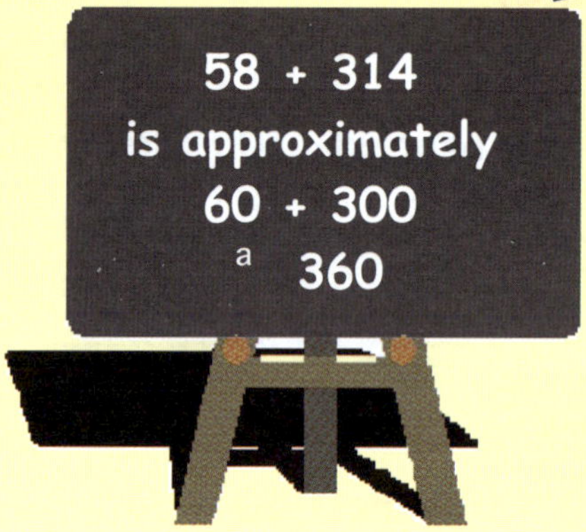

22 + 69
is approximately
20 + 70
≈ 90

58 + 314
is approximately
60 + 300
≈ 360

"≈" approximately equal to.

Exercise 10

1. Round each number to **1 figure accuracy**, then give an **estimate** to :-

   a   19 + 42   b   31 + 48   c   26 + 43   d   58 + 33
   e   93 + 19   f   89 + 43   g   98 + 49   h   58 + 88
   i   109 + 39   j   192 + 29   k   208 + 38   l   58 + 314
   m   589 + 73   n   391 + 43   o   411 + 291   p   422 + 488

2. a   Jack has 194 Jinju cards, Paul has 88.

      Approximately, how many do they have in total ?

   Yoshi   Tishu

   b   Maggie has saved £196. Lisa has saved £312.

      Approximately, how much have they saved in total ?

   c   Calculate, **approximately**, the perimeter of the rectangle shown.

   59 cm
   28 cm

3. Give an **approximate** answer to each of the following :-

   a   77 – 39   b   99 – 41   c   316 – 96   d   507 – 190
   e   913 – 479   f   788 – 512   g   821 – 697   h   781 – 59

4. Round each number to **1 figure accuracy**, then give an **estimate** to :-

   a   38 + 31 + 29   b   198 + 314 + 289   c   59 + 789 + 99   d   612 + 304 + 179
   e   12 × 9   f   67 × 9   g   31 × 99   h   316 × 98

this is Chapter One   page 22   WHOLE NUMBERS

Using a Calculator

Exercise 11

You may use a calculator for this exercise.

1. Calculate :-

   a 162 + 49   b 316 + 78   c 426 + 243   d 578 + 833
   e 3793 + 1923   f 4589 + 1243   g 9458 + 4679   h 1058 + 7688
   i 107 − 39   j 232 − 179   k 7208 − 4798   l 9858 − 7989
   m 89 × 14   n 39 × 43   o 153 × 176   p 87 × 208
   q 1751 ÷ 17   r 3128 ÷ 23   s 32 778 ÷ 54   t 960 × 12 ÷ 18

2. a A car travels 276 kilometres of a 750 kilometre journey.

   How far has the car still to travel ?

   b    Jack grows a 197 metre high beanstalk.
   The beanstalk needs to grow another
   154 m to reach the giant.

   How high in total does the beanstalk
   need to be to reach the giant ?

   c A case of 12 bottles of champagne costs £444.

   How much does 1 bottle cost ?

   d    An airport runway has width 35 metres
   and length 2875 metres.

   Calculate the perimeter of the runway.

   e A Noodle Pot weighs 89 grams.

   Calculate the weight of 12 Pots.

   f    A garage can buy a 50 litre drum
   of Super Oil for £63.

   How much would it cost for 6 drums ?

   g The perimeter of a rectangle is 366 centimetres.

   (i) If the length is 74 cm, calculate the breadth.

   (ii) Calculate the area (length × breadth).

this is Chapter One   page 23   WHOLE NUMBERS

Topic in a Nutshell

1. Write out the number 9318 fully **in words**.

2. Write these numbers **using digits** :-
   a   eight thousand seven hundred and sixty one.
   b   forty two thousand and ten.

3. Rearrange the numbers given below in order, starting with the **largest**.
   3039   4090   4101   3992   4001   4010.

4. a   What numbers are represented by P, Q, R and S on the given scales?

   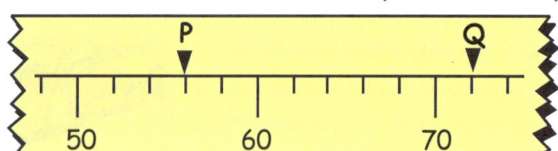   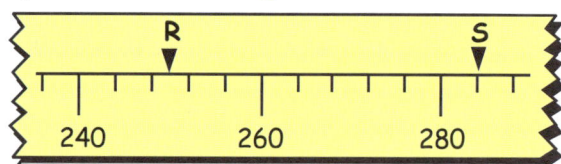

   b   What is the reading on this thermometer?

   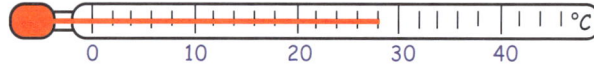

5. What number lies **halfway** between :-
   a   1300 and 1700 ?   b   370 and 430 ?

6. Do the following mentally (**no working should be seen**) :-
   a   59 + 77   b   138 + 99   c   2700 + 3300   d   83 − 29
   e   1700 − 250   f   10 000 − 5700 g   9999 + 1200   h   5000 − 62.

7. Try this question **mentally** :-
   A bus leaves the station with 27 passengers.
   At the first stop 10 people get off and 5 people get on.
   At the second stop 7 people get off and 14 people get on.
   How many passengers were on the bus when it left the second stop?

   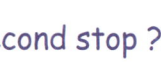

8. Set down the following and show your working :-
   a   5264   b   6327 − 1851   c   7896   d   10000
       + 2927   + 999   − 2947

9. Attempt these problems, showing all working :-

a A train carried 1479 passengers from Glasgow to London. On the return journey there were 1592 passengers.

What was the total number of passengers on both trips ?

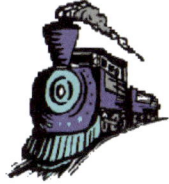

b A shopkeeper buys televisions at £265 each.

How much would it cost him for 9 televisions ?

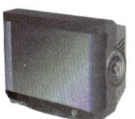

c Brad can process 2765 forms in a five day week.

How many forms does he process in one day ?

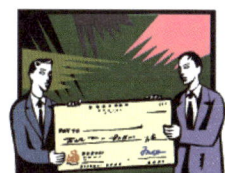

d Henry raised £3216 for charity. Sebastian raised £5197. How much more money did Sebastian raise than Henry ?

10. Do the following **mentally** :-

a 35×10 b 10×2160 c 401×100 d 100×700

e $7900 \div 10$ f $2000 \div 10$ g $53\,000 \div 100$ h $9000 \div 1000$.

11. Copy the following and complete :-

a $\begin{array}{r} 52 \\ \times\ 5 \\ \hline \end{array}$ b $\begin{array}{r} 8132 \\ \times\ 7 \\ \hline \end{array}$ c 708×9 d 6×1234.

12. Copy and do the following :-

a $7\overline{)378}$ b $4135 \div 5$ c $\dfrac{7314}{6}$ d $2052 \div 9$.

13. There were 3993 spectators at Wimbledon one day. Round this number to the nearest :-

(i) 10 (ii) 100.

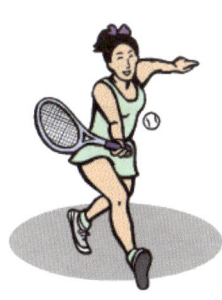

14. Find **mentally** an ***APPROXIMATE*** answer to :-

$$397 + 1188.$$

15. Find **mentally** :-

a 70×30 b 800×90.

Chapter 2

Symmetry

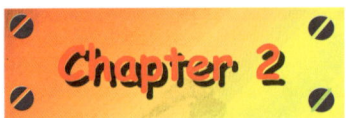

Line Symmetry

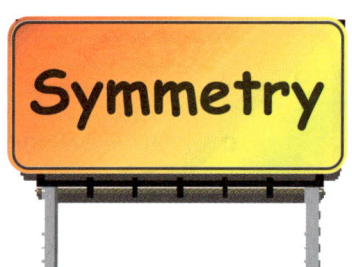

A shape has a **line of symmetry** if :-

when you fold the shape over the line
the 2 halves **exactly** match.

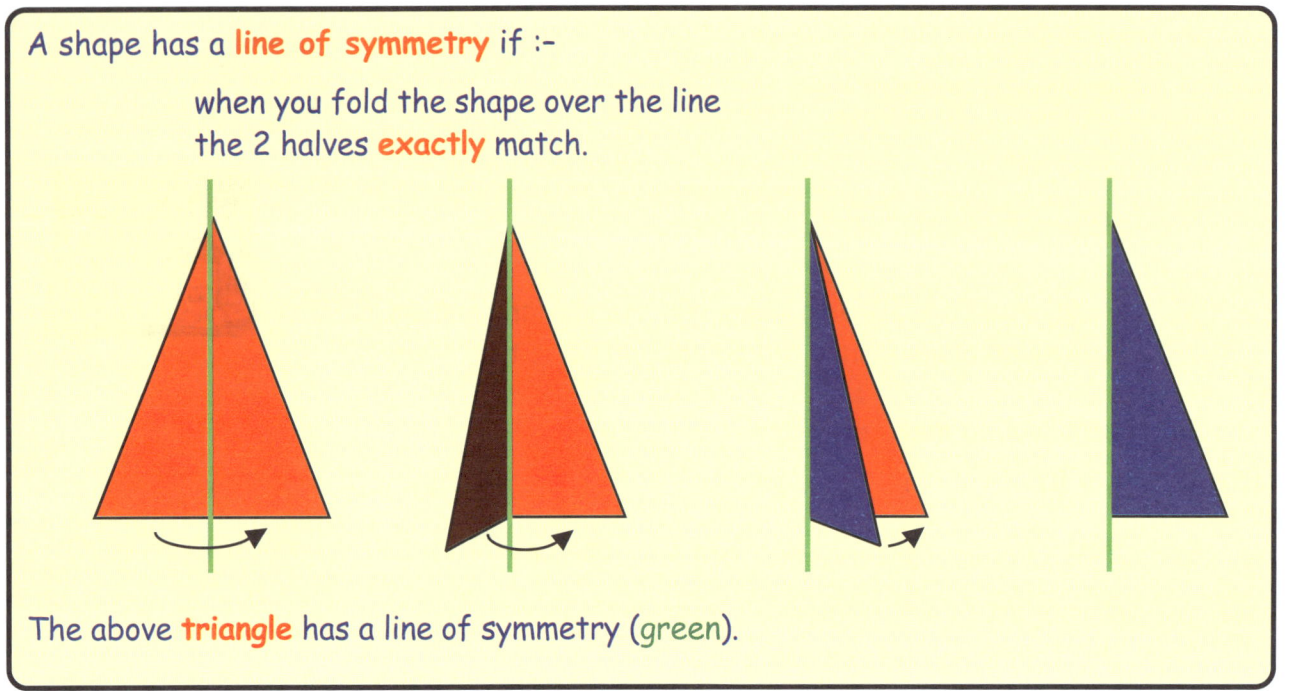

The above **triangle** has a line of symmetry (green).

Exercise 1

You will need a ruler and tracing paper.

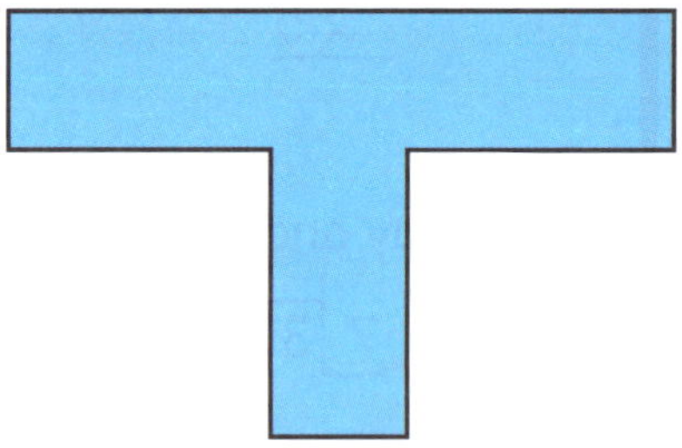

1. a Trace this shape neatly.
   b Either cut it out and fold it (or just fold it).
   c Check it has 1 line of symmetry.

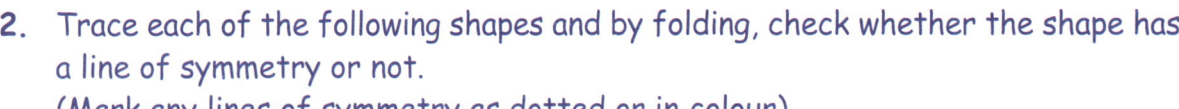

2. Trace each of the following shapes and by folding, check whether the shape has a line of symmetry or not.
   (Mark any lines of symmetry as dotted or in colour)

a b c d

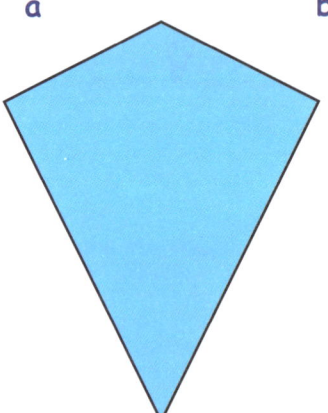

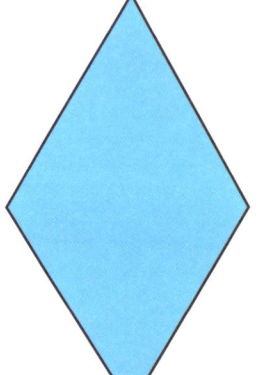

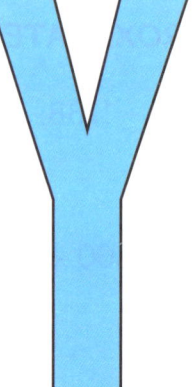

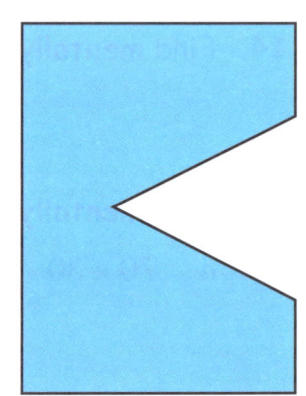

3. Either trace the following shapes **or make a neat copy of each in your jotter**. Mark any lines of symmetry on your drawings (you can check by folding).

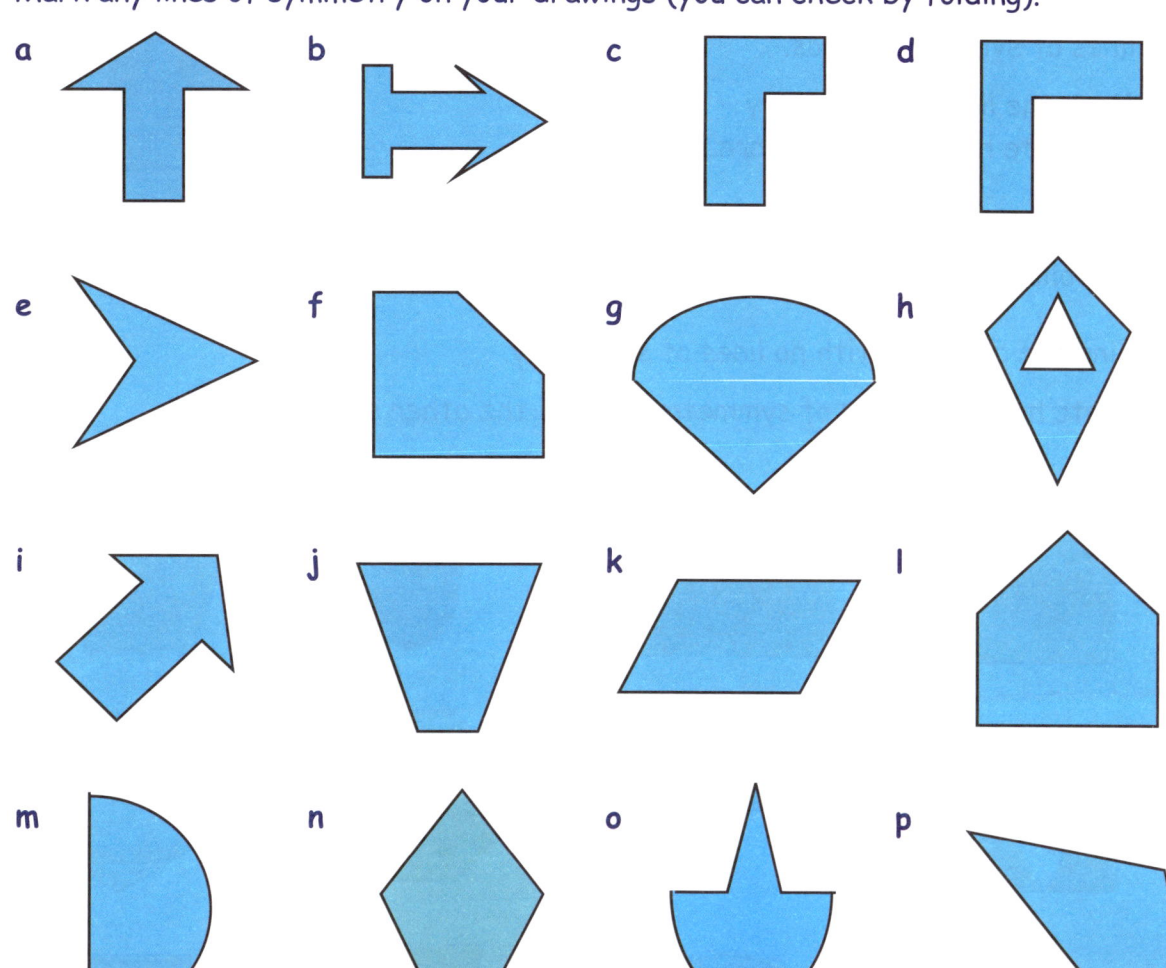

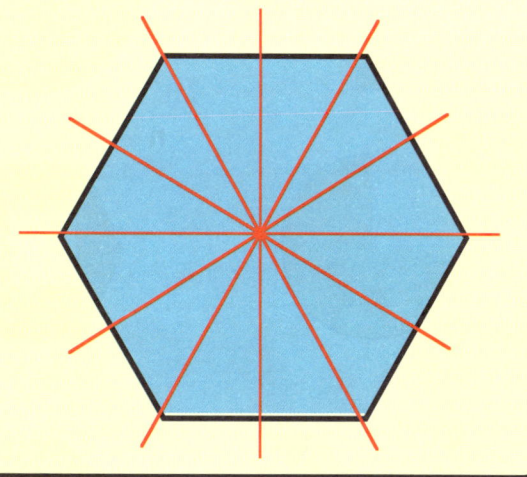

Some shapes have more than 1 line of symmetry.

This **hexagon** has **6**.

They are shown in red.

4. Trace the above hexagon, fold it, then check that it has in fact got **6** lines of symmetry.

5. How many lines of symmetry does this square have? (Check your answer by tracing the square and folding).

6. **a** Trace the **equilateral** triangle.

    b Fold it to check how many lines of symmetry it has.

    c Mark the lines of symmetry and state how many there are.

7. Of the following shapes, **five** of them have **NO** lines of symmetry.

    (i) Find the 5 shapes with no lines of symmetry.

    (ii) State how many lines of symmetry each of the other shapes has.

this is Chapter Two   page 28   SYMMETRY

Creating a Symmetrical Shape

If you are given **half** a symmetrical shape with the line of symmetry shown, it is fairly straightforward to create the **other half**.

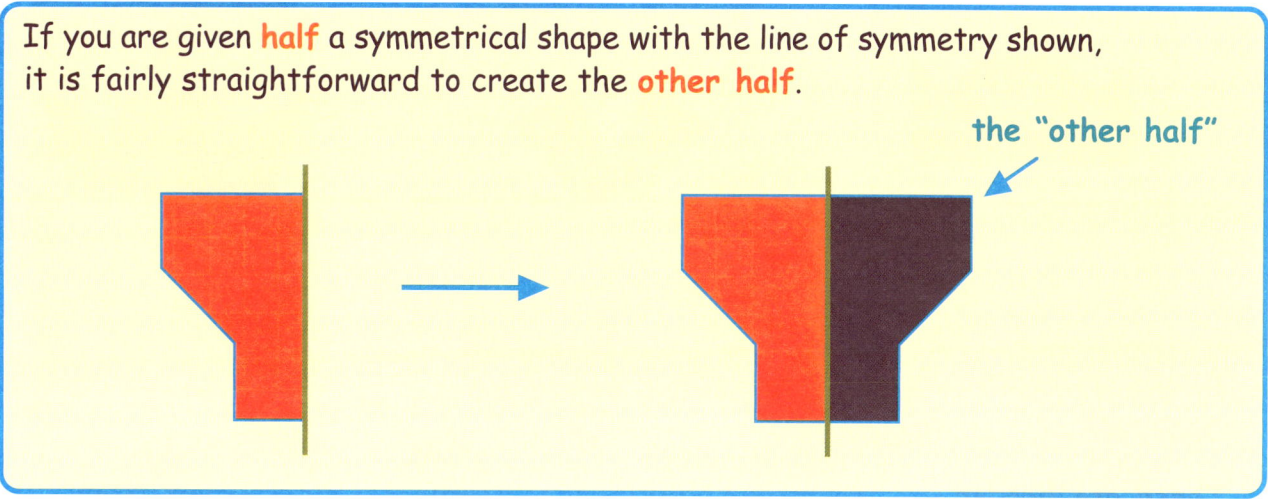

Exercise 2

1. a Copy this shape onto squared paper. (or into your jotter)

    b Now draw in and shade/colour the other half such that the **green** line is a line of symmetry.

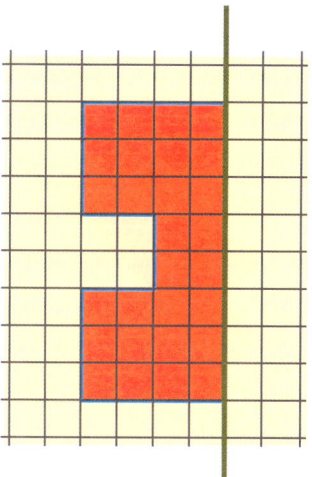

2. Copy each of the following shapes neatly onto squared paper, then complete each shape so that the **green** line is a line of symmetry.

   a

   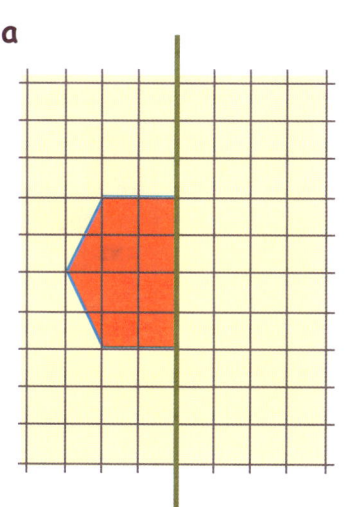

   b

   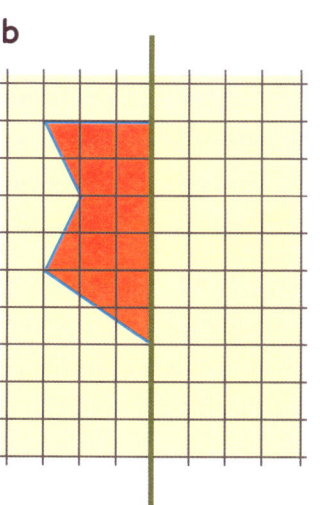

   c

   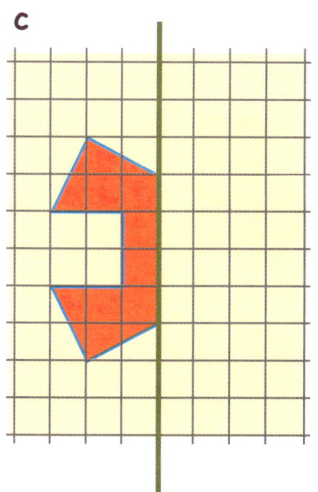

3. Copy each of the following shapes neatly onto squared paper, then complete each shape so that the green line is a line of symmetry.

a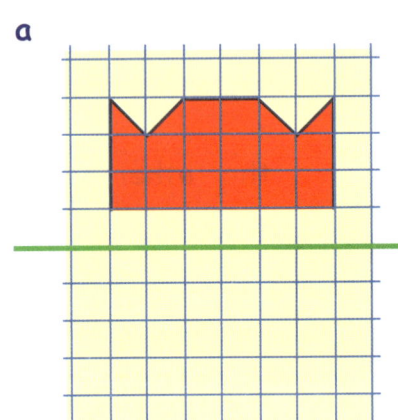
b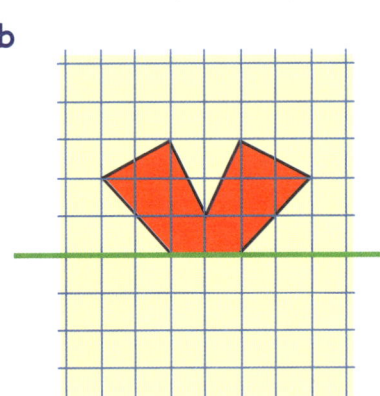
c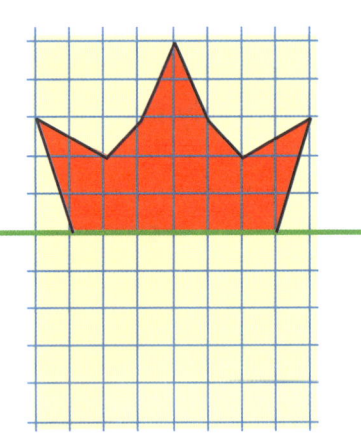

4. **These are harder**.
   Copy and draw the other half of the following symmetrical shapes :-

a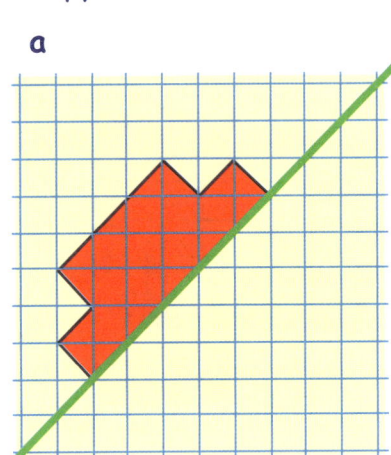
b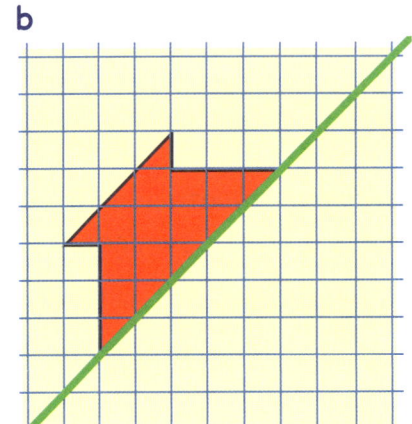
c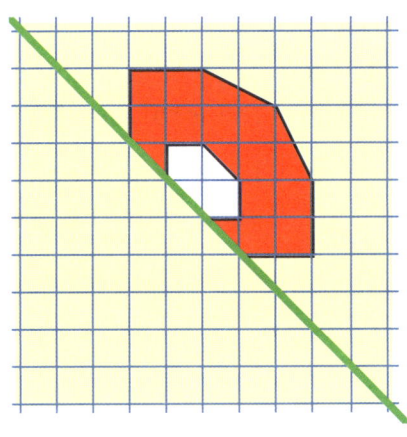

5. This time, each shape has 2 lines of symmetry, each shown in green :-

a b c

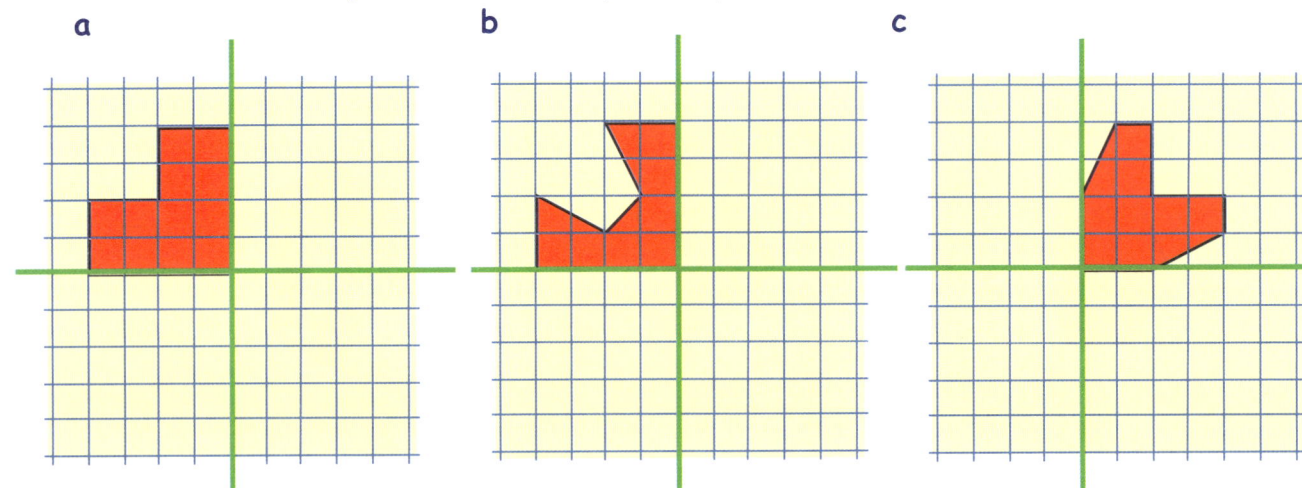

Copy and draw the other 3 parts of each shape.

6. Shown below is a set of computer fonts.

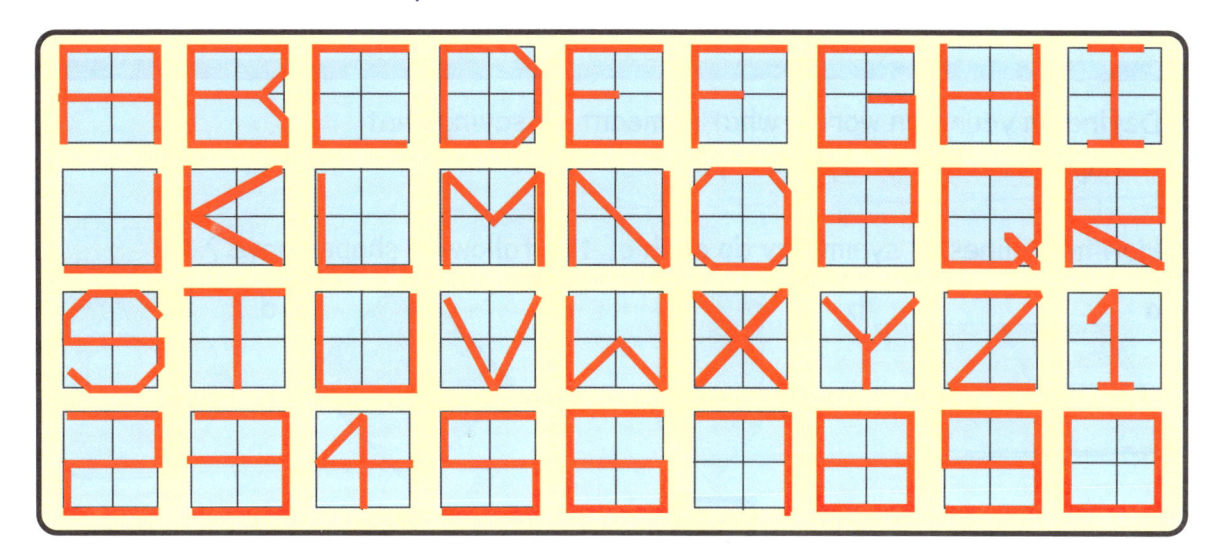

   a   Which of the above letters/numbers have exactly 1 line of symmetry ?
   b   Which of them have 2 lines of symmetry ?
   c   Which have no lines of symmetry ?

7. Neatly, write out your name on squared paper using the above set of fonts.

8. Shown is the letter **A** created on a 4 by 4 grid.

   Try to create a set of fonts showing all 26 letters (and 10 numbers) using a 4 by 4 grid each time.

9. **Class Project.**

   Bring in pictures, labels, charts, adverts, etc., which show lines of symmetry and display them on a poster.
   [Either work as a class, in groups or as individuals].

10. Ask your teacher for some **isometric** paper or triangular spotted paper.

    a   Draw the shape shown opposite carefully
    b   Complete the shape so that the green line is a line of symmetry.

this is Chapter Two   page 31   SYMMETRY

Topic in a Nutshell

1. Define, in your own words, what is meant by saying that a shape has a **line of symmetry**.

2. How many lines of symmetry do each of the following shapes have?

   a 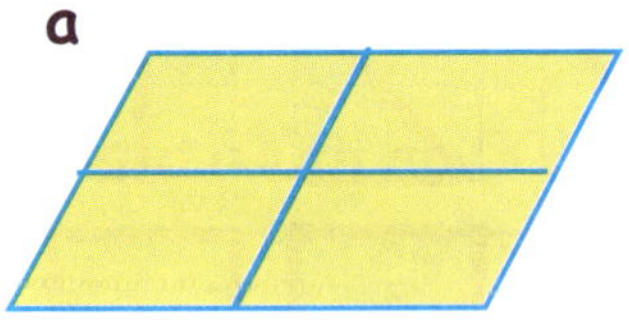   b 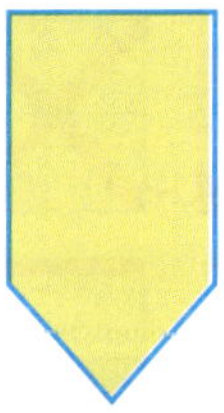   c    d

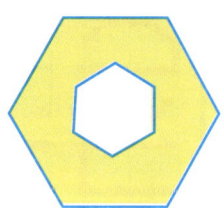

   e    f    g    h

3. Draw these shapes **NEATLY** onto squared paper.

   a 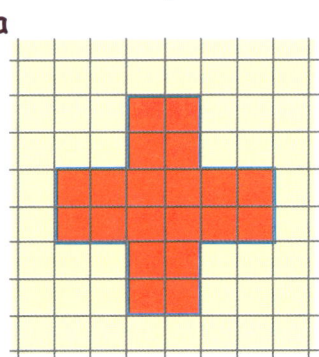   b 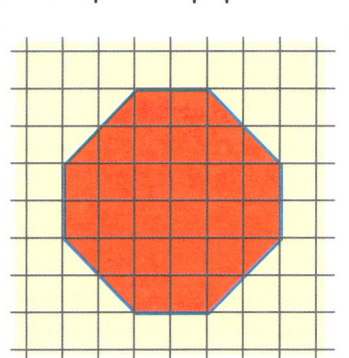   c

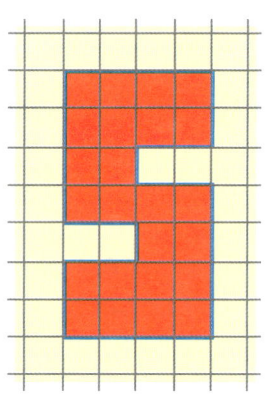

   Mark on in colour, or with a dotted line, **ALL** the lines of symmetry.

4. Copy the following shapes neatly and draw in the **other half** so the **green** line is a line of symmetry.

   a 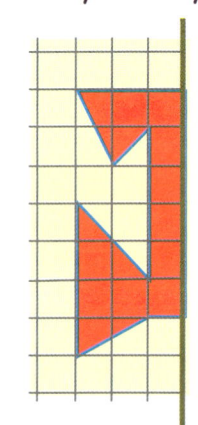   b

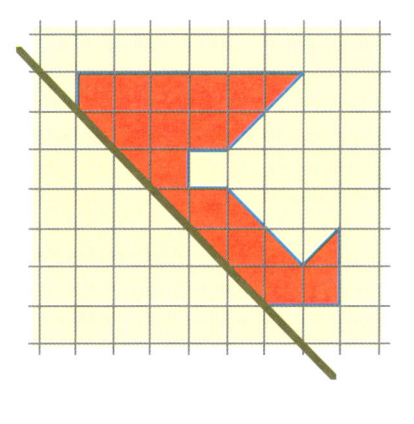

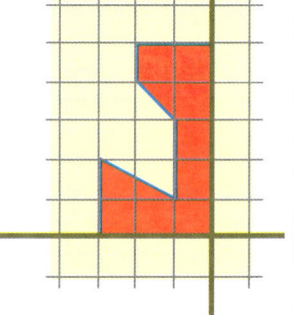

5. Copy this shape and draw the other **3 parts** so that the **green** lines are both lines of symmetry.

this is Chapter Two — page 32 — SYMMETRY

Chapter 3

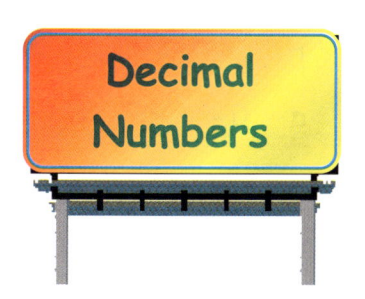

Decimal Numbers

Do you know what a DECIMAL is ?

In chapter 1, we dealt with units, 10's, 100's and 1000's.

When you take a single unit and divide it into 10 (or 100 or 1000) bits, what we then have are **decimal fractions** of a whole number.

For example, let us look at a rectangular tray of toffee as our "**UNIT**" of measure.

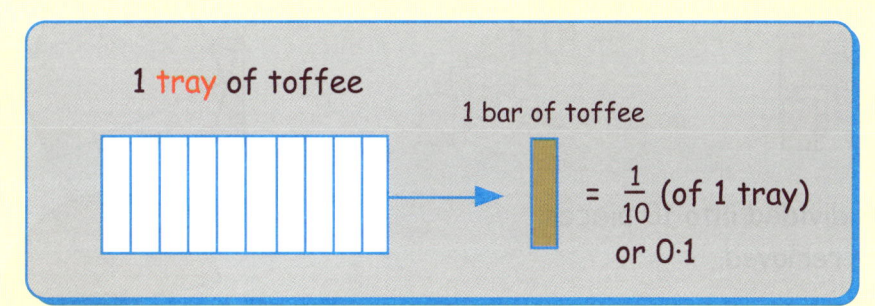

1 tray of toffee

1 bar of toffee = $\frac{1}{10}$ (of 1 tray) or 0·1

The tray of toffee shown above has been cut into 10 equal bars.
Each bit is $\frac{1}{10}$ of the whole tray and is written as 0·1. (called 1 tenth).
In the decimal number, 0·**7**, the "**7**" refers to **7 tenths** or $\frac{7}{10}$.

Exercise 1

1. In this question, ▭ stands for 1 tray of toffee (1 whole number).

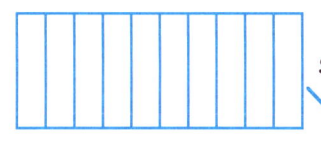

   ▮ stands for 1 bar (0·1).

   What decimal numbers do the following diagrams represent ?

   a 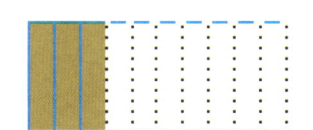   b 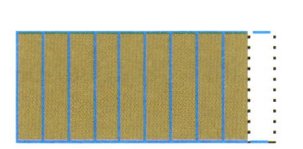   c 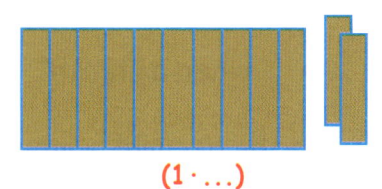 (1·...)

   d 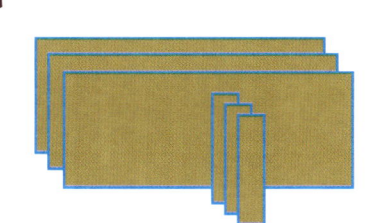   e 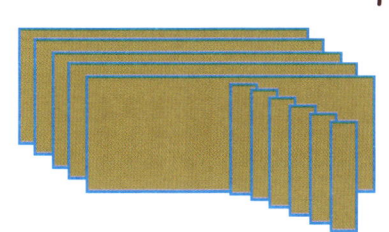   f

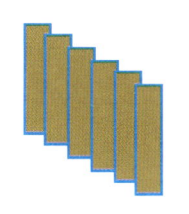

this is Chapter Three   DECIMALS 1

2. Draw neat pictures, in the same style as shown in question 1, to represent :-

    a 0·4   **b** 1·3   **c** 2·5   **d** 4·8

3. Shown opposite is a whole dish of lasagna which has been divided into 10 bits.

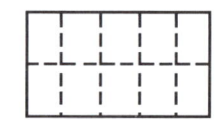

What numbers are represented in the following diagrams ?

    a   **b** 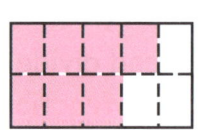   **c**

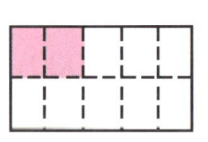

    d 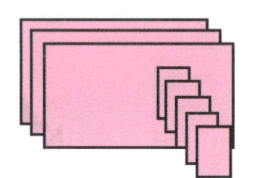   **e** 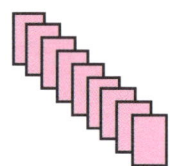   **f**

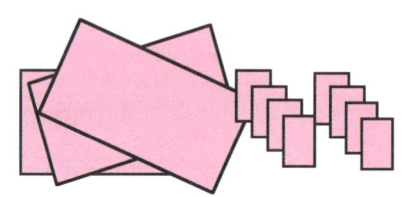

4. A round pizza is divided into 10 pieces. Three pieces are removed.

What decimal does the remaining shaded part represent ?

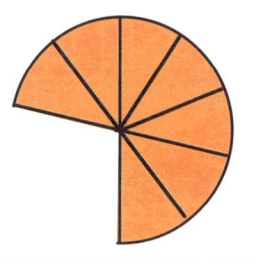

The Second Decimal Place

When our 1 tray of toffee was divided into 10 equal bars, each bar was called 1 tenth ($\frac{1}{10}$). What happens when each **bar** of toffee is cut into 10 equal **blocks** ?

1 whole tray (cut)   1 bar $\frac{1}{10}$ $\frac{1}{10}$ of 1 bar (cut)   1 block

$\frac{1}{100} = \frac{1}{10}$ of $\frac{1}{10}$ or 0·01

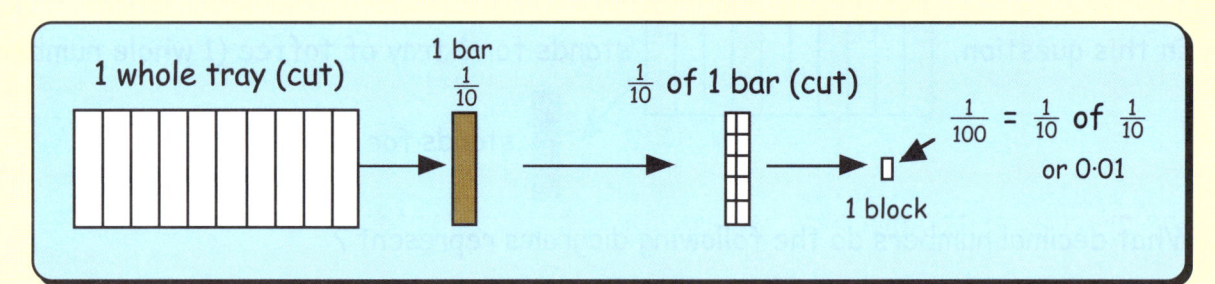

=> when a "tenth" is then cut into 10 equal blocks each bit is ($\frac{1}{10}$ of $\frac{1}{10}$) = $\frac{1}{100}$.

In the decimal number, 0·04, the "4" refers to **4 hundredths** or $\frac{4}{100}$.

---

5. What decimal numbers are represented in the diagrams below ?

    a   **b**   **c**

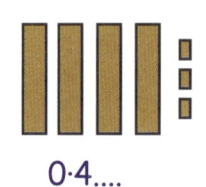

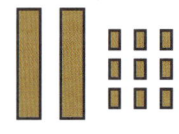

    0·4....   0·....   0·....

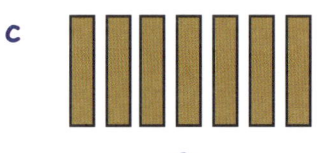

6. Here are another two diagrams. What numbers do they show?

   a   stands for 1 unit.

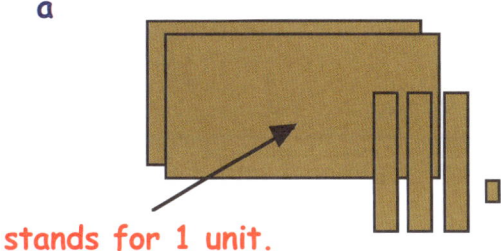

   b

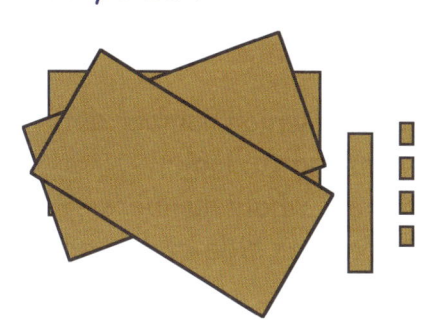

7. Draw neat pictures, in the same style as shown in questions 5 and 6, to represent :-
   a 0·12   b 1·34   c 2·26   d 3·09

8. In the decimal number 24·58, what does the   a 5 mean?   b 8 mean?

9. What does the "3" stand for in these numbers :-
   a 32·81   b 43·29   c 12·31   d 57·83 ?

10. Arrange the following numbers in order, **smallest** first :-

    0·95,   1·16,   0·17,   1·04,   0·09,   1·61.

11. What number is :-
    a $\frac{1}{10}$ up from 1·2   b $\frac{3}{10}$ down from 2·6   c $\frac{7}{10}$ up from 3·1

    d $\frac{3}{100}$ up from 0·14   e $\frac{2}{100}$ down from 1·18   f $\frac{5}{100}$ up from 1·25 ?

12. What number lies **half way** between :-
    a 0·1 and 0·3   b 0·7 and 0·9   c 2·6 and 2·8
    d 2·3 and 2·7   e 1·2 and 1·3   f 0·4 and 0·5 ?

13. The **average** of two numbers lies right in the middle of the numbers.

    a Alice is 1·3 metres tall and Johnnie is 1·6 metres tall.

       What is their **average** height.

    b One wooden broom handle is 1·8 metres long and another is 2·1 metres long.

       What is their **average** length. 

    c Jenny weighs 34·5 kg. The **average** weight of Jenny and Linda is 36 kg.

       What must Linda's weight be?

this is Chapter Three   DECIMALS 1

Reading Decimal Scales

One Decimal Place

Before deciding which number an arrow is pointing to, look firstly at the 2 whole numbers which lie on either side of the arrow.

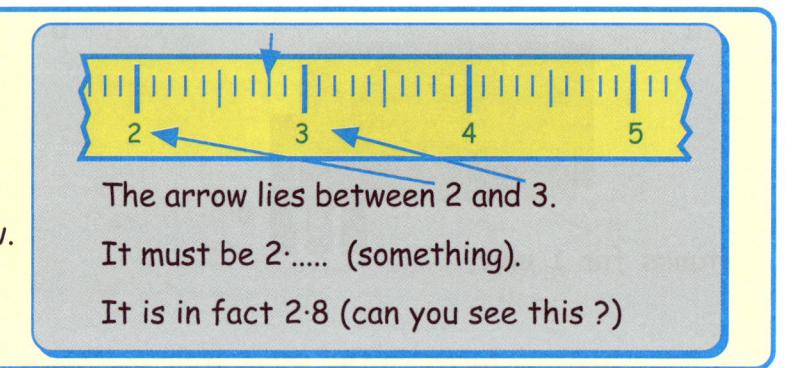

The arrow lies between 2 and 3.

It must be 2·..... (something).

It is in fact 2·8 (can you see this ?)

Exercise 2

1. Write down the length of each car in metres :-

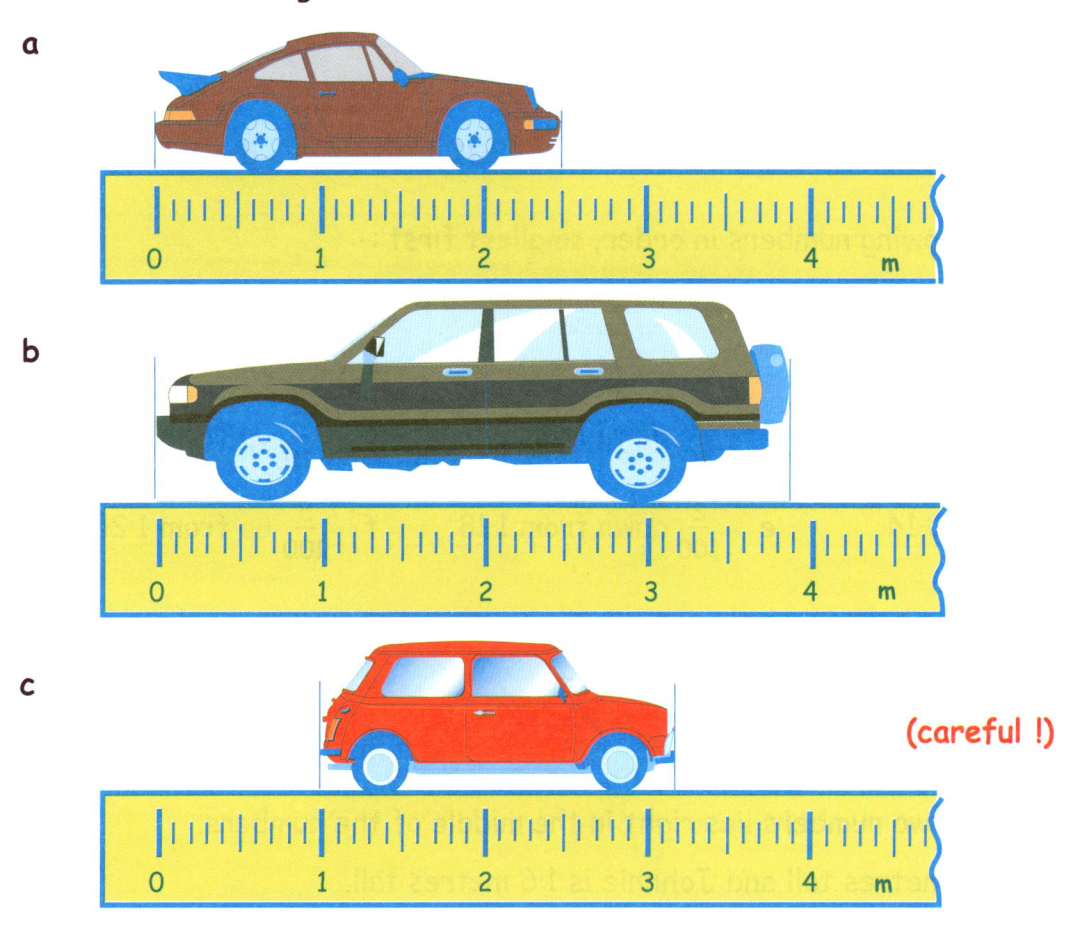

   a

   b

   c (careful !)

2. To what decimal numbers are the arrows pointing ?

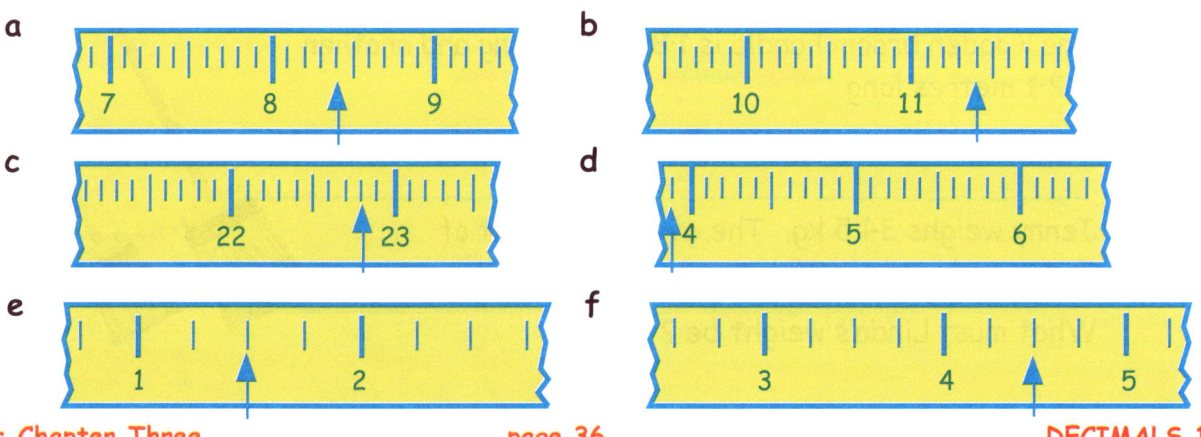

   a

   b

   c

   d

   e

   f

this is Chapter Three   page 36   DECIMALS 1

3. Look at these diagrams. What number is the arrow pointing to in each case?

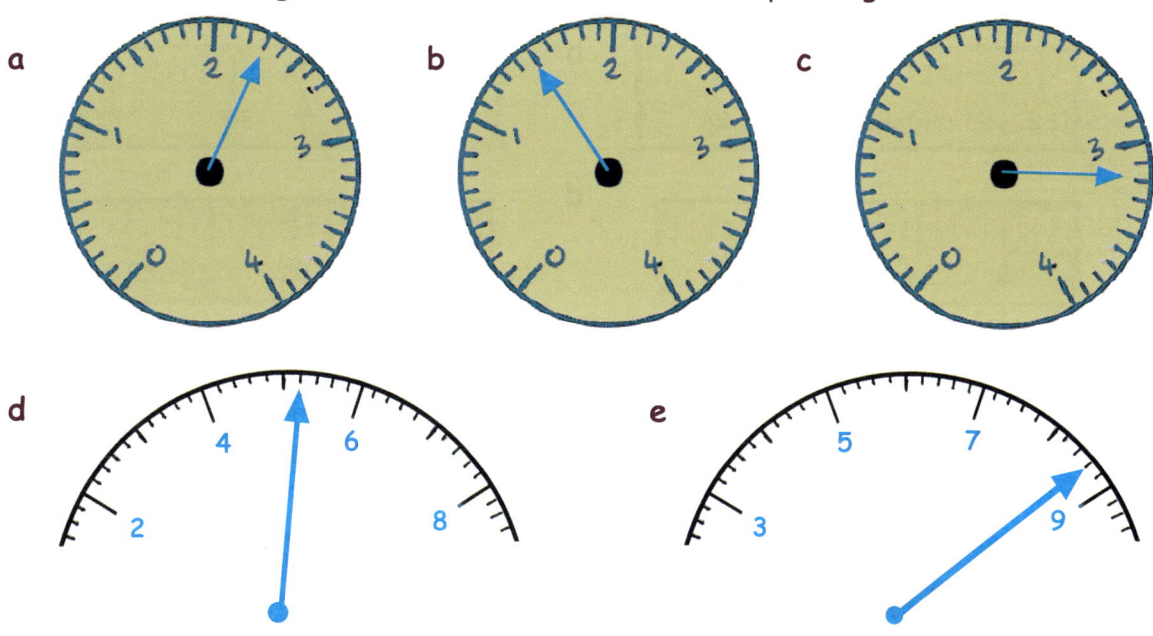

a   b   c

d   e

Two Decimal Places

Look at the 2 decimal numbers shown on the scale which lie on either side of the arrow. (the 1·3 and 1·4).

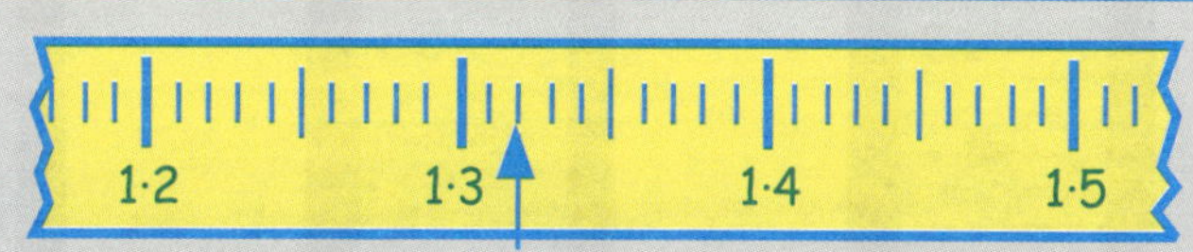

The arrow points to between 1·3 and 1·4.
It has to be 1·3.... (1·3 something)
It points to **1·32** (can you see this?)

4. Write down the length of each cartoon insect :-

a

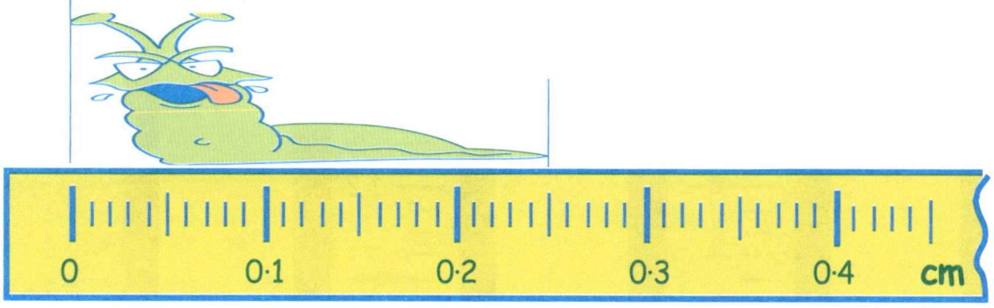

b

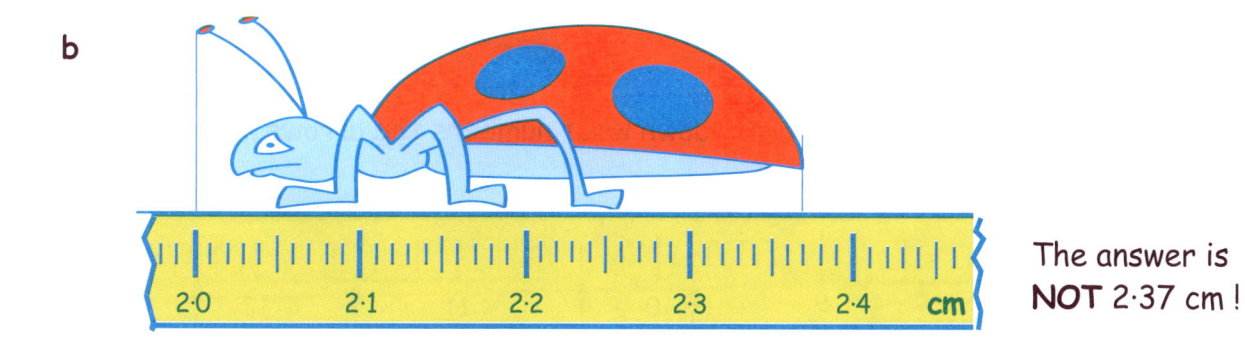

The answer is **NOT** 2·37 cm !

this is Chapter Three   page 37   DECIMALS 1

5. To what numbers are the arrows pointing?

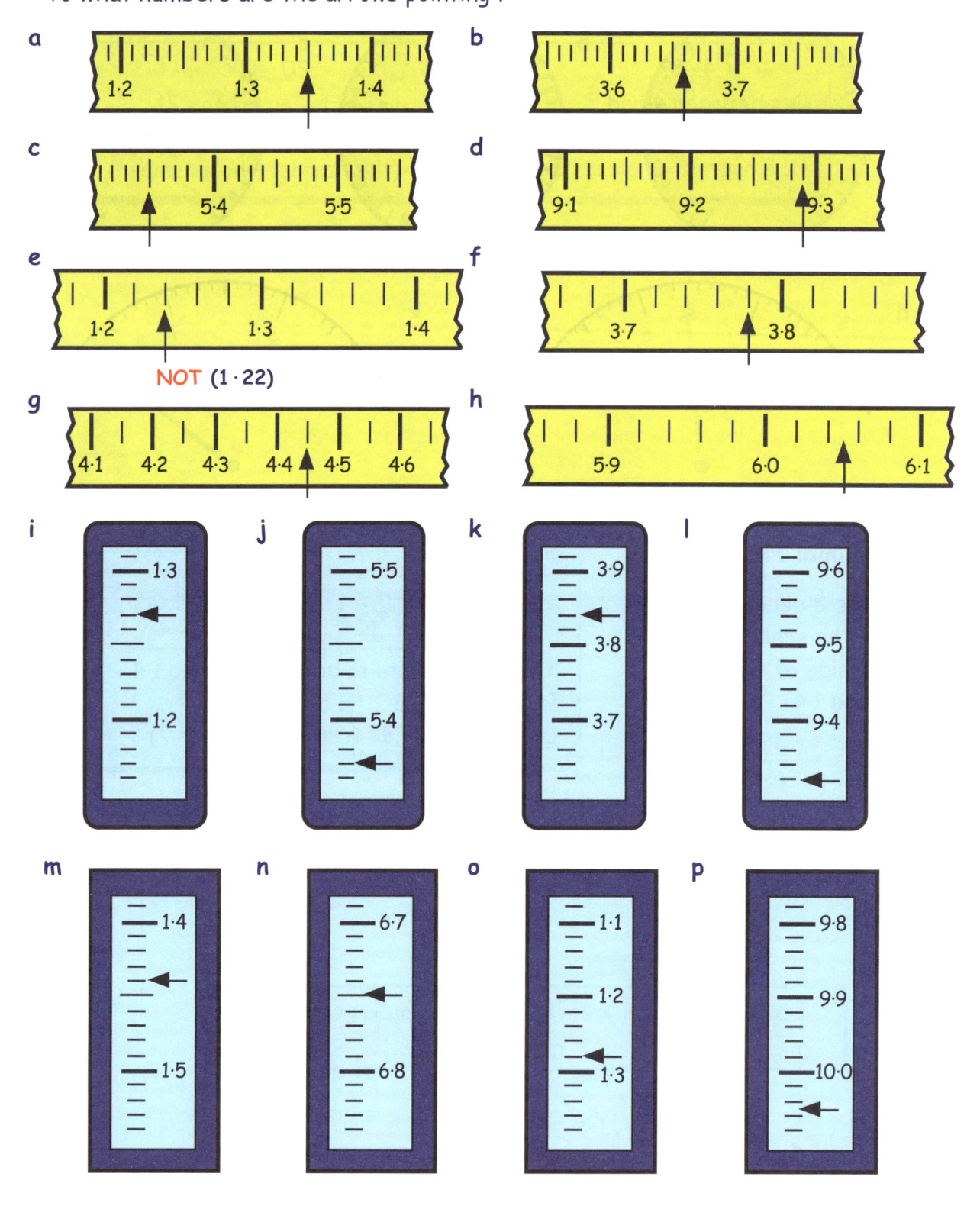

6. Look at the scale below and write down what numbers the arrows A, B, C..... are pointing to.

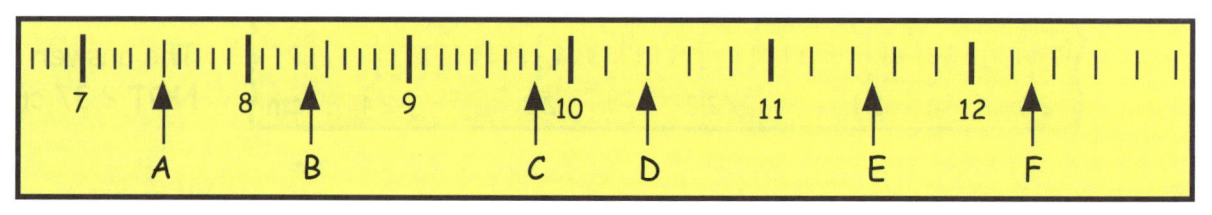

this is Chapter Three   page 38   DECIMALS 1

Rounding to the nearest Whole Number

4·37
lies between 4 and 5.
It is closer to 4
(the nearest whole number).

20·81
lies between 20 and 21.
It is closer to 21
(the nearest whole number).

When rounding to **the nearest whole number** :-

=> look at **the first digit which comes just after the decimal point** :-

if it is a 5, 6, 7, 8 or 9 => round **up** to the next whole number.

if it is a 0, 1, 2, 3 or 4 => **leave** the whole number before the point as it is.

Examples :- 2·4 = 2 to the nearest whole number.

2·7 = 3 to the nearest whole number.

2·5 = 3 to the nearest whole number.

2·488888 = 2 to the nearest whole number.

Exercise 3

1. When each decimal is rounded to the nearest whole number, which of the two numbers in the brackets is the correct answer :-

   a 4·2   (**4** or **5**) ?   b 6·7   (**6** or **7**) ?
   c 3·9   (**3** or **4**) ?   d 1·4   (**1** or **2**) ?
   e 10·16 (**10** or **11**) ?   f 14·97 (**14** or **15**) ?
   g 8·5   (**8** or **9**) ?   h 8·05   (**8** or **9**) ?
   i 40·75 (**40** or **41**) ?   j 100·39 (**100** or **101**) ?

2. Copy and complete these statements :-

   a 6·7 lies between 6 and 7 .   It is closer to ?
   b 4·3 lies between 4 and ?   It is closer to ?
   c 7·5 lies between ? and ?   It is closer to ?   (**remember the rule**)
   d 1·58 lies between ? and ?   It is closer to ?
   e 5·34 lies between ? and ?   It is closer to ?
   f 0·83 lies between ? and ?   It is closer to ?
   g 10·8 lies between ? and ?   It is closer to ?
   h 23·52 lies between ? and ?   It is closer to ?
   i 58·81 lies between ? and ?   It is closer to ?

this is Chapter Three   DECIMALS 1

3. Round these to the nearest **whole £** :-

   a £4·10   b £5·90   c £3·40   d £8·70
   e £12·80   f £14·50   g £17·39   h £18·72
   i £0·34   j £0·51   k £0·50   l £101·49

4. Round these measurements to the nearest **whole centimetre** :-

   a 7·4 cm   b 8·6 cm   c 9·8 cm   d 2·1 cm
   e 3·47 cm   f 6·85 cm   g 15·29 cm   h 20·63 cm
   i 25·27 cm   j 33·99 cm   k 42·14 cm   l 68·50 cm

5. To round numbers like 3·87487 to the nearest whole number :-

   Step 1 - check what two numbers it lies between - (**3** and **4**)
   Step 2 - decide which whole number it is closer to —> **4**

   Round these numbers to the nearest whole number, in the same way :-

   a 2·41784 —>   b 3·958744 —>   c 7·28719 —>
   d 9·386743 —>   e 5·48794 —>   f 8·097412 —>
   g 11·755874 —>   h 12·074874 —>   i 25·66875 —>
   j 0·824111 —>   k 28·265741 —>   l 32·09999 —>

6. **Use your calculator** to do the following divisions.
   Write down the answers, correct to the nearest whole number :-

   a 30 ÷ 7   b 45 ÷ 6   c 78 ÷ 15
   d 104 ÷ 27   e 215 ÷ 46   f 400 ÷ 39
   g 840 ÷ 350   h 1000 ÷ 76   i 2500 ÷ 104
   j 15 ÷ 14   k 0·2 ÷ 0·3   l 85·6 ÷ 100

   m A group of 4 janitors won £3525 on the lottery. How much did they **each** get ?

   n A piece of wood 84 cm long is sawn into 5 logs. How long is **each** log ?

   o 20 litres of juice is shared between 11 children. How much does **each** get ?

   Here is how you can find **remainders** using your calculator.

   137 ÷ 7 —>   • Use your calculator to show 137 ÷ 7 = **19**·571......
                 • Now find 7 × **19** = 133
                 • Now find 137 − 133 —> remainder = 4

7. Find the remainder in each of the following (using the method shown above) :-

   a 317 ÷ 6   b 409 ÷ 8   c 362 ÷ 5   d 1000 ÷ 11.

Adding & Subtracting Decimals

When you add or subtract decimal numbers, it is important to **line up the decimal point**.

For example :-   To add 4·6 and 2·82   =>

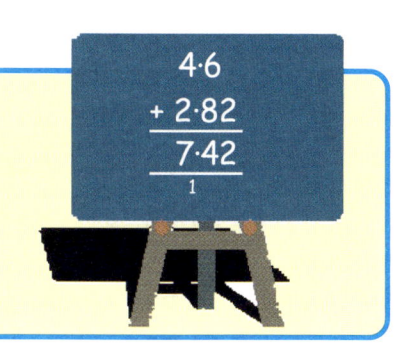

```
  4·6
+ 2·82
──────
  7·42
    1
```

Exercise 4

1. Try to do the following **mentally**. Write down the answers to :-

   a 3·7 + 4·2   b 5·7 + 3·1   c 3·9 + 7·1   d 9·7 + 1·6
   e 0·24 + 0·35   f 0·48 + 0·31   g 0·53 + 0·74   h 0·33 + 0·96
   i 4·2 + 5·34   j 8·1 + 1·45   k 3·7 + 4·22   l 2·8 + 5·35
   m 6·8 – 6·5   n 8·6 – 1·2   o 9·8 – 0·7   p 3·5 – 0·5
   q 6·8 – 1·9   r 7·4 – 1·6   s 7 – 0·75   t 5 – 0·32

2. What is the total length of each of the following tools ? (Try to do it **mentally**).

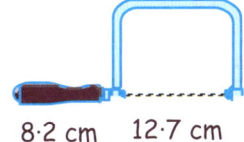

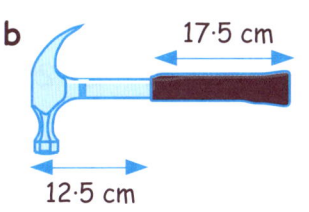

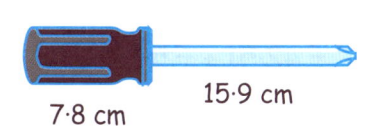

   a 8·2 cm   12·7 cm

   b 17·5 cm   12·5 cm

   c 7·8 cm   15·9 cm

3. Try the following **mentally** :-

   a An empty watering can weighs 4·5 kilograms.
      2·6 kilograms of weedkiller are poured into the can.
      What is the combined weight ?

   b Mary lives 8·3 miles from the nearest Post Office.
      The bus takes her 7·9 miles along the way.
      How far has Mary still to walk ?

   c Three girls received pocket money.
      Ann got £8·30, Jan got £5·50
      and Fran got £6·10.
      What was their total amount of pocket money ?

   d Bob cycles 2·4 km from his home to meet Joe.
      Joe travels 3·2 km from his home to meet Bob.
      After their meeting, they both return to their own homes.
      What is the **total** distance of both their journeys ?

4. Copy the following and find :-

a	4·6 + 2·5	b	17·3 + 8·9	c	14·7 + 55·8	d	74·8 + 26·9
e	7·35 + 1·43	f	4·48 + 3·01	g	7·04 + 2·59	h	8·57 + 5·72
i	5·72 + 1·39	j	13·56 + 12·78	k	28·14 + 2·87	l	32·94 + 24·09
m	8·5 − 2·3	n	43·8 − 21·6	o	72·4 − 25·7	p	35·18 − 27·93
q	7·58 − 6·31	r	8·49 − 4·27	s	5·08 − 2·01	t	9·54 − 1·12
u	5·24 − 3·17	v	8·67 − 4·96	w	5·01 − 2·43	x	7·15 − 5·26

5. Calculate :-

a £4·62 + £3·07
b £34·54 + £26·27
c £42·51 + £5·22
d £7·26 + £8·55
e £28·37 + £9·28
f £35·94 + £42·70
g £8·48 − £5·27
h £7·74 − £4·13
i £5·72 − £5·68
j £74·56 − £40·26
k £74·80 − £7·29
l £24·50 − £3·87

6. Blythe bought a swimming costume for £25·50 and a swimming cap at £8·25.

    How much did she spend **altogether** ?

7. James bought a skate board for £9·75 but sold it the following year for £7·90.

    How much did he lose on the deal ?

8. In a diving competition the UK judge awarded 2·7 points less than the French judge. The French judge gave the diver 9·3 points.

    What mark did the UK judge award ?

this is Chapter Three   page 42   DECIMALS 1

9. The postman is delivering two parcels.
   One weighs 17·7 kg, the other weighs 32·8 kg.

   What is the total weight of the parcels ?

10.
Burgh of Renfrew	
Bishopbriggs	13·07
Chryston	15·02

   From Renfrew to Bishopbriggs is 13·07 miles.
   From Renfrew to Chryston is 15·02 miles.

   How far is it from Bishopbriggs to Chryston ?

11. In any one week a Potted Blue plant can grow 0·85 cm.
    The Potted Red plant can grow 1·23 cm.

    How much taller can the Potted Red be than the Potted Blue after one week ?

12. A computer football game priced at £39·95 actually appeared on the Internet for £29·99.

    How much of a saving was this ?

13. Tanya weighs 62·73 kilograms and Lisa weighs 54·58 kilograms.

    a   What is their combined weight ?

    b   By how much is Tanya heavier than Lisa ?

14. Two cars and a lorry are shown.

    a   How much longer is the lorry than

        (i) the red car   (ii) the blue car ?

    b   Calculate the difference in length between the red car and the blue car.

    (red car: 4·35 m, blue car: 3·07 m, lorry: 6·13 m)

15. The fares for the crossing from Wumiss Bay to the Island of Hute are shown in the table.

Adult	£8·45
Child	£5·48
Car	£28·69
Bus	£36·72

    a   What price for :-

        (i)   1 adult and 1 child ?

        (ii) 1 car with 1 adult ?

        (iii) 2 buses ?

    b   What change will you get from £50 if you pay for 1 car with 1 adult and 1 child ?

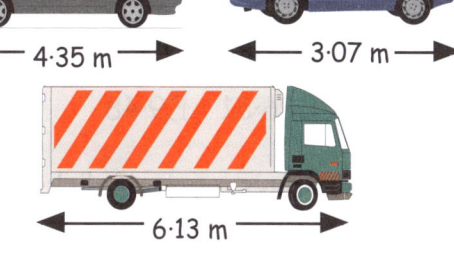

Topic in a Nutshell

1. What decimal number is represented by this diagram?

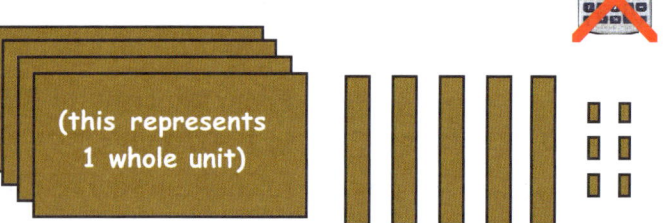

   (this represents 1 whole unit)

2. In the decimal number 73·94, what does the :-

   a 7 stand for   b 3 stand for   c 9 stand for   d 4 stand for?

3. What decimal numbers are the arrows pointing to?

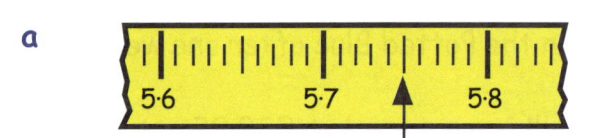

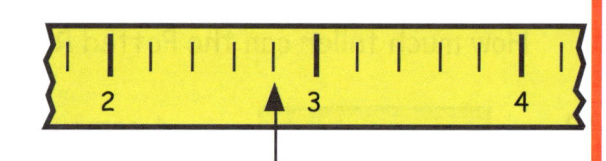

   a (ruler showing 5·6, 5·7, 5·8 with arrow)
   b (ruler showing 2, 3, 4 with arrow)

4. Round the following to **the nearest whole number**.

   a 9·4   b 6·7   c 31·39   d 58·62.

5. Do the following **mentally** (*no working*) :-

   a 4·7 + 5·2   b 5·3 + 3·45   c 7·5 − 3·1   d 0·81 − 0·14.

6. Copy the following and find :-

   a 6·82
      + 1·49

   b 27·45
      + 5·58

   c 9·6
      − 5·1

   d 9·48
      − 3·97

   e £3·69 + £4·75   f £26·39 + £3·18   g £4·75 − £3·69
   h £26·31 − £9·48   i £29·41 − £8·58   j £36·61 − £19·38.

7. Jason buys a box of disks for £3·94 and a CD cleaner for £5·87. How much change should he receive from £10?

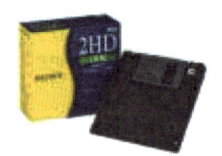

8. Mr Porter bought a pair of windscreen wiper blades at £4·25 each and 6 car air-fresheners at £1·24 each.

   a How much did it cost him in total? (*show all your working*)
   b He handed over a £20 note. How much change did he get?

9. Calculate the **perimeter** of this rectangular lawn.

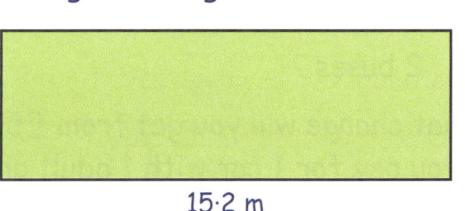

   4·95 m
   15·2 m

this is Chapter Three   DECIMALS 1

Chapter 4

Time

12 hr & 24 hr Times

We usually think of the time of day in terms of 1 to 12 o'clock a.m. (ante-meridian - morning) and 1 to 12 o'clock p.m. (post- meridian - after noon/night), but pilots and sailors need a system that causes no confusion.

Imagine turning up for your plane to Florida at 8.00 (p.m.) to find it had flown away at 8.00 (a.m.) and you missed your holiday !

The 24 hour Clock :-

12 hour times

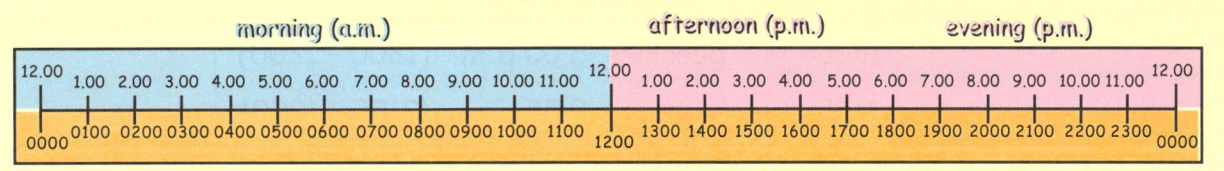

morning (a.m.) — afternoon (p.m.) — evening (p.m.)

12.00 1.00 2.00 3.00 4.00 5.00 6.00 7.00 8.00 9.00 10.00 11.00 12.00 1.00 2.00 3.00 4.00 5.00 6.00 7.00 8.00 9.00 10.00 11.00 12.00

0000 0100 0200 0300 0400 0500 0600 0700 0800 0900 1000 1100 1200 1300 1400 1500 1600 1700 1800 1900 2000 2100 2200 2300 0000

24 hour times

Example :- Can you see that morning times in 24 hour format stay the same ?

8.00 a.m.	becomes	0800 hrs
7.45 a.m.	becomes	0745 hrs
10.50 a.m.	becomes	1050 hrs

but for afternoon and evening times you always **add on 12 hours** :-

2.00 p.m.	becomes	1400 hrs (2 hours past 12.00 o'clock)
5.15 p.m.	becomes	1715 hrs (5.15 + 12.00)
10.50 p.m.	becomes	2250 hrs (10.50 + 12.00)

Exercise 1

1. Copy and complete the following, showing how to change to 24 hour format :-

   a   7.00 a.m. is **before** mid-day.   —> 7.00 a.m. = 0700.

   b   9.45 a.m. is ...... mid-day.   —> 9.45 a.m. = ...

   c   4.00 p.m. is **after** mid-day.   —> 4.00 p.m. = 0400 + 1200 = 1600.

   d   10.35 p.m. is ...... mid-day.   —> 10.35 a.m. = 1035 + ... = ...

2. Change the following 12 hour clock times to <u>**24 hour clock times**</u> :-

a	8·40 am	b	1·45 am	c	6 am
d	3·20 pm	e	2·25 pm	f	9 at night
g	6·35 am	h	8·50 pm	i	5 past 4 in the morning
j	9·58 am	k	noon	l	12·05 am
m	12·05 pm	n	11·32 pm	o	1·52 am
p	10·40 pm	q	11·44 pm	r	midnight

Example :- Can you see that in 24 hour format times before 1300 stay the same ?

> 0900   becomes 9.00 **a.m.**
> 1245   becomes 12.45 **p.m.**

but for times from 1300 onwards, you must **subtract 12 hours** :-

> 1800   becomes 6.00 **p.m.** (1800 – 1200)
> 2155   becomes 9·55 **p.m.** (2155 – 1200)

3. Copy and complete the following, showing how to change from 24 hour format :-

a   0600 is **before** 1300   —>   0600 = 6.00 a.m.

b   1045 is .... 1300.   —>   1045 = ...

c   1700 is **after** 1300.   —>   1700 = 1700 – 1200 = 5.00 p.m.

d   1850 is ...... 1300.   —>   1850 = 1850 – .... = ... p.m.

4. Change the following 24 hour clock times to <u>**12 hour clock times**</u> :-

a	0330	b	1150	c	0920
d	1545	e	1740	f	2225
g	0240	h	1845	i	2120
j	1812	k	1200	l	0650
m	0345	n	1525	o	2345
p	2105	q	0040	r	0505

5. The British Airways plane left New York at 10.50 pm and touched down at Heathrow at 6.35 am.

Write these times in 24 hour form.

6. On a Spring night, the sun set at 2015 and rose the following morning at 0555.

Write these times out in 12 hour form.

Time Intervals, Timetables, Programme Guides

Counting on :- The easiest way of finding how long something lasts is by "counting on".

Example :- A film starts at 8·45 pm and ends at 11·25 pm. How long was the show ?

Answer :-

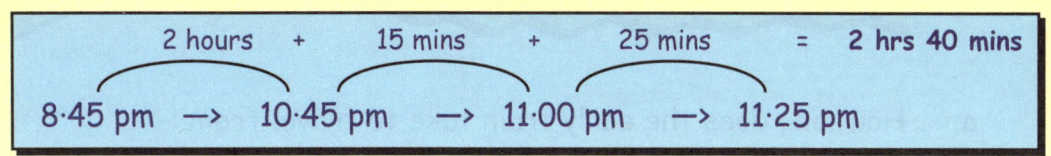

```
           2 hours    +    15 mins    +    25 mins     =   2 hrs 40 mins
         8·45 pm  -->  10·45 pm  -->  11·00 pm  -->  11·25 pm
```

Exercise 2

1. Use the method of **counting on** to find how long it is from :-

   a   3·15 pm to 6·15 pm   b   7 am to 10·30 am
   c   midnight to 5·30 am   d   5·30 pm to 9·40 pm
   e   9·55 am to 10·15 am   f   2·50 am to 8·25 am
   g   0830 to 1055   h   1655 to 1810
   i   1950 to 2115   j   2350 to 0300 (next day ?)

2. Calculate the **finishing times** of the following TV programmes :-

	Film A	Film B	Film C	Film D	Film E
Prog started	3·30 pm	2·15 pm	8·25 pm	9·45 am	11·30 pm
Prog lasted	2 hr 30 mins	1 hr 40 mins	2 hr 35 mins	45 mins	1 hr 45 mins

3. The two clocks show when a TV film started and finished one Saturday night.

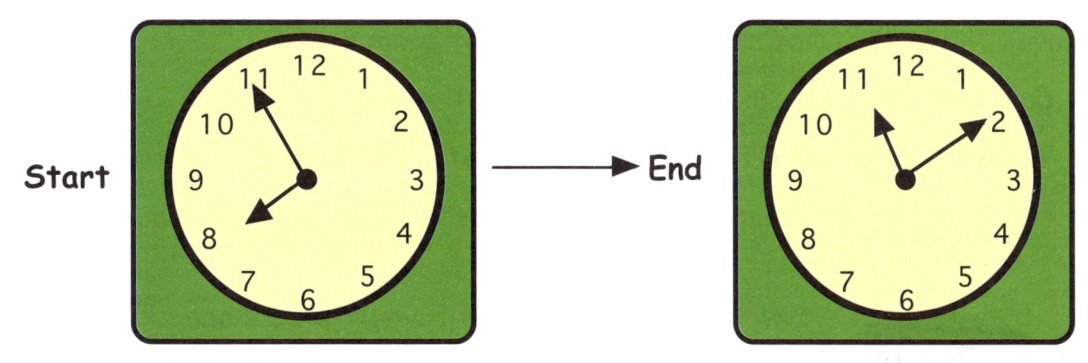

   Start → End

   How long did the film last ?

4. The Grand Prix began at 10·25 am.
   Billy McLaren crossed the finish line at 2·08 pm.
   What was Billy's time for the race ?

this is Chapter Four   page 47   TIME

5. Shown is part of the train timetable from Barrow to Highgate.

	Barrow ➤ Lorne ➤ Stove ➤ Ferny ➤ Highgate
Early Train	8·10 am 9·20 am 11·30 am 12·15 pm 3·00 pm
Late Train	10·05 am 11·15 am 4·55 pm

a How long does the early train take to travel from :–

   (i) Barrow to Lorne ?   **(ii)** Stove to Ferny ?   **(iii)** Barrow to Highgate ?

b Assuming that the late train travels at the same speed as the early train, when would it be expected to arrive at :–

   (i) Stove ?   (Hint ! Notice how long the early train takes from Lorne to Stove)

   (ii) Ferny ?

6. Tony set off one morning at 6·35 am for a walk in the hills. He returned (exhausted) at 5·00 pm.

For how long had Tony been walking ?

7. A tanker set sail from Southampton at 1850 on Sunday.

It docked at a French port at 0525 (British time) on Monday morning.

How long was the tanker's journey ?

8. A little bus runs on a circular route around a tropical island. It leaves the post office at 0845 and passes it again at 1020.

   a Calculate the time taken for 1 circuit of the island.

   b When should the bus next pass the post office ?

   c How many complete circuits can it make between 6 am and 10 pm ?

9. Two girls played their 5 favourite CD's one after the other. Julie began at 1355 and her 5th CD finished at 1815. Tricia began to play hers at 1640 and they ended at 2055.

Which girl's CD's lasted longer and by how much ?

Minutes and Seconds

For accuracy, especially in sport, time is measured in minutes and seconds (and the seconds are sometimes measured to 1 or 2 decimal places).

Adding Times :-

```
   4 mins   40 secs
+  2 mins₁  50 secs
   ─────────────────
   7 mins   30 secs
```
90 secs = 1 min 30 secs

Exercise 3

1. Round the following times to the **nearest second** :-

   a   23·7 secs   b   19·45 secs   c   54·09 secs

   d   2 mins 15·8 secs   e   5 mins 9·38 secs   f   22 mins 59·9 secs

2. A pop song lasted 195 seconds.
   Write this time in **minutes** and **seconds**.

3. Change each of these to **minutes** and **seconds** :-

   a   100 secs   b   153 secs   c   230 secs

4. Change each of these to **hours** and **minutes** :-

   a   95 mins   b   265 mins   c   500 mins

5. Copy the following and complete :-

   a   5 mins 30 secs   b   3 mins 50 secs   c   9 mins 55 secs
      + 4 mins 25 secs   + 1 mins 30 secs   + 3 mins 45 secs
         ─────────────────   ─────────────────   ─────────────────

   d   6 mins 40 secs   e   5 mins 55 secs   f   7 mins 30 secs
      − 3 mins 35 secs   − 1 mins 05 secs   − 4 mins 40 secs
         ─────────────────   ─────────────────   ─────────────────

6. Michelle sang 3 songs in her spot on the "TV IDOL" audition.

   "Lonely" - 3 mins 25 secs,   "High Spirit" - 2 mins 40 secs,   "Pain" - 3 mins 15 secs.

   How long did her songs last altogether ?

7. Two babies were born at Ravenmoore Maternity hospital.
   Lucy was born on the 31st December 2002 at 11.50 pm.
   Raymond was born at 1.20 am on the 1st January 2003.

   How much older was Lucy than Raymond ?

This stopwatch shows the time in minutes and seconds.

The time shown is 2 minutes 17·6 seconds.

8. State the times shown on each of the following stopwatches :-

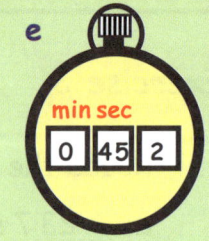

   a   3 min 25 sec 4
   b   5 min 17 sec 1
   c   9 min 04 sec 8
   d   6 min 00 sec 9
   e   0 min 45 sec 2

9. The "tachograph" on a lorry shows how long a driver has driven his lorry. The times are in hours, minutes and seconds. Write down these times :-

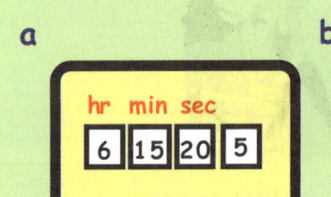

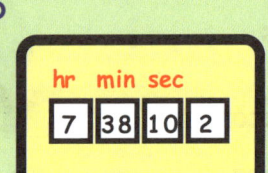

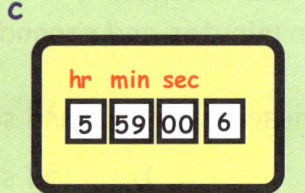

   a   6 hr 15 min 20 sec 5
   b   7 hr 38 min 10 sec 2
   c   5 hr 59 min 00 sec 6

10. Jordan won the race in a time of 1 minute 13·6 seconds. Nicolas was only $\frac{7}{10}$ of a second behind him.

    What was Nicolas' time ?

11. Look at the practice lap times for 2 racing drivers.

    a   Who was faster, Bill or Ben ?

    b   How much faster was one than the other ?

    BILL 2 min 58 sec 7
    BEN   3 min 00 sec 4

12. George's practice lap time in the same race was 2 minutes 54·8 seconds.

    a   How much faster was George than Bill ?

    b   The slowest time was by Brian. His time was 15·8 seconds slower than Bill.

    What was Brian's time ?

13. It took Parminder 7 minutes 5 seconds to walk to the top of the Wallace Monument in Stirling.

    It took him 4 minutes 35 seconds to come down.

    How much longer did it take him going up than coming down ?

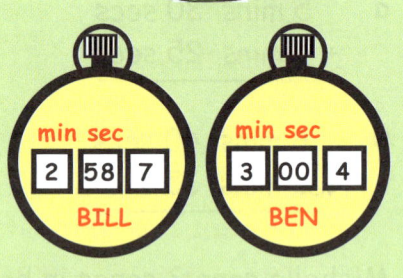

this is Chapter Four   page 50   TIME

Topic in a Nutshell

1. Change these times to **24 hour format** :-

   a   6·50 am   b   3·05 pm   c   20 to midnight

   d   Noon   e   half past midnight   f   10 to 11 at night.

2. Write the following in **12 hour format** :-   (remember to use am or pm)

   a   0705   b   1450   c   1057   d   2257

3. I set off for a meeting in Aberdeen at 0945 and got back home at 1425.

   How long had I been away from home ?

4. A van driver started his deliveries at 25 past 8 in the morning. It took him 7 hours and 45 minutes to do all his deliveries.

   At what time did the driver finish ?

5. The "Happy Traveller" paddle steamer sails a circular route in Loch Durness. The times of the first 2 sails, from the pier, are shown below in the table.

	Pier	Eagle Point	Pine Harbour	Strum Castle	Bruce's Cave	Royal Gardens	Pier
1st Sail	0950	1005	1040	1115	1145	1225	1320
2nd Sail	1415	1430	1505				

   a   How long did it take from Strum Castle to Bruce's Cave ?

   b   How long in total was the 1st sail from pier to pier ?

   c   Assuming both sails took the same time, at what time would the 2nd sail reach the the Royal Gardens ?

6. New York time is 5 hours **behind** British time.
   This means that when it is 9·00 pm here, it is only 4·00 pm in New York.
   I flew from Manchester Airport to New York at 1305.

   If the flight took 8 hours 15 minutes, at what time, (New York time), would I arrive at New York Airport ?

7. Lucy and Jane are friends who ran in the Aberdeen 10 km race for charity.

   Jane's time is shown on the 1st stopwatch.

   Lucy was 25·4 seconds slower than Jane.

   Copy the blank stopwatch and fill in Lucy's time.

   Jane: min 48, sec 50, 3

Chapter 5

Statistics

Organising and Interpreting Information

Data can often appear untidy and difficult to understand.

Organising such data into tables and graphs can make it easier to interpret.

Frequency tables

Example

Shown are the times (in minutes) taken to complete an obstacle course.

Organise the data into a **frequency table**.

12	15	13	13	14	16
17	13	14	14	14	17
15	14	12	13	13	15
12	14	16	14	13	12

Time	Tally	Frequency
12	II	
13	III	
14		
15		

Frequency is the same as number.

Tally marks are grouped in fives
||||| ||| = 8

Exercise 1

1. Copy and complete the frequency table in the example above.

2. Pupils were asked to name their favourite sport.

football	darts	snooker	football
snooker	tennis	football	rugby
tennis	football	football	tennis
darts	football	snooker	football

Sport	Tally	Frequency
darts		
tennis		
football		
rugby		
snooker		

    a   Copy and complete the frequency table.

    b   How many pupils chose tennis ?

    c   What was the most popular sport ?

    d   How many **more** pupils chose football than rugby ?

    e   How many pupils were asked to name their favourite sport ?

3. Twenty four boxes of sweets are opened and the number of sweets in each box is counted.

   The results are shown in the table.

44	41	41	39	40	42	42	44
41	42	44	41	40	41	41	41
39	42	40	41	42	38	40	41

Sweets	Tally	Frequency
38		
39		

   a   Copy and complete the frequency table.
   b   How many boxes contained 40 sweets?
   c   How many boxes contained **more than** 41 sweets?

4. Each year the Inter House school trophy is awarded to the best year-group in Dunstoon High School.

   This table shows the results over a 21 year period.

   DUNSTOON H.S.

1984 Sec 1	1991 Sec 5	1998 Sec 6
1985 Sec 2	1992 Sec 6	1999 Sec 3
1986 Sec 4	1993 Sec 1	2000 Sec 5
1987 Sec 6	1994 Sec 3	2001 Sec 1
1988 Sec 1	1995 Sec 5	2002 Sec 3
1989 Sec 1	1996 Sec 6	2003 Sec 4
1990 Sec 5	1997 Sec 6	2004 Sec 6

   a   Make up your own frequency table to show how many times each year group has won.
   b   Which year group has won the most trophies?
   c   Which year group do you think has been the **poorest**? Why?

   Pictographs and bar graphs can also be used to display information.

5. The pictograph shows the number of trees that were planted in the school grounds. (Each symbol represents 2 trees.)

   Key: 🌲 stands for 2 trees.

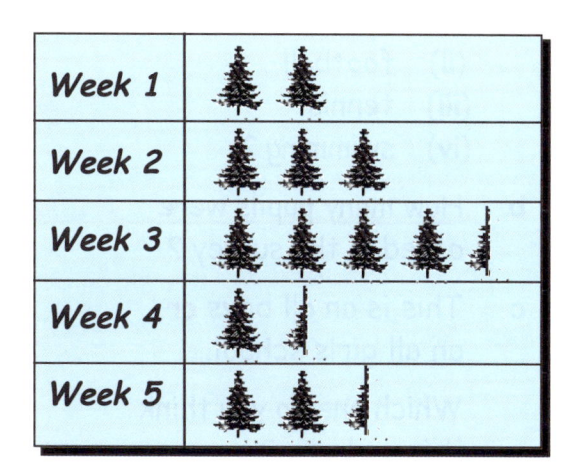

   a   How many trees were planted in :-
      (i)   week 1 (the answer is **not** 2)
      (ii) week 2   (iii) week 3
      (iv) week 4   (v) week 5?
   b   How many trees were planted altogether?

Week 1	🌲🌲
Week 2	🌲🌲🌲
Week 3	🌲🌲🌲🌲🌲
Week 4	🌲🌲
Week 5	🌲🌲🌲

this is Chapter Five   STATISTICS

6. The **pictograph** shows the number of pupils who made a purchase at the tuck shop.
   (Remember to look at the key first).

   Key: 👤 stands for 4 pupils.

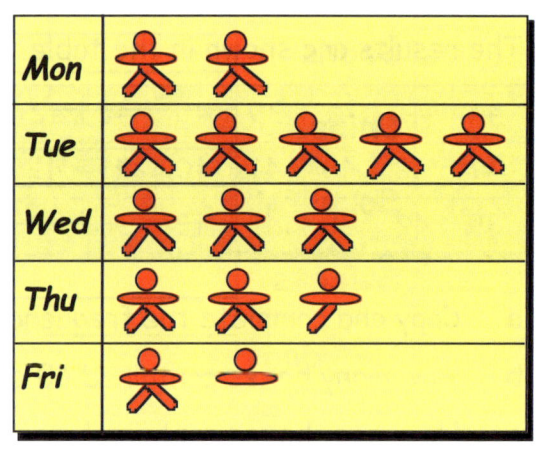

   a How many pupils made a purchase on :-

   (i) Monday (the answer is **not** 2)

   (ii) Tuesday (iii) Wednesday

   (iv) Thursday (v) Friday ?

   b How many **more** pupils were there on Tuesday than on Friday ?

Mon	👤 👤
Tue	👤 👤 👤 👤 👤
Wed	👤 👤 👤
Thu	👤 👤 👤(half)
Fri	👤 👤(half)

7. Teachers at some primary schools were asked to name their favourite year group. The results are shown in the **bar graph** below.

   a How many teachers chose :-

   (i) P3 (ii) P4

   (iii) P6 (iv) P7

   b What was the most popular year group ?

   c How many teachers were asked ?

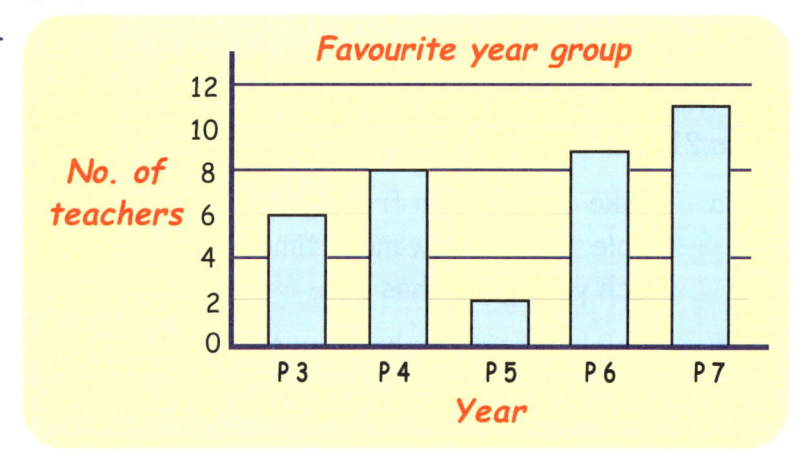

   Favourite year group — bar graph: P3 = 6, P4 = 8, P5 = 2, P6 = 9, P7 = 11. No. of teachers vs Year.

8. Pupils were asked to name their favourite sport. The results are shown in the **bar graph** below.

   a How many pupils chose :-

   (i) hockey
   (ii) football
   (iii) tennis
   (iv) swimming ?

   b How many pupils were asked in the survey ?

   c This is an all boys **or** an all girls school.

   Which one do you think it is and why ?

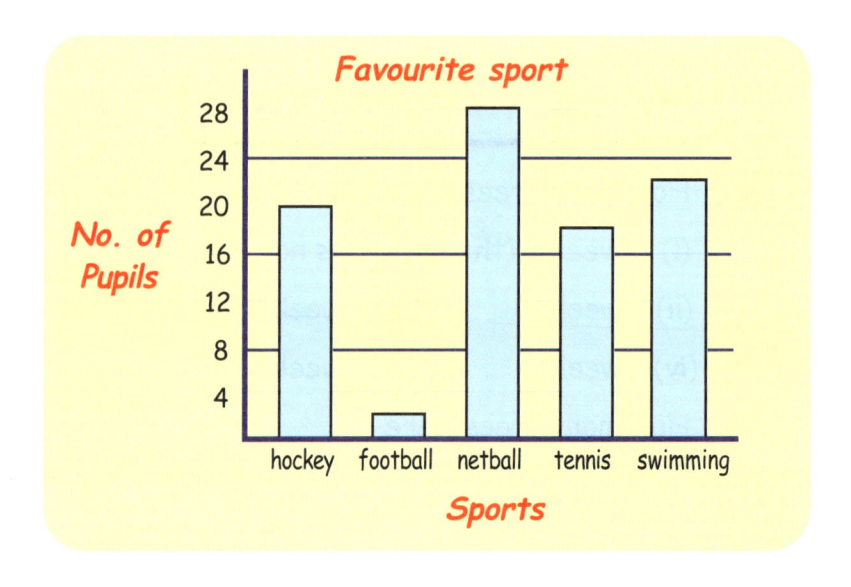

   Favourite sport — bar graph: hockey = 20, football = 2, netball = 29, tennis = 18, swimming = 23. No. of Pupils vs Sports.

this is Chapter Five   page 54   STATISTICS

9. Primary 1 classes in some schools were asked to name their favourite food.

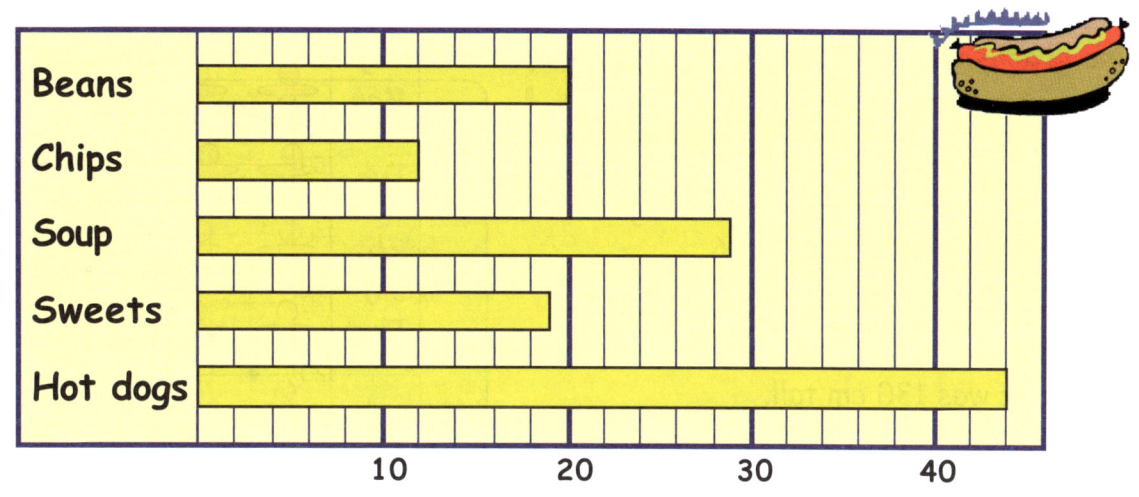

- Beans: 20
- Chips: 15
- Soup: 30
- Sweets: 25
- Hot dogs: 45

a How many Primary 1's liked :-

  (i) Beans   (ii) Chips   (iii) Sweets   (iv) Soup   (v) Hot dogs ?

b What was the favourite food ?

c How many **more** pupils chose soup than sweets ?

d How many pupils were asked altogether ?

10. A primary 7 class were asked about the pets they had.

cat	dog	rabbit	hamster	snake	budgie
6	8	3	7	1	5

Draw and label a neat **bar graph** to show this information.

11. An insurance secretary was given six different types of insurance forms to complete.

Draw and label a neat **bar graph** to show this information.

Car Insurance	– 16	Life Insurance	– 12
Pet Insurance	– 8	House Insurance	– 20
Contents Insurance	– 18	Holiday Insurance	– 15

12. Pupils in a P6 and P7 class were asked their national test levels for Mathematics.

A B D E E E D B A C C E D E D C D B C A
B C B D D D D D E E D B C B D D A C D
E C C A E E D D E D B B C D B C D D E C

a Make a **frequency table** and use tally marks to complete it.

b Draw and label a neat **bar graph** from your frequency table.

Line graphs

Line graphs can be used to compare values which change with time.

Example :-

This line graph shows Joe's height from the age of 6 up to 16.

The yellow shaded line shows that when Joe was 10 years old he was 130 cm tall.

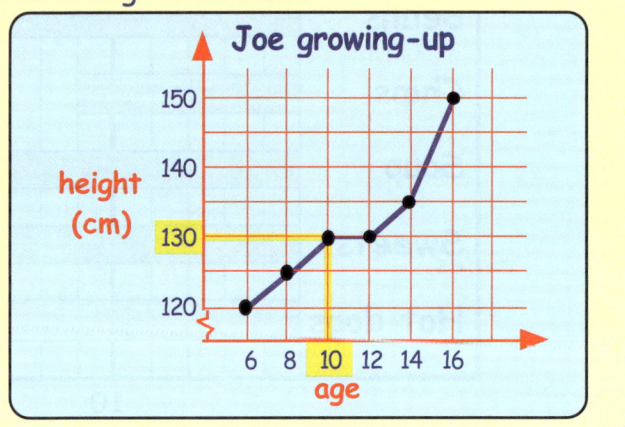

Exercise 2

1. Use the **line graph** above to answer the following :-

    a   How tall was Joe at the age of   (i) 6   (ii) 12   (iii) 14 ?

    b   How old was Joe when he was 150 cm tall ?

    c   How old was Joe when he was 125 cm tall ?

    d   Estimate the height of Joe at 7 years of age.

2. The **line graph** shows the number of cars per hour that were passing over a bridge one Monday.

    a   How many cars were passing over the bridge at :-

    (i)   6 am   (ii)   8 am
    (iii) 10 am   (iv)   noon
    (v)   1 pm ?   (vi)   9.30 am

    b   At what time were there 350 cars per hour going over the bridge ?

    c   At what times (approx) were there 250 cars per hour going over the bridge ?

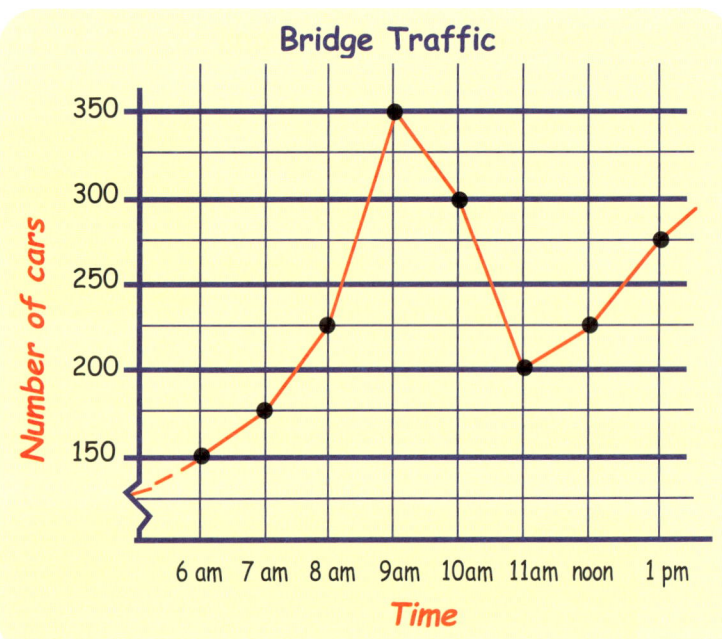

    d   Between what two times was the biggest increase in traffic ?

    e   Why do you think the traffic was busiest around 9 am ?

3. The **line graph** shows the ice cream sales (**in 100's**) by **Tony's Van** from March to December 2002.

ICE CREAM SALES

Sales (100's) vs Month (Mar–Dec)

a How many ice creams did Tony sell in May ? (**in 100's**)

b How many ice creams did Tony sell in :-

  (i) April (ii) July (iii) October ?

c By how much did the sales **increase** between June and July ?

d Between which two consecutive months did sales :-

  (i) rise the most ? (ii) fall the most ?

e How many ice creams did Tony sell altogether from May to September ?

f Why do you think the sales go up and down in this way ?

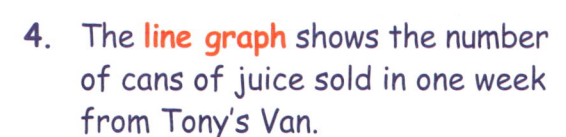

4. The **line graph** shows the number of cans of juice sold in one week from Tony's Van.

JUICE SALES

Number Sold vs Day (Mon–Sun)

  a How many cans of juice were sold on :-

  (i) Monday
  (ii) Friday
  (iii) Saturday ?

  b On what days were more than 30 cans sold ?

  c One day the van would not start. Which day must it have been ?

  d One of the days was a very hot day.
   Which day was very hot ? Explain why it is likely to have been this day.

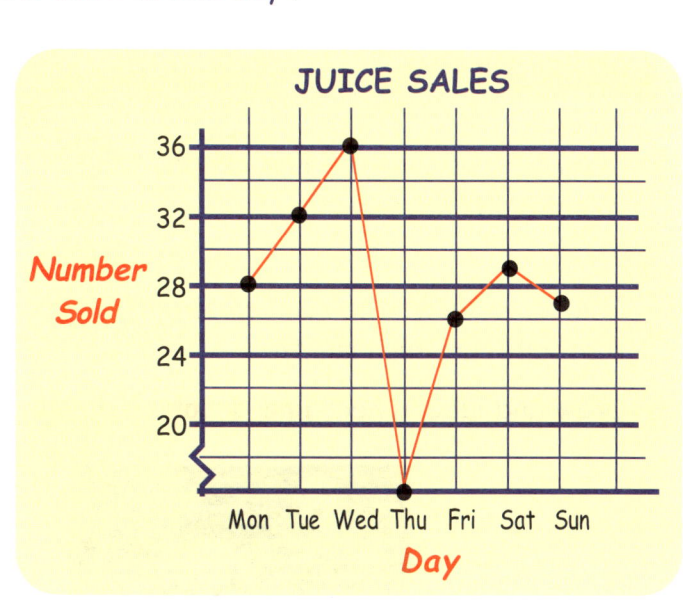

this is Chapter Five   page 57   STATISTICS

5. The **comparative** line graph shows the sales from two different car showrooms, **Cars-R-Us** and **Best Cars**.

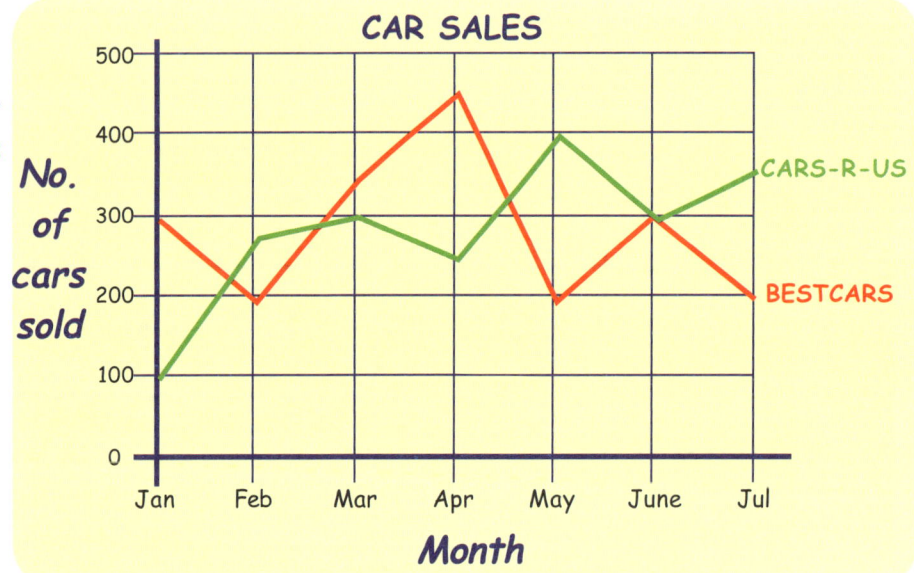

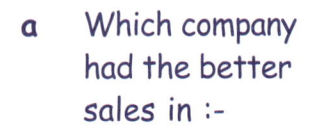

   a   Which company had the better sales in :-

   (i)   February
   (ii) April
   (iii) May
   (iv) June ?

   b   How many cars were sold by each company in :-   (i) May   (ii) March   (iii) April ?

   c   Over the months shown, which company had the better (**total**) sales ?

6. Rachael recorded her height from the age of 6 up to 16.

   Draw and label a neat **line graph** to show this information.
   (**Hint** : look at the example on page 93)

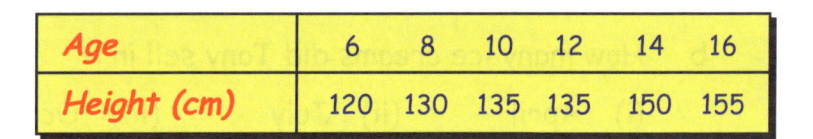

Age	6	8	10	12	14	16
Height (cm)	120	130	135	135	150	155

7. Mary recorded how many flies her pet spider ate each day.

Day	Mon	Tue	Wed	Thu	Fri
No. of flies	3	7	1	3	10

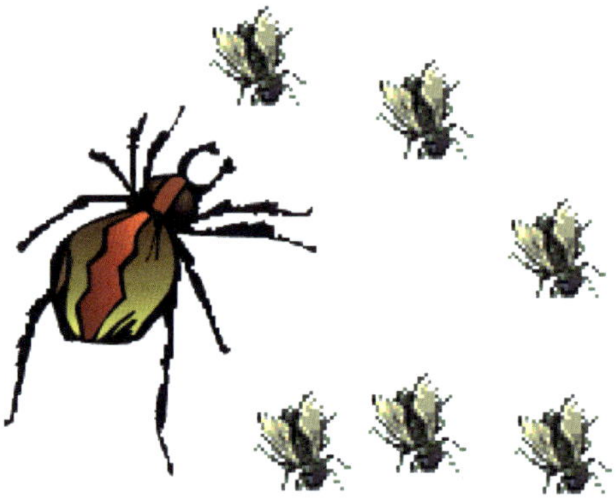

   Draw and label a neat **line graph** to show this information.

8. The table shows the number of goals scored by a school football team each month.

   Draw and label a neat **line graph** to display this data.

Month	Goals
Aug	20
Sept	30
Oct	15
Nov	45
Dec	10
Jan	25

Pie charts

Pie charts are also useful for displaying information.

The pie chart displays the results of a survey conducted to find the most popular pet in a class.

The chart shows that the cat was the most popular pet.

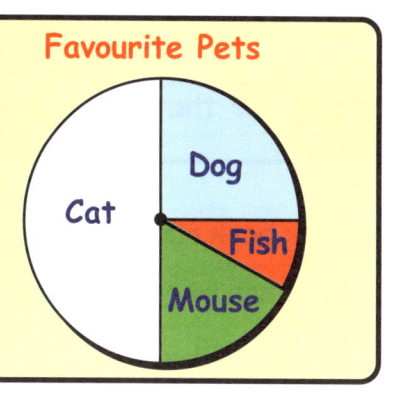

Favourite Pets

Exercise 3

1. a From the diagram above, write down the **least** popular pet.

   b Make a **list** of the pets from **most** popular to **least** popular.

2. The class also surveyed the most popular drink.

   a Write down the classes' favourite drink.

   b List the drinks in order, from **most** popular.

Favourite Drinks

This pie chart has been divided into 10 equal "**sectors**".

Each "bit" is $\frac{1}{10}$ of the whole pie.

The chart shows that the **green sector (A)** is $\frac{5}{10}$.

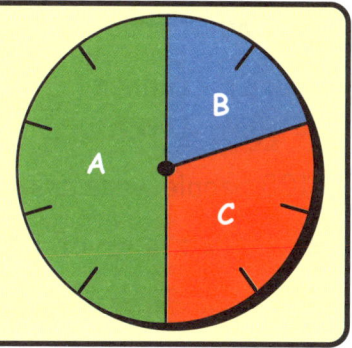

3. a From the pie chart **above**, how many tenths are shown by B **(the blue sector)** ?

   b What fraction does C **(the red sector)** represent ?

4. The pie chart shows the results of a class survey into favourite restaurant food.

   a Write down the fraction of the class who chose :-

   (i) Indian ($\frac{?}{10}$)   (ii) Chinese
   (iii) Italian   (iv) French.

   b List the foods in order, from **most** popular to **least** popular.

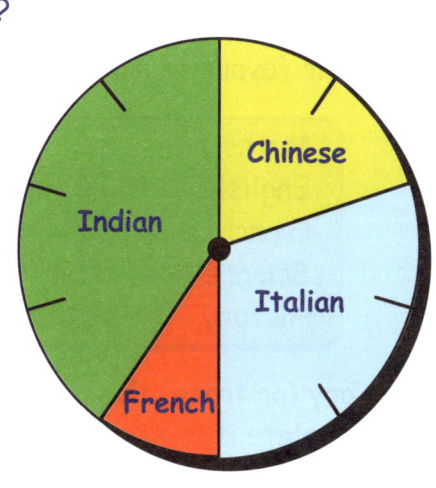

this is Chapter Five   page 59   STATISTICS

> Look back at the pie chart from question 4.
>
> > Italian was $\frac{3}{10}$. If there were 20 in the class, Italian is $\frac{3}{10}$ of 20 = 20 ÷ 10 × 3 = 6.
>
> **Can you see that 6 pupils chose Italian ?**

5. Look back again at the pie chart from question 4.

   If there were 20 pupils in the class, how many chose :-

   a French   **b** Chinese   **c** Indian ?

   (Check that your answers to Italian, French, Chinese and Indian add to give 20 pupils).

6. Fifty people were asked to name their favourite holiday destination.

   The results are shown in the pie chart. Calculate how many people chose :-

   a America   **b** Spain

   c France   **d** Italy ?

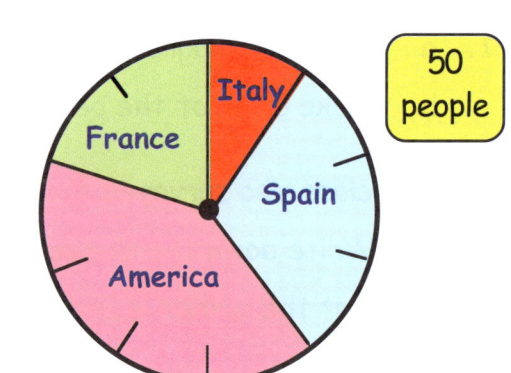

7. This pie chart has been divided into **20 equal parts**.

   a What fraction does each part stand for ?

   b What fraction represents :-

   (i) Dinner ($\frac{?}{20}$)   (ii) Supper
   (iii) Lunch   (iv) Breakfast ?

   100 people were asked in the survey.

   c What is $\frac{1}{20}$ of 100 ?

   d **How many** people chose :-

   (i) Dinner   (ii) Supper
   (iii) Lunch   (iv) Breakfast ?

8. 100 people were asked to name their favourite school subject.

   Maths - 50
   English - 20
   French - 5
   Science - 15
   History - 10

   Copy (or trace) the blank pie chart, and complete it showing the above information.

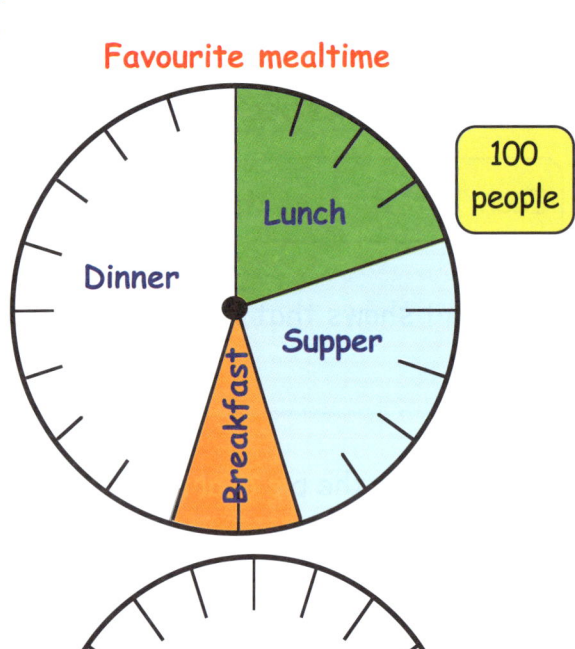

Interpreting tables

Exercise 4

	Fri	Sat	Sun
Apples	5	7	12
Oranges	12	14	27

1. The table shows the number of pieces of fruit sold over a weekend.

    a   How many **apples** were sold on :-

    (i) Sunday   (ii) Saturday   (iii) Friday   (iv) altogether ?

    b   How many **oranges** were sold on :-

    (i) Sunday   (ii) Friday   (iii) altogether ?

    c   Over the three days, how many **more** oranges were sold than apples ?

2. Using Asha's timetable below, answer the following questions :-

Period	1	2	3	4	5
Monday	Maths	French	P.E.	History	Art
Tuesday	English	Maths	Geog	R. E.	French
Wednesday	Music	English	History	Maths	Maths
Thursday	Geog	French	English	P.E.	P.E.
Friday	H.E.	French	Music	Maths	English

    a   How many periods in a week are given to :-

    (i) Maths   (ii) English   (iii) P.E.   (iv) Art ?

    b   Which subject does Asha have on :-

    (i) Monday 2   (ii) Friday 3   (iii) Thursday 4   (iv) Tuesday 4 ?

    c   Write down which days and which periods Asha has :-

    (i) Maths   (ii) French   (iii) Music   (iv) Art.

3. Jason takes his dad to buy a new bike.

    The table shows the cost of bikes of different sizes and standards.

	Small	Medium	Large
Economy	£24	£28	£32
Standard	£25	£30	£35
Deluxe	£30	£36	£40

    a   How much would it cost for each of these bikes :-

    (i) small economy

    (ii) medium standard

    (iii) large standard

    (iv) deluxe large ?

    b   Jason's dad paid £25 for his bike.

    Which bike did Jason get ?

4. Mr. Wilson is looking at the holiday table shown opposite.

	1 week	2 weeks	3 weeks	4 weeks
Beach Hotel	£217	£289	£329	£349
Bay Hotel	£227	£311	£335	£350
Sun Hotel	£249	£299	£349	£399

   a   How much would it cost Mr. Wilson to stay at the :-

   (i)   Beach Hotel for one week ?

   (ii) Bay Hotel for two weeks ?

   (iii) Sun Hotel for four weeks ?

   (iv) Bay Hotel for four weeks ?

   b   Mr. Wilson paid £299 for his holiday. Where did he stay and for how long ?

   c   The table prices shown are for each person. How much would it cost altogether for Mr. **and** Mrs. Boney to stay at the :-

   (i)   Beach Hotel for one week ?   (ii) Sun Hotel for two weeks ?

5. This holiday table shows the prices for each adult and each child.

   How much would it cost for each of the following holidays :-

	One week Adult	One week Child	Two weeks Adult	Two weeks Child
Majorca	£149	£79	£189	£99
Portugal	£179	£69	£199	£89
Malta	£229	£99	£279	£129

   a   Majorca, 1 adult for 1 week ?

   b   Malta, 1 adult for 2 weeks ?

   c   Portugal, 2 adults for 1 week ?

   d   Malta, 1 adult and 1 child for 2 weeks ?

   e   Mr. Podge, his wife and 3 children for two weeks in Portugal ?

6. The charges for a delivery service are shown in the table.

   a   What is the charge for each of the following deliveries :-

Weight \ Distance	under 5 km	between 5-10 km	above 10 km
1 - 5 kg	£5·50	£6·00	£8·50
6 - 10 kg	£7·50	£8·50	£10·50
11 - 20 kg	£8·50	£9·00	£12·50
above 20 kg	£10·50	£11·00	£15·00

   (i)   2 kg delivered 3 km ?

   (ii) 14 kg delivered 12 km ?

   (iii) 9 kg delivered 7 km ?

   (iv) 11 kg delivered 2 km ?

   b   I paid £9 for a package delivery.

   Give an example of the weight of the package and how far it was delivered.

Topic in a Nutshell

1. A class were asked to name their favourite sportswear label. Shown opposite are their answers.

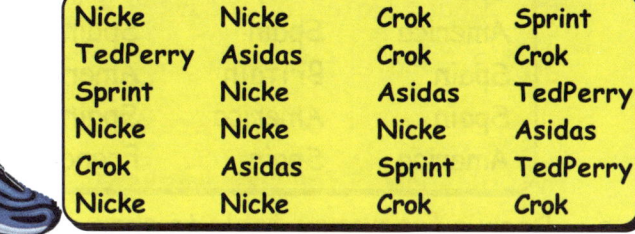

Nicke	Nicke	Crok	Sprint
TedPerry	Asidas	Crok	Crok
Sprint	Nicke	Asidas	TedPerry
Nicke	Nicke	Nicke	Asidas
Crok	Asidas	Sprint	TedPerry
Nicke	Nicke	Crok	Crok

   a Copy and complete the **frequency table**.

   b How many pupils were in the class ?

   c Which was the **most** popular sports wear ?

Label	Tally	Frequency
Nicke		
Crok		
Asidas		
Ted Perry		
Sprint		

   COPY

2. The **pictograph** shows the number of pupils who attended football practice.

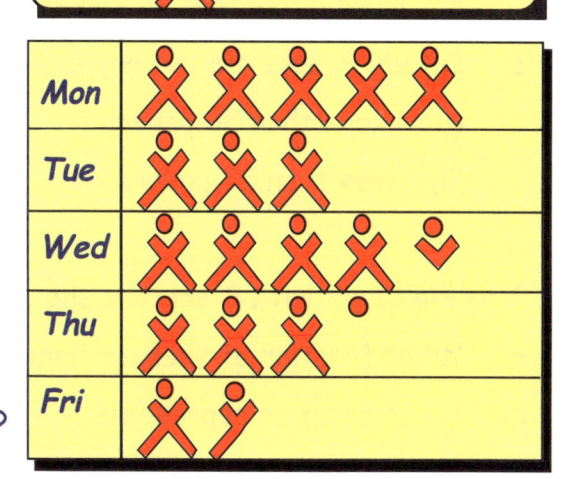

   Key: ✗ stands for 5 pupils.

   a How many pupils attended on :-

   (i)   Monday ?

   (ii) Tuesday ?

   (iii) Friday ?

Mon	✗ ✗ ✗ ✗ ✗
Tue	✗ ✗ ✗
Wed	✗ ✗ ✗ ✗ ✗
Thu	✗ ✗ ✗
Fri	✗ ✗

   Mr. Sampson needs at least **90 pupils** to attend practice each week, otherwise he will cancel next week's practice.

   b Will next week's practice be cancelled ? Explain your answer.

3. The **bar graph** shows the number of bags of crisps sold at the school tuck shop one day.

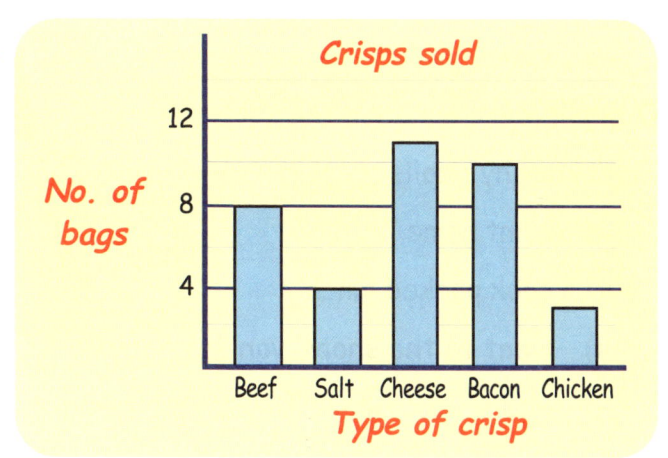

   a How many of each type was sold ?

   b How many bags were sold altogether ?

   Crisps sold

   No. of bags — Beef 8, Salt 4, Cheese 11, Bacon 10, Chicken 3

   Type of crisp

4. People were asked to name their favourite holiday destination.

America	Spain	Italy	France	Britain
Spain	Italy	Britain	America	America
America	Spain	Spain	Spain	America
Spain	Britain	America	Spain	France
Spain	America	Spain	Britain	France
America	Spain	France	Spain	Britain

   a Draw a **frequency table** to show this information with the use of **tally marks**.

   b Now draw and label a neat **bar graph** to help represent this information.

5. The **line graph** shows the number of newspapers delivered by a paper boy one week.

   a Write down the number of papers the boy delivered each day.

   b How many deliveries did the boy make altogether this week ?

   c On which days did the boy deliver :-

   (i) **more** than 36 papers ?

   (ii) **less** than 33 papers ?

6. This Pie Chart with **8 sectors** shows where pupils go for lunch.

   a What fraction of them go **home** for lunch ?

   b What fraction represents :-

   (i)   packed lunch ?

   (ii) shops/van ?

   (iii) school dinner ?

   40 pupils were asked in the survey.

   c How many pupils :-

   (i)   went home ?

   (ii) took packed lunch ?

   (iii) went to the shops/van ?

   (iv) had school dinner ?

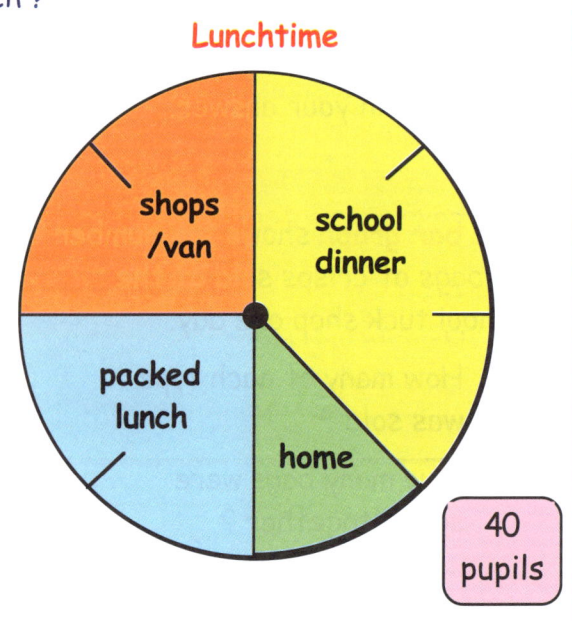

7. Theatre ticket prices are shown in the table.

	Mon – Thu Adult	Mon – Thu Child	Fri – Sat Adult	Fri – Sat Child
Stalls	£15	£9	£22	£15
Circle	£12	£7	£19	£12
Upper Circle	£10	£5	£17	£11

a How much would it cost for :-

   (i) one adult stalls ticket on Tuesday ?

   (ii) one child circle ticket on Friday ?

   (iii) **Two** adult upper circle tickets on Saturday ?

   (iv) One adult **and** one child upper circle ticket on Wednesday ?

b Mr. and Mrs. Bruce take their two children on a Friday and buy upper circle tickets.

Calculate the total cost for the tickets.

c How much would they have saved if they had gone on **Thursday** instead ?

Conducting a survey

When carrying out a survey you need to consider several points :-

- the type of questions you will ask.
- who you will ask.
- how will you organise your answers.
- how will you display your answers.

You may wish to use a **frequency table**, **bar graph**, **line graph** or **pie chart**.

1. Choose **one** from the list below and carry out a survey.

   a The shoe sizes in your class.
   b Which month of the year were the members of your class born ?
   c Favourite class cartoon character.
   d Favourite international football team.
   e Favourite pop star.
   f Most popular breakfast.
   g How do you get to school ?
   h Number of words each member of your class can write in 30 seconds.
   i Heights of each pupil in your class.

2. Choose **another** from the list - or make one up for yourself - and conduct a survey. (Make sure that this survey is different from your first. You could work in groups – Display your graphs and charts).

Chapter 6

Decimals 2

Multiply and Divide Decimals

Multiplication by 10 and 100.

Learn these rules for decimals :-

If you multiply by 10,

=> move all the figures **ONE place LEFT**
(*or move the point one place right*)

```
  2·54
  × 10
  ————
  25·4
```

If you multiply by 100,

=> move all the figures **TWO places LEFT**
(*or move the point two places right*)

```
  26·725
  × 100
  ——————
  2672·5
```

Exercise 1

1. Write down the answers to these multiplications :-
   a 3·7 × 10
   b 4·5 × 10
   c 4·52 × 10
   d 10 × 7·21
   e 10 × 12·78
   f 0·94 × 10
   g 10 × 3·008
   h 0·0147 × 10

2. Write down the answers to :-
   a 5·96 × 100
   b 8·74 × 100
   c 100 × 2·05
   d 100 × 2·6
   e 5·47 × 100
   f 100 × 2·68
   g 100 × 0·0589
   h 0·0068 × 100

3. A bag of Uncle Bob's rice weighs 1·16 kg. What is the weight of :-
   a 10 bags
   b 100 bags ?

4. There are **100 centimetres** in **1 metre**. How many centimetres are there in :
   a 4·14 m
   b 27·6 m
   c 0·9 m
   d 0·003 m ?

5. There are **10 millimetres** in **1 centimetre**. How many millimetres are there in :-
   a 90·0 cm
   b 0·9 cm
   c 9·9 cm
   d 0·09 cm ?

6.  Granny Smith gives her 10 grandchildren pocket money.
   She uses the loose change in her purse.
   Last week, the grandchildren **each** received £2·36.

   How much loose change must Granny Smith have had ?

7. Each of the 100 men in the bowling club's "100 Club" received £500·80 for getting "5 numbers up" in the lottery.

   What was the total prize that night for the five winning numbers ?

> **Division by 10 and 100.**
>
> **Learn these rules for decimals :–**
>
> If you divide by 10,
>
> => move all the figures **ONE place RIGHT**
> (or move the point one place left)   10)47·8 = 4·78
>
> If you divide by 100,
>
> => move all the figures **TWO places RIGHT**
> (or move the point two places left)   100)247·3 = 2·473

Exercise 2

1. Write down the answers to the following divisions :–

    a 14·2 ÷ 10   b 35·9 ÷ 10   c 7·84 ÷ 10   d 247·5 ÷ 10
    e 23·82 ÷ 10   f 478·27 ÷ 10   g 57·02 ÷ 10   h 46 ÷ 10
    i 8 ÷ 10   j 0·34 ÷ 10   k 0·2 ÷ 10   l 0·047 ÷ 10

2. Try the following :–

    a 488·4 ÷ 100   b 417·12 ÷ 100   c 15·8 ÷ 100   d 42·04 ÷ 100
    e 470 ÷ 100   f 9 ÷ 100   g 5·6 ÷ 100   h 0·6 ÷ 100

3. a When 100 paper clips are weighed, their total weight is 42·7 grams.
       What is the weight of 1 paper clip ?

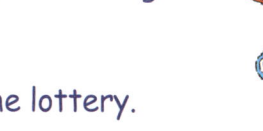

    b 100 people form a group who get 5 numbers up in the lottery.
       Their **total** winnings come to £70 803·00.
       How much will **each** person receive ?

    c Grandpa Jones gives his 10 grandchildren pocket money, monthly.
       He puts his loose change into a tin for this purpose.
       Last month, Grandpa had saved £25·20 of loose change in his tin.
       How much did he give **each** of his grandchildren ?

4. There are **10 millimetres** in **1 centimetre**. How many centimetres are equal to :–

    a 60 mm   b 80·3 mm   c 427 mm   d 0·6 mm ?

5. **1 metre = 100 centimetres**. How many metres are the same as :–

    a 303 cm   b 4510 cm   c 65 cm   d 7 cm ?

6. Mr Devlin buys 100 jotters for a total of £35.
    What is the cost of **one** jotter ?

Multiplication by a Single Digit.

* It is very important for you know your multiplication tables.

Example 1   34·8 × 6

```
  34·8
×    6
------
 208·8
   2 4
```
note that the points stay in line

Example 2   45·29 × 7

```
  45·29
×     7
-------
 317·03
   3 2 6
```
Again the points stay in line

Exercise 3

1. How well do you know your tables? Write the answers to :-

   a 4 × 8   b 5 × 6   c 6 × 8   d 7 × 4
   e 8 × 5   f 3 × 9   g 7 × 5   h 8 × 6
   i 6 × 9   j 9 × 5   k 9 × 6   l 5 × 9
   m 9 × 7   n 4 × 9   o 7 × 6   p 10 × 10
   q 6 × 7   r 8 × 7   s 5 × 8   t 8 × 9
   u 9 × 8   v 7 × 7   w 9 × 9   x 7 × 9

2. Copy and complete each calculation :-

   a   4·9   b   5·8   c   15·3   d   92·3
      × 2   × 3   × 4   × 5

   e   41·7   f   32·6   g   36·6   h   52·7
      × 6   × 7   × 8   × 9

   i   4·87   j   6·52   k   45·8   l   3·87
      × 7   × 6   × 4   × 8

   m   5·67   n   8·26   o   65·8   p   6·84
      × 3   × 5   × 7   × 9

3. Put each of these in the form shown above, then carry out the multiplication :-

   a 3·4 × 2   b 2·7 × 3   c 8·6 × 4   d 5·7 × 3
   e 5 × 6·4   f 4 × 18·6   g 3·17 × 7   h 6 × 2·83
   i 8 × 5·74   j 5 × 6·98   k 46·3 × 6   l 9 × 27·6

this is Chapter Six   page 68   DECIMALS 2

4. Try these problems. **Show all your working !**

   a   A notebook costs £6·48.

   What is the cost of 4 identical notebooks ?

   No calculator

   b   Emma works in a baker's shop on a Saturday.

   If she works 8 hours at £5·46 per hour how much does she get paid ?

   c   A 10p coin is 2·37 cm wide.

   How long will a line of 9 coins be ?

   d   A dictionary is 8·29 cm thick.

   How high would a pile of 6 dictionaries be ?

   e   It says on the packet that the weedkiller will cover 25·8 m^2 of pathway.

   What area of pathway can be treated with 7 packets ?

   f   Carol hires a bike at £2·35 per hour.

   If she stays out on the bike for 6 hours how much will it cost her ?

   g   What is the cost of 5 identical CD's if one costs £12·68 ?

   h   A snail covered 17·4 metres in the space of 1 hour.

   At this speed, how far will it cover in 8 hours ?

   i   A wall tile is 9·37 cm wide.

   What width of wall will a pack of 6 tiles cover ?

   j   Last winter, 6·28 centimetres of snow fell every day for a week.

   What depth of snow fell during this period ?

   k   A ten pack of chicken drumsticks weighs 3·85 kg.
   Mrs Bain buys 4 of these packs.

   What weight will she be carrying home ?

Division by a Single Digit

* **Again** - very important for you know your multiplication tables.

    Example 1   16·8 ÷ 6

    Example 2   29·26 ÷ 7

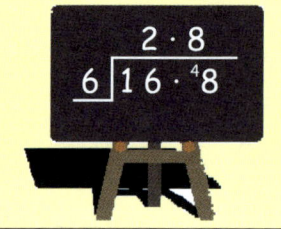

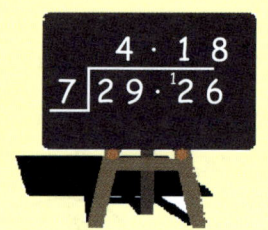

$$\begin{array}{r}2.8\\6\overline{)16.^48}\end{array} \qquad \begin{array}{r}4.18\\7\overline{)29.^12^26}\end{array}$$

Exercise 4

1. **How well do you know your tables?** Copy and complete :-

a	32 ÷ 8	b	30 ÷ 6	c	48 ÷ 8	d	28 ÷ 4
e	40 ÷ 5	f	27 ÷ 9	g	35 ÷ 5	h	48 ÷ 6
i	54 ÷ 9	j	45 ÷ 5	k	54 ÷ 6	l	45 ÷ 9
m	63 ÷ 7	n	36 ÷ 9	o	42 ÷ 6	p	80 ÷ 10
q	42 ÷ 7	r	56 ÷ 7	s	40 ÷ 8	t	72 ÷ 9
u	72 ÷ 8	v	49 ÷ 7	w	81 ÷ 9	x	63 ÷ 9

2. Copy and complete each calculation :-

a	2)8·4	b	3)9·6	c	4)6·8	d	5)6·5
e	6)13·8	f	7)44·1	g	8)53·6	h	9)37·8
i	2)7·36	j	3)7·35	k	4)7·56	l	5)9·75
m	6)1·56	n	7)9·73	o	8)9·84	p	9)9·54

3. Write each of these in the form shown above, then carry out the division :-

a	9·4 ÷ 2	b	7·2 ÷ 3	c	7·6 ÷ 4	d	5·45 ÷ 5
e	20·4 ÷ 6	f	74·2 ÷ 7	g	90·4 ÷ 8	h	70·29 ÷ 9
i	7·14 ÷ 6	j	1·04 ÷ 8	k	9·72 ÷ 9	l	7·88 ÷ 4
m	7·38 ÷ 2	n	8·25 ÷ 3	o	8·36 ÷ 4	p	51·5 ÷ 5
q	2·22 ÷ 6	r	8·54 ÷ 7	s	9·76 ÷ 8	t	9·81 ÷ 9
u	27·2 ÷ 4	v	5·61 ÷ 3	w	8·89 ÷ 7	x	0·80 ÷ 8

this is Chapter Six   DECIMALS 2

4. Try these problems. **Show all your working !**

   a   6 packets of biscuits weigh 1·74 kilograms.
       What is the weight of 1 packet ?

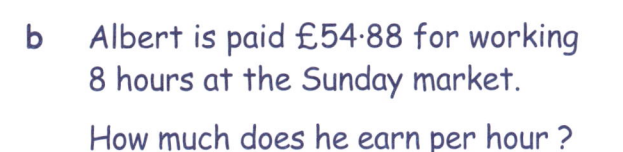

   b   Albert is paid £54·88 for working
       8 hours at the Sunday market.
       How much does he earn per hour ?

   c   To find a "third" of something, you simply **divide by 3**.

      (i)   What is a third of 38·7 ?   (ii) What is a quarter of 5·88 ?
      (iii) What is a fifth of 7·05 ?   (iv) What is a sixth of 7·56 ?
      (v)   What is a eighth of 92·0 ?   (vi) What is a ninth of 1·71 ?

   d   A pile of 7 identical books is 30·66 cm tall ?
       What is the thickness of 1 book ?

   e   Four girls went to the cinema.
       The tickets cost £10·92 in total.
       What is the cost of 1 ticket ?

   f   A tray of 6 potted sunflowers costs £5·34.
       How much is it for one pot ?

   g   Joyce put £7·02 into the parking meter.
       She left her car parked there from 8 am until 5 pm.
       How much is it to park next to the meter for 1 hour ?

   h   To raise money for charity, school pupils held a sponsored "sing-along".
       All pupils had to sing non-stop for 90 minutes.
       Unfortunately a few of the pupils had stopped singing one quarter
       of the way through.
       For how many minutes had they sang ?

   i   9 children decided to split the cost of
       a box of fireworks.
       If the cost of the fireworks was £5·13,
       how much did each have to pay ?

   j   I poured 8 glasses of lemonade from a 2·4 litre jug.
       I managed to pour an equal amount into each glass.
       How much juice was in each glass ?

this is Chapter Six   page 71   DECIMALS 2

Mixed Problems

In this exercise, you have to decide whether to ADD, SUBTRACT, MULTIPLY or DIVIDE.

You **MAY** use a calculator, but show what type of calculation you are doing.

Do not just write down an answer.

Exercise 5

1. Rona buys a handbag for £25·85 and a pair of gloves at £17·99.

   What is the total cost ?

2. The band "Aquaria" have two CD's out at the moment.
   One lasts for 42·3 minutes, the other for only 37·8 minutes.

   How much longer does the first CD last than the second ?

3. Donald works for 8 hours on a Saturday for £8·95 per hour.
   His brother, Dougal, gets paid only £8·29 per hour, but he works
   for 9 hours on a Saturday.

   Who comes home with the higher pay packet and by how much ?

4. Sally paid out £85·68 for 6 driving lessons.

   How much did this work out for each lesson ?

5. Sidney bought 3 computer games, priced £28·99, £32·45 and £23·10.

   How much change did he get from nine £10 notes ?

6. Mandy is putting edging slabs round her lawn.
   The total length around the lawn is 18 metres.
   Each concrete edging slab is 2·3 metres long.

   Mandy buys 7 slabs. Is this enough ? Explain !

7. Mrs Grace is the manager of a retail company.
   She saw this advert in a magazine and sent off
   an order for 5 staplers and 4 hole punches.
   When her order arrived she noticed that her bill
   was for £12.

   How much had she been overcharged ?

   SPECIAL OFFER
   Staplers -   £1·48
   Hole Punches - £0·94

8. David hires a carpet cleaner from the local store. It costs him £7·75 deposit
   plus £2·65 per hour. He returned the carpet cleaner after 3 hours use.

   How much had he to pay ?

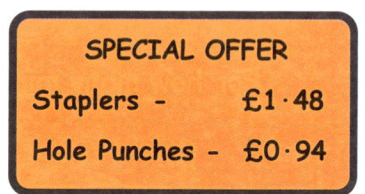

9. Sandy bought 8 packets of chewing gum, each costing £0·63, 4 packets of toffees at 92p each and 2 bottles of cola at £1·23 each.
    His sister, Rose, offered to split the total cost equally with him.

    She gave Sandy a £5 note. Was this enough ? **Explain !**

10. George hired an electric drill.
    It cost £32·96 for a 4 hour hire.

    How much did that work out at, per hour ?

11. Barry fills his motor bike with petrol.
    He puts in 9 litres at a cost of £0·78 per litre.

    How much does he get back from one £5 note and 3 pound coins ?

12. The good ship Galileo used 46·8 litres of fuel during a 6 hour trip.

    How much fuel is used in one hour ?

13. A group of 16 children pay a total of £56·80 to have a night out at the theatre.

    What is the cost of one ticket ?

14. Find the total cost (including parking) for each of the following groups to visit the castle :-

    a 20 adults in a coach.
    b 15 children in a minibus.
    c 2 adults and 2 children in a car.

    VISIT THE CASTLE
    Entrance
    Adult £1·34   Child 69p
    Parking
    Coach £2·50   Car £1·15   Minibus £1·92

15. Look again at the entry fees for visiting the castle.

    If a group of 12 travelling by coach pays a total of £15·33 for parking and visiting the castle, how many of them were adults and how many were children ?

16. The times of the five fastest runners in a school's sports event were :-

    28·7 seconds   30·1 seconds   31·3 seconds   31·7 seconds   32·7 seconds

    Calculate the **average** time taken by these five runners.

this is Chapter Six   page 73   DECIMALS 2

Topic in a Nutshell

1. Set down and find :-

   a 3·24 × 9   b 5 × 4·68   c 7·44 ÷ 4   d 9·59 ÷ 7.

2. Write down the answers to these multiplications and divisions :-

   a 5·1 × 10   b 74·3 × 10   c 7·96 × 10   d 3·2 × 100

   e 56·34 × 100   f 5·74 × 100   g 4·81 ÷ 100   h 5 ÷ 100

3. Six long-life light bulbs cost £22·32.

   What does one cost ?

4. One bag of cement covers 8 square metres of ground when laid thinly.

   a How many **full** bags will I need for a piece of ground with an area of 126 square metres ? (**careful**)

   b At £7·46 per bag, what will I have to pay ?

5. A group of 25 children and 4 adults are going to a Water Park. The cost is £8·46 per adult and **half-price** for each child.

   Work out the cost for :-

   a the adults.   b the children.   c the whole group.

6. Hazel and five of her friends bought a bag of chips and one pickled onion each. The total bill came to £9·36.

   If the cost of a bag of chips was £1·22, calculate :-

   a the cost of the chips for everyone

   b the total cost of the pickled onions

   c the cost of one pickled onion.

7. Maitland's are selling boxes of 20 salmon for £69·40.
   Marshall's are selling their salmon at £82·32 for a box of 24.

   By working out the cost of 1 salmon in each shop, find which fishmonger sells the cheaper fish.

Chapter 7 — Algebra

Revision Work

Basic "Equations"

Example 1 :-   Look at this simple statement (**an equation**).

   5 + * = 11   -   what does the " * " stand for ?

=> By using your finger to **cover up** the star, ask yourself :-

   " 5 plus **what** equals 11

   => the answer of course is "6".

   5 + = 11
   => * = 6

3 further examples :-

   3 × * = 15
   =>   * = 5

   10 − * = 4
   =>   * = 6

   $\frac{*}{6} = 3$
   =>   * = 18

3 different examples :-

Which of the 4 symbols, +, −, × or ÷ should replace the ☐ box each time ?

   12 ☐ 6 = 6
   => ☐ is "−"

   2 ☐ 3 = 5
   => ☐ is "+"

   2 ☐ 3 = 6
   => ☐ is "×"

Exercise 1

1. Copy each of the following and find what * stands for each time :-

   a   4 + * = 7
       => * = ...

   b   10 − * = 2
       => * = ...

   c   * × 4 = 20
       => * = ...

2. Find the value of * in each of the following :-

   a   6 + * = 20
   b   3 + * = 3
   c   18 + * = 30
   d   * + 11 = 19
   e   12 − * = 3
   f   20 − * = 10
   g   9 − * = 0
   h   7 − * = 7
   i   * − 4 = 7
   j   * − 10 = 19
   k   * − 3 = 0
   l   * − 5 = 4
   m   3 × * = 21
   n   6 × * = 48
   o   * × 5 = 35

p $9 \times * = 0$ q $\dfrac{*}{3} = 6$ r $\dfrac{*}{8} = 5$

s $\dfrac{20}{*} = 10$ t $36 \div * = 4$ u $27 \div * = 9$

3. In each of the following, the symbol ☐ stands for +, −, × or ÷.
   Decide which symbol is needed each time here :−

   a   6 ☐ 4 = 10   b   12 ☐ 2 = 10   c   2 ☐ 5 = 10
   d   30 ☐ 3 = 10   e   5 ☐ 1 = 4   f   5 ☐ 1 = 5
   g   5 ☐ 1 = 6   h   8 ☐ 2 = 4   i   30 ☐ 3 = 33
   j   36 ☐ 4 = 32   k   42 ☐ 6 = 7   l   50 ☐ 10 = 500

4. By inserting each of +, −, × or ÷, in place of ●, find **all** the possible answers to 20 ● 4.

5. Replace ● and ✱ by any of the symbols +, −, × or ÷ in turn to produce all 16 answers to   24 ● 6 ✱ 2.

6. Look at the scales shown below and find the weight of the **brown** box each time :−

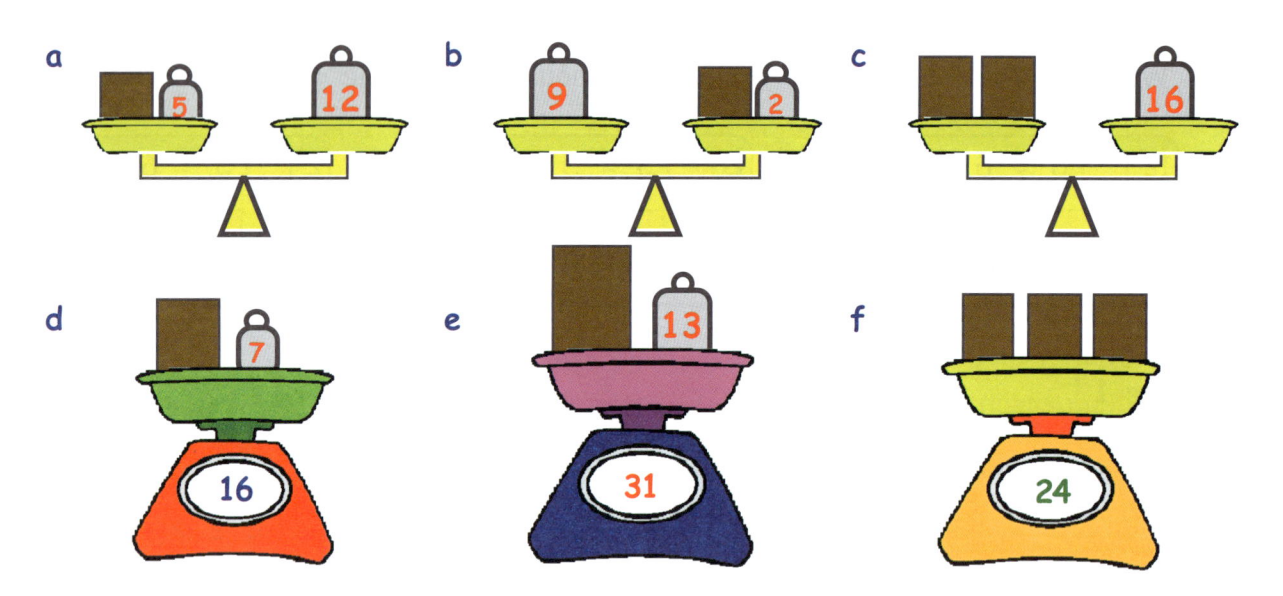

   a (brown box + 5 balances 12)   b (9 balances brown box + 2)   c (2 brown boxes balance 16)

   d (brown box + 7 on scale reads 16)   e (brown box + 13 on scale reads 31)   f (3 brown boxes on scale reads 24)

7. Which of the 2 cakes is heavier, and by how much is it heavier than the other ?

   CAKE A (cake + 3 balances 8 + 8)   CAKE B (9 + 7 balances 4 + cake)

8. What must the length of the red piece of wood be each time here?

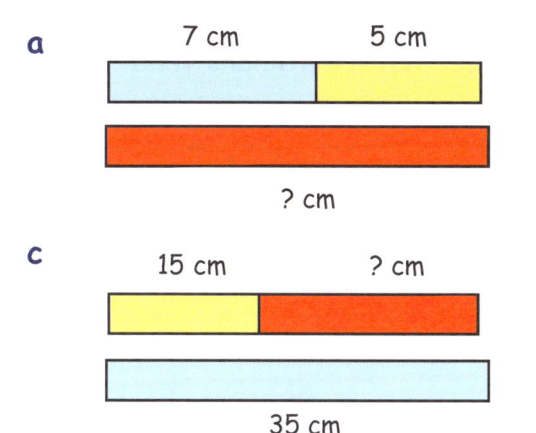

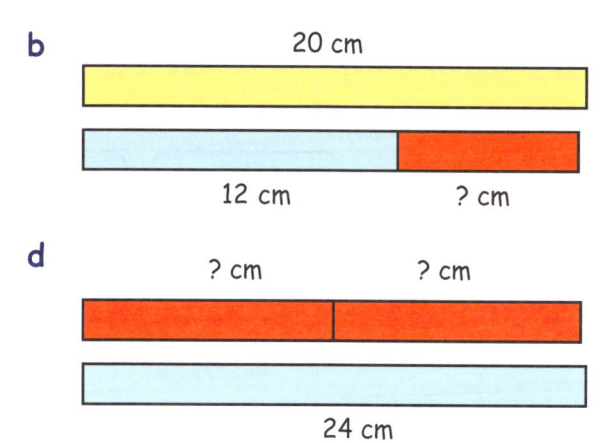

a 7 cm   5 cm
   ? cm

b 20 cm
   12 cm   ? cm

c 15 cm   ? cm
   35 cm

d ? cm   ? cm
   24 cm

9. Jane and Lucy compare how much money each has.
Jane has 13p and together they have 22p.

   a Write down a statement using 13p, 22p and *p (Lucy's money).

   b Find out how much money Lucy has.

10. For each of the following problems, make up a statement (equation) involving +, −, × or ÷ along with a * to stand for the unknown quantity and find the value of * each time.

   a A chocolate bar had 16 squares.
Nick ate some squares and found he was then left with 5 squares.

      How many squares did Nick eat? (start with 16 − * = 5)

   b 5 identical coins weigh 100 grams.

      What does 1 coin weigh? (**Make up an equation first**).

   c When a small lottery win was shared between 4 people, each person received £7.

      What was the value of the total lottery win?

   d When George stood on the bathroom scales holding his pet dog, their total weight was 56 kg.

      If George himself weighed 47 kg, what was the weight of his dog?

   e 4 new tyres cost Mr Brown £160.

      What is the cost of 1 tyre?

   f When a 42 metre piece of rope is cut into identical lengths, the length of each piece is 6 metres.

      How many cut pieces of rope were there?

   g When Mrs White was asked her age, she fibbed and said she was only 39.

      If she had taken 8 years off her true age, how old was Mrs White?

this is Chapter Seven   ALGEBRA

Equations

Instead of using " * " to represent a missing value, mathematicians tend to use letters instead. "*x*" is a firm favourite.

Examples :-

[use **cover up**]

$x + 2 = 7$ => $x = 5$

$x - 4 = 5$ => $x = 9$

$2 \times x = 12$ => $x = 6$

$\frac{x}{10} = 7$ => $x = 70$

These are examples of **equations**.

Exercise 2

1. Copy each equation and solve it to find the value of *x* :-

   a $x + 4 = 11$ b $x + 10 = 13$ c $7 + x = 19$

   d $x + 7 = 7$ e $x - 5 = 2$ f $x - 9 = 1$

   g $x - 6 = 6$ h $10 - x = 5$ i $20 - x = 9$

   j $3 \times x = 18$ k $5 \times x = 35$ l $10 \times x = 60$

   m $x \times 20 = 40$ n $\frac{x}{2} = 11$ o $\frac{x}{9} = 5$

   p $x \div 8 = 3$ q $x \div 4 = 4$ r $30 \div x = 5$

2. Though *x* is a firm favourite, any letter can be used to stand for a missing quantity. Copy each of the following and find the missing values each time :-

   a $y + 7 = 15$ b $t - 3 = 11$ c $4 \times p = 20$

   d $\frac{m}{3} = 7$ e $g + 8 = 8$ f $w - 10 = 20$

   g $f \times 7 = 49$ h $h \div 6 = 1$ i $1.5 + q = 4.5$

   j $27 - z = 9$ k $8 \times s = 40$ l $36 \div d = 4$

3. For each of the following :-

   (i) make up an equation using the letter shown.

   (ii) solve the equation to find the value of the letter.

   a (scale showing x and weight 4, balance reads 11)

   b (scale showing y and weight 9, balance reads 20)

   c (scale showing t and t, balance reads 18)

d scale: n n n n = 32

e scale: p p p = 150

f scale: f, 30 = 50

4. John and Sandra's combined ages are 29. John is 13.

Make up an equation and solve it to find Sandra's age.

5. When a melon was cut into 4 identical pieces, each piece weighed 300 grams.

Make up an equation and solve it to find the total weight of the melon.

6. Wee Jimmy, the Janni, was asked to count how many tables had been laid out in the hall for an exam.
He counted the legs instead and found there were 240 legs.

Make up an equation and solve it to find how many tables there were.

7. When 250 ml of water was poured from a kettle into a cup, there were 1230 ml left in the kettle.

Make up an equation and solve it to find how much water was in the kettle to begin with.

8. I walked 3 kilometres to my friend's house and it took me 36 minutes.

Make up an equation and solve it to find how long it would take me to walk 1 kilometre if I walked at the same speed.

9. The combined number of apple and pear trees in an orchard is 42. There are 18 pear trees.

Make up an equation and solve it to find how many apple trees there are.

10. When a box of chocolates is shared equally, Ned, Ted and Fred each get 13 chocolates.

Make up an equation and solve it to find how many chocolates are in the box before sharing.

this is Chapter Seven   page 79   ALGEBRA

Function Machines (Revision)

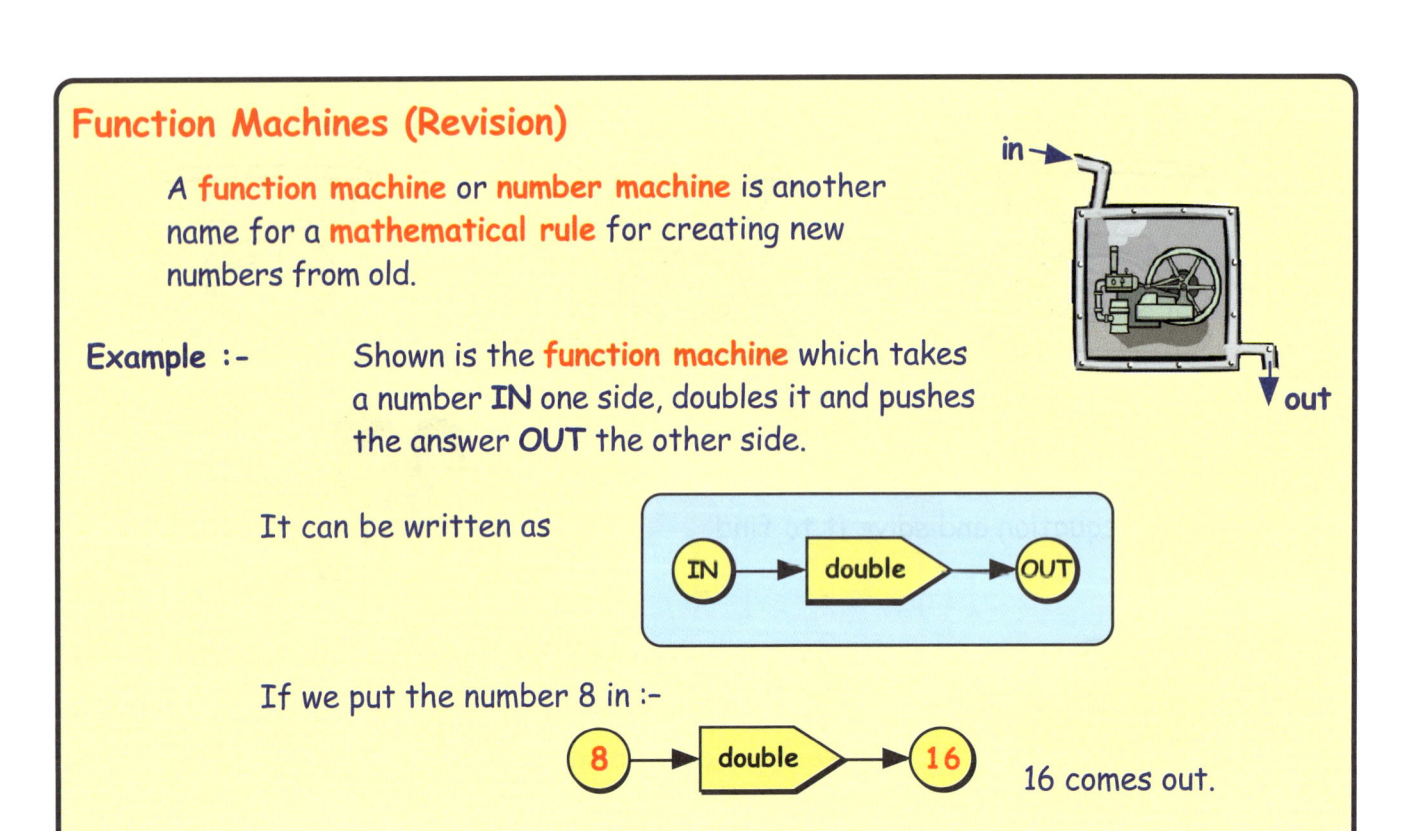

A **function machine** or **number machine** is another name for a **mathematical rule** for creating new numbers from old.

Example :- Shown is the **function machine** which takes a number **IN** one side, doubles it and pushes the answer **OUT** the other side.

It can be written as

IN → double → OUT

If we put the number 8 in :-

8 → double → 16   16 comes out.

Exercise 3

1. Look again at the **double** function machine.

   IN → double → OUT

   a   What comes **out** when you put **in** the number :-

   (i) 7   (ii) 10   (iii) 50   (iv) 1·2   (v) 0 ?

   b   What number must have been put **in** to produce the answer

   (i) 6   (ii) 30   (iii) 5000   (iv) 6·4   (v) 9 ?

2. Here is a new function machine.   IN → + 11 → OUT

   a   What comes **out** of this machine when you put in the number :-

   (i) 7   (ii) 2   (iii) 0   (iv) 25   (v) 6·5 ?

   b   What number must have been put **in** to produce the answer :-

   (i) 25   (ii) 22   (iii) 50   (iv) 11·5   (v) 6311 ?

3. Shown below are some function machines.

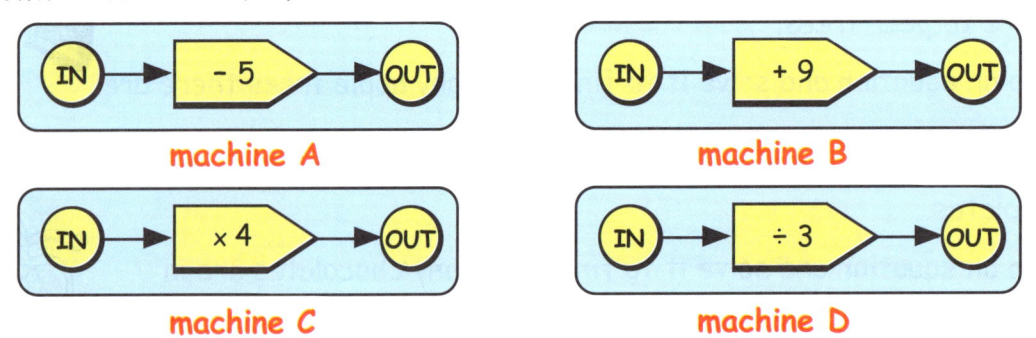

   IN → − 5 → OUT   IN → + 9 → OUT

   machine A   machine B

   IN → × 4 → OUT   IN → ÷ 3 → OUT

   machine C   machine D

a   What comes out when you put **5** into machine **C** ?

b   What comes **out** when the following numbers are put into these machines :-

   (i)   7 into machine A   (ii)   24 into machine D   (iii)   17 into machine B ?

c   What numbers must have been put **in** to get the following numbers out :-

   (i)   10 out of machine A   (ii)   36 out of machine C   (iii)   9 out of machine D ?

4.   Look at the diagram showing costs of lollypops.

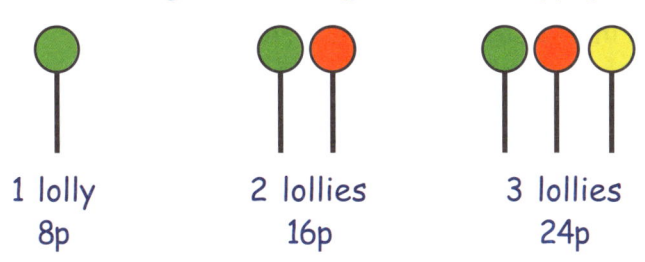

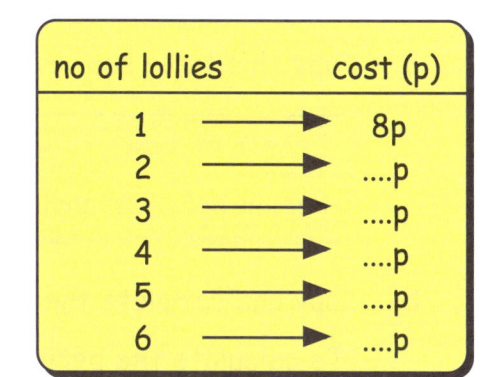

1 lolly — 8p
2 lollies — 16p
3 lollies — 24p

no of lollies	cost (p)
1	8p
2	….p
3	….p
4	….p
5	….p
6	….p

a   Make a neat copy of this table and complete it.

b   Copy this sentence and complete it :-

   "To calculate the total cost of a number of lollies, you multiply the number of lollies by ……."

c   This can be represented by a function machine.

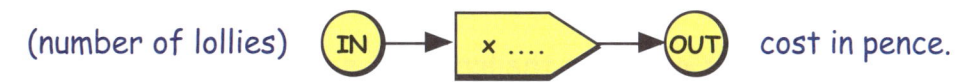

   (number of lollies) IN → × …. → OUT   cost in pence.

   Copy the function machine and fill in the value of the middle box.

d   Use the function machine to find the cost of 10 lollies.

5.   The rule for making a good pot of tea is to use :-

   "1 teabag per person + 1 for the pot".

This can be shown in the table :-

No. of people	1	2	3	4	5	6
No. of teabags	2	3	…	…	…	…

a   Copy this table and complete it.

b   Copy and complete the rule for making a good cup of tea.

   "If there are a number of people wanting tea, you simply ………… to this number to find how many teabags are needed".

c   Copy and complete this function machine to show your rule.

   (no. of people) IN → + …. → OUT (no. of teabags)

this is Chapter Seven   page 81   ALGEBRA

6. The **PERIMETER** of a shape is the total distance round all of its edges.

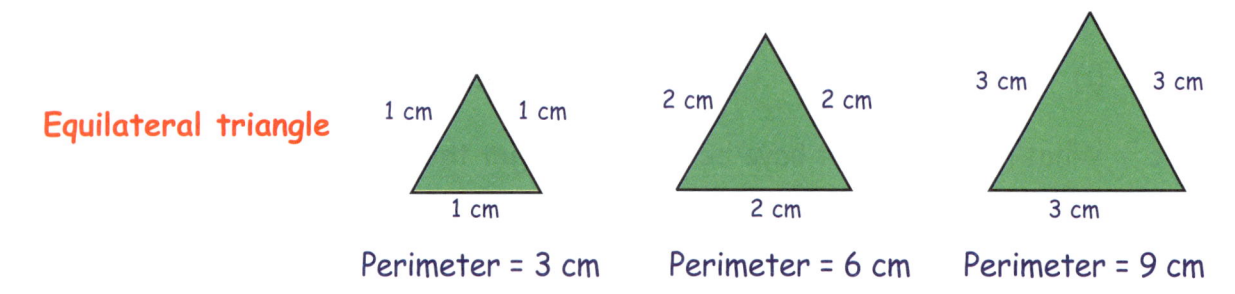

Equilateral triangle

Perimeter = 3 cm   Perimeter = 6 cm   Perimeter = 9 cm

a   Copy this table showing the perimeter of equilateral triangles.

Length of side	1 cm	2 cm	3 cm	4 cm	5 cm	6 cm
Perimeter of triangle	3 cm	6 cm	...	...	...	...

b   Copy and complete the sentence :-

"To calculate the perimeter of an equilateral triangle you :-

.... the length of the side by .... "

c   Draw up the function machine which shows how to calculate the perimeter.

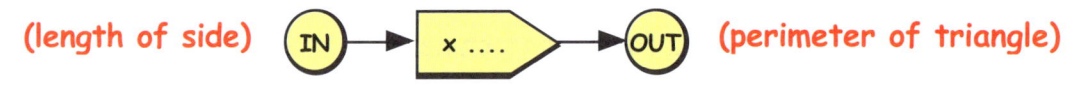

(length of side) IN → × .... → OUT (perimeter of triangle)

d   What perimeter **comes out** when the length of side is 10 cm ?

7. Look at the following **Pentagons**.

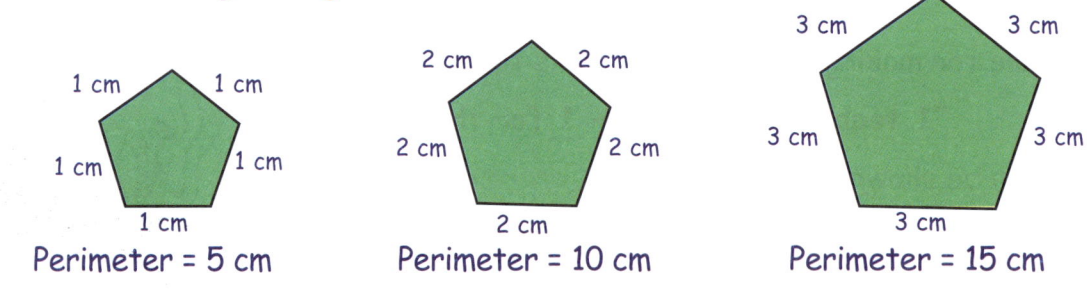

Perimeter = 5 cm   Perimeter = 10 cm   Perimeter = 15 cm

a   Copy and complete this table.

Length of side	1 cm	2 cm	3 cm	4 cm	5 cm	6 cm
Perimeter of pentagon	5 cm	...	...	...	...	...

b   Draw up the function machine which shows how this works.

c   If the number coming **out** of the function machine (the perimeter) is 400, what number must have gone **in** (the length of the side) ?

this is Chapter Seven   page 82   ALGEBRA

8. It is possible to **combine** 2 or more function machines.

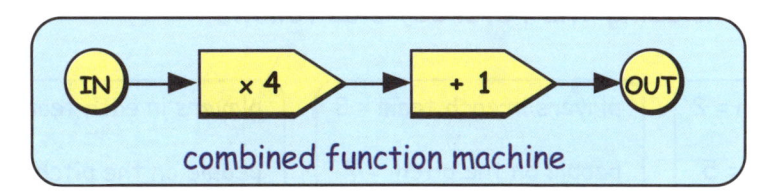

    IN → x 4 → + 1 → OUT
    combined function machine

    a   What finally comes out of this function machine if you put 5 **in**?

    b   What comes out of the machine when the following numbers are put in :-
        (i) 3   (ii) 4   (iii) 10   (iv) 0   (v) $\frac{1}{2}$?

9. Look at these 2 function machines.

    IN → x 2 → + 3 → OUT   IN → + 3 → x 2 → OUT
    Machine **A**   Machine **B**

    a   What comes out when 6 is put in :-   (i) machine A   (ii) machine B ?
    b   What comes out when 10 is put in :-   (i) machine A   (ii) machine B ?
    c   Both machines take in numbers and at some point multiply by 2 and add 3.
        Do both machines produce the same result each time ?

10. Shown are several combined function machines.

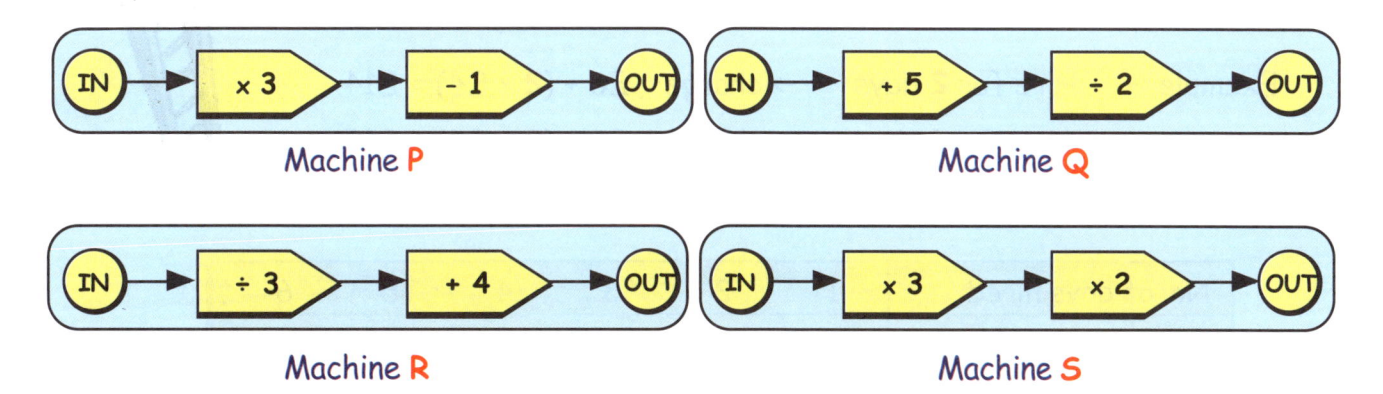

    IN → x 3 → − 1 → OUT   IN → + 5 → ÷ 2 → OUT
    Machine **P**   Machine **Q**

    IN → ÷ 3 → + 4 → OUT   IN → x 3 → x 2 → OUT
    Machine **R**   Machine **S**

    What numbers come out of the machines when the following are put in :-

    a   7 in machine P   b   3 in machine Q   c   12 in machine R
    d   4 in machine S   e   0 in machine R   f   4 in machine Q ?

11. In this function machine, when 3 is put in, the number 32 comes out.

    What number must * represent ?

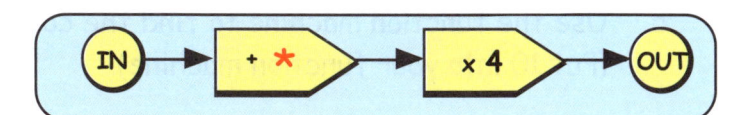

    IN → + * → x 4 → OUT

this is Chapter Seven   page 83   **ALGEBRA**

12. In a game, if each team has a certain number of players, then the total number of people on the pitch (**including the referee**) is as follows :-

- players in each team = 2
- people on the pitch = 5

- players in each team = 3
- people on the pitch = 7

- players in each team = 4
- people on the pitch = 9

a Copy and complete this table.

Players in each team	1	2	3	4	5	6
People on the pitch	...	5	7	...	...	...

b This can be shown as a function machine.

players in each team → IN → x ? → + ? → OUT → people on the pitch

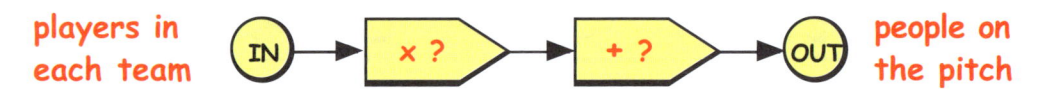

Draw the function machine and complete it.

c Use your machine to find the number of people on the pitch if there are 11 players in each team.

13. If you wish to hire a ladder from "Hire-It-All", the cost is as follows :-

"Hire-It-All" charges you
- £6 to hire it
- plus £4 for every day of hire.

Example :- Hire for **2** days → charge = £6 + (**2** × £4) = £14.

Hire for **3** days → charge = £6 + (**3** × £4) = £18.

a Copy this table showing "Hire-It-All" charges.

No. of days hired	1	2	3	4	5	6
Total hire cost	...	£14	£18	...	...	...

b This can be shown as a function machine. Copy and complete :-

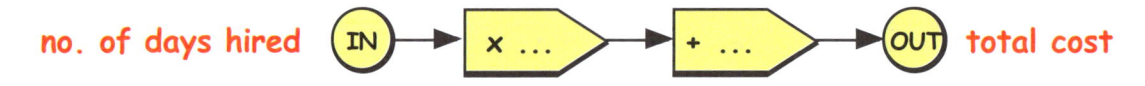

no. of days hired → IN → x ... → + ... → OUT → total cost

c Use the function machine to find the cost of hiring a ladder for 10 days. (Put 10 **into** your function machine).

Topic in a Nutshell

1. Copy the following and find what * stands for :-

   a $9 + * = 15$
      $* = ...$

   b $10 - * = 6$
      $* = ...$

   c $3 \times * = 21$
      $* = ...$

2. What number does ☐ stand for each time here :-

   a $4 + ☐ = 11$
   b $☐ \times 5 = 30$
   c $\frac{☐}{3} = 10$

   d $☐ - 7 = 7$
   e $\frac{20}{☐} = 4$
   f $4 \times ☐ = 0$

   g $\frac{☐}{2} = 1\cdot 5$
   h $☐ + 2\cdot 1 = 3\cdot 3$
   i $☐ - 25 = 0$

3. In each of the following, the symbol ☐ stands for **+, −, ×** or **÷**. Decide which symbol is needed each time here :-

   a $6 \,☐\, 2 = 4$
   b $6 \,☐\, 2 = 12$
   c $6 \,☐\, 2 = 3$

   d $6 \,☐\, 2 = 8$
   e $12 \,☐\, 3 = 4$
   f $4 \,☐\, 2 = 8$

   g $1\cdot 5 \,☐\, 1\cdot 5 = 3$
   h $8 \,☐\, 8 = 0$
   i $8 \,☐\, 8 = 1$

4. Solve the following equations (**find the value of the letter**) :-

   a $x + 5 = 11$
   b $x - 3 = 17$
   c $5 \times w = 50$

   d $\frac{a}{6} = 4$
   e $y - 9 = 9$
   f $24 \div m = 8$

5. Gina weighs 38 kg and Tina weighs * kg. Their combined weight is 70 kg.

   a Make up an **equation** using *.

   b Solve it to find Tina's weight.

6. 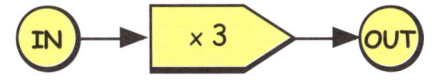 Machine **A**: IN → ×3 → OUT   Machine **B**: IN → −6 → OUT

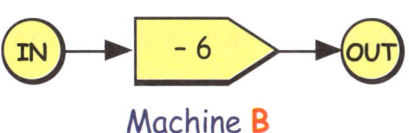

   a What number comes out when :-

   (i) 7 is put into machine A   (ii) 12 is put into machine B ?

   b What number has gone in when :-

   (i) 15 comes **out** of machine A   (ii) 11 comes **out** of machine B ?

7. A Rover car has 5 tyres (4 + 1 spare)

  a Copy the table showing total number of tyres.

No. of cars	1	2	3	4	5	6
No. of tyres	5	...	...	...	...	...

  b Make up a function machine to show how to calculate the number of tyres if you know the number of cars.

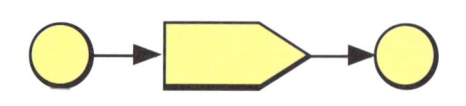

8. Look at this combined function machine.

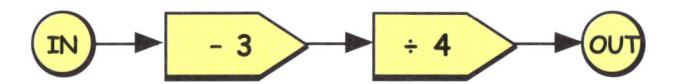

  IN → − 3 → ÷ 4 → OUT

  a What comes **out** when 23 is put **in**?

  b A number was put in and the number **2** came out. What number must have been put in?

9. A box weighs 30 grams.
A rubber weighs 12 grams.

  The total weight of the box and **2** rubbers is
  (**2** × 12) + 30 = 54g.

  The total weight of the box and **3** rubbers is
  (**3** × 12) + 30 = 66g.

  a Copy and complete this table to show the total weight of box and rubbers.

No. of rubbers	1	2	3	4	5	6
Total weight	...	54g	66g	...	...	...

  b This can be shown as a function machine.

  no. of rubbers IN → × ... → + ... → OUT **total weight**.

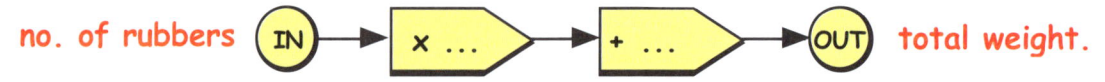

  Copy and complete the function machine.

  c Use the function machine to find the total weight of a full box containing 10 rubbers.

Chapter 8

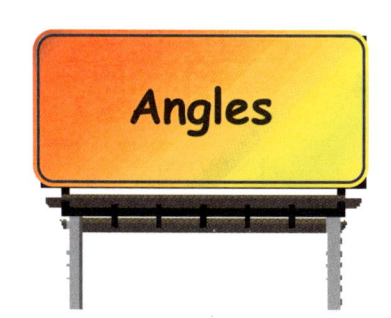

Angles

Types of Angles

Below are ways to describe the different "type" of angles.

- acute
- right
- obtuse
- straight
- reflex

Exercise 1

1. Use a word from the above list to describe each of the red angles below :-

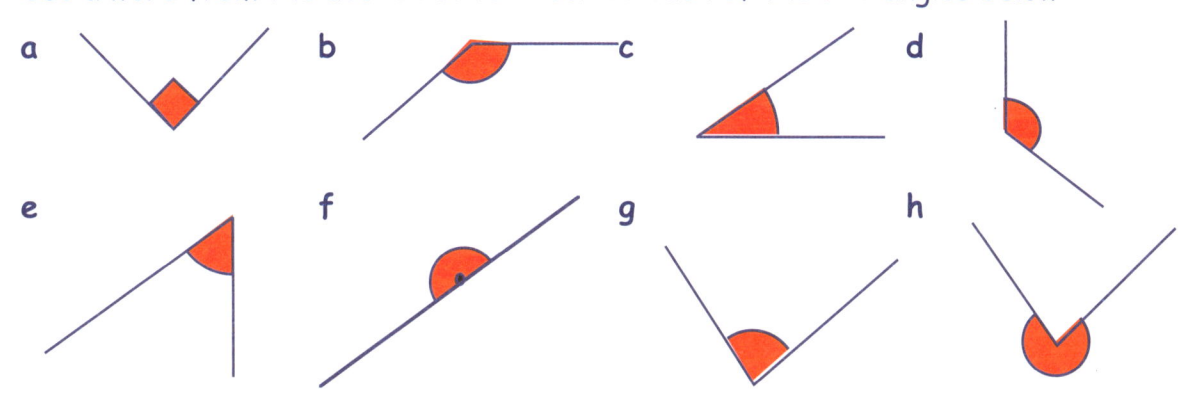

   a   b   c   d
   e   f   g   h

2. What **type** of angle is marked blue in these triangles :-

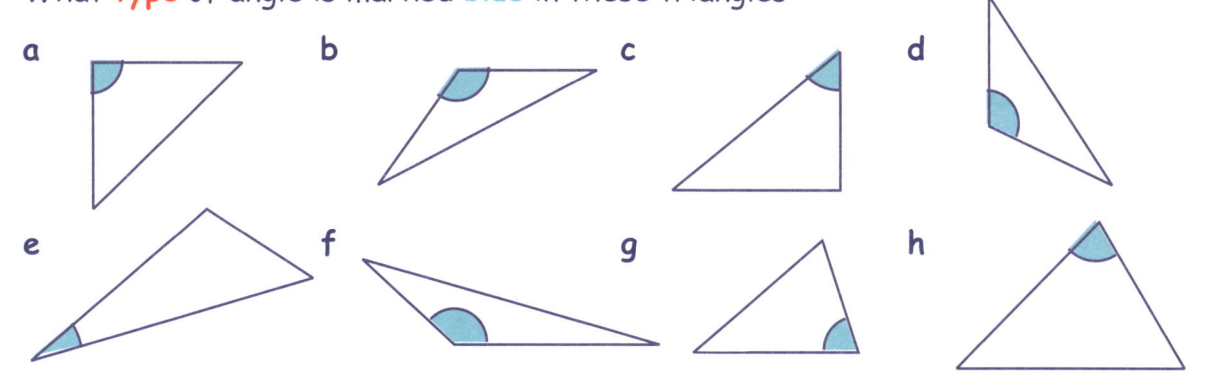

   a   b   c   d
   e   f   g   h

3. What **type** of angle is marked pink in these shapes :-

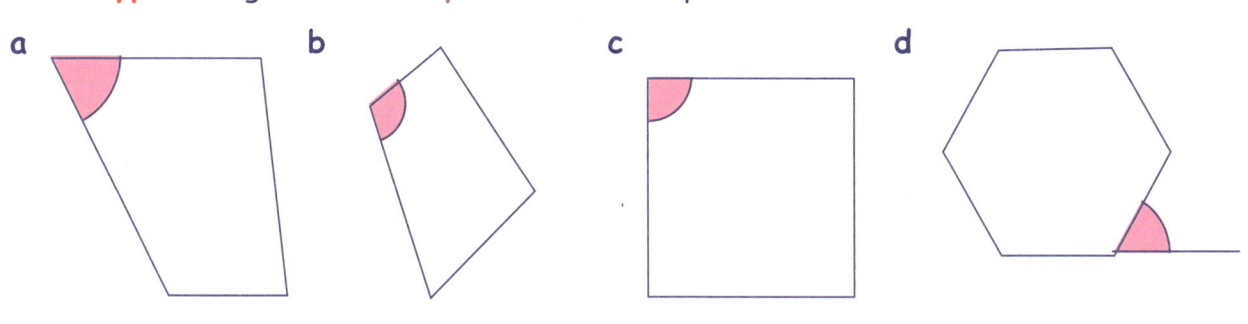

   a   b   c   d

this is Chapter Eight   page 87   ANGLES

4. **Copy** the diagram below and match the **type** of angle with the given sizes :-

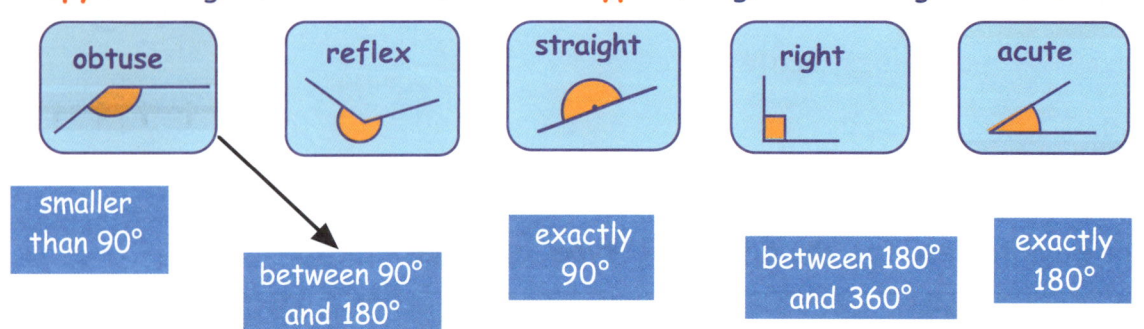

| obtuse | reflex | straight | right | acute |

smaller than 90°   between 90° and 180°   exactly 90°   between 180° and 360°   exactly 180°

5. Look at the angle sizes listed below :-

   210°, 88°, 110°, 17°, 60°, 180°, 176°, 91°, 90°, 335°, 31°, 169°

   Write down the sizes of those angles that are :-

   a acute   **b** obtuse   **c** straight   **d** right   **e** reflex.

Naming Angles

Remember that an angle is made up of two **arms** and a **vertex** (corner).

You name an angle using three capital letters.

The vertex must always be the middle letter.

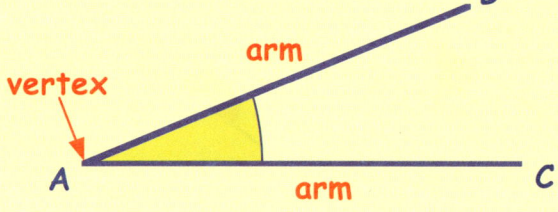

–BAC is a short way of writing angle BAC.

Exercise 2

1. Use 3 LETTERS each time to name the **red** angle :-

   (remember to use the "–" sign).

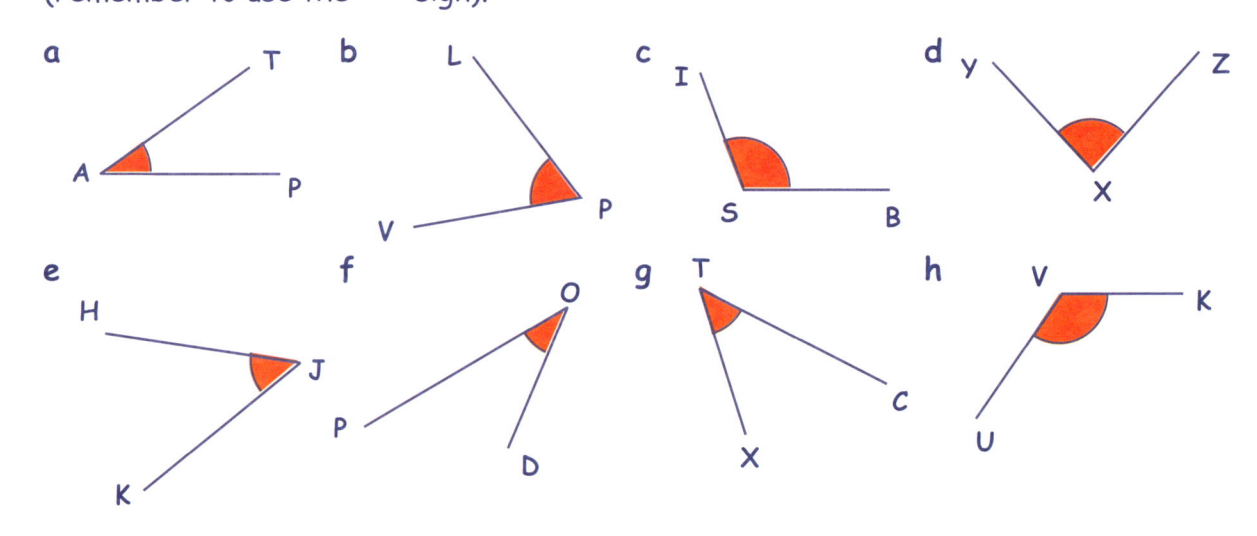

   a, b, c, d, e, f, g, h

this is Chapter Eight   page 88   ANGLES

2. Use **THREE** letters to name each angle and say what **TYPE** of angle it is :-

   Example -   ∠GTF is an **acute** angle.

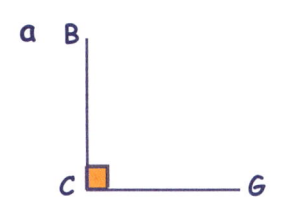

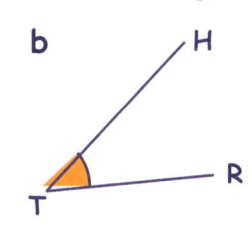

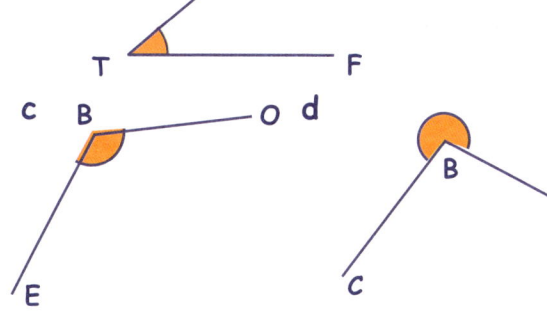

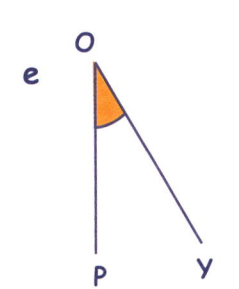

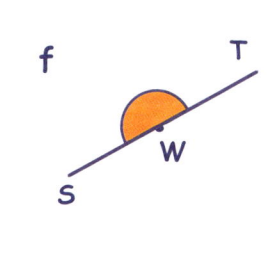

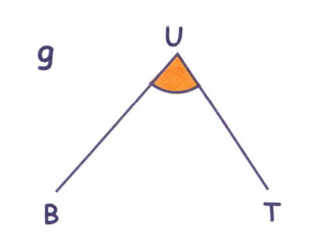

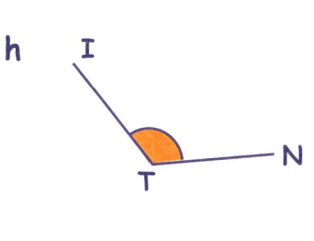

   a   **b**   **c**   **d**

   e   **f**   **g**   **h**

3. Look at triangle TSV :-

   ∠TSV is **green**.

   ∠STV is **red**.

   ∠TVS is **blue**.

   Now look at the triangles below :-

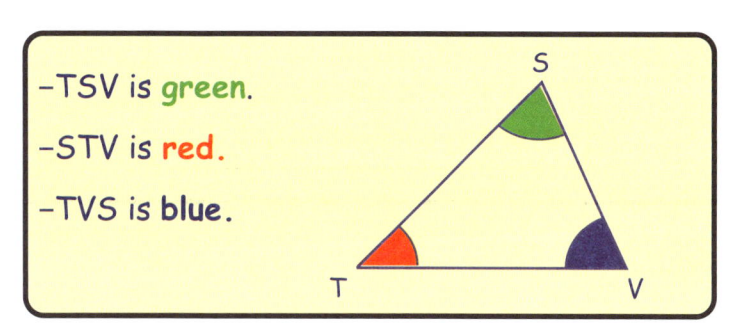

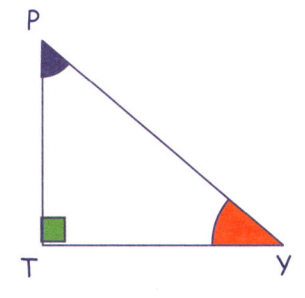

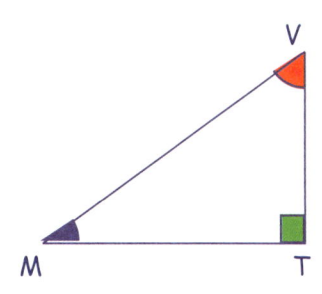

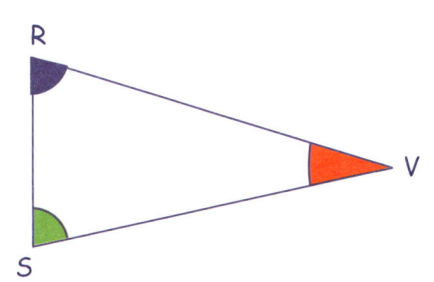

   From the triangles above, name each :-

   a **red** angle   **b** **green** angle   **c** **blue** angle.

4. Copy the diagram shown.
   ∠ACD is marked **yellow**.

   Colour or mark :-

   a ∠EDC **red**

   b ∠CED **green**

   c ∠ACB and ∠DCE **blue**

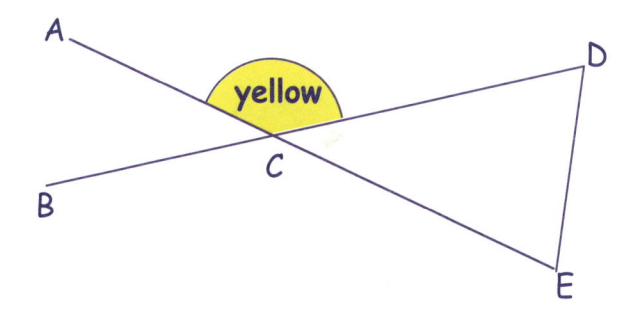

   d ∠ECB **yellow**. (Why do you think ∠ACD and ∠BCD are both coloured yellow ?)

   this is Chapter Eight   page 89   ANGLES

Measuring Angles

Remember : to measure an angle with a protractor :-

Step 1 : place the centre of the protractor on the vertex

Step 2 : turn the protractor until the zero line lies along an arm

Step 3 : count from the zero (inside or out) and read the value where the arm cuts the scale.

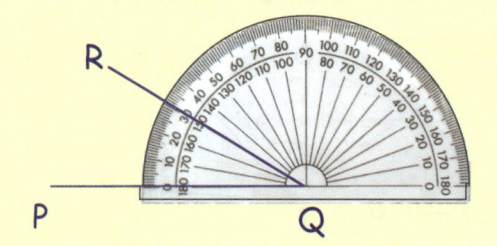

Use outside scale ∠ PQR = 30°

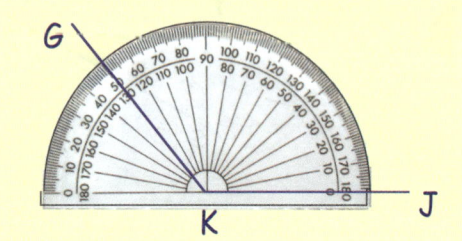

Use inside scale ∠ GKJ = 130°

You should always estimate the size of angle (in degrees) **before** you measure it.

Exercise 3

1. Name and write down the size of each angle below (example ∠ PQR = 30°) :-

   a, b, c, d, e, f, g, h, i

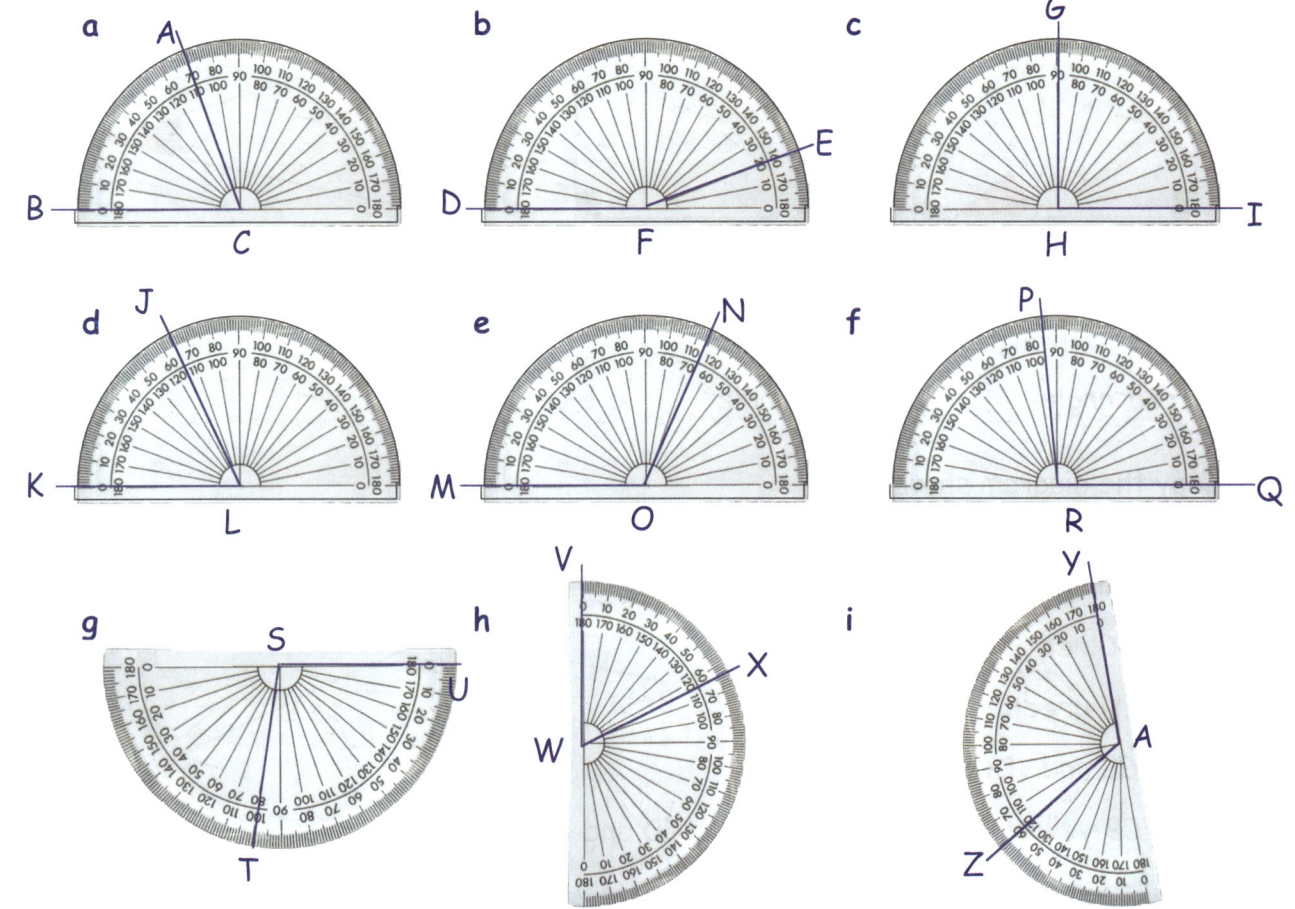

this is Chapter Eight   ANGLES

2. Do **not** use a protractor in this question.
   Choose the estimate closest to what you think the angle is :-

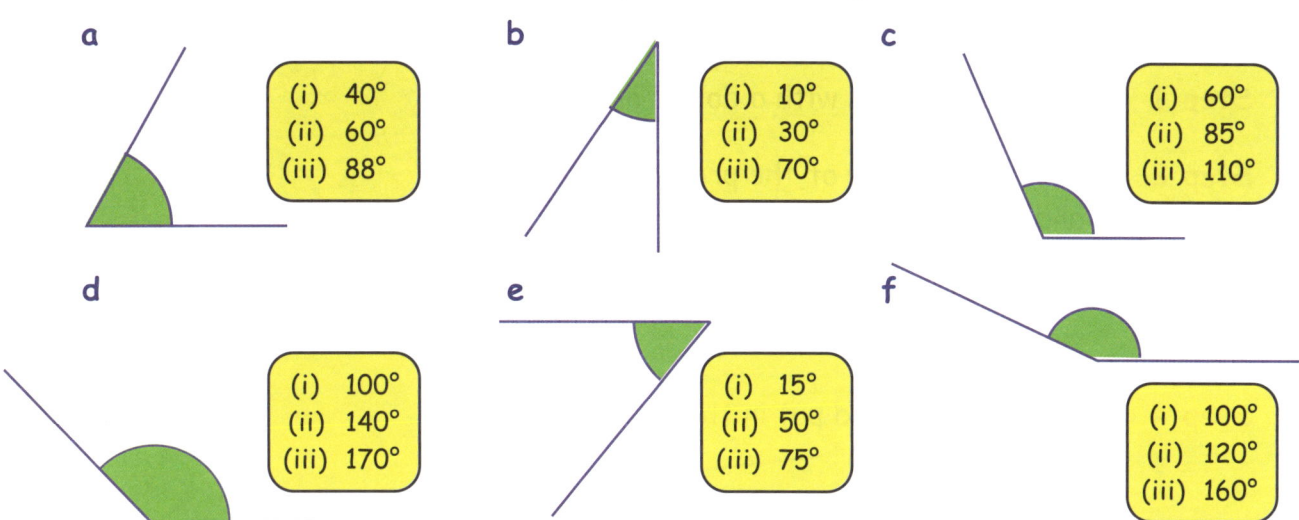

   a (i) 40° (ii) 60° (iii) 88°

   b (i) 10° (ii) 30° (iii) 70°

   c (i) 60° (ii) 85° (iii) 110°

   d (i) 100° (ii) 140° (iii) 170°

   e (i) 15° (ii) 50° (iii) 75°

   f (i) 100° (ii) 120° (iii) 160°

3. For each **red** angle :-   (i) estimate its size (then)
   (ii) use a protractor to find the size of each angle.

   a   b   c

   d   e   f

   g   h   i

   j   k   l

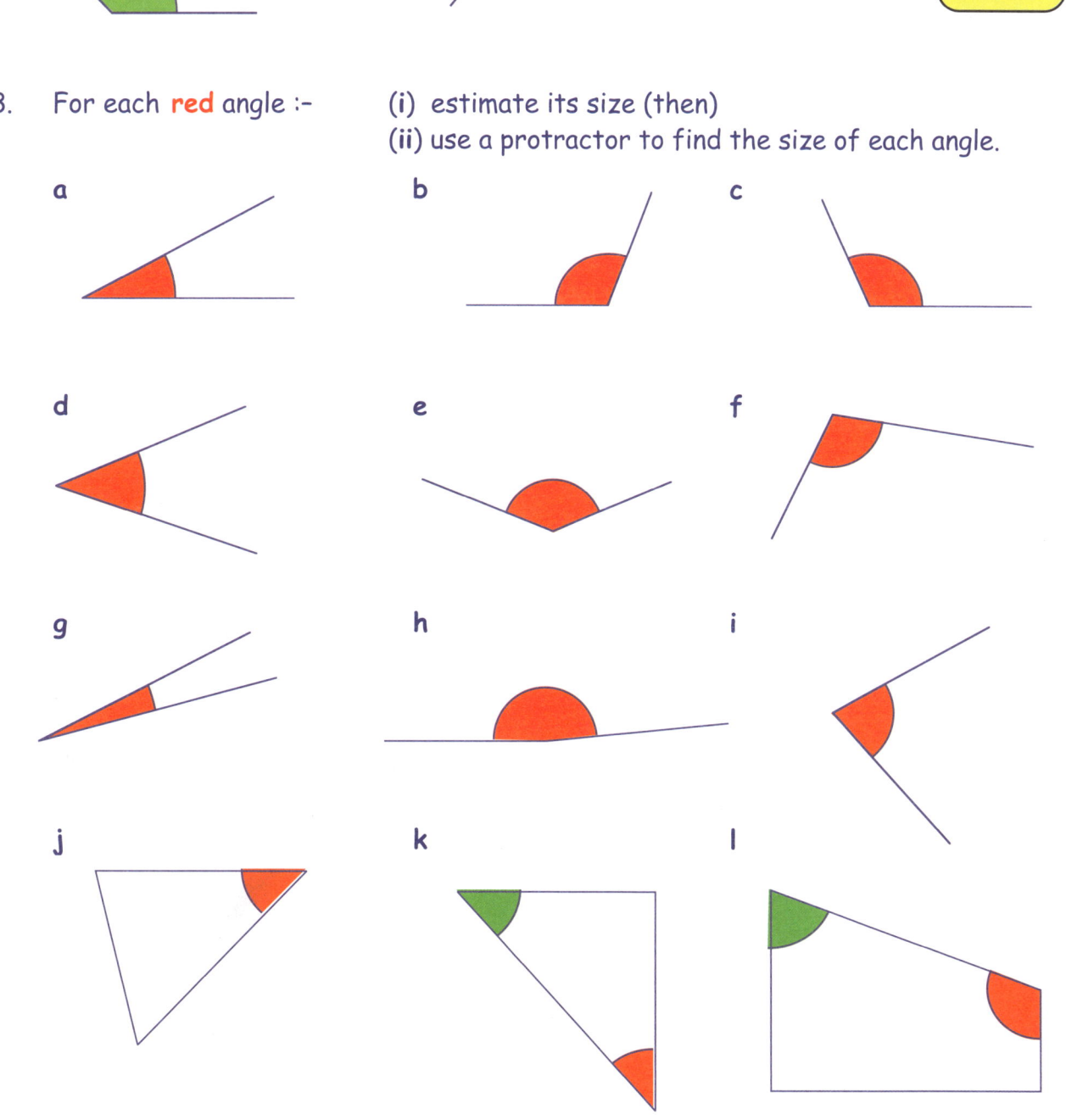

this is Chapter Eight   page 91   ANGLES

Drawing Angles

Example :- To draw ∠ABC = 40°

Step 1 : Start with a line with a dot at one end

Step 2 : Put the crossbar of the protractor on the dot and line up with the line

Step 3 : Count round from the zero line to the 40° mark and mark with a dot

Step 4 : Join the dots and put in the letters (middle letter B)

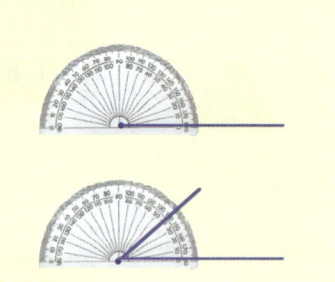

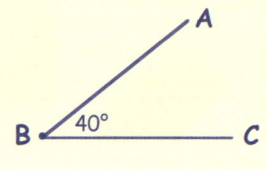

Exercise 4

1. Draw a 6 centimetre line and put a dot on the end (left side).
    Use your protractor to show ∠BFG = 30°.

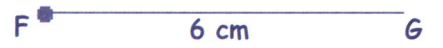

2. Use the same method to draw and label these angles :-

    a ∠ABC = 50°   b ∠PTY = 90°   c ∠LMK = 10°   d ∠RWT = 20°

    e ∠RAT = 100°   f ∠WXY = 110°   g ∠ACT = 150°   h ∠QET = 130°

    i ∠YUM = 45°   j ∠HJK = 75°   k ∠SWA = 15°   l ∠BUM = 135°

3. (Harder) Draw and label these angles :-

    a ∠ABH = 38°   b ∠XTC = 22°   c ∠KLM = 49°   d ∠STV = 76°

    e ∠PIJ = 96°   f ∠TRG = 108°   g ∠DAZ = 173°   h ∠YUK = 123°

    i ∠FST = 8°   j ∠REW = 111°   k ∠JIL = 144°   l ∠BAD = 190°

4. Shown is a small sketch of ΔPQR. To draw it accurately, follow these steps :-

    Step 1 : Draw the line QR = 6 cm. (Put Q and R on your diagram).

    Step 2 : Put your protractor at Q and draw an angle of 40°.

    Step 3 : Put your protractor at R and draw an angle of 60°.

    Step 4 : Where the lines cross, call this point P.

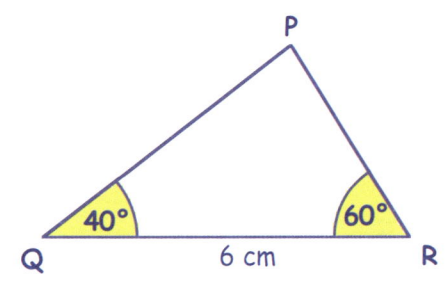

this is Chapter Eight   page 92   ANGLES

5. Try making full size accurate drawings of these triangles :-

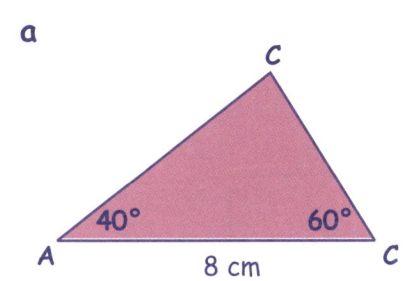

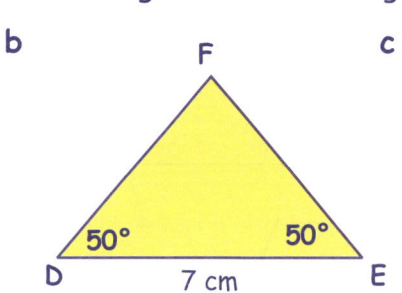

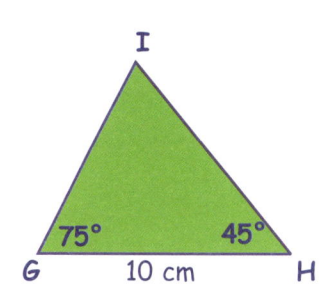

a) Triangle ABC with angle A = 40°, angle C = 60°, AC = 8 cm (C at top)

b) Triangle DEF with angle D = 50°, angle E = 50°, DE = 7 cm (F at top)

c) Triangle GHI with angle G = 75°, angle H = 45°, GH = 10 cm (I at top)

Calculating Missing Angles

Remember :

A right angle is 90°   Two right angles make 180°   Four right angles make 360°
                          (a straight line)   (a complete turn).

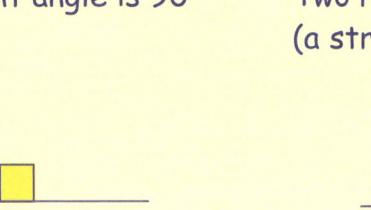

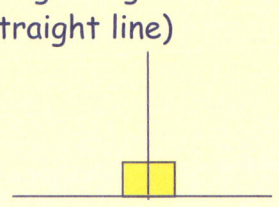

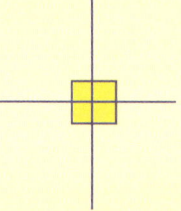

If we are asked to calculate the size of an angle we do not always need a protractor.

Examples   Find the value of ? in each of the following :-

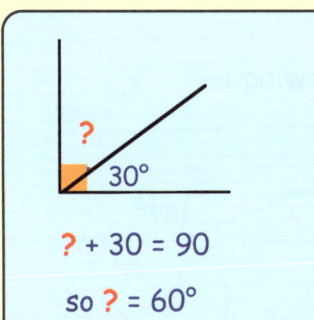

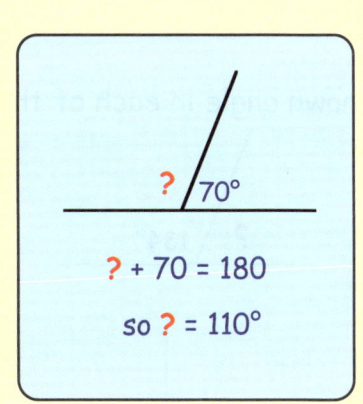

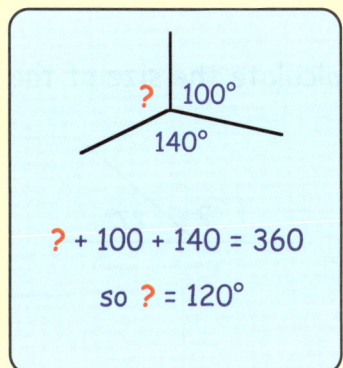

| ? + 30 = 90 | ? + 70 = 180 | ? + 100 + 140 = 360 |
| so ? = 60° | so ? = 110° | so ? = 120° |

Exercise 5

1. Calculate the value of ? in each of the following :-

   a) ? with 30° (right angle on base)

   b) ? with 70° (right angle on base)

   c) ? with 45° (right angle on base)

this is Chapter Eight   page 93   ANGLES

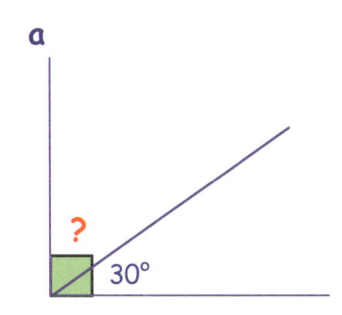

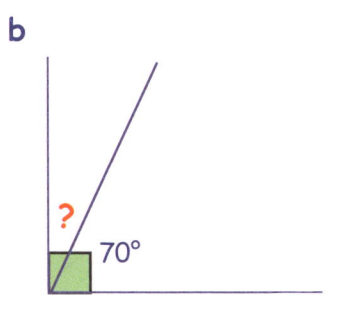

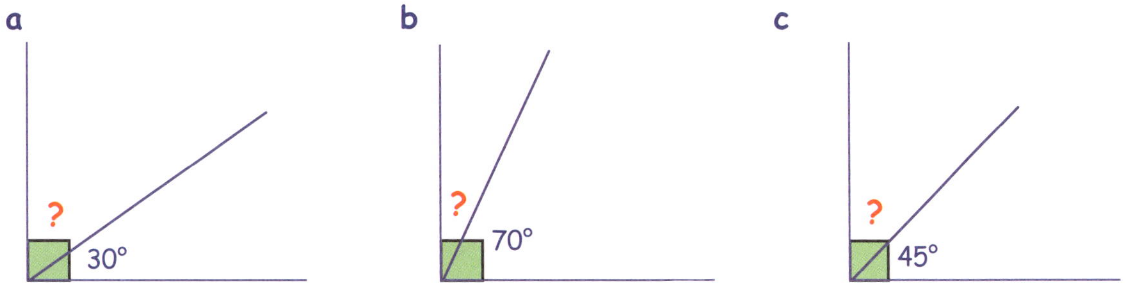

d 25° ?

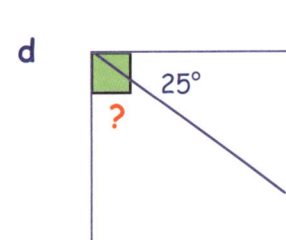

e 75° ?

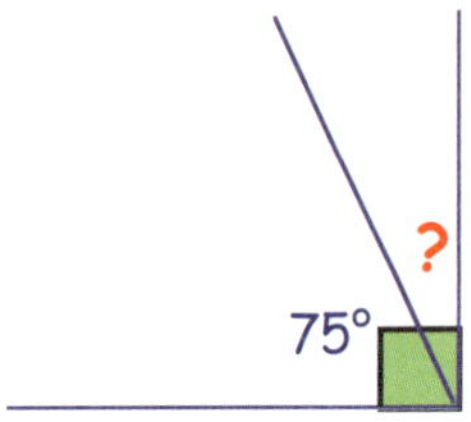

f ? 43°

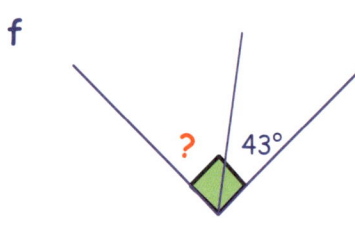

g ? 30°

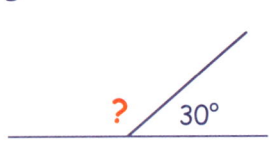

h ? 140°

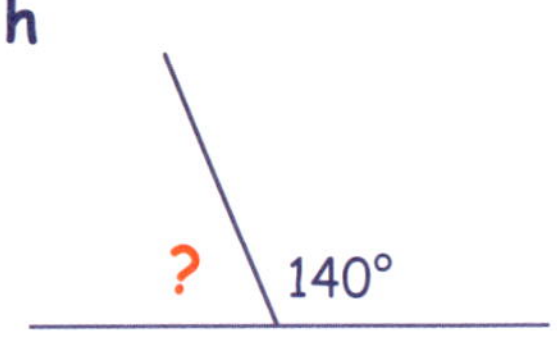

i ?

j 50° ?

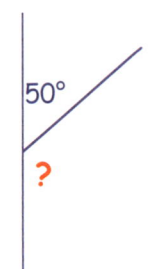

k ? 125°

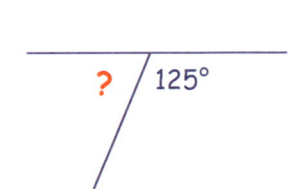

l 35° ?

m 120° 130° ?

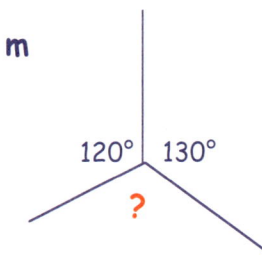

n ? 140°

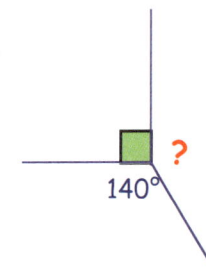

o 30° ? 140°

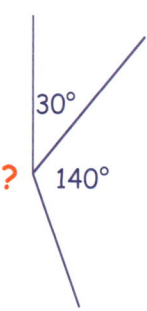

2. Calculate the size of the unknown angle in each of the following :-

a ? 27°

b ? 134°

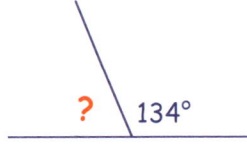

c ? 167°

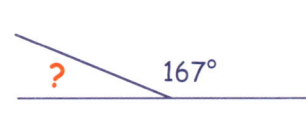

d 119° 137° ?

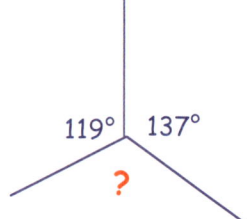

e ? 157° 112°

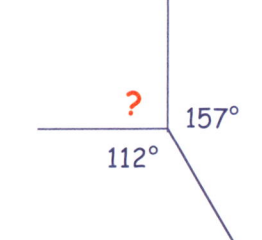

f ? 199° 133°

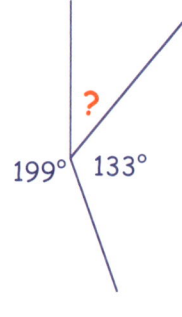

g 139° 89° ?

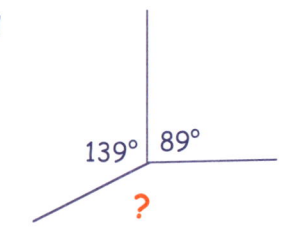

h ? 135° 135°

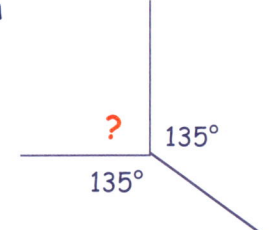

i 39° 83° ?

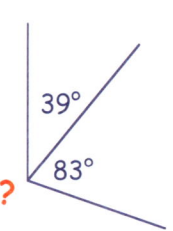

this is Chapter Eight page 94 ANGLES

Vertically Opposite Angles

Exercise 6

1. Shown are two lines which cross at a point. 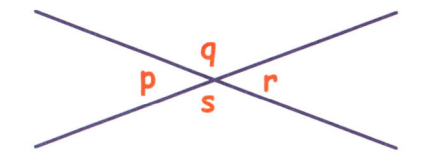

   a Measure angles marked **p**, **q**, **r** and **s**.

   b What do you notice about **p** and **r** ?

   c What do you notice about **q** and **s** ?

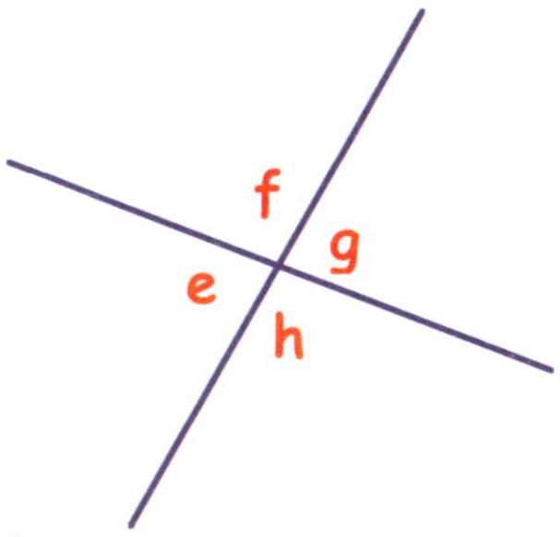

2. a Measure angles **e**, **f**, **g** and **h**.

   b What do you notice about
   (i) **e** and **g**   (ii) **f** and **h** ?

3. When two lines cross at a point, what do you think is **always** true about the opposite angles ?

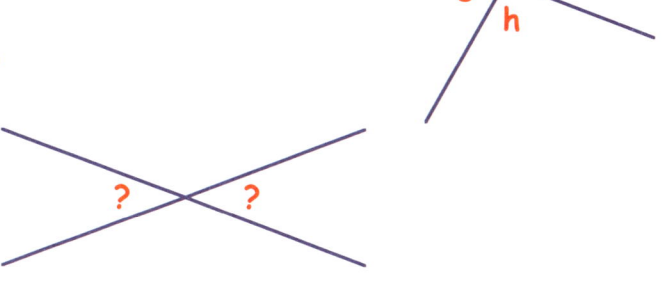

4. Write down the sizes of the angle represented by the letters **a, b, c, ...** :–

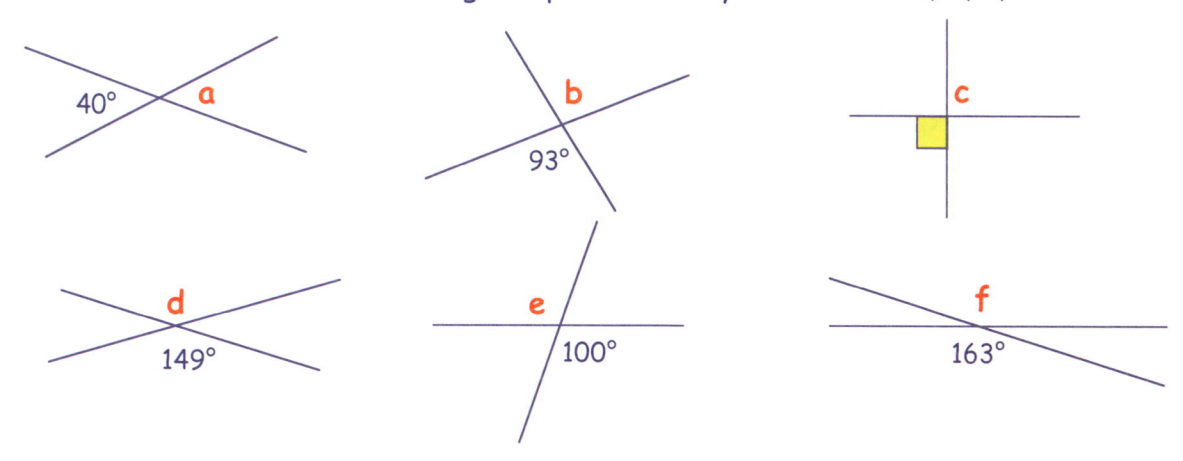

   40° a

   b 93°

   c

   d 149°

   e 100°

   f 163°

5. In the diagram shown, one angle is 38°.
   Notice that :–

   green angle + 38 = 180°.

   Write down the value of the :–

   a **green** angle   *(Do **NOT** measure)

   b **red** angle

   c **blue** angle.

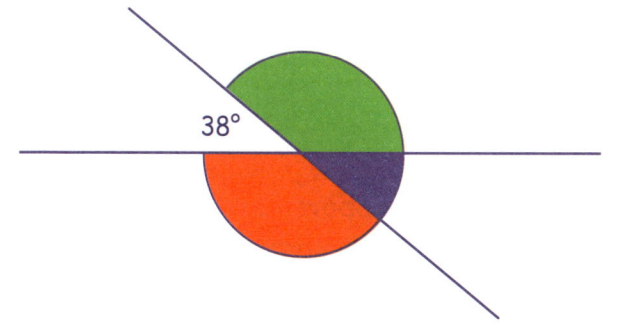

6. a Make a sketch of each of the diagrams in **Question 4**.

   b Fill in the sizes of **all** the angles in your figures.

"F" and "Z" Angles

Corresponding Angles

Many diagrams like the one shown have parallel lines that make an F angle.

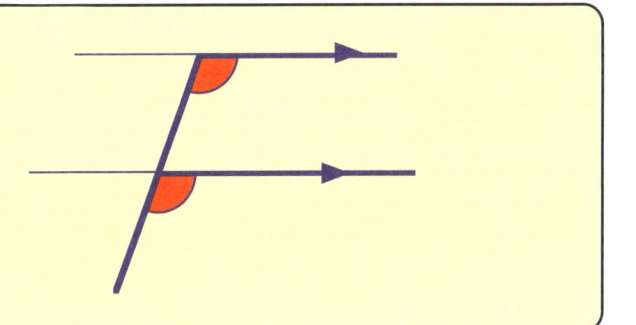

F angles are usually referred to as **corresponding angles**.

Exercise 7

1. Measure the red angles in the diagram above.
   What do you notice about the sizes of the red angles?

2. (Can you see a pair of F angles in this diagram?)
   Measure the red angles in this diagram.
   What do you notice about the sizes of these corresponding angles?

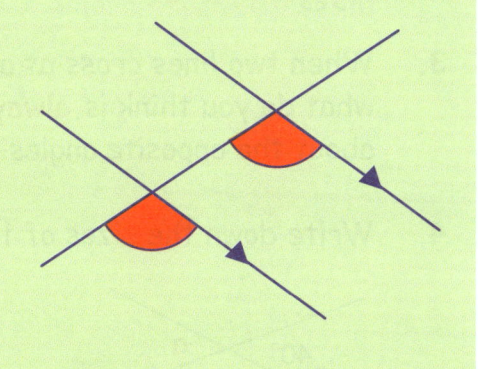

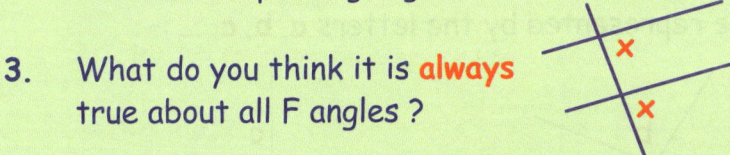

3. What do you think it is **always** true about all F angles?

4. Write down the sizes of the angles marked a, b and c.

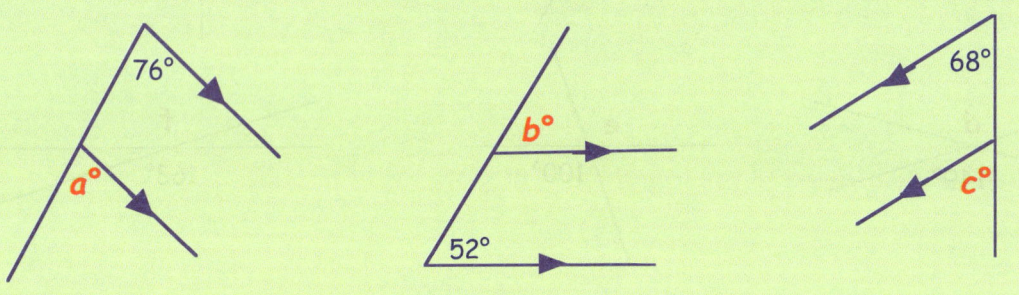

   76°   a°

   b°   52°

   68°   c°

5. **Remember :-**   150° → 30°   and   150° / 150°

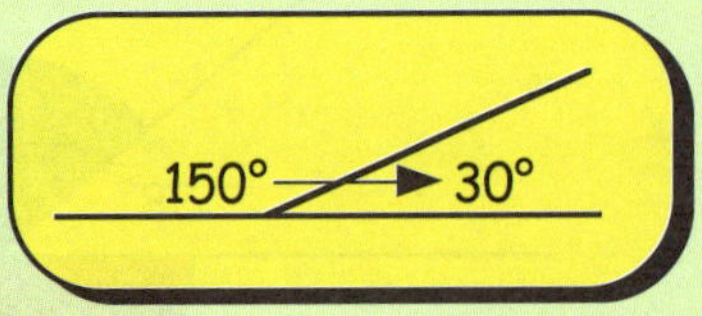

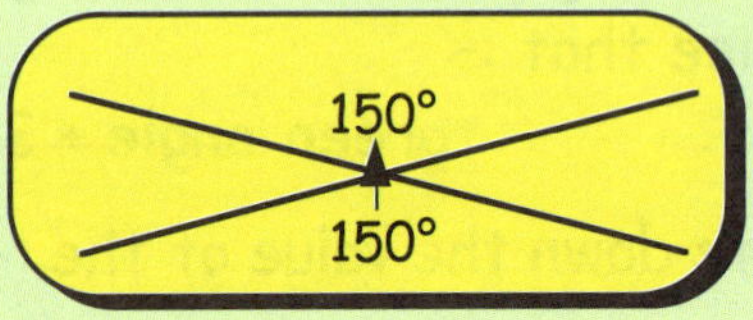

   Using the above facts and corresponding (F) angles,
   COPY the diagrams below and enter **all** the missing angles :-

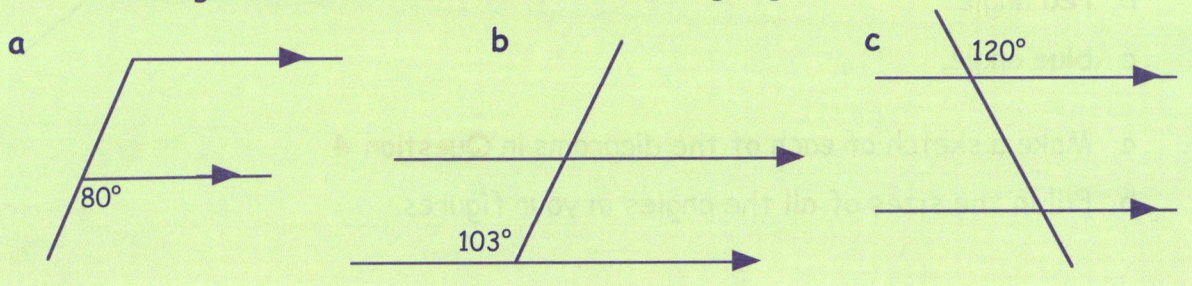

   a) 80°

   b) 103°

   c) 120°

this is Chapter Eight   page 96   ANGLES

Alternate Angles

Many diagrams like the one shown have parallel lines that make a Z angle.

Z angles are usually referred to as **alternate angles**.

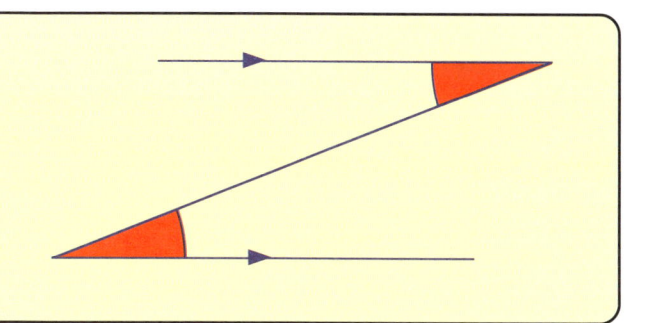

6. Measure the red angles in the diagram above.
   What do you notice about the sizes of the 2 red angles ?

7. (Can you see a Z angle in this diagram ?)
   Measure the green angles in this diagram.
   What do you notice about the sizes of these alternate angles ?

8. What do you think is true about all Z angles ?

9. Write down the sizes of the angles marked a, b and c.

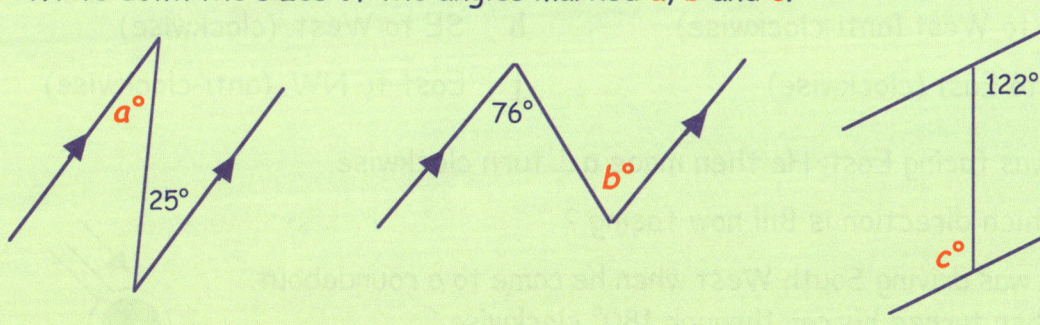

10. Copy the diagrams below and fill in all the angles :-

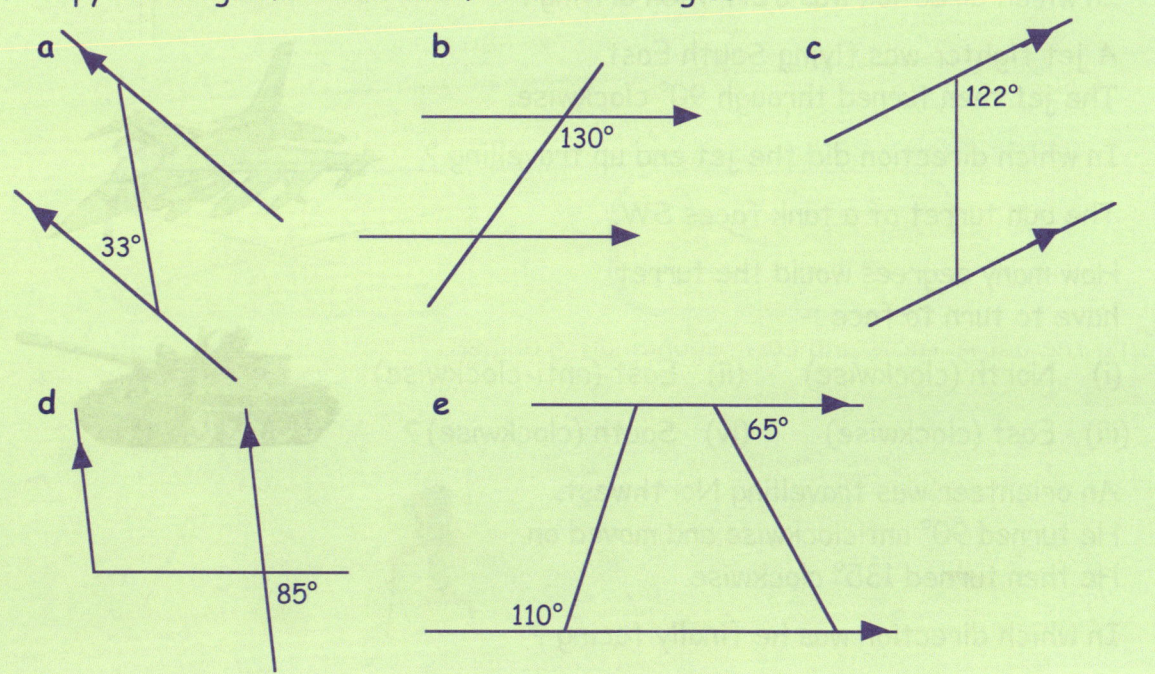

this is Chapter Eight   page 97   ANGLES

Compass Points

The four points of the compass **North, South, East and West** can be extended into an eight point compass rose as shown.

NE stands for North-East etc.

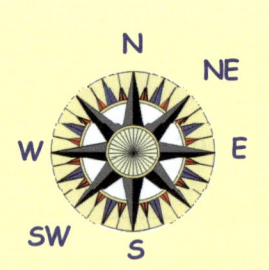

Remember :
360° = 1 full turn
180° = $\frac{1}{2}$ turn
90° = $\frac{1}{4}$ turn

Exercise 8

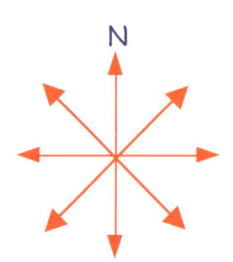

1. Copy and complete the 8 points of the compass from the diagram shown.

2. How many degrees are there from :-
   - a North to East (clockwise)
   - b East to South (clockwise)
   - c North to West (anti-clockwise)
   - d North to West (clockwise)
   - e North to North East (clockwise)
   - f North to South East (clockwise)
   - g East to West (anti-clockwise)
   - h SE to West. (clockwise)
   - i NW to East (clockwise)
   - j East to NW. (anti-clockwise)

3. a Bill was facing East. He then made a $\frac{1}{4}$ turn clockwise.

   In which direction is Bill now facing ?

   b Jeff was driving South West when he came to a roundabout. He then turned his car through 180° clockwise.

   In which direction was Jeff then driving ?

   c A jet fighter was flying South East. The jet then turned through 90° clockwise.

   In which direction did the jet end up travelling ?

   d The gun turret of a tank faces SW.

   How many degrees would the turret have to turn to face :-
   - (i) North (clockwise)
   - (ii) East (anti-clockwise)
   - (iii) East (clockwise)
   - (iv) South (clockwise) ?

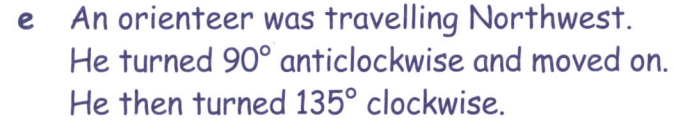

   e An orienteer was travelling Northwest. He turned 90° anticlockwise and moved on. He then turned 135° clockwise.

   In which direction was he finally facing ?

f Zak was facing South-East.
He turned clockwise 270°.
He then turned anti-clockwise 45°.

In which direction was Zak then facing.

g A ship is sailing North-West. The ship turns anti-clockwise and now faces North-East.

By how many degrees had the ship turned through ?

h A submarine, facing East, is trying to avoid being tracked.
The captain issues the following orders :-

- *Turn anticlockwise 135° for 100 metres.*
- *Turn clockwise 45° for 50 metres.*
- *Turn clockwise 225° for 75 metres.*
- *Turn 180° anticlockwise.*

In which direction was the submarine then facing ?

4. A soldier is given the location of several points of interest.

a In which direction does the soldier need to travel to get to :-

(i) the tree

(ii) HQ

(iii) the jeep

(iv) the tank ?

b You are standing at HQ.

From there, in which direction is :-

(i) the huts   (ii) the helicopter

(iii) the jeep   (iv) the tank ?

c The soldier moves to the helicopter.
He flies to the tree, then to HQ, and finally to the tank.

Describe the soldiers movements using compass points.

d Another helicopter is facing North-East. It then spins 405° (clockwise) out of control. In which direction is this helicopter now facing ?

Three Figure Bearings

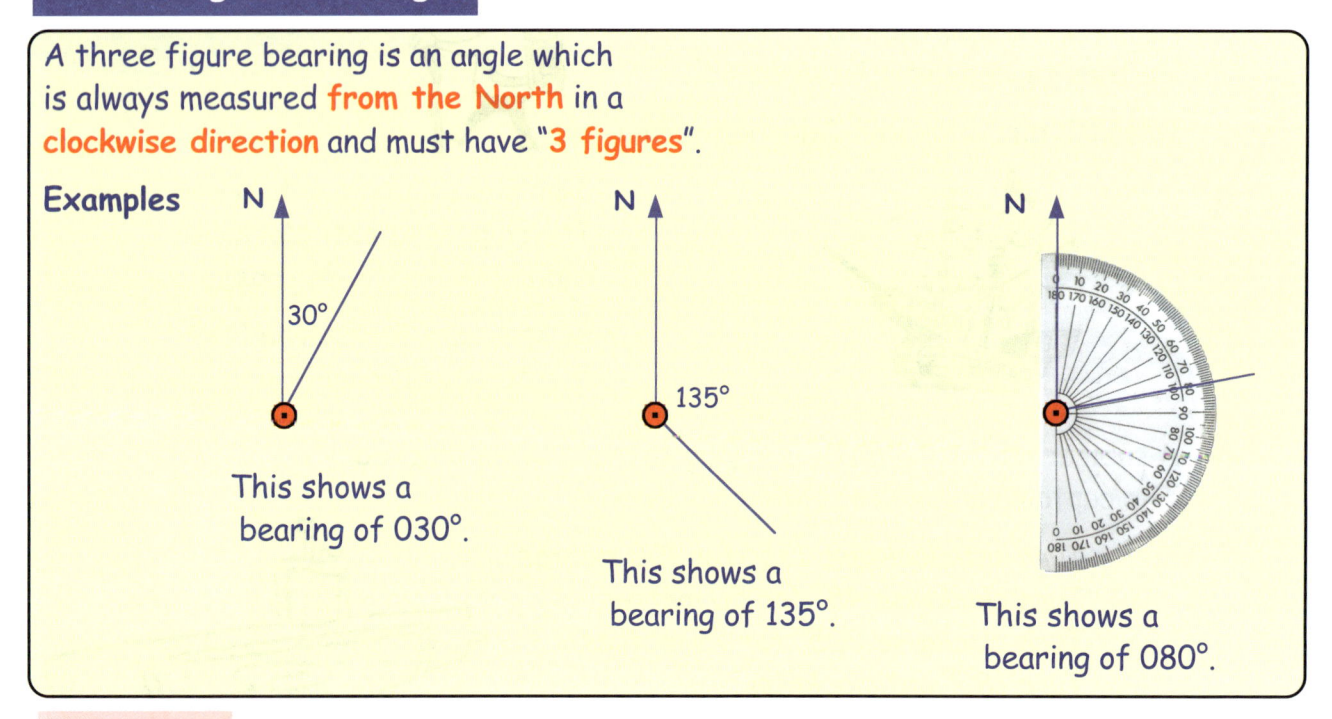

A three figure bearing is an angle which is always measured **from the North** in a **clockwise direction** and must have "**3 figures**".

Examples

This shows a bearing of 030°.

This shows a bearing of 135°.

This shows a bearing of 080°.

Exercise 9

1. Write down the 3-figure bearing for each of the following :–

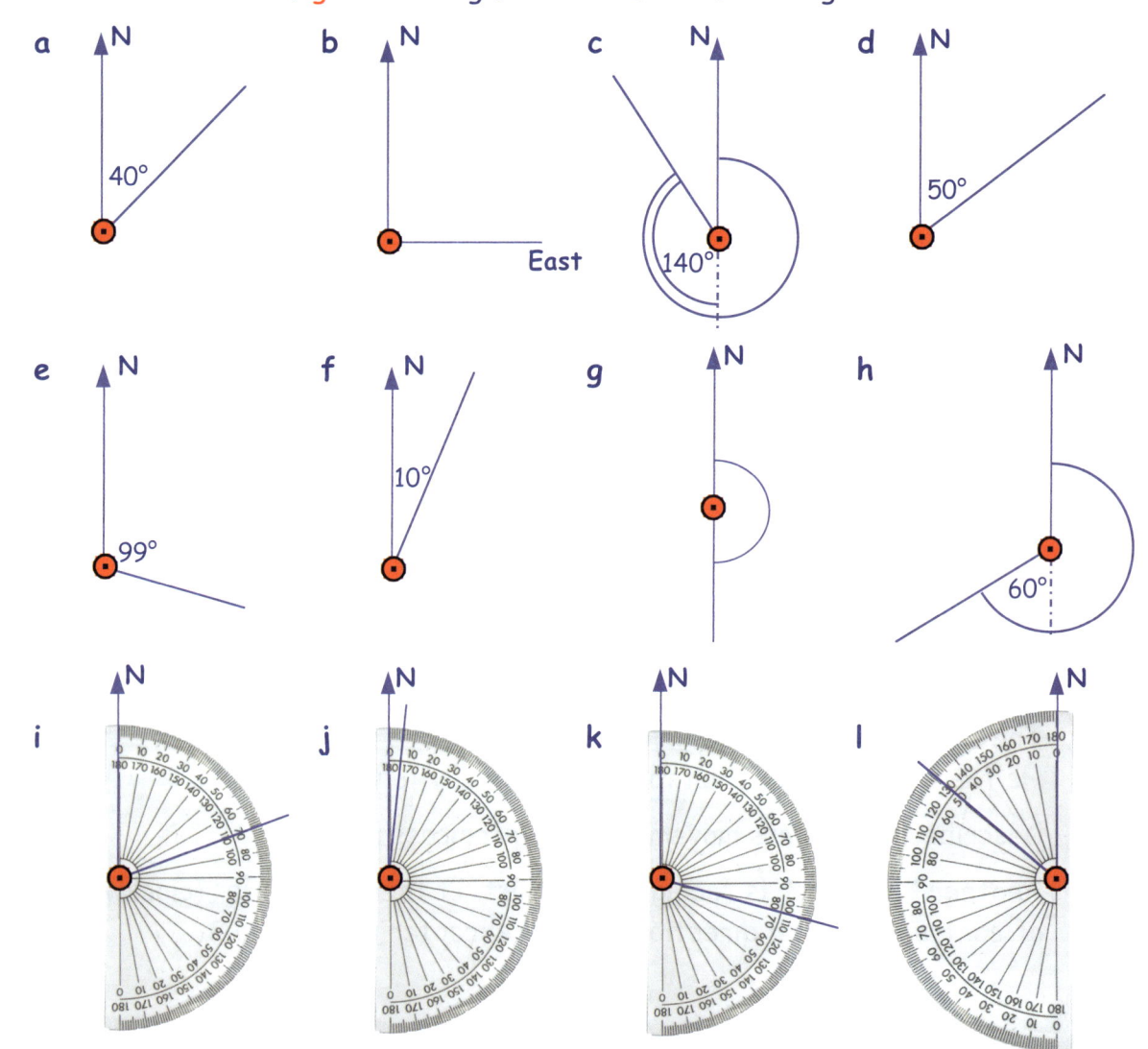

   a   40°

   b   East

   c   140°

   d   50°

   e   99°

   f   10°

   g

   h   60°

   i

   j

   k

   l

this is Chapter Eight   page 100   ANGLES

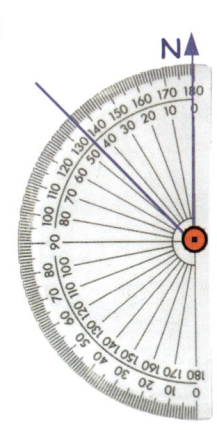

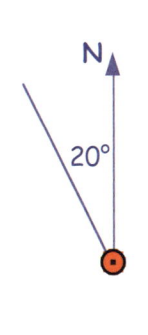

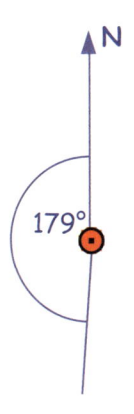

2. Use a protractor to measure the 3-figure bearing of each angle :-

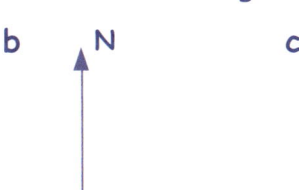

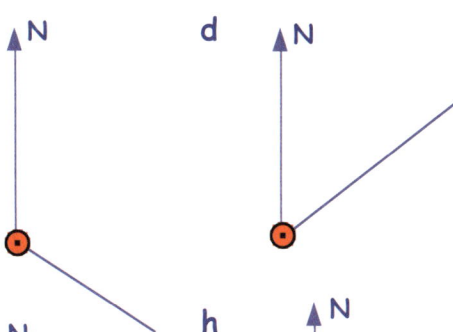

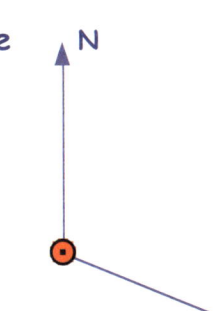

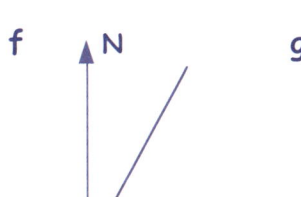

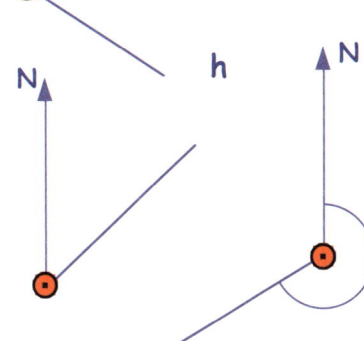

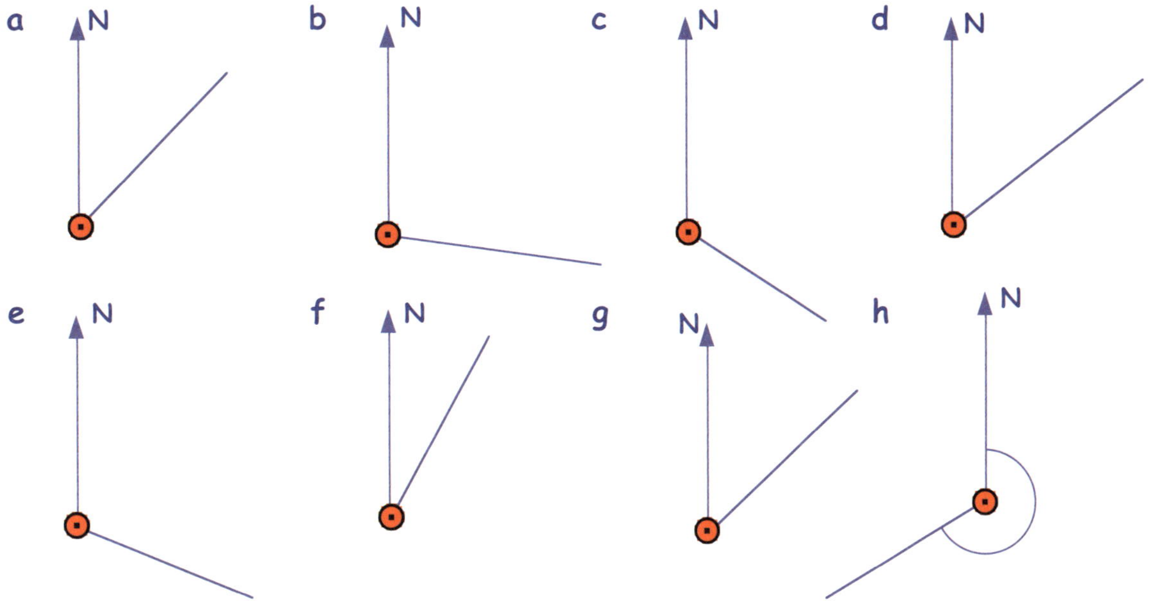

a   b   c   d

e   f   g   h

3. Write down the 3-figure bearing of the following directions :-
   a East 
   b West
   c North-East
   d North.

Even if the direction you are dealing with is further round than **south**, you still measure it "**clockwise**" from the North.

Can you see that Beetown, in this figure, is 40° **further round** than south ?

=> it is (40° + 180°) = 220° round from North

=> the 3-figure bearing of Beetown **from** Aytown is **220°**.

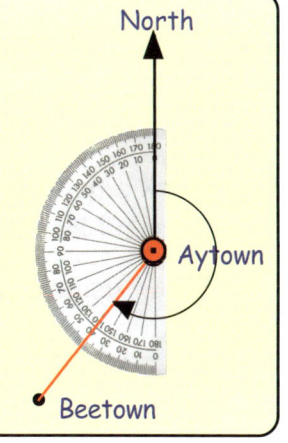

4. Write down the 3-figure bearing for each of the following :-

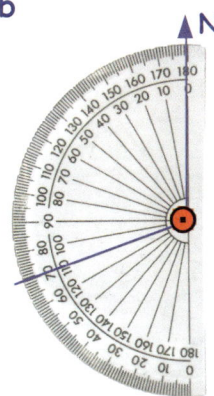

a   b   c (20°)   d (179°)

this is Chapter Eight   page 101   ANGLES

5. Use a protractor to measure the 3-figure bearing of each town **from** Aytown :-

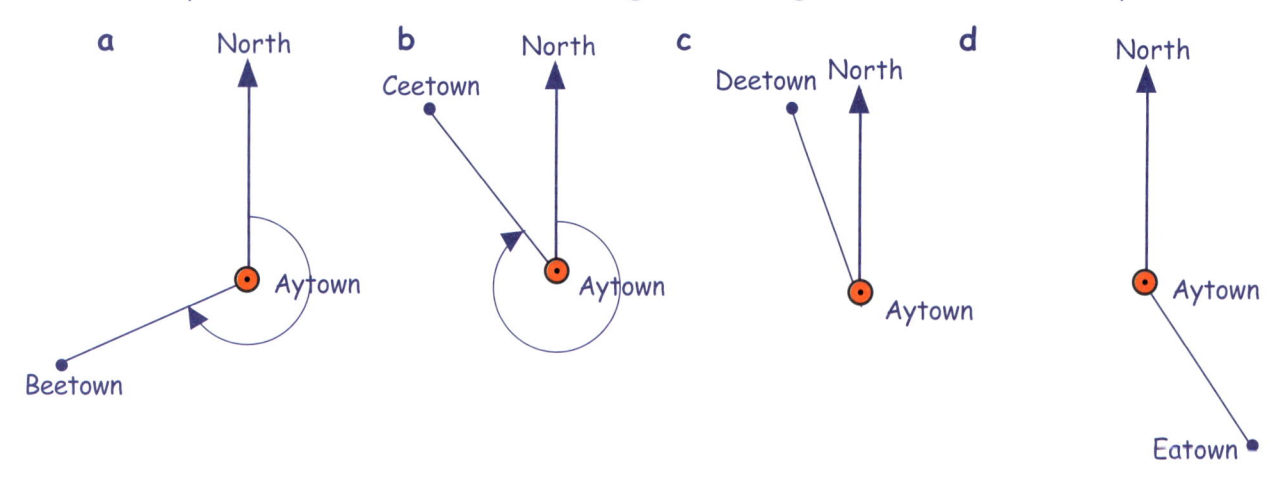

a Beetown   **b** Ceetown   **c** Deetown   **d** Eatown

6. Use a protractor to write down the 3-figure bearing for each of these towns **from** Arton.

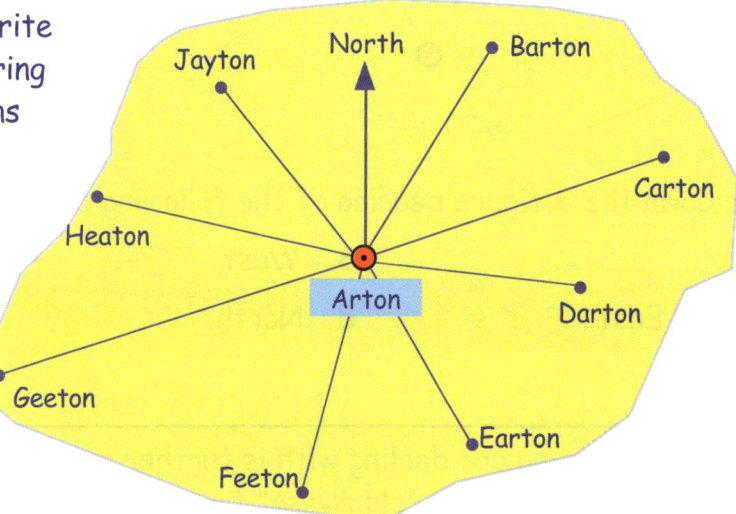

(Towns: Jayton, Barton, Carton, Darton, Earton, Feeton, Geeton, Heaton)

7. Mark a point on the page of your jotter and call it A. Draw a North line from your point.

Show, using a protractor, a bearing of 050°.

8. Repeat Question 7 to show each of the following bearings :-

    a 020°   **b** 090°   **c** 120°   **d** 045°

    e 190°   **f** 260°   **g** 325°   **h** 005°

9. A soldier leaves his base (**A**) on a bearing of 070° to go to hill (**B**).

If the soldier leaves hill B to go back to A, what bearing would he have to take ? (Do **NOT** measure it).

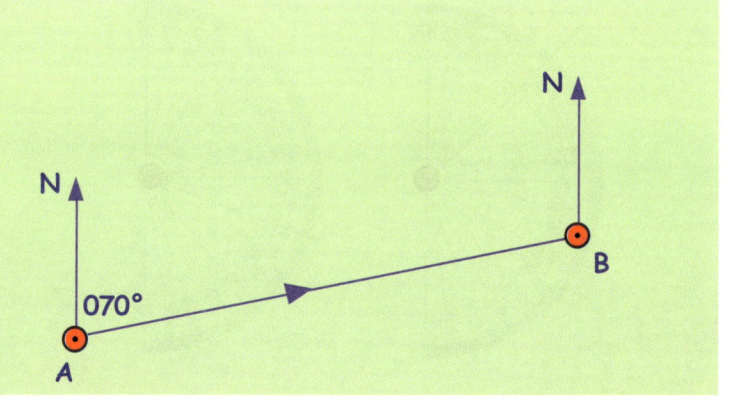

this is Chapter Eight   ANGLES

Topic in a Nutshell

1. Use a word from " **acute, right, obtuse, straight** or **reflex**" to describe each type of the **red** angles below :-

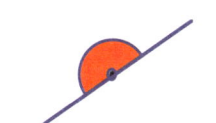

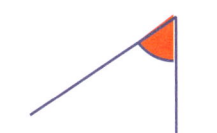

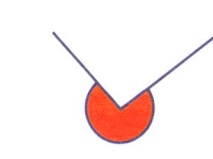

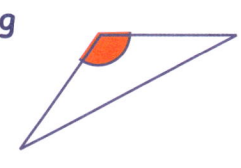

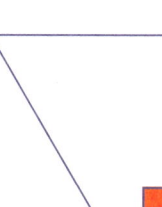

   a   b   c   d

   e   f   g   h

2. Look at the angle sizes listed below :-

   54°, 122°, 90°, 189°, 200°, 4°, 179°, 99°, 40°, 67°, 111°, 180°.

   Make lists of angles which are :-

   a acute   **b** obtuse   **c** right   **d** straight   **e** reflex.

3. Use 3 letters to name each **brown** angle :-

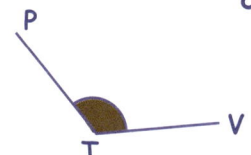

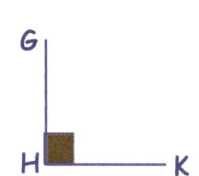

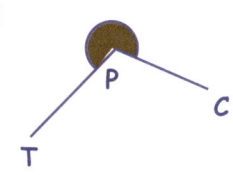

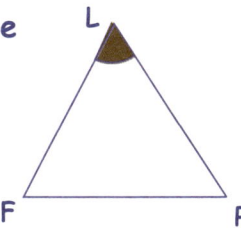

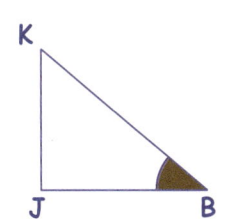

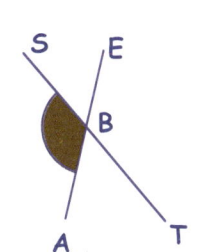

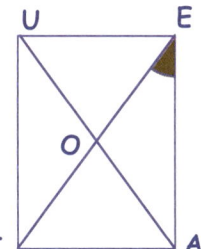

   a   b   c   d

   e   f   g   h

4. For each **green** angle : (i)   estimate its size.
   (ii) use a protractor to measure the size of the angle.

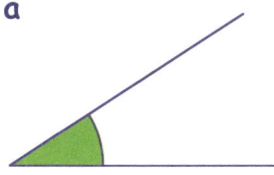

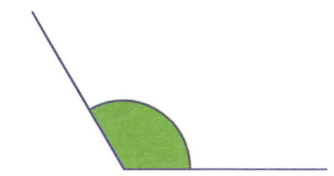

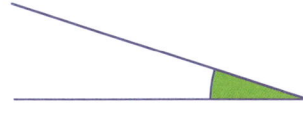

   a   b   c

this is Chapter Eight   page 103   ANGLES

d   e   f

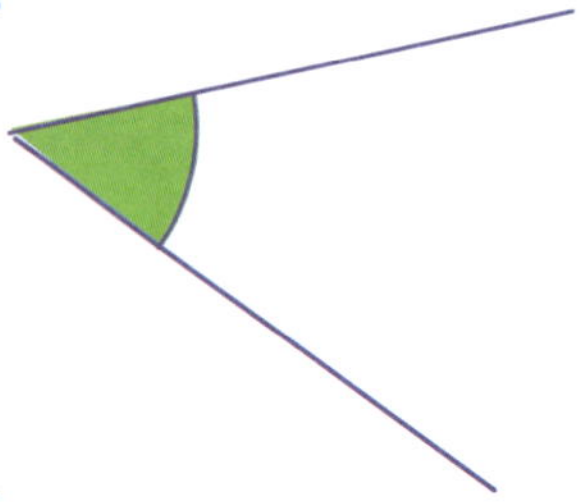

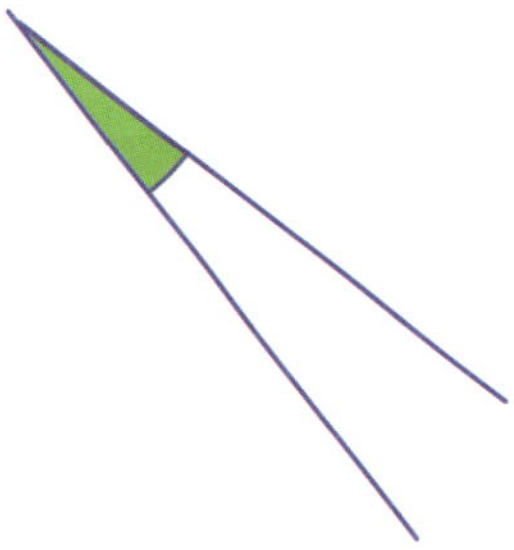

g 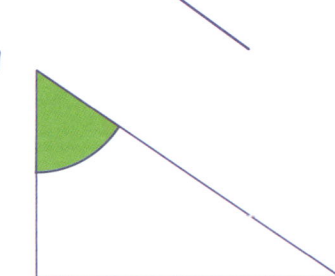   h 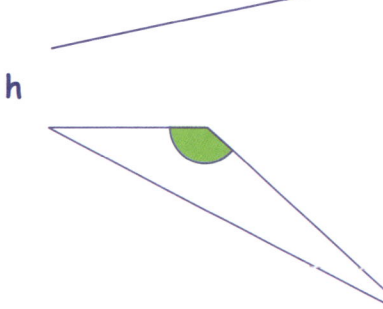   i

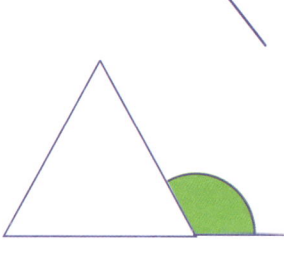

5. Carefully draw each of the following angles and label them with their letters :-

   a ∠ABC = 40°   b ∠GXD = 70°   c ∠PKT = 100°   d ∠TWG = 160°
   e ∠TPH = 25°   f ∠MNB = 123°   g ∠JKL = 190°   h ∠DFG = 300°

6. Make a full size accurate drawing of these triangles :-

   a 40° 50° 6 cm
   b 120° 20° 4 cm

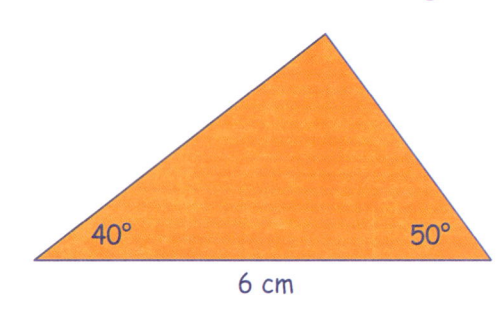

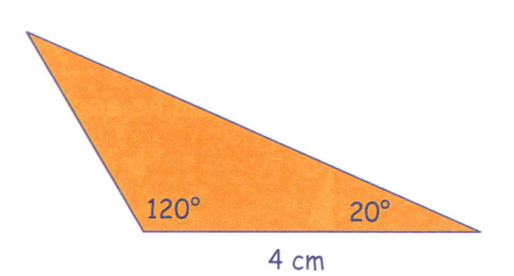

7. **Calculate** the sizes of the coloured angles :-

   a 60°
   b 27°
   c 40°
   d 150°
   e 120° 140°
   f 145°

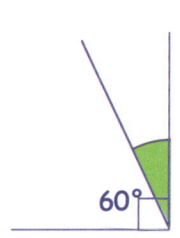

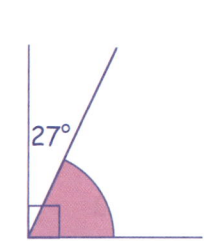

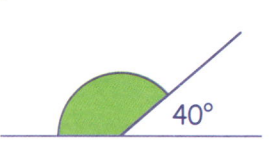

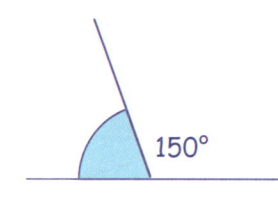

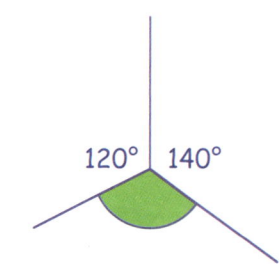

this is Chapter Eight   page 104   ANGLES

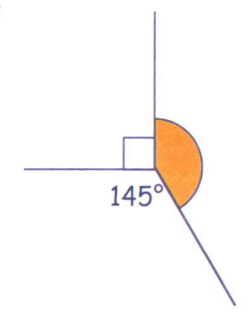

8. Copy each diagram and fill in the sizes of **all** the angles :- (do **NOT** measure)

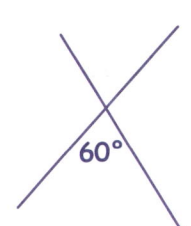

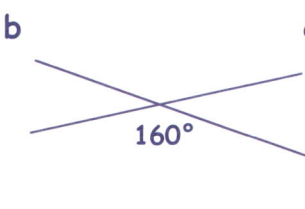

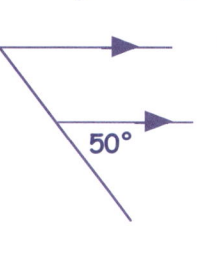

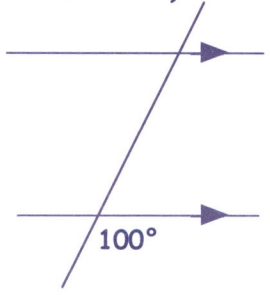

    a 60°   b 160°   c 50°   d 100°

9. How many degrees are there from :-

    a East to South (clockwise)
    b East to North (clockwise)
    c North to South-West (anti-clockwise)
    d North-East to West (clockwise) ?

10. a Jane drove her Land Rover North-West.
       She then made a **quarter turn clockwise**.
       In which direction was she then driving ?

    b A yacht sailing South-West turns 135° anti-clockwise.
       In which direction is the yacht now sailing ?

    c Later, the yacht was sailing South-East then
       turned clockwise and sailed West.
       Through how many degrees had the yacht turned ?

11. Write down the **3-figure bearing** shown in each diagram :-

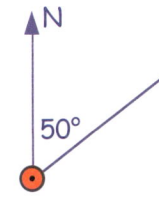

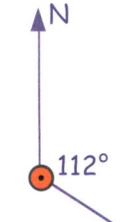

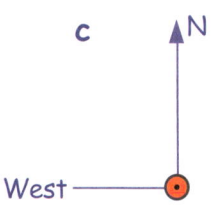

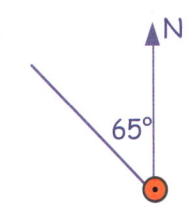

    a 50°   b 112°   c West   d 65°

12. Use a protractor to measure the **3-figure bearing** of each direction below :-

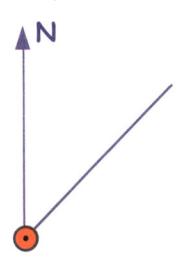

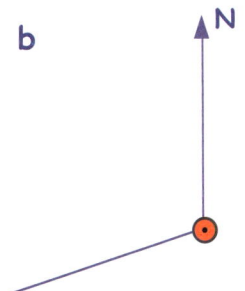

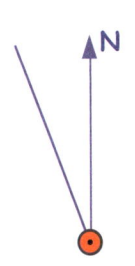

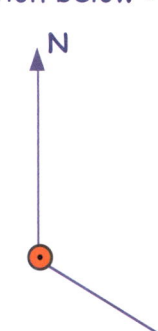

    a   b   c   d

13. Use a protractor to show each of these 3-figure bearings :-

    a 040°   b 075°   c 155°   d 300°.

this is Chapter Eight   page 105   ANGLES

Chapter 9

Money

How much is my Money worth ?

The Pound £

a £5 note **is worth the same as** FIVE pound coins

a £10 note **is worth the same as** TWO £5 notes

a £20 note **is worth the same as** TWO £10 notes

Exercise 1

1. How many **£1 coins** will I get for :-

   a two £5 notes
   b seven £5 notes
   c three £10 notes
   d six £10 notes
   e one £5 and three £10 notes
   f one £5, one £10 and one £20 note ?

2. How many **£5 notes** will I get for :-

   a two £10 notes
   b one £10 and one £20 note
   c four £10 and one £20 note
   d two £10 and two £20 notes
   e three £20 notes
   f three £10 notes and two £20 notes ?

3. David has these notes and coins in his wallet. He buys an ink cartridge costing £15·80 for his PC.

   Which of these notes and coins make up the £13·80 ?

4. Sammy buys a box of sweets for £2·69. She hands over a £10 note.

   a How much change should she get ?

   b Give an example of what notes and coins might make up her change.

5. Jason goes to Hamburger Palace and buys food costing £13·27. He pays with a £20 note.

   a How much change should Jason get ?

   b Give an example of what notes and coins he might have in his change.

Add, Subtract, Multiply and Divide using Money

Addition and Subtraction

When you ADD or SUBTRACT money, it is important to **line up the decimal points**.

Examples **Addition**

£7·85
+ £1·43
───────
£9·28
 1

Subtraction

£4·25
− £1·64
───────
£2·61

* Your teacher will show you how to subtract.

Multiplication and Division

It is important that you know your multiplication tables.

Examples **Multiplication**

£1·23
× 6
───────
£7·38
 1 1

Division

£1· 32
7)£9·²2⁴

Exercise 2

1. Copy the following and find :-

   a £2·45   b £2·53   c £1·35   d £2·72
      + £1·34   + £3·14   + £3·46   + £4·84

   e £12·54   f £14·67   g £ 5·72   h £ 7·67
      + £ 5·68   + £ 3·74   + £13·19   + £11·85

   i £5·72   j £4·89   k £6·28   l £8·21
      − £1·61   − £2·53   − £3·19   − £6·84

   m £15·98   n £17·43   o £12·15   p £19·67
      − £ 3·81   − £ 1·28   − £ 6·79   − £ 8·77

   q £4·49   r £8·12   s £12·14   t £13·36
      + £9·91   − £1·61   + £ 3·79   − £ 3·37

   u £ 1·92   v £14·00   w £14·66   x £20·00
      + £11·66   − £ 1·45   + £ 5·34   − £19·25

2. Set down these additions and subtractions in the same way as question 1 and work out the answers :-

a £4·25 + £3·54   b £6·57 − £1·26   c £13·84 + £1·19
d £17·42 − £6·54   e £10 + £3·42   f £10 − £5·17
g £15 + £4·98   h £15 − £6·98   i £7·56 + £12·34
j £13 − £1·99   k £9·94 + £9·99   l £18·04 − £0·35

3. Copy the following and complete each multiplication :-

a £1·25 × 2   b £2·15 × 3   c £1·26 × 4   d £3·40 × 5
e £3·46 × 5   f £4·57 × 4   g £6·19 × 3   h £9·97 × 2
i £3·14 × 6   j £2·35 × 7   k £1·54 × 8   l £2·06 × 9

4. Copy the following and complete each division :-

a 2) £2·60   b 3) £9·63   c 4) £8·48   d 5) £5·50
e 6) £6·06   f 7) £14·00   g 8) £8·16   h 9) £9·27
i 2) £16·36   j 3) £16·11   k 4) £7·32   l 5) £18·95
m 6) £1·44   n 7) £17·64   o 8) £19·60   p 9) £0·54

5. Write each of these in the forms shown above, then work out the answers :-

a £8·57 × 2   b £19·36 ÷ 2   c £4·17 × 3   d £17·46 ÷ 3
e £18·16 ÷ 4   f £3·81 × 4   g £3·85 ÷ 5   h £13·45 ÷ 5
i £3·17 × 6   j £9·42 ÷ 6   k £0·63 ÷ 7   l £2·95 × 7

ADDITIONAL PRACTICE (if required).

6. Try these additions :-

a	£12·50 + £8·40	b	£16·75 + £7·55	c	£35·90 + £4·60
d	£4·50 + £56·85	e	£6·85 + £28·90	f	£5·65 + £47·80
g	£23·48 + £21·40	h	£59·58 + £25·50	i	£18·80 + £47·97
j	£35·16 + £48·48	k	£26·64 + £14·46	l	£27·25 + £21·74
m	£57·67 + £26·47	n	£17·48 + £67·67	o	£39·31 + £19·99
p	£36·59 + £37·16	q	£38·34 + £66·46	r	£43·98 + £56·02

7. Try these subtractions :-

a	£17·50 – £9·20	b	£18·25 – £4·55	c	£25·90 – £5·90
d	£34·25 – £6·45	e	£26·10 – £8·90	f	£45·65 – £6·65
g	£21·48 – £10·47	h	£32·27 – £16·90	i	£54·62 – £23·81
j	£48·65 – £27·88	k	£55·47 – £38·57	l	£37·87 – £14·98
m	£31·84 – £26·07	n	£72·24 – £57·32	o	£49·31 – £19·99
p	£46·46 – £45·38	q	£84·01 – £74·32	r	£100 – £48·97

8. Try these multiplications :-

a	£15·25 × 2	b	£29·48 × 2	c	£17·35 × 3
d	£46·19 × 3	e	£15·55 × 4	f	£21·18 × 4
g	£12·75 × 5	h	£19·96 × 5	i	£9·45 × 6
j	£14·78 × 6	k	£6·37 × 7	l	£13·45 × 7
m	£7·64 × 8	n	£12·39 × 8	o	£10·58 × 9
p	£11·07 × 9	q	£2·99 × 10	r	£28·30 × 10

9. Try these divisions :-

a	£90·50 ÷ 2	b	£65·38 ÷ 2	c	£73·71 ÷ 3
d	£89·82 ÷ 3	e	£89·96 ÷ 4	f	£79·96 ÷ 4
g	£82·25 ÷ 5	h	£95·45 ÷ 5	i	£88·08 ÷ 6
j	£79·56 ÷ 6	k	£99·61 ÷ 7	l	£44·87 ÷ 7
m	£90·24 ÷ 8	n	£78·88 ÷ 8	o	£46·53 ÷ 9
p	£95·22 ÷ 9	q	£15·40 ÷ 10	r	£72·90 ÷ 10

Mixed Money Problems

This exercise consists of a mixture of money problems.

CALCULATORS may be used here, but **all working should be shown**.

Exercise 3

1. The local chemist shop puts out a notice to customers in the area, telling them of the special offers for the week.

   This week's special offers are shown below.

   shampoo £2·95
   comb 58p
   soap £1·28
   toothbrush £1·99
   toilet roll 78p
   talcum powder £4·15
   toothpaste £3·50
   kitchen towel £1·60
   duster 28p
   polish £3·99

   How much would it cost for :-

   a a bottle of shampoo and a bar of soap ?
   b a duster and a tin of polish ?
   c a tube of tooth paste and 2 tooth brushes ?
   d 3 tins of talc and 4 combs ?
   e 5 kitchen towels and 4 toilet rolls ?

2. Sandra looked at her weekly bill from Andy's Newsagent shop.

   a Copy the bill and complete it.
   b Sandra handed over one £10 note and four one pound coins.

   How much change did she receive ?

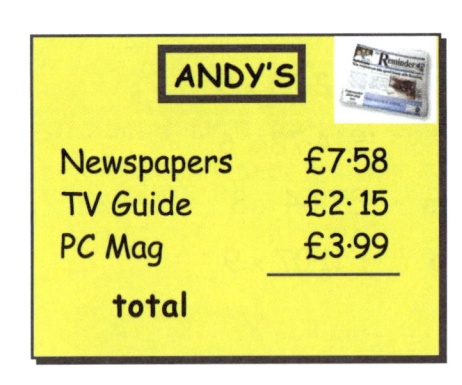

   ANDY'S
   Newspapers   £7·58
   TV Guide   £2·15
   PC Mag   £3·99
   total

3. **Gordon's Go-Karts**
   (for 10 minutes)
   Adult   £7·45
   Child   £4·85
   Parent/Child £15·65
   (1 adult + 2 kids)

   Mr Baxter took his 2 children Go-Karting.

   a How much did it cost to buy 1 adult and 2 children's tickets for a ten minute ride ?
   b How much would they have saved by buying the Parent/Child ticket ?

this is Chapter Nine   page 110   MONEY

4. Sarah goes swimming 5 nights per week.

Langbank Baths
Single Session :-
non member £2·64
member £1·99
Membership :- FREE !

a How much does it cost her each week as a non-member ?

She decides to join the swimming club which meets nightly at 8p.m.

b How much does it now cost her to swim the 5 times per week ?

c How much does she save per week by joining the club ?

5. The table below shows how much money four young children raised for charity by holding a sponsored stay-awake sleepover.

Sponsors	Joe	Jan	Dawn	Dave
Neighbours	£4·20	£2·00	£2·94	£7·82
Friends	£5·00	£6·20	£1·30	£2·80
Family	£8·57	£8·75	£14·38	£7·10
Others	£0·89	£3·17	£1·67	£0·12

a How much did each of the children raise individually ?

b Who raised the most and who raised the least ?

c By how much was the highest total larger than the second highest total ?

d Compare how much the children got in total from their **families** with how much they got from "**others**".

6. The total cost for 6 men to go on a chairlift to the top of a mountain was £18·84.

What was the cost for one man ?

7. It costs £1·95 for a PC games magazine and £2·98 for a Playzone games magazine.

a How much will it cost altogether for 3 PC and 4 Playzone games magazines ?

b What change will you get back from £20 ?

8. Adam's the Butchers, have lamb chops on special offer. A pack of 6 costs £19·68 and a pack of 4 costs £13·16.

Which is the better deal ?
(*Explain your answer with working*).

this is Chapter Nine   page 111   MONEY

9. Copy and complete the following bills **and say what change is left from £20 in each case** :-

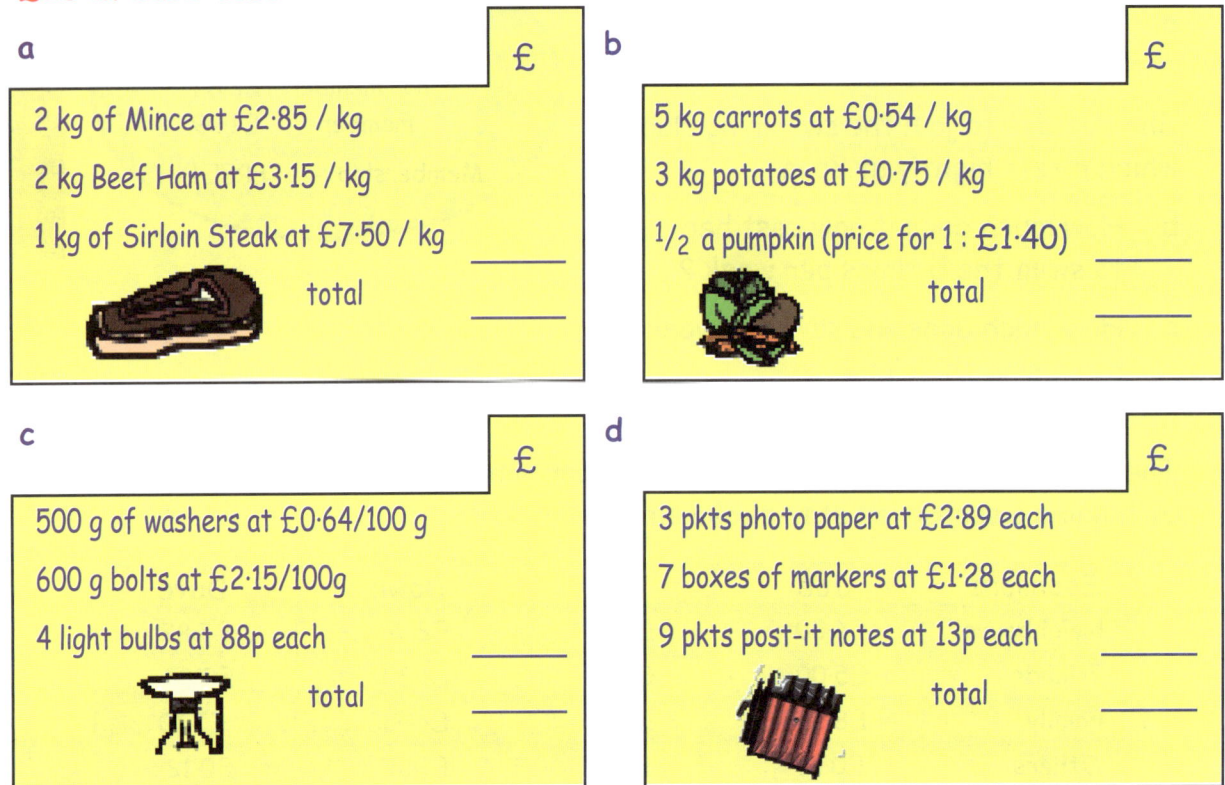

   a   £
   2 kg of Mince at £2·85 / kg
   2 kg Beef Ham at £3·15 / kg
   1 kg of Sirloin Steak at £7·50 / kg _____
                                total   _____

   b   £
   5 kg carrots at £0·54 / kg
   3 kg potatoes at £0·75 / kg
   ½ a pumpkin (price for 1 : £1·40) _____
                                total   _____

   c   £
   500 g of washers at £0·64/100 g
   600 g bolts at £2·15/100g
   4 light bulbs at 88p each   _____
                        total   _____

   d   £
   3 pkts photo paper at £2·89 each
   7 boxes of markers at £1·28 each
   9 pkts post-it notes at 13p each   _____
                               total   _____

10. I bought a calculator, a pen and a novelty pencil case from the corner shop and the bill came to £17·12. I remembered that the calculator was £6·75 and the pen was £2·99.

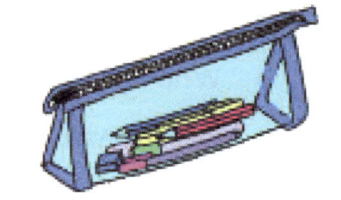

    What must the pencil case have cost me ?

11. The bill for 4 of us in Burger House, including drinks, came to £19·12. Since it was my birthday, I paid for the drinks (£3·56) and the rest of the bill was split evenly between the four of us.

    a   What did it cost each of my friends for their food only ?

    b   What did it cost ME for my meal and the drinks at Burger House ?

12. Lemon Fresh washing conditioner comes in 2 sizes, as shown opposite.

    The small one (300 g) costs £4·44.

    The larger one (500 g) costs £6·65.

    By calculating the cost of 100 grams of conditioner for each size of box, say which is the better deal.

13. I bought 8 Christmas decorations on the Internet for a total of £14·36 **plus** £2·66 for postage and packing.

I saw the same decorations on the QVC channel priced £2·19 **each** plus £1·80 for postage and packing.

How much had I saved altogether by buying the decorations on the Internet ?

14. Lyle and his sister work at Govan Market on a Saturday morning. He gets paid £0·29 less **per hour** than his sister.

If they both work for 4 hours and his sister gets paid a total of £18·24, how much does Lyle get paid for his shift ?

15. I bought a pair of matching candlesticks at an auction for a total of £14·92. My wife didn't like them ! So, I sold one of them for £7·99 and the second one, because it was rusty, for £2·55.

How much did I lose in this deal ?

16. Two chicken suppers and a sausage supper cost me £11·98.

If the sausage supper was priced at £2·40, what was the price of a chicken supper ?

17. The bill for 2 lemon teas and 3 rounds of sandwiches at the Beneagles Hotel came to £18·70 !

If the price of 1 lemon tea was £1·58, how much must each round of sandwiches have cost me ?

18. Seven friends went for breakfast before work. If the total bill had been shared amongst the 7 of them, each would have had to pay £2·94. Because Freddie left before the bill arrived, the others had to split the bill 6 ways.

How much did each of them then have to pay ?

19. Gordon borrowed a sum of money from his friend Tony. He paid him back the entire amount (eventually).

He paid Tony £2·55 the first week and followed this with 9 payments of £1·45 each.

How much must Gordon have borrowed from Tony ?

Topic in a Nutshell

1. Rockie buys a pair of boxing gloves costing £14·25.
   He pays with a £20 note.

   a How much change should Rockie get ?

   b Give an example of what notes and coins he might have in his change.

2. Work out the answers to these :–

   a £5·29 + £3·72   b £8·36 − £1·64   c £1·83 × 5   d £4·35 ÷ 3

   e £12·57 + £6·98   f £19·05 − £11·08   g £2·37 × 8   h £13·93 ÷ 7

3. Hannah is out at the ice-cream van.
   She buys one large cone at £1·45, one packet of chewing gum at 46p and eight 1 penny chews.

   What change will Hannah get from a £5 note ?

4. Norah goes out with £20 in her purse.
   She buys two fashion magazines in the newsagent's at £4·75 each.

   a How much change will Norah get from her £20 ?

   She now goes for a half-hour session on a sunbed where the cost is £3·95 for 10 minutes.

   b How much will this cost Norah ?

   c When she goes to pay for her time on the sunbed she finds that she does not have enough money ! How much is she short ?

5. The total cost for 9 men to go for a game of crown bowls was £13·95.

   By working out the cost for one man, calculate how much it will cost old Mr Bryant **and** his 3 cronies who intend to go bowling tomorrow.

6. Frank's Fruit Store are running a special promotion on melons..........

   £5·76 for six   OR   £7·52 for eight

   a By working out the cost of 1 melon in each deal, find which deal is cheaper.

   b Melanie buys **two** lots of 8 melons and hands Frank a £20 note.

   How much change should she get ?

this is Chapter Nine   page 114   MONEY

Chapter 10

Two Dimensions

2D Work

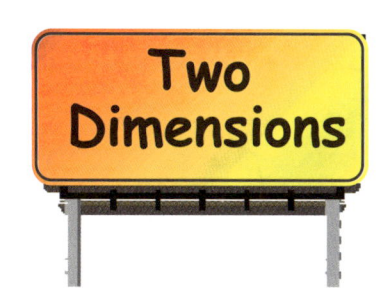

Exercise 1

1. Name the following shapes :-

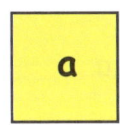

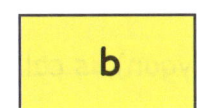

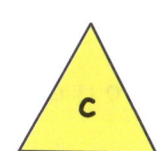

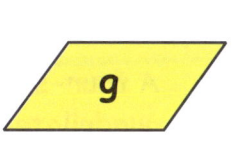

   a, b, c, d, e, f, g

2. Identify the (2 Dimensional) mathematical shapes in the following figures :-

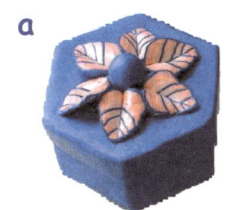

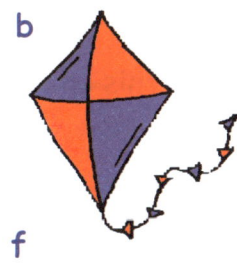

   a, b, c, d, e, f, g, h

3. A **polygon** is a mathematical name for a shape with "**many sides**". By many, we usually mean more than **4**.

   a   Copy or trace this shape.
   b   Write the name of this polygon shape beneath your drawing.
   c   How many edges does it have ?
   d   How many angles does it have ?

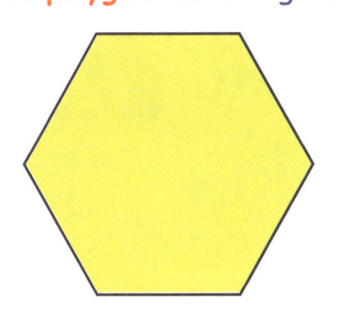

4. This **polygon** has 6 edges.

   a   How many angles does it have ?
   b   Copy or trace this polygon.
   c   Write down the special name of this polygon beneath your drawing.

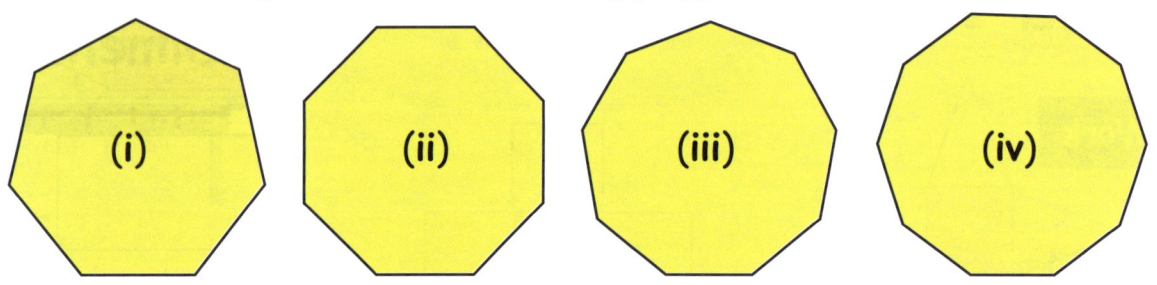

5. a   Make a tracing of each of the following polygons :-

    (i)   (ii)   (iii)   (iv)

    b   Try to find the special names for each of these polygons and write their names down under each shape.

6. A **four-sided polygon**, (though we don't refer to it as a polygon), is called a **quadrilateral** (4-sided figure).

    a   What is the special name for this quadrilateral ?

    b   What do you call the special type of angle at each corner of this shape ?

    c   Copy, trace or draw a similar quadrilateral to this one and draw in all of its diagonals (*see definition below*).

    Definition :-   a **diagonal** is a line joining one corner of the shape to any other corner that is not directly next to the 1st corner.

    d   How many diagonals does a square have ?

7. Copy or trace the **pentagon** shown opposite.

    a   From each of the 5 corners, draw in **all** the diagonals of the pentagon.

    b   How many diagonals does a pentagon have ?

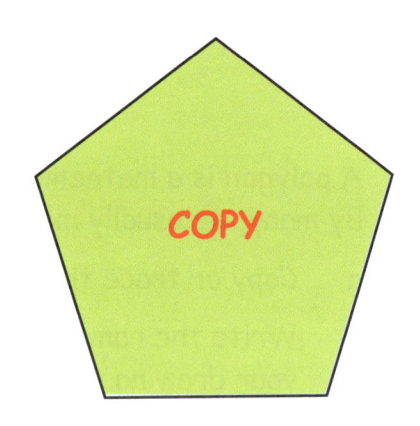

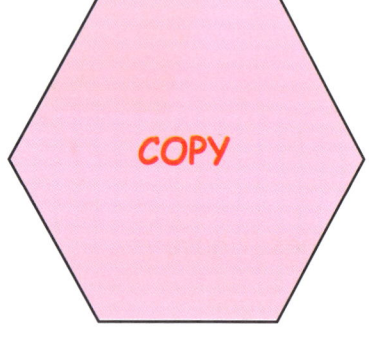

8. Copy or trace the **hexagon** shown opposite.

    a   From each of the 6 corners, draw in **all** the diagonals of the hexagon.

    b   How many diagonals does a hexagon have ?

9. Use your drawings in Question 5 to find how many diagonals each of the other polygons have.

this is Chapter Ten   TWO DIMENSIONS

10. This shape consists of **1 square** and **2 triangles**.
    Describe each of the following in the same way :-

a

b

c

d

e

f

g

h

i

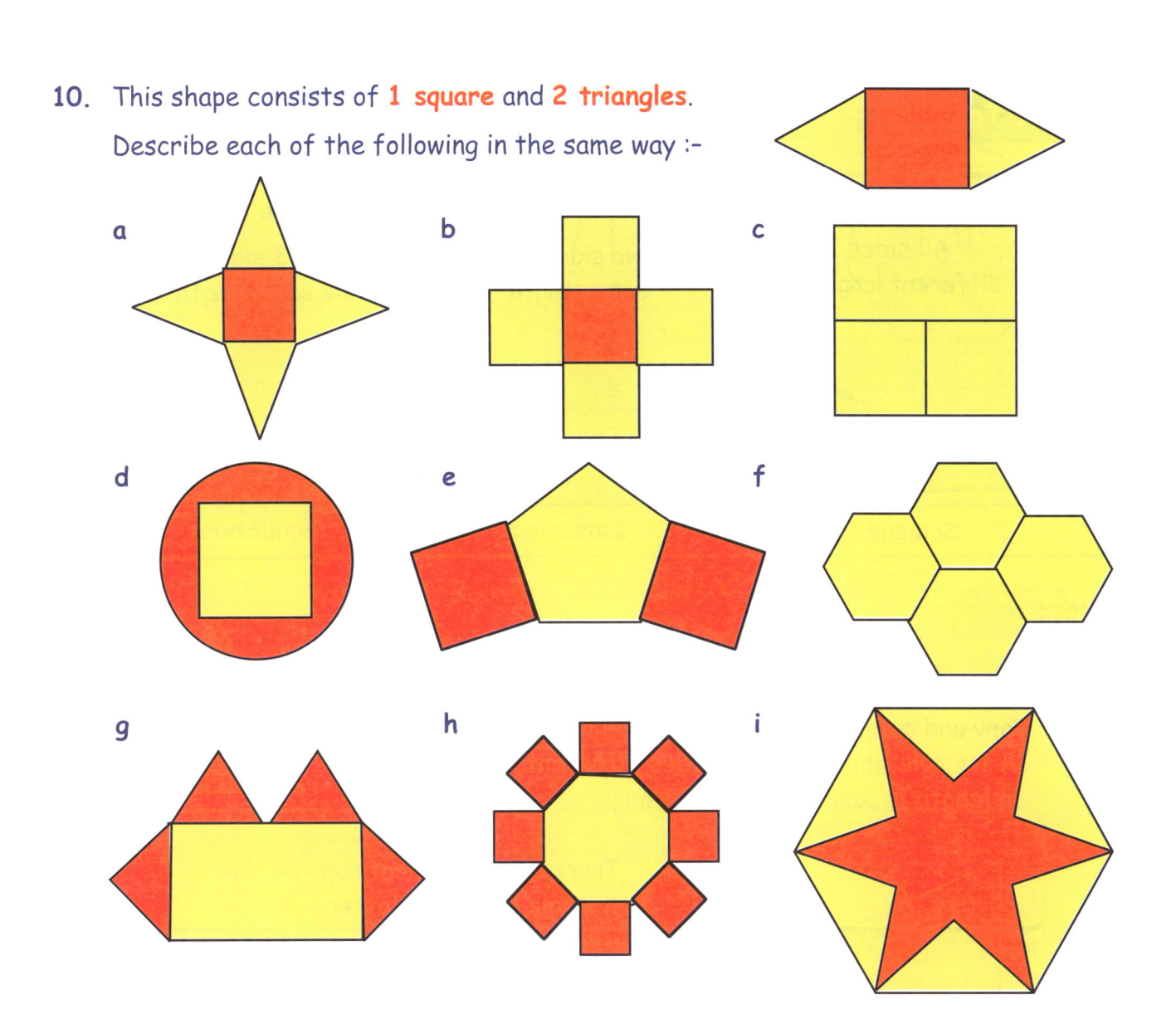

11. a   Neatly, design some shapes consisting of **squares**, **rectangles**, **triangles**, **circles**, **pentagons**, **hexagons**, etc.

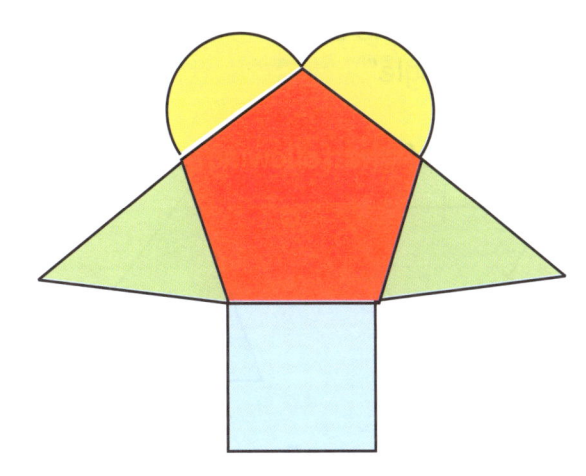

    b   Draw your best shapes onto white cardboard, colour them and make a wall display.

Special Triangles

Side Properties :– There are **3 types of triangles** based on their side lengths.

All sides different lengths	Two sides the same length	All 3 sides the same length
Scalene	Isosceles	Equilateral

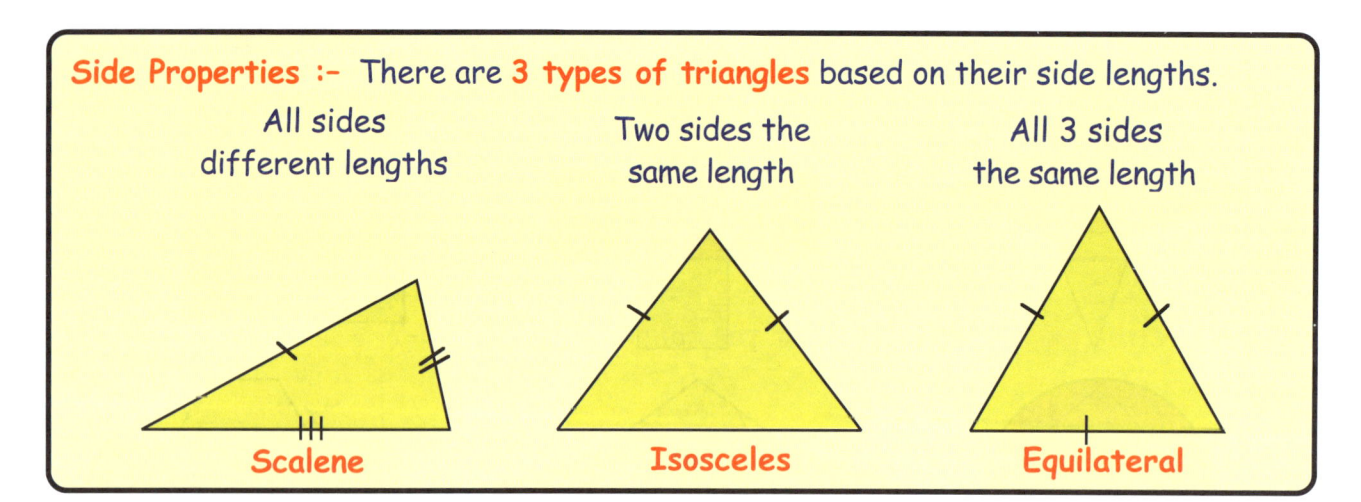

Exercise 2

1. a   Trace or make a neat copy of this triangle into your jotter.

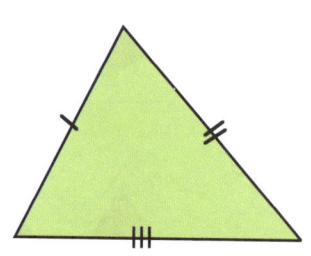

    b   Copy and complete :–
        "A triangle which has all 3 sides different in length is called a .... triangle".

2. a   Trace or make a neat copy of this triangle into your jotter.

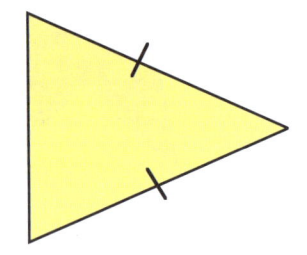

    b   Copy and complete :–
        "A triangle which has 2 of its sides equal in length is called a .... triangle".

3. a   Trace or make a neat copy of this triangle into your jotter.

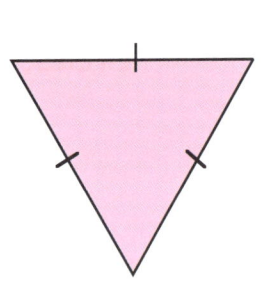

    b   Copy and complete :–
        "A triangle which has all 3 sides the same length is called a .... triangle".

4. State which type of triangle each of the following is :–

    a 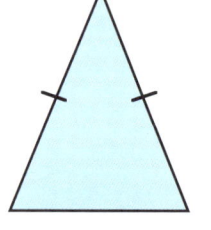   b 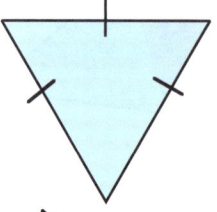   c 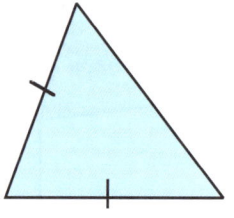   d

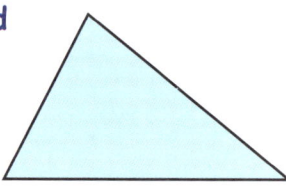

    e 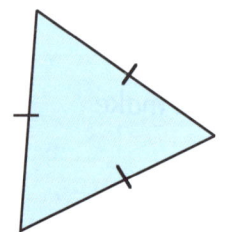   f 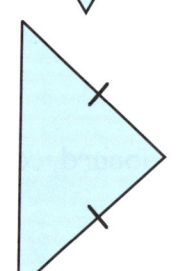   g 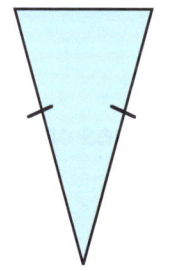   h

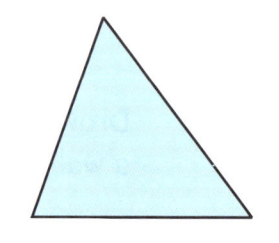

this is Chapter Ten   page 118   TWO DIMENSIONS

The **PERIMETER** of a shape is the total distance around its outside.

Perimeter = 3 cm + 4 cm + 6 cm + 5 cm = 18 cm.

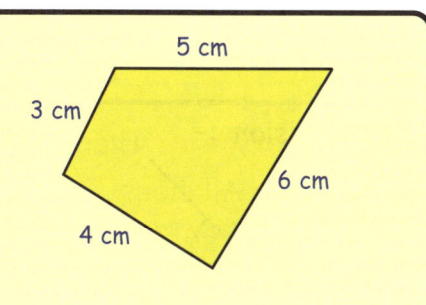

5. Calculate the **perimeter** of each of the following triangles :-

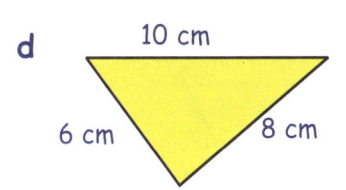

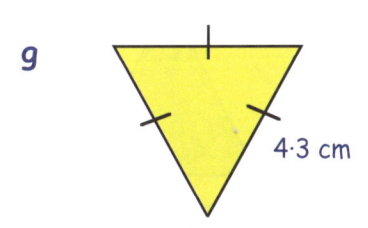

a) 6 cm, 15 cm, 14 cm
b) 10 cm, 8 cm (isosceles, two equal sides marked)
c) 11 cm (isosceles, two equal sides marked)
d) 10 cm, 6 cm, 8 cm
e) 3·6 cm, 2·1 cm (isosceles, two equal sides marked)
f) 55 mm, 125 mm (isosceles, two equal sides marked)
g) 4·3 cm (equilateral)
h) 8 m, 6·5 m, 9·5 m
i) 15·6 cm, 27·8 cm (isosceles, two equal sides marked)

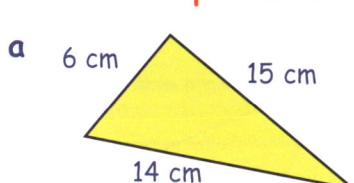

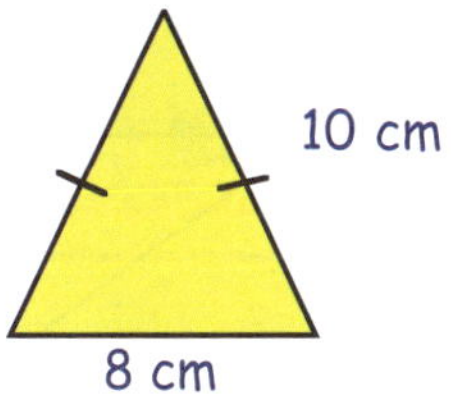

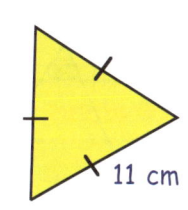

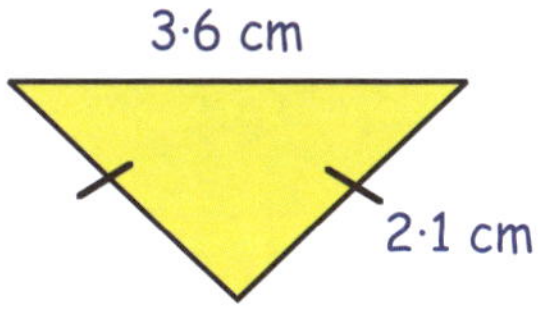

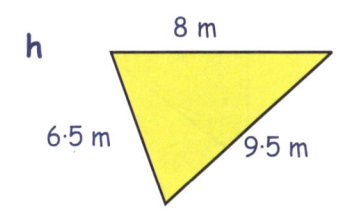

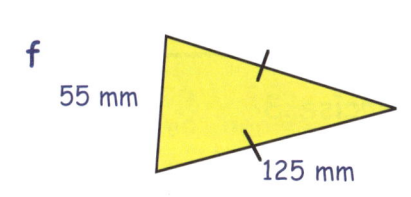

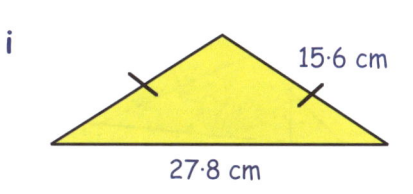

6. In each of the following triangles, the **perimeter** is given. Calculate the lengths of the missing sides :-

a) ?, 11 cm, 14 cm — Perimeter = 34 cm
b) 9 cm, 12 cm, ? — Perimeter = 36 cm
c) 10 cm (isosceles), ? — Perimeter = 35 cm
d) ?, 16 cm (isosceles, two equal sides marked) — Perimeter = 42 cm
e) ? (equilateral) — Perimeter = 30 cm
f) 7 cm, ? (isosceles, two equal sides marked) — Perimeter = 25 cm

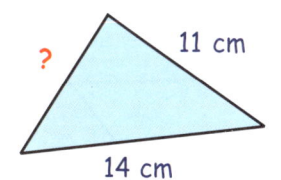

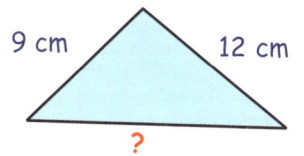

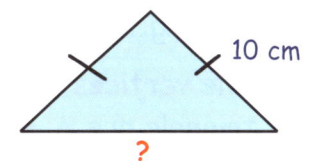

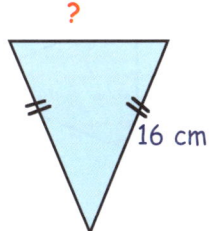

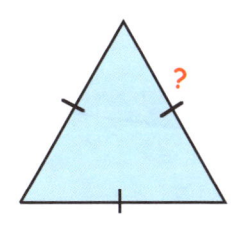

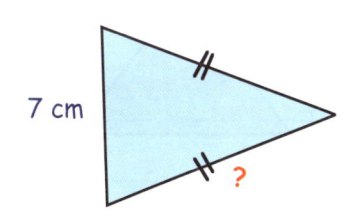

this is Chapter Ten   page 119   TWO DIMENSIONS

Angle Properties :- Triangles can be described in 3 different ways dependent on their angle sizes.

Revision :-   **Types of Angles**

acute   right   obtuse   reflex

New :-   **Types of Triangles**

All angles are smaller than 90°   One angle is equal to 90°   One angle is bigger than 90°

acute angled triangle   **right** angled triangle   **obtuse** angled triangle

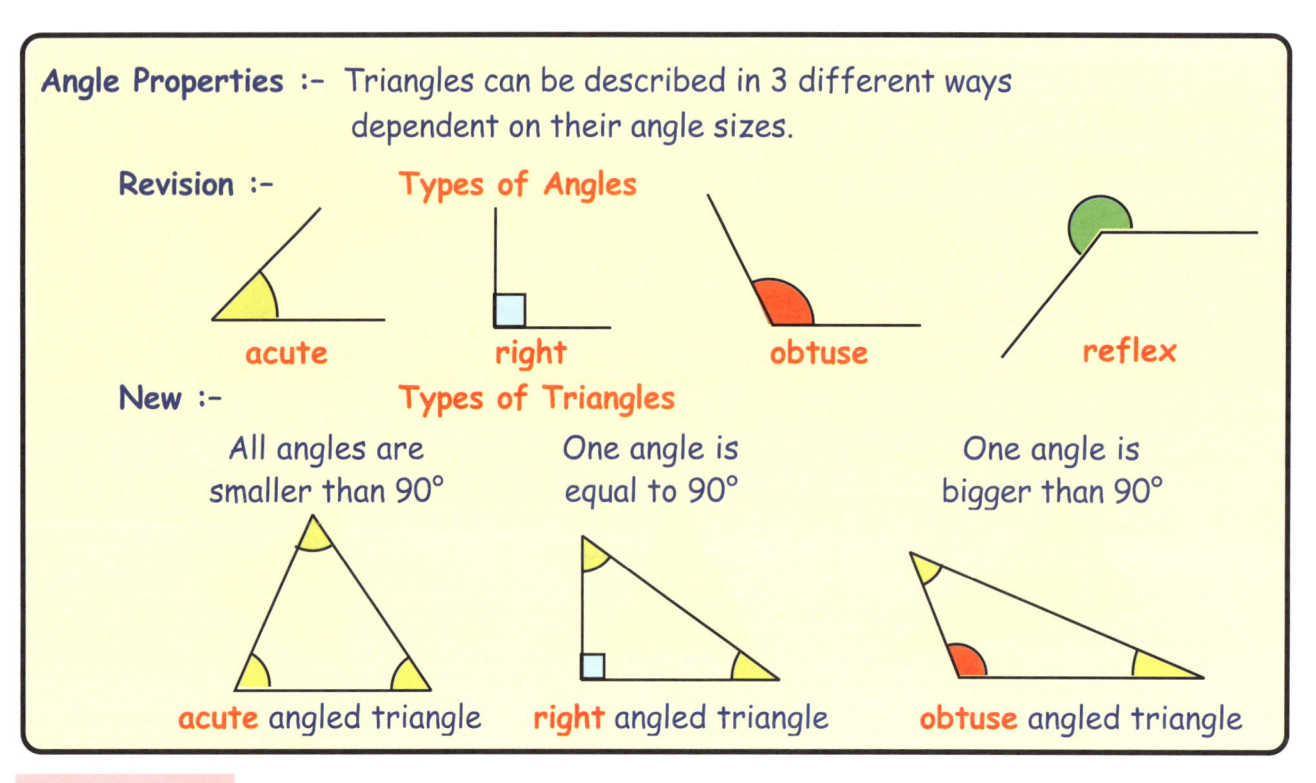

Exercise 3

1. State whether each of the following is an **acute** angled, **right** angled or **obtuse** angled triangle :-

   a   b 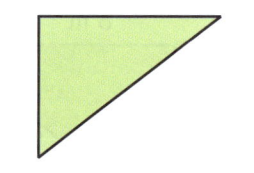   c

   d 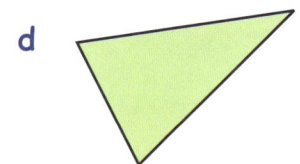   e 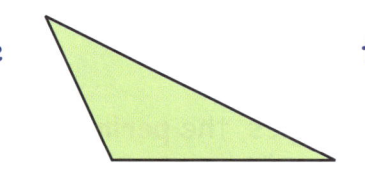   f

2. Naming triangles using **3 letters**.

   The **vertices** (corners) of this triangle are **A**, **B** and **C**.
   It is called triangle ABC (or △ABC for short)

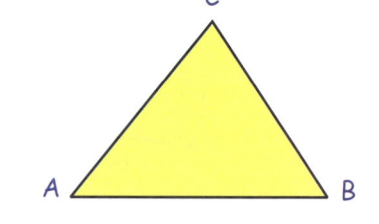

   Name each of the following triangles (Capital letters) :-

   a   G, E, T   b   F, L, K   c   M, I, Q

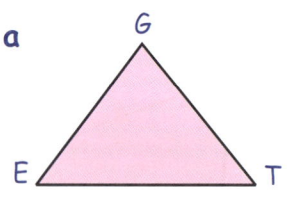

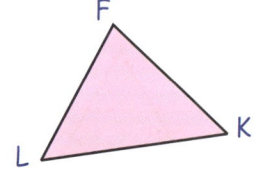

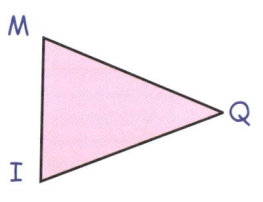

   d   R, L, D   e   N, P, H   f   V, S, J

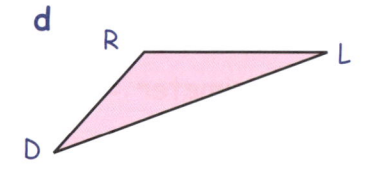

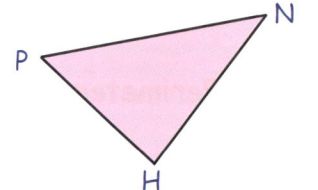

this is Chapter Ten   page 120   TWO DIMENSIONS

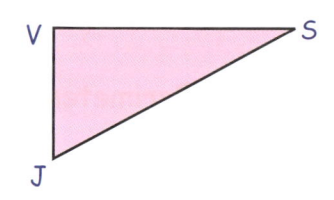

We can describe a triangle as follows :-

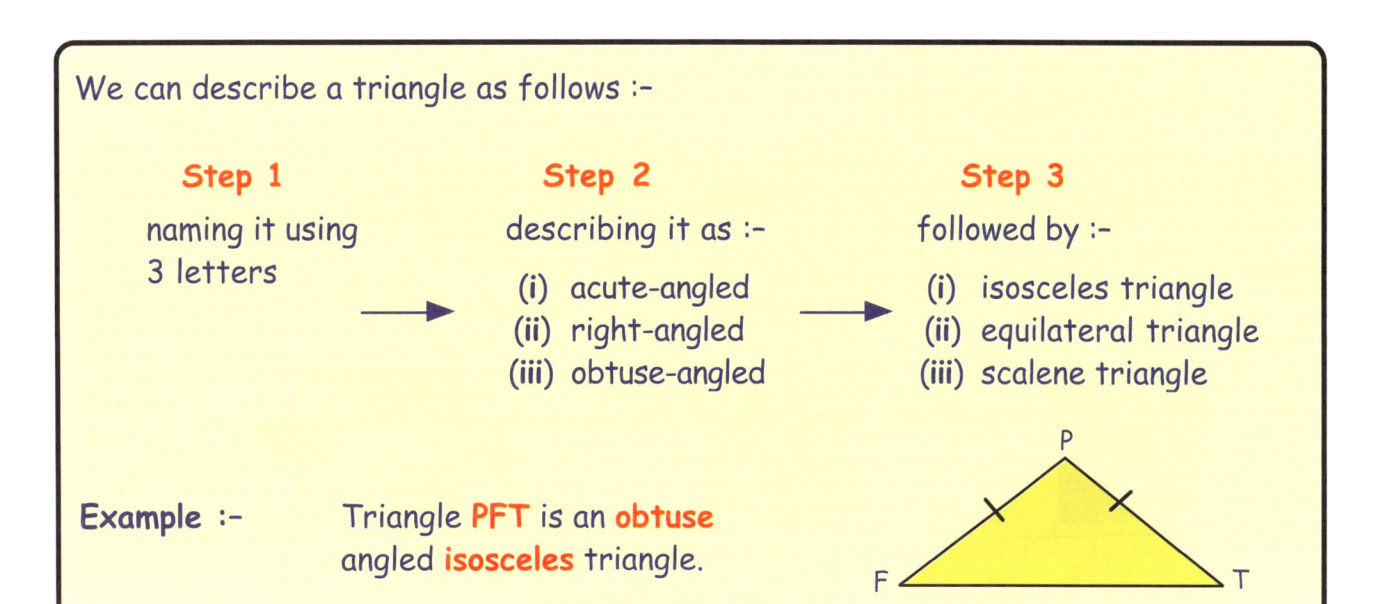

Step 1
naming it using 3 letters

Step 2
describing it as :-
(i) acute-angled
(ii) right-angled
(iii) obtuse-angled

Step 3
followed by :-
(i) isosceles triangle
(ii) equilateral triangle
(iii) scalene triangle

Example :- Triangle **PFT** is an **obtuse** angled **isosceles** triangle.

3. Describe this triangle in the same way :-

   "D.......... is a .... angled .... triangle".

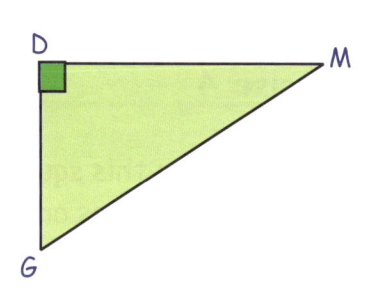

4. 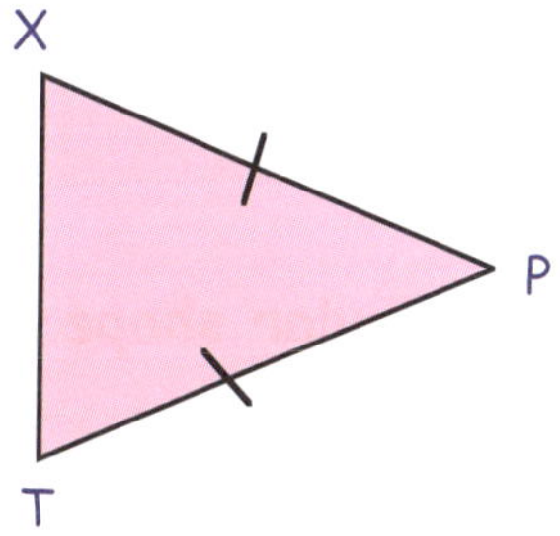 Describe this triangle in the same way :-

   "D.......... is an .... angled .... triangle".

5. Describe each of the following triangles in the same way :-

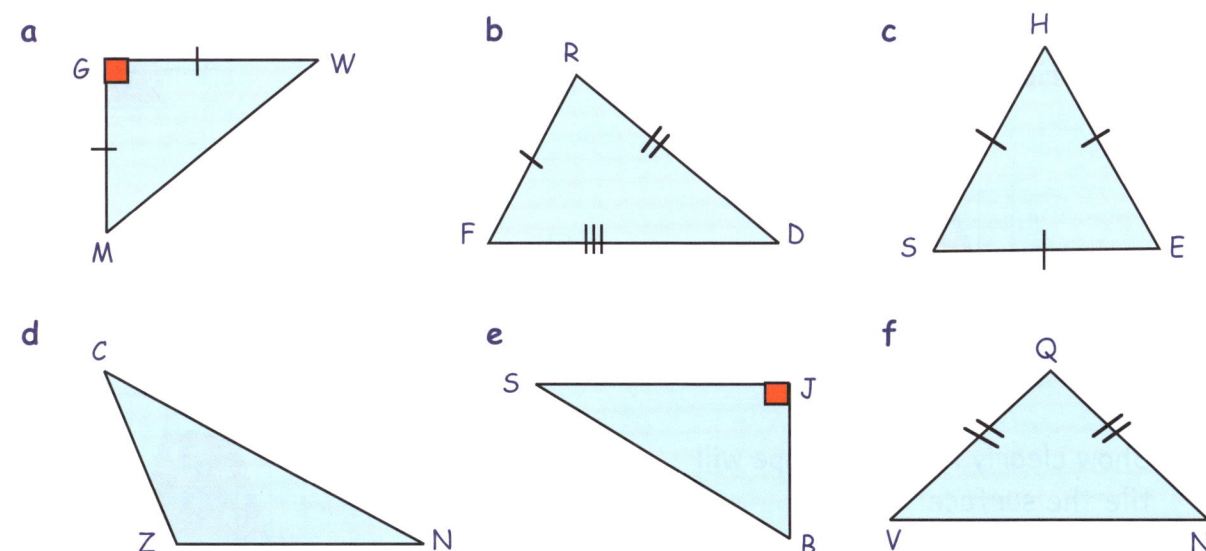

   a   b   c

   d   e   f

this is Chapter Ten   page 121   TWO DIMENSIONS

Tilings using 2-D Shapes

If you can cover a flat surface without any gaps using one type of shape we say that :-

"the shape TILES the surface".

Shown above are some examples of shapes which tile.

Exercise 4

1. a   Draw this **square** tile measuring 2 boxes by 2 boxes and colour or lightly shade it.

    b   By completely surrounding the shape with similar squares, show that the square tiles.

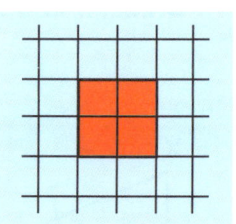

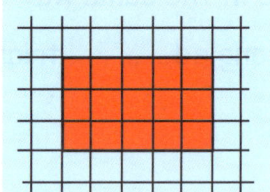

2. a   Copy this 3 by 5 **rectangular shape**.

    b   Surround it with similar rectangles to show that the rectangle tiles.

3. a   Copy this **isosceles triangle** and colour or lightly shade it.

    b   Completely surround the shape with similar **triangles** to show that it tiles the plane.

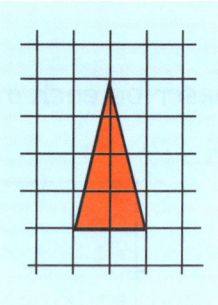

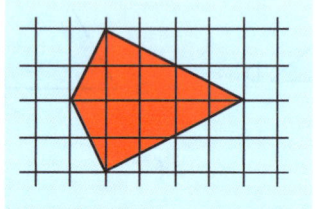

4. Show clearly how this **kite shape** will tile the surface.

5. Show clearly how this shape will tile the surface.
    (Do you know the name of this shape ?)

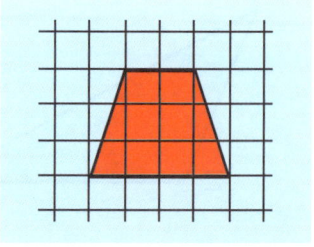

this is Chapter Ten   page 122   TWO DIMENSIONS

6. Decide which of the following shapes will tile.

For those that do, show how they do so by surrounding the given tile.

a   b 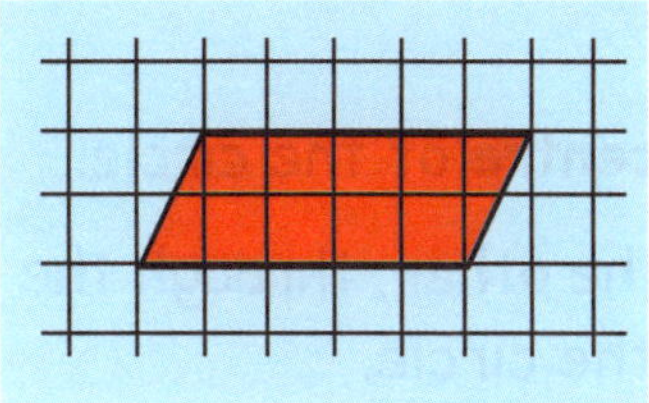   c

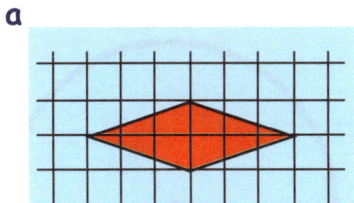

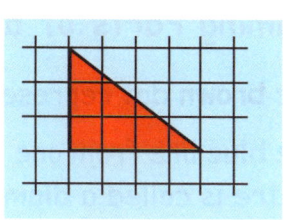

d 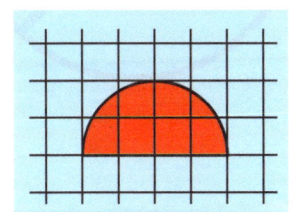   e 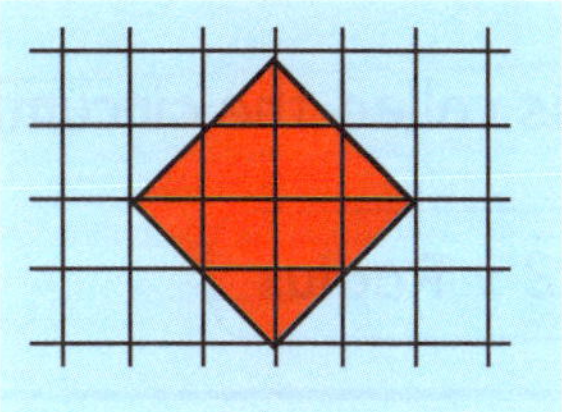   f

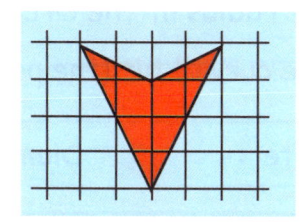

g 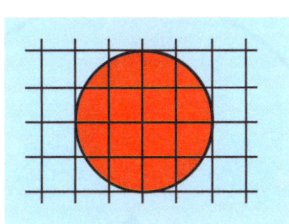   h 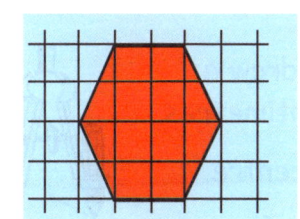   i

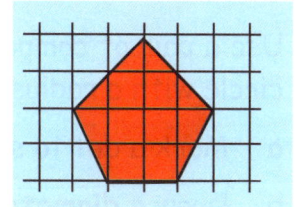

7. a   Trace or copy this **T-shape** onto a small piece of card and cut it out carefully.

b   Show how to tile the surface by using the T-shape as a **template** to cover a piece of paper with the shape.

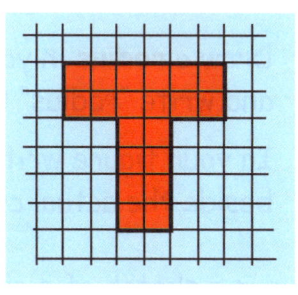

8. 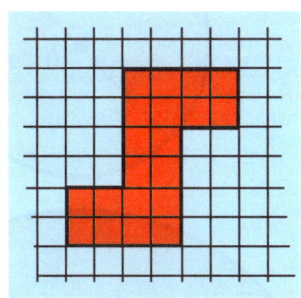   a   Trace or copy this **S-shape** onto a small piece of card and cut it out carefully.

b   Show how to tile the surface by using this S-shape as a **template** to cover a piece of paper with the shape.

9. a   Trace or copy this shape onto a small piece of card and cut it out carefully.

b   Show how to tile the surface by using the shape as a **template** to cover a piece of paper with the shape.

this is Chapter Ten   page 123   TWO DIMENSIONS

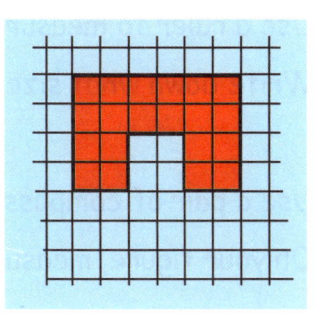

Circular Shapes

Naming Parts of a Circle

The **brown** dot represents the **centre** of the circle.

The **blue** line from one edge to the other, through the centre is called a **diameter** of the circle.

The small **green** line from the centre to the edge is called the **radius** of the circle.

The **curved bit** (the perimeter) is called the **circumference**.

Note :-   Diameter = 2 × **Radius**

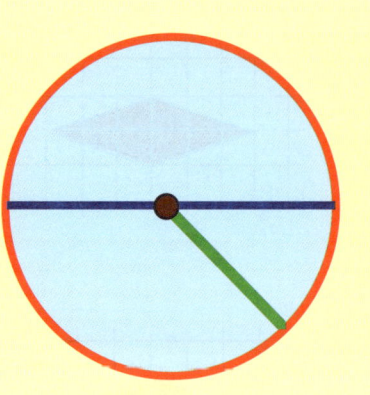

Exercise 5

1. Use a pair of compasses to draw a circle with a radius of 3 centimetres.

   a Mark a dot to show its centre.

   b Draw a **diameter** in your figure and write "diameter" beside it.

   c Draw a **radius** in your figure and and write "radius" beside your line.

   d In your figure write the word "**circumference**" beside the actual circumference.

2. This is a sketch of a circle whose diameter is 16 cm.

   What must the length of its **radius** be ?

3. The radius of a circle is 23 millimetres.

   What must the length of its diameter be ?

4. Look at this **semi-circle**.

   a Use a ruler to measure its diameter.

   b Write down what size its radius must be.

5. a Use a pair of compasses to draw a semi-circle with a radius of 6 cm.

   b On your figure, measure and show what length its diameter must be.

this is Chapter Ten   TWO DIMENSIONS

6. Shown is a sketch of 3 touching circles surrounded by a rectangular box.

The **radius** of each circle is 7 cm.

Calculate what the length and breadth of the box must be.   (*do **not** use a ruler*)

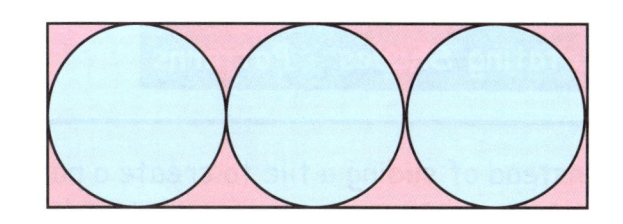

7. The length of the shape below is 50 cm.

    a What must the height of the shape be ?

    b What must the length of the **radius** of each circle be ?

8. This shape has four identical semi-circles on top of a rectangle.

    a Calculate the length of the diameter of **one** circle.

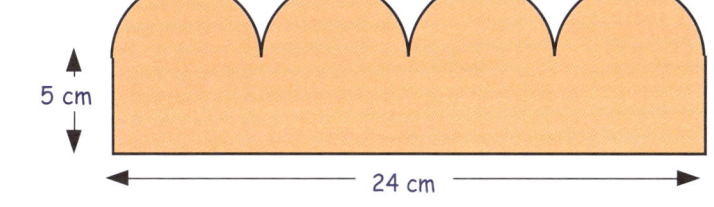

    b What must the **radius** be ?

    c Now calculate the **height** of the shape.

5 cm

24 cm

9. Use your compasses to create this flower pattern :-

Start by drawing a circle with radius 4 cm.

Next, put your compass point on any point (P) on the circumference, and with radius still 4 cm, "step" round the circle moving from one point to the next.

Carefully colour your design and display the best ones.

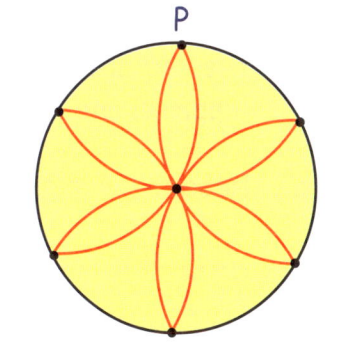

10. Here are 2 more designs created in almost the same way.

Draw each of them using a fixed radius of 5 cm.

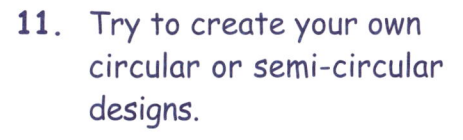

11. Try to create your own circular or semi-circular designs.

Make a display of the most imaginative and well drawn designs.

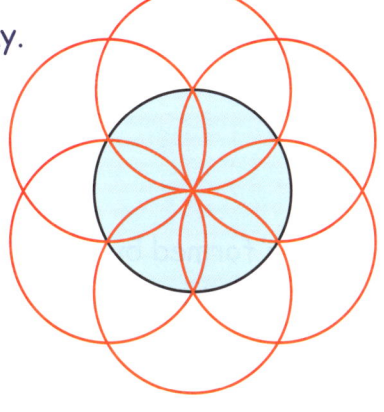

this is Chapter Ten   TWO DIMENSIONS

Rotating Shapes - Patterns

Instead of **sliding** a tile to create a pattern as in Page 122, we can **rotate** it instead.

Can you see that :-

- the **brown** shape has been **spun** (or **rotated**) by 90° about the **black** dot to form the **blue** shape,

- the **blue** shape was then rotated by 90° to form the **green** shape and

- the **green** shape was finally spun by 90° to form the **red** shape.

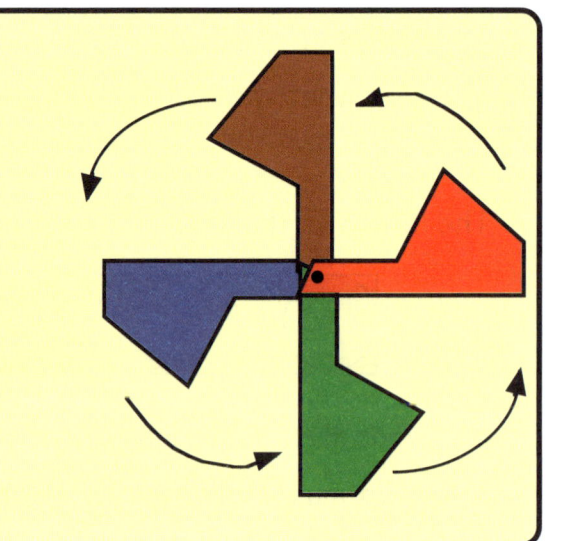

Exercise 6

1. a   Trace (or copy) this triangular shape onto a small piece of stiff card, mark a dot on it as shown and carefully cut it out.

    b   Draw round your "template" onto your jotter. By putting a pin (or compass point) through the red dot, spin your triangle by 90° (approx) and draw round it again.

    c   Repeat twice more to create this "windmill".

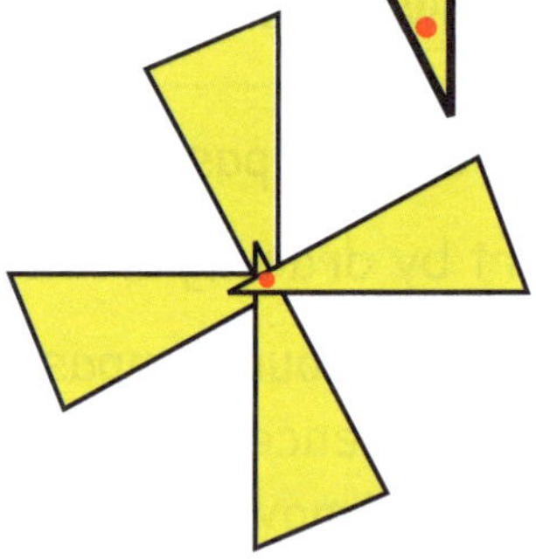

2. Try doing the same with each of the following "tiles" :-

    a   b 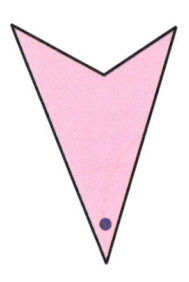   c    d

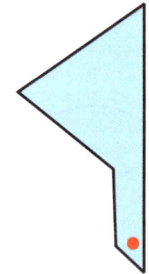

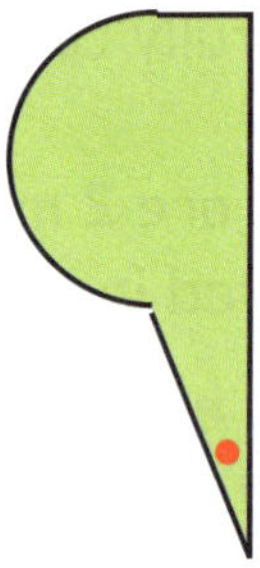

3. Sometimes nice patterns can be formed by rotating the shape by 120°, 60°, 45° or other angles.

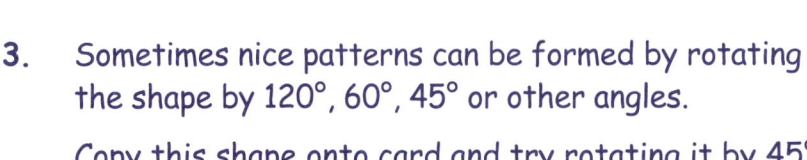

    Copy this shape onto card and try rotating it by 45° each time to create a symmetrical pattern.

4. Now do a few of your own (bigger) and make a display of the nicest, most imaginative designs.

this is Chapter Ten   page 126   TWO DIMENSIONS

Topic in a Nutshell

1. Write down the special names for each of these two polygons.

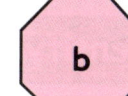

2. Name all the mathematical shapes you can see in the following figure.

3. Calculate the **perimeter** of each of the following 2 triangles :-

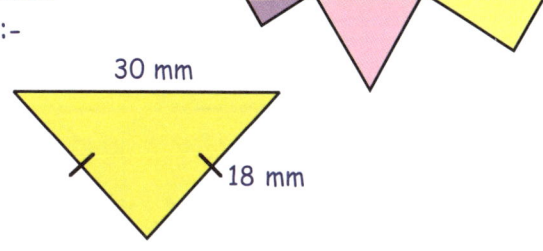

   a   17 cm, 10 cm, 15 cm

   b   30 mm, 18 mm

4. Describe each of these triangles by using an expression from **both** lists.

   right angled
   acute angled
   obtuse angled

   scalene triangle
   isosceles triangle
   equilateral triangle

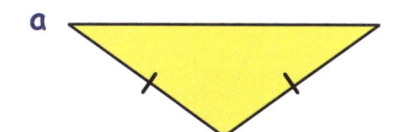

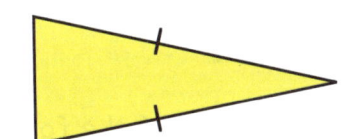

   a   b   c

5. Copy the following shape onto squared paper.

   Show that the shape **tiles** by completely surrounding the shape with identical tiles.

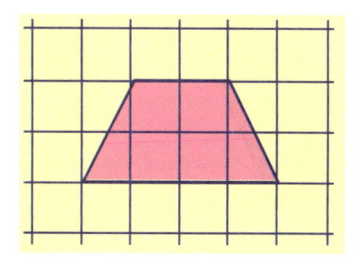

6. 18 cm

   The diameter of a circle is 18 centimetres. Write down the length of its radius.

7. This shape consists of a rectangle measuring 8 metres by 10 metres, with a semi-circle on its end.

   Calculate the **length** of the shape.

   (Do NOT measure it with a ruler)

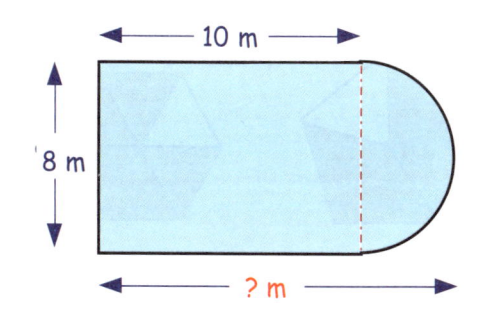

   10 m, 8 m, ? m

this is Chapter Ten   page 127   TWO DIMENSIONS

Chapter 11

Fractions

Identifying Fractions

A fraction consists of 2 parts :-

$\dfrac{2}{3}$ ← the **NUMERATOR** tells you the number or "how many" of the thirds (in this case 2).

← the **DENOMINATOR** tells you the type of fraction you are dealing with (thirds here).

Examples :-

This shape shows 3 out of 4 equal parts are green.

$\dfrac{3}{4}$ of this shape is green.

This shape shows 3 out of 5 equal parts are pink.

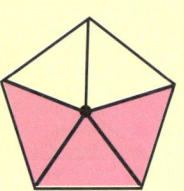

$\dfrac{3}{5}$ of this shape is pink.

$\dfrac{2}{5}$ of this shape is **not** pink.

Exercise 1

1. For each of the following, write the fraction that is shaded green :-

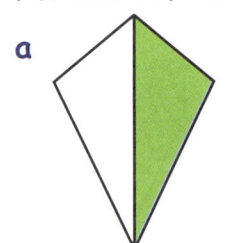

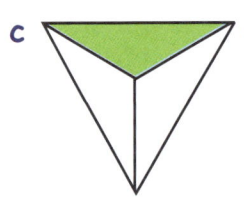

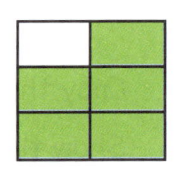

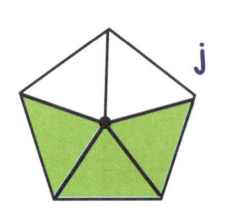

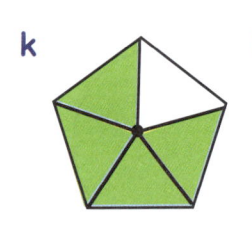

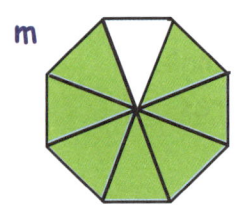

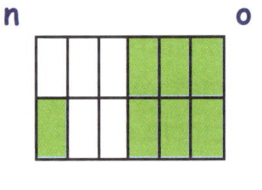

   a b c d e

   f g h i j

   k l m n o

2. For each shape in question 1, write the fraction that is **not** shaded green.

this is Chapter Eleven   page 128   FRACTIONS

The picture shows 15 animals.

(Can you see that 2 out of the 15 animals are cats, so $\frac{2}{15}$ are cats ?)

3. Write down what fraction of the animals are :-

    a   dogs ($\frac{?}{15}$)   b   cows   c   pigs   d   elephants ?

4.   a   Use a ruler to draw this rectangle measuring 6 boxes by 2 boxes. Shade in any 7 boxes.

       (Can you see that $\frac{7}{12}$ of the rectangle is shaded ?)

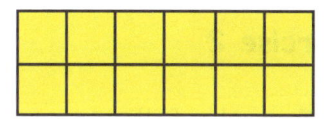

    b   Draw the same box again. This time shade or colour in $\frac{5}{12}$ of the shape.

    c   Draw the same box again. This time shade or colour in $\frac{1}{6}$ of the shape.

       (Hint : for every 6 equal parts shade in 1 part)

    d   Draw the same box again. This time shade or colour in $\frac{1}{4}$ of the shape.

    e   Draw the same box again. This time shade or colour in $\frac{3}{4}$ of the shape.

       (Hint : for every 4 equal parts shade in 3 parts)

    f   Draw the same box again. This time shade or colour in $\frac{2}{3}$ of the shape.

    g   Draw the same box again. This time shade or colour in $\frac{6}{12}$ of the shape.

    h   Draw the same box again. This time shade or colour in $\frac{1}{2}$ of the shape.

    i   What do you notice about the answers **g** and **h** ?

Equivalent Fractions

Two fractions might look different because they have different **numerators** and different **denominators** but they might still represent the same number.

Look at the these diagrams representing fractions :-

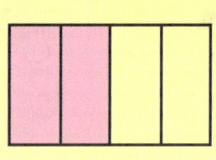

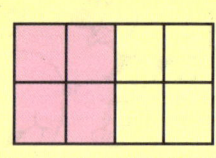

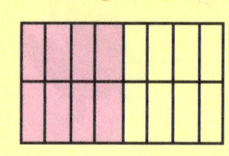

fig. 1   fig. 2   fig. 3

$\frac{2}{4}$ coloured $\frac{4}{8}$ coloured $\frac{8}{16}$ coloured

In each shape $\frac{1}{2}$ has been coloured.   This means $\frac{1}{2} = \frac{2}{4} = \frac{4}{8} = \frac{8}{16}$.

These are called **equivalent** fractions.

Exercise 2

1. Copy the following and write down underneath each figure what fraction is shaded.

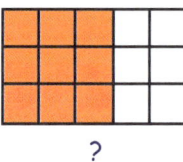

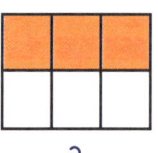

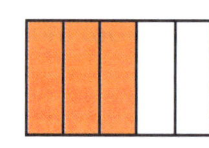

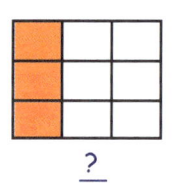

   $\frac{1}{2}$ $\frac{?}{?}$ $\frac{?}{15}$ $\frac{?}{6}$ $\frac{?}{?}$ $\frac{?}{9}$

   a   From the pictures you can see another fraction equal to $\frac{1}{2}$. ($\frac{1}{2} = \frac{?}{?}$)

   b   The second and last diagrams show that $\frac{1}{3}$ is the same as $\frac{?}{?}$.

   c   The third and the fifth diagram shows that $\frac{?}{15}$ is the same as $\frac{?}{?}$.

It is possible to find a fraction **equivalent** to $\frac{1}{4}$ by simply "multiplying the numerator and the denominator by any number" :-

=> $\frac{1}{4}$ becomes $\frac{1 \times 5}{4 \times 5} = \frac{5}{20}$ numerator × 5
denominator × 5

2. a   Multiply the top and the bottom of $\frac{1}{4}$ by 2 to create a new fraction. What is it ?

   b   Multiply the top and the bottom of $\frac{1}{4}$ by 3 to create a new fraction. What is it ?

3. a Multiply the top and the bottom of $\frac{3}{4}$ by 2 to create a new fraction. What is it ?

    b Multiply the top and the bottom of $\frac{3}{4}$ by 3 to create a new fraction. What is it ?

    c Find at least 4 more fractions equivalent to $\frac{3}{4}$.

4. Multiply the top and bottom of each fraction by 3 to create a new fraction equivalent to the one given :-

    a $\frac{1}{2}$ b $\frac{3}{5}$ c $\frac{4}{7}$ d $\frac{3}{8}$ e $\frac{7}{10}$ f $\frac{13}{20}$

5. Repeat question 4, but multiply the top and bottom of each fraction by 4.

6. Multiply the top and bottom of each fraction by a number of your own choice to create a new fraction equivalent to the one given :-

    a $\frac{2}{3}$ b $\frac{3}{7}$ c $\frac{2}{9}$ d $\frac{5}{8}$ e $\frac{3}{10}$ f $\frac{11}{20}$

We can **SIMPLIFY** fractions (like $\frac{12}{15}$) by "dividing" top and bottom by a number.

=> $\frac{12}{15}$ becomes $\frac{12 \div 3}{15 \div 3} = \frac{4}{5}$ (This cannot be simplified any further).

---

7. Divide the top line and bottom line of each fraction by 3, to simplify each one :-

    a $\frac{3}{6}$ b $\frac{3}{9}$ c $\frac{12}{15}$ d $\frac{15}{27}$ e $\frac{9}{33}$ f $\frac{27}{30}$

8. Divide the top line and bottom line of each fraction by 4, to simplify each one :-

    a $\frac{4}{12}$ b $\frac{8}{20}$ c $\frac{12}{28}$ d $\frac{24}{28}$ e $\frac{32}{44}$ f $\frac{24}{60}$

9. For each of the following fractions, divide the numerator and the denominator by a number to simplify the fraction :-

    a $\frac{12 \div 4}{16 \div 4}$ b $\frac{4}{6}$ c $\frac{3}{18}$ d $\frac{6}{18}$ e $\frac{7}{21}$ f $\frac{10}{30}$

    g $\frac{10}{18}$ h $\frac{9}{27}$ i $\frac{14}{35}$ j $\frac{10}{35}$ k $\frac{15}{55}$ l $\frac{16}{18}$

    m $\frac{50}{100}$ n $\frac{5}{100}$ o $\frac{11}{33}$ p $\frac{8}{14}$ q $\frac{20}{60}$ r $\frac{44}{64}$

this is Chapter Eleven   page 131   FRACTIONS

Fractions of a quantity

To find $\frac{1}{3}$ of something, you divide by 3.

To find $\frac{1}{4}$ divide by 4

To find $\frac{1}{5}$ divide by 5.

Examples :-

Find: a $\frac{1}{3}$ of 15   b $\frac{1}{4}$ of 28   c $\frac{1}{5}$ of 20

a
15 ÷ 3
= 5

b
28 ÷ 4
= 7

c
20 ÷ 5
= 4

Exercise 3

1. Find :-

   a $\frac{1}{3}$ of 12   b $\frac{1}{4}$ of 16   c $\frac{1}{5}$ of 15

   d $\frac{1}{4}$ of 32   e $\frac{1}{3}$ of 27   f $\frac{1}{5}$ of 45

   g $\frac{1}{5}$ of 60   h $\frac{1}{4}$ of 48   i $\frac{1}{3}$ of 39

   j $\frac{1}{2}$ of 40   k $\frac{1}{6}$ of 18   l $\frac{1}{2}$ of 7

2. Find :-

   a $\frac{1}{6}$ of 42   b $\frac{1}{7}$ of 42   c $\frac{1}{8}$ of 40

   d $\frac{1}{9}$ of 72   e $\frac{1}{6}$ of 84   f $\frac{1}{7}$ of 77

   g $\frac{1}{9}$ of 36   h $\frac{1}{8}$ of 800   i $\frac{1}{10}$ of 300

3. a There are 40 people on a bus.
      $\frac{1}{2}$ of them are children.
      How many children are on the bus?

b There were 30 drinks served at a bar.
$\frac{1}{6}$ of the drinks were cocktails.
How many of the drinks were cocktails ?

c Brenda baked 24 muffins.
$\frac{1}{4}$ of the muffins had currants.
How many muffins contained currants ?

d There were 50 pencils in a jar.
$\frac{1}{5}$ of the pencils needed sharpening.
How many pencils needed sharpening ?

e The cat and dog home has 48 animals.
$\frac{1}{8}$ of the animals were dogs.
   (i)   How many dogs were at the home ?
   (ii) How many cats were at the home ?

f There are 30 apples in a box. $\frac{1}{3}$ of the apples are green.
   (i)   How many apples are green ?
   (ii) How many apples are **not** green ?

4. **a** Of the twenty seven babies born yesterday in a busy hospital, a third of the babies were boys.
How many baby boys were born at the hospital yesterday ?

b One seventh of the thirty five children in a group are girls.
   (i)   How many girls are in the group ?
   (ii) How many boys are in the group ?

5. There are 24 pets in the pet shop.
A third of the pets are kittens
A quarter of the pets are puppies.
A sixth of the pets are rabbits.
An eighth of the pets are snakes.
The rest are birds.

Find, the number of :-

   a kittens   **b** puppies   **c** rabbits
   d snakes   **e** birds   **f** animals with 4 legs ?

Harder fractions

To find $\frac{3}{4}$ of a number (like 20), you do it <u>using 2 steps</u>.

Step 1 :- Find $\frac{1}{4}$ of 20 first (÷ 4) => $\frac{1}{4}$ of 20 = 20 ÷ 4 = 5

Step 2 :- Now find $\frac{3}{4}$ of 20 by (× 3) => $\frac{3}{4}$ of 20 = 5 × 3 = 15

Set the working down as follows :-

$\frac{3}{4}$ of 16 => (16 ÷ 4) => 4 × 3 = 12

$\frac{2}{5}$ of 35 => (35 ÷ 5) => 7 × 2 = 14

$\frac{3}{7}$ of 42 => (42 ÷ 7) => 6 × 3 = 18

Rule :-

To multiply by a fraction like $\frac{3}{4}$

=> "divide by the denominator" (4)
=> then "multiply by the numerator" (3)

Exercise 4

1. **Without using a calculator** do the following :-

    a $\frac{2}{3}$ of 21 = (21 ÷ 3) => 7 × 2 = ...

    b $\frac{3}{5}$ of 40 = (40 ÷ ...) => ... × 3 = ...

    c $\frac{2}{3}$ of 24   d $\frac{3}{4}$ of 28   e $\frac{4}{5}$ of 45

    f $\frac{2}{7}$ of 49   g $\frac{2}{5}$ of 55   h $\frac{5}{8}$ of 56

    i $\frac{4}{9}$ of 63   j $\frac{7}{10}$ of 80   k $\frac{9}{10}$ of 120

    l $\frac{5}{6}$ of 48   m $\frac{2}{15}$ of 30   n $\frac{9}{20}$ of 60.

2. a A small aeroplane carried 36 passengers.
    $\frac{2}{3}$ of the passengers were asleep.
    How many passengers were asleep ?

    b A cafe served 45 customers in an hour.
    Three fifths of the customers ordered tea.
    How many customers did **not** order tea ?

this is Chapter Eleven   FRACTIONS

Topic in a Nutshell

1. For each shape, say what fraction has been shaded :-

   a 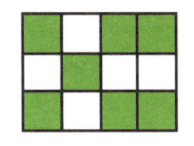   b 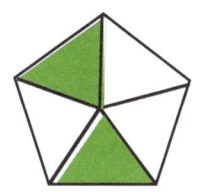   c

2. For each shape in question 1, write down the fraction **not** shaded.

3. Copy and complete :-

   a $\dfrac{1}{2} = \dfrac{?}{6}$ b $\dfrac{3}{4} = \dfrac{15}{?}$ c $\dfrac{7}{?} = \dfrac{21}{27}$

4. Write down **two** fractions equivalent to :-

   a $\dfrac{1}{4}$ b $\dfrac{2}{5}$ c $\dfrac{7}{8}$

5. Write each of these fractions in their **simplest** form :-

   a $\dfrac{5}{10}$ b $\dfrac{9}{27}$ c $\dfrac{24}{36}$

6. Find :-

   a $\dfrac{1}{2}$ of 22   b $\dfrac{1}{3}$ of 21   c $\dfrac{1}{4}$ of 28

   d $\dfrac{1}{7}$ of 42   e $\dfrac{1}{8}$ of 48   f $\dfrac{1}{12}$ of 36

7. Shirley had saved £36 for her day out.
   She spent half her money on food and
   a third of her money on presents. 

   a How much money did she spend on food ?

   b How much money did she spend on presents ?

   c How much money did she have left ?

8. Find :-

   a $\dfrac{2}{3}$ of 24   b $\dfrac{3}{4}$ of 28   c $\dfrac{5}{8}$ of 56

this is Chapter Eleven   FRACTIONS

Chapter 12

Coordinates

The Coordinates of a Point

The position of an object or point can be described by using a **coordinate grid system**.

The position of a point is given by stating which **two lines** the point is on.

You need to remember the following:-

- you always start at O, go **ALONG** first, then **UP**
- always put **BRACKETS** round the two numbers
- always put a **COMMA** between the two numbers.

Example :-

To find the coordinates of point **H** :-

Start at **O**,

go 4 boxes **ALONG**,
then go 2 boxes **UP**.

"H is the point **(4,2)**"
    or
"the coordinates are given as **H(4,2)**"

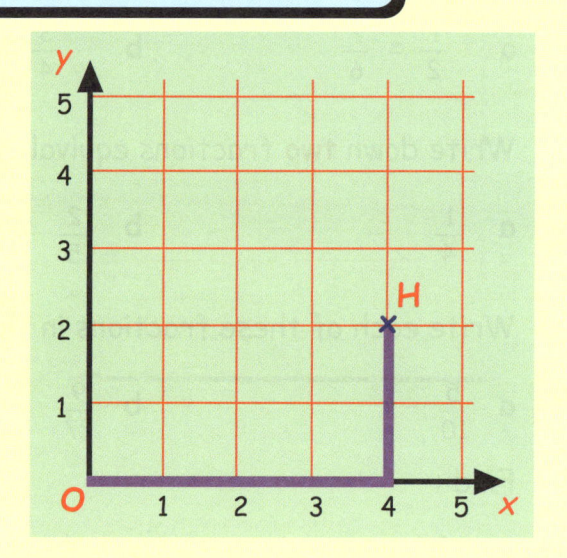

Notes :-   the point **O(0,0)** is called the **ORIGIN**.

the "ALONG" **black** line is called the *x-axis*.

the "UP" **black** line is called the *y-axis*.

Exercise 1

1. Five places in a town are shown in the coordinate grid.

   Write down the coordinates of :-

   a   the church **C**.

   b   the butcher's shop **B**.

   c   the supermarket **S**.

   d   the football ground **F**.

   e   the video shop **V**.

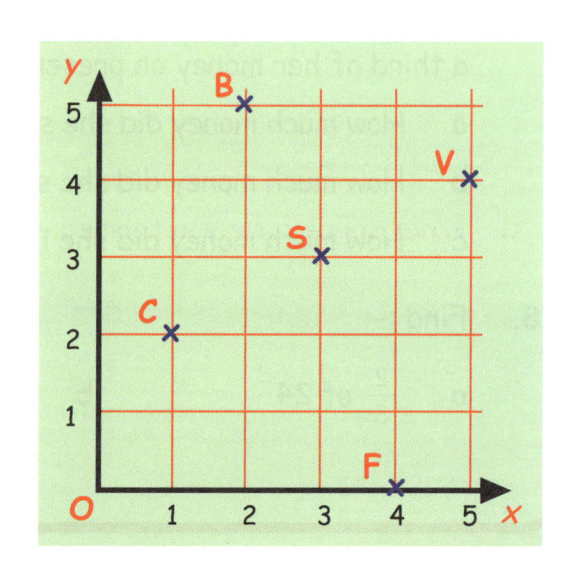

2. Write down the capital letter representing each point and put its coordinates next to it.

For example :-

A (2,7).

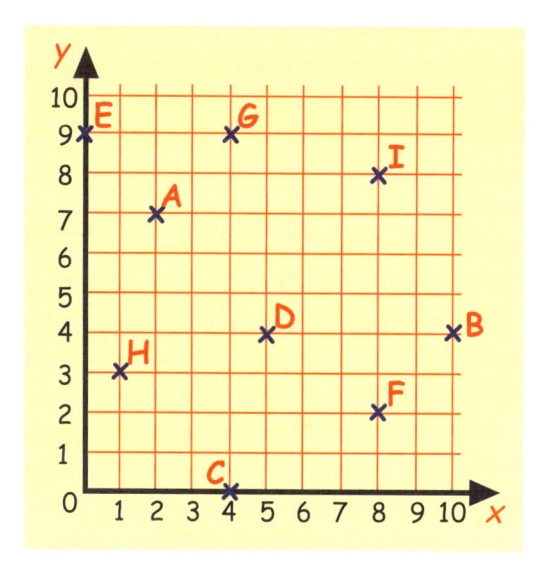

3.

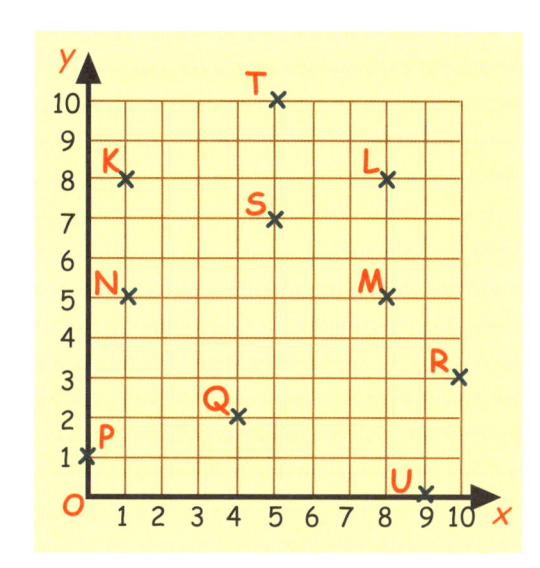

a Which point has coordinates :-

(i)   (5,10)   (ii)   (0,1)
(iii) (4,2)   (iv) (8,5)?

b Write down the coordinates of :-

(i)   K   (ii)   S
(iii) N   (iv) U.

c When four of the points are joined a rectangle is formed.

(i)   Which four points ?
(ii) Write down their coordinates.

4. Now its your turn to plot points.

a Draw up a coordinate grid like the one in question 3 on squared paper.
Make the horizontal and vertical axes both go up from 0 to 10.

b Mark with a small neat cross the position of the following points :-

E(7,2),   F(3,0),   G(1,8),   H(9,1),   I(5,5),   J(4,10),
K(7,4),   L(3,5),   M(10,10), N(7,8),   R(8,9),   S(1,2).

c Join point G to point N; join point N to point E; join point E to point S. Now join point S to point G.

d What shape have you formed ?

5. a Draw a new grid (from 0 to 6 in each axis).

b Mark with a dot the following six points :-

P(2,1) Q(4,1) R(5,$2\frac{1}{2}$) S(4,4) T(2,4) U(1,$2\frac{1}{2}$)

c When the six points are joined, what shape is formed ?

this is Chapter Twelve   page 137   COORDINATES

More about the *x*-axis and the *y*-axis

Remember :-
- the grid used is called a **coordinate grid**.
- the point **O(0,0)** is called the **origin**.
  This is where the *x*-axis meets the *y*-axis.
- the horizontal axis (the "along" axis) is called **the *x*-axis**.
- the vertical axis (the "up" axis) is called **the *y*-axis**.

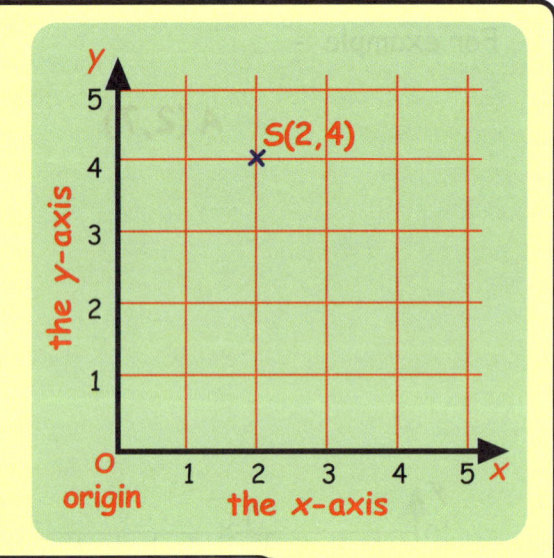

RULE :- go **ALONG** the *x*-axis first, then go **UP** the *y*-axis.

Exercise 2

1. Look at the coordinate grid.

   Each time you mention a point, say what object is at that point.

   a Which point has an *x*-coordinate of 4 ?

   b Which point has a *y*-coordinate of 5 ?

   c What is the *x*-coordinate of **A** ?

   d What is the *y*-coordinate of **F** ?

   e Which point has its *x*-coordinate the same as its *y*-coordinate ?

   f Which point lies on the *x*-axis ?

   g Which point lies on the *y*-axis ?

   h Which 2 points have the same *y*-coordinate ?

      Write down their coordinates.

   i Which 2 points have the same *x*-coordinate ?

      Write down their coordinates.

   j From **D** to **E** is "1 along and 2 up".

      Which other two points have the same rule to get from one to the other ?

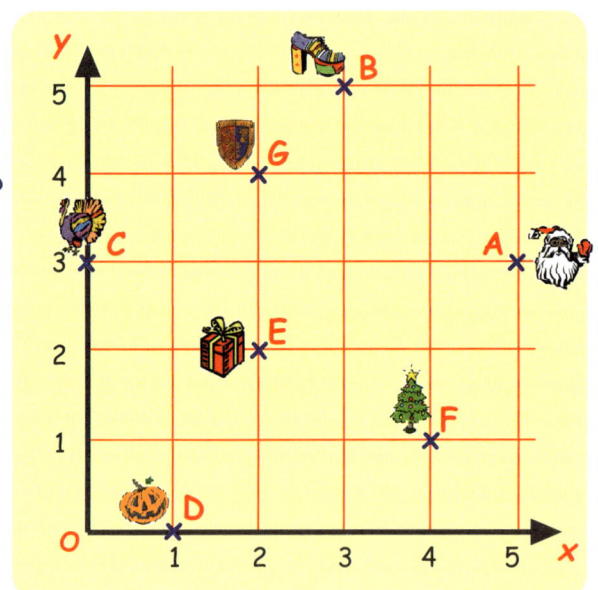

2. Look at this coordinate grid.
   a   What are the coordinates of **Q**?
   b   Which point has coordinates (7, 9)?
   c   Which point has the same *y*-coordinate as **U**?
   d   Which point has the same *x*-coordinate as **P**?
   e   3 points have the same *y*-coordinate. Name them and write down their coordinates.
   f   Which point lies on the *y*-axis?
   g   Which point has the same *x* and *y*-coordinate?
   h   Is the *y*-axis known as the horizontal axis or the vertical axis?

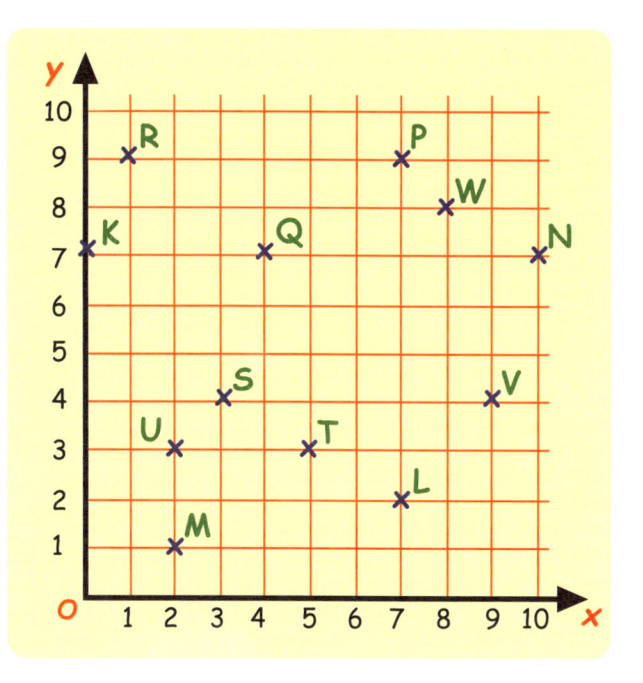

3. Draw up a 5 by 5 coordinate grid as shown.
   a   Plot the points **A**(1, 1), **B**(1, 5) and **C**(5, 5).
   b   **D** is a point to be put on the grid so that figure **ABCD** is a **square**.
       On your diagram plot the point **D** and write down its coordinates.
   c   Join **A** to **C** and join **B** to **D**. You now have the two **diagonals** of the square.
       Write down the coordinates of the point where the two diagonals meet.

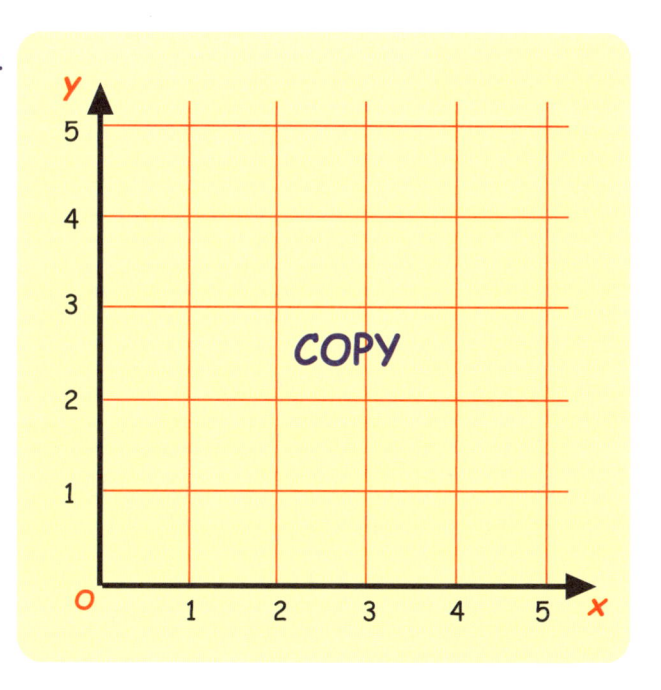

4. Draw up another 5 by 5 coordinate grid as shown above.
   a   Plot the points **P**(5, 2), **Q**(1, 2) and **R**(1, 4).
   b   **S** is a point to be put on the grid so that figure **PQRS** is a **rectangle**.
       On your diagram plot the point **S** and write down its coordinates.
   c   Join **P** to **R** and join **Q** to **S**.
       You now have the two diagonals of the rectangle.
       Write down the coordinates of the point where the two diagonals meet.

this is Chapter Twelve   page 139   COORDINATES

5. You will need to draw 5 more coordinate grids. (Make each of them 5 by 5).

   On separate grids :-
   - plot each set of points.
   - join each of them up in the correct order.
   - write below each one, the name of the shape you have formed.

   a   Join R(1,0) to S(1,5) to T(4,5) to U(4,0), back to R.
   b   Join K(3,3) to L(3,5) to M(5,5) to N(5,3), back to K.
   c   Join A(2,4) to B(3,2) to C(2,0) to D(1,2), back to A.
   d   Join E(4,4) to F(2,0) to G(0,4) to H(2,5), back to E.
   e   Join H(2,1) to I(1,2) to J(2,3) to K(4,3) to L(5,2) to M(4,1), back to H.

   You should have found a diamond, a hexagon, a rectangle, a kite and a square - but not in that order !

   (Do you know the mathematical name for a **diamond** ?)

Coordinates for fun

Exercise 3

Pictures can be drawn using coordinates. Make a coordinate grid for each picture (you are guided as to what size). Plot the points in order and join them up as you move from one point to the next.

1. Highest x-coordinate **15**.   Highest y-coordinate **16**.

   (5,2) (5,12) (3,12) (9,16) (15,12) (13,12) (13,2) (5,2) Stop.
   (6,8) (6,10) (8,10) (8,8) (6,8) Stop.
   (10,8) (10,10) (12,10) (12,8) (10,8) Stop.
   (7,13) (7,14) (11,14) (11,13) (7,13) Stop.
   (8,2) (8,5) (10,5) (10,2) Stop.

2. Highest x-coordinate **14**.   Highest y-coordinate **8**.

   (3,5) (3,2) (8,2) (14,5) (14,8) (8,5) (3,5) (9,8) (14,8) Stop.
   (8,2) (8,5) Stop.

3. Highest x-coordinate **17**.   Highest y-coordinate **10**.

   (3,2) (3,10) (16,10) (16,2) (3,2) Stop.
   (4,3) (4,9) (15,9) (15,3) (4,3) Stop.
   (5,4) (5,8) Stop.   (6,8) (6,4) (8,4) (8,6) (6,6) Stop.
   (9,8) (11,8) (11,6) (9,6) (9,4) (11,4) Stop.
   (12,4) (12,8) (14,8) (14,4) (12,4) Stop.

4. Highest *x*-coordinate **25**.   Highest *y*-coordinate **22**.

(7,15) (6,13) (5,13) (4,12) (4,11) (5,10) (6,10) (5,7) (6,6) (8,7) (8,9) (6,10) Stop.

(6,6) (7,4) (9,3) (12,3) (16,7) (16,8) (17,8) (18,9) (19,11) (18,14) (17,15) (15,14) Stop.

(18,12) (17,14) (16,13) (16,10) (17,11) (17,13) (16,13) Stop.

(8,17) (7,15) (8,16) (9,15) Stop.

(8,12) (9,14) (8,15) (7,14) (7,13) (8,13) (8,14) (7,14) Stop.

(12,3) (16,4) (20,6) (22,6) (21,7) (23,6) (21,8) (24,9) (22,9) (25,10) (22,10) (25,12) (22,12) (25,15) (22,14) (23,18) (20,16) (20,19) (19,17) (19,21) (18,18) (17,22) (15,19) (15,22) (14,19) (13,22) (12,18) (11,21) (10,18) (9,20) (9,18) (7,20) (8,17) Stop.

(8,17) (13,14) (15,14) Stop.

5. Highest *x*-coordinate **22**.   Highest *y*-coordinate **32**.

(5,12) (5,11) (6,9) (5,7) (5,6) (7,3) (5,2) (9,2) (9,3) (10,6) (13,9) (12,6) (12,5) (14,3) (12,2) (16,2) (16,6) (19,9) (19,11) (17,15) (13,21) (18,24) (19,23) (20,24) (19,24) (19,25) (22,26) (19,26) (12,24) (8,21) (7,22·5) (7,14) (6,15) (6,11) (5,12) Stop.

(7,22·5) (6,24) (11,25) (12,25) (12,24) Stop.

(6,24) (5,24) (6,22) (6,24) Stop.

(7,22·5) (7,22) (6,22) (6,15) Stop.

(6,22) (3,14) (5,12) Stop.

(3·5,15) (2,15) (2,18) (3,21) (2,23) (4,25) (4,24) (3,23) (4,22) (4,23) (5,22) (4,21) (5·5,20) Stop.

(11,25) (11,27) (12,27) (13,28) (13,29) (12,30) (11,30) (7,29) (7,28) (4,28) (6,24) Stop.

(5,28) (5,26) Stop.

(5·5,25) (7,25) (8,26) Stop.

(7,29) (8,29) (8,28) (7,28) Stop.

(11,30) (11,29) (12,30) (11,28) Stop.

(7,29) (6,29) (5,30) (7,30) (11,31) (12,32) (12,30) Stop.

(7,30) (6,31) (11,32) (11,31) Stop.

this is Chapter Twelve   page 141   COORDINATES

Topic in a Nutshell

1. a Which point has coordinates :-
     (i) (9,3)   (ii) (2,0)
     (iii) (5,8) (iv) (3,10) ?

   b Write down the coordinates of :-
     (i) L   (ii) R
     (iii) F   (iv) W.

   c When 4 of the points are joined a square is formed.
     (i) Which 4 points ?
     (ii) Write down their coordinates.

   d Which point lies :-   (i) on the *x*-axis ?   (ii) on the *y*-axis ?

   e Name any 2 points with :-   (i) the same *x*-coordinate
                                  (ii) the same *y*-coordinate.

   f Which point has its *x*-coordinate the same as its *y*-coordinate ?

2. Draw up a 5 by 5 coordinate grid as shown below.

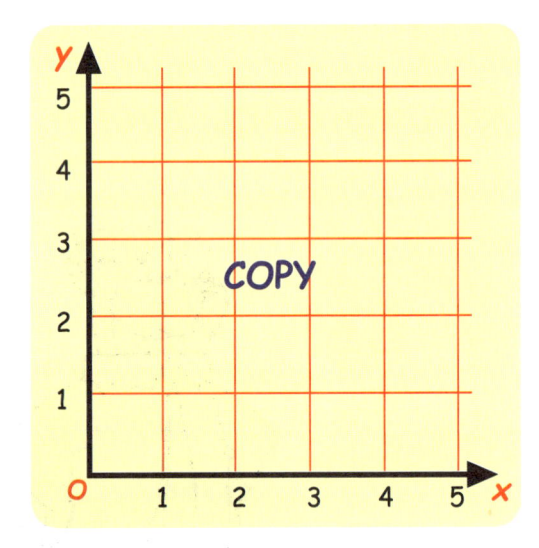

   a Plot the points E(2,0), F(3,0) and G(3,5).

   b H is a point to be put on the grid so that figure EFGH is a **rectangle**.
      On your diagram plot the point H and write down its coordinates.

   c Join E to G and join F to H.
      You now have the two diagonals of the square.
      Put a dot where the two diagonals meet and write down the coordinates of this point. (bit harder)

this is Chapter Twelve   page 142   COORDINATES

Chapter 13 — Percentages

Percentages

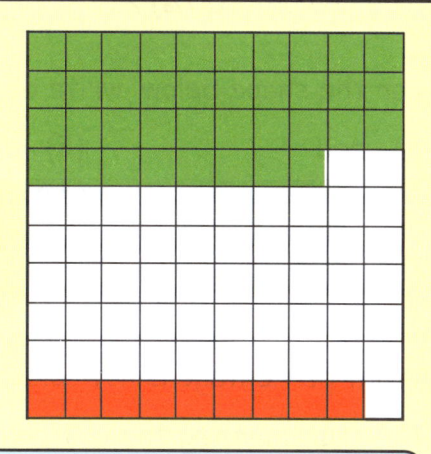

When a shape is divided into 100 "bits", each bit is called "**1 percent**".

We use the symbol "**%**" for percent.

This square has 38 bits out of 100 **green**.

This is written as **38%**.

There are 9 bits out of a hundred **red**.

This is written as **9%**.

38% means $\frac{38}{100}$ = 38 ÷ 100 = **0·38**

9% means $\frac{9}{100}$ = 9 ÷ 100 = **0·09**

Exercise 1

1. Each of these squares has been divided into 100 bits.
   Write down each colour as a percentage :-

   a   Green : 50%
       Red   : ...%

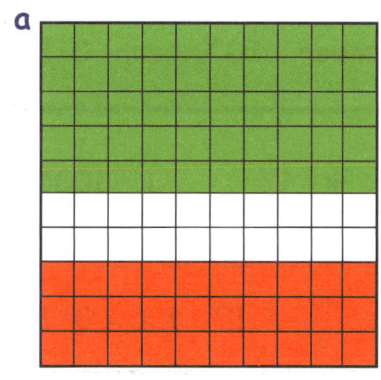

   b   Green : ...%
       Red   : ...%

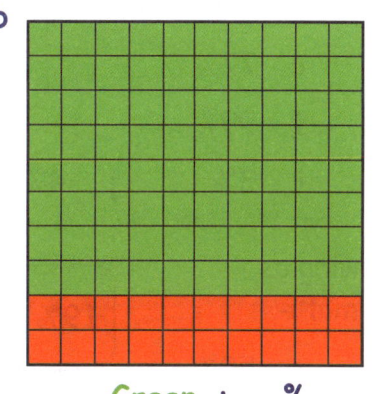

   c

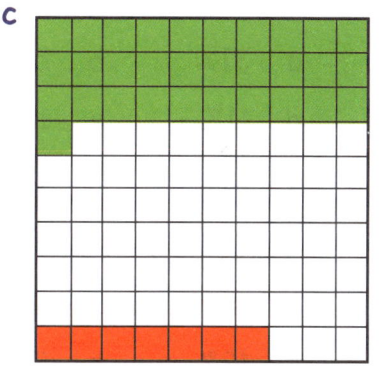

   d

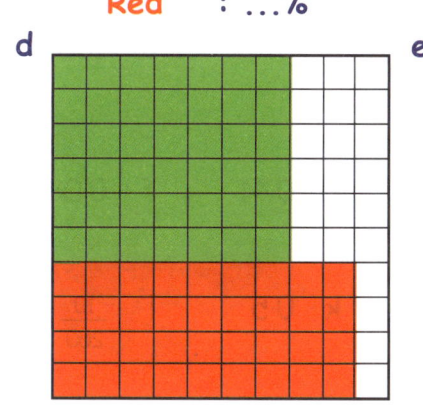

   e

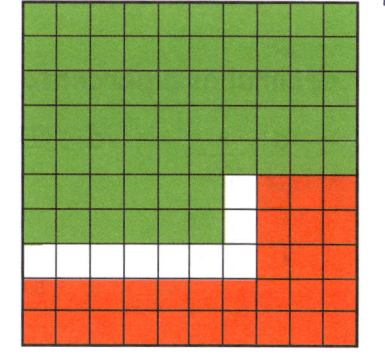

   f

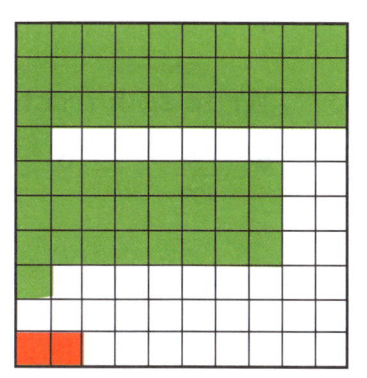

this is Chapter Thirteen   page 143   PERCENTAGES

2. a Write down what each coloured section is as a percentage of the rectangle.

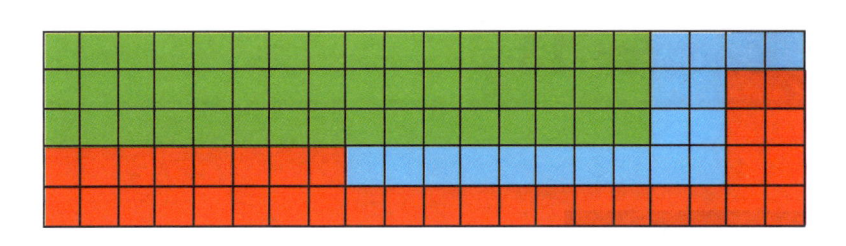

    b Add your 3 answers together.
       (Did you get **100%**) ?

3. a For the shape below, write down the percentage of :-

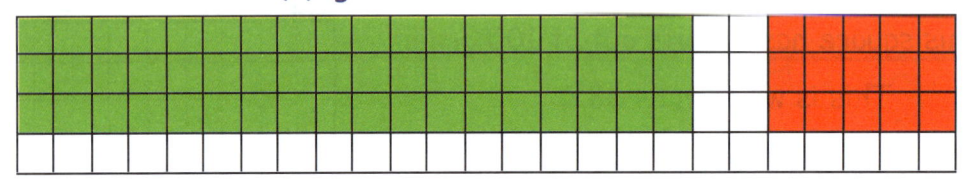

       (i) red   (ii) green.

    b What percentage is not coloured ?

    c Without counting the white squares, explain how could you answer part **b** ?
       (**Hint :** use part "**a**" answers).

4. Write each of the following as a **fraction** :-

    a 23%   b 49%   c 60%
    d 14%   e 99%   f 17%
    g 66%   h 8%   i 3%   j 4%   k 1%   l 100%

    Remember : 47% means $\frac{47}{100}$

5. Write each of the following as a **decimal** :-

    a 31%   b 59%   c 77%
    d 11%   e 18%   f 99%
    g 9%   h 8%   i 3%   j 4%   k 1%   l 100%

    Remember : 53% means 0·53

6. Write each of the following as a **fraction** and as a **decimal** :-

    19% means $\frac{19}{100}$ = 19 ÷ 100 = 0·19

    a 12%   b 33%   c 50%
    d 25%   e 10%   f 19%   g 68%   h 40%   i 13%
    j 2%   k 5%   l 6%   m 1%   n 3%   o 100%

7. Write each **fraction** or **decimal** as a **percentage** :

    a $\frac{19}{100}$ b $\frac{79}{100}$ c $\frac{8}{100}$ d 0·89   e 0·41   f 0·08

    g 0·62   h $\frac{1}{100}$ i 0·01   j $\frac{93}{100}$ k 0·5   l $\frac{10}{200}$

Linking Fractions, Decimals & Percentages

Remember :– $\frac{19}{100} = 19 \div 100 = 0.19 = 19\%$.

We can change **any fraction** into a **decimal** then into a **percentage**.

Examples

Change each of the following fractions into decimals then into a percentage :–

a $\frac{3}{50} = 3 \div 50 = 0.06 = 6\%$

b $\frac{3}{4} = 3 \div 4 = 0.75 = 75\%$

Exercise 2

1. Copy and complete each of the following :–

   a $\frac{7}{25} = 7 \div 25 = 0.\ldots = \ldots\%$
   b $\frac{8}{10} = 8 \div \ldots = 0.\ldots = \ldots\%$

   c $\frac{3}{5} = \ldots \div \ldots = 0.\ldots = \ldots\%$
   d $\frac{18}{40} = \ldots \div \ldots = 0.\ldots = \ldots\%$

2. Change each of the **fractions** shown to a **decimal** then to a **percentage** :–

   a $\frac{12}{60}$ b $\frac{6}{40}$ c $\frac{4}{5}$ d $\frac{56}{200}$ e $\frac{87}{150}$ f $\frac{14}{140}$

   > You must be careful with answers like 0·1. (This is **NOT** 1%).
   > The "1" is in the **tenths** column so **0·1 = 10%**.

3. **Carefully,** change each of these **fractions** to **percentages** :–

   a $\frac{1}{5}$ b $\frac{7}{35}$ c $\frac{12}{20}$ d $\frac{22}{110}$ e $\frac{9}{30}$ f $\frac{222}{5550}$

4. Bobby scored $\frac{60}{80}$ in a Maths test.
   Change his score to a percentage.

5. Jay scored $\frac{69}{92}$ in her English test, $\frac{56}{70}$ in her French test and $\frac{39}{50}$ in her History test.

   a Change each mark to a percentage.
   b In which subject did she score the **highest** test mark ?
   c In which subject did she score the **lowest** test mark ?

Common percentages

Some percentages are used frequently.

$50\% = \frac{50}{100} = \frac{1}{2}$ $25\% = \frac{25}{100} = \frac{1}{4}$ $10\% = \frac{10}{100} = \frac{1}{10}$

Examples

a Find 50% of £20
   $= \frac{1}{2}$ of £20
   $= £10$

b Find 25% of 32 kg
   $= \frac{1}{4}$ of 32 kg
   $= 8$ kg

c Find 10% of 50 ml
   $= \frac{1}{10}$ of 50 ml
   $= 5$ ml

Exercise 3

1. Copy and complete the following :-

   a Find 50% of £60
      $= \frac{1}{2}$ of £60
      = ...

   b Find 25% of 24p
      $= \frac{1}{4}$ of 24p
      = ...

   c Find 10% of 90 cm
      $= \frac{1}{10}$ of 90 cm
      = ...

2. Calculate each of the following :-

   a 50% of £26
   b 50% of 56 km
   c 50% of 124 mm
   d 25% of $8
   e 25% of 48 ml
   f 25% of 800 m
   g 10% of 600 m
   h 10% of 200 ml
   i 10% of 100 cm
   j 50% of £900
   k 10% of 800 mm
   l 25% of 64p
   m 50% of £15
   n 25% of £10
   o 10% of £13

3. a Harry had £30. He gave 50% of this money to charity.
      How much did Harry give to charity ?

   b Jackie weighed 80 kilograms.
      She went on a diet and lost 25% of her weight.
      How many kilograms did she lose ?

   c Fred weighed 90 kg. He only lost 10% of his weight.
      How much weight did Fred lose ?

4. The sale sign read 10% off.

   a How much would be taken off a book costing £12 ?
   b How much would it now cost for the book ?

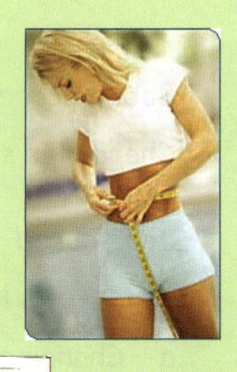

10% OFF

Topic in a Nutshell

1. Write down each colour as a percentage of each shape :-

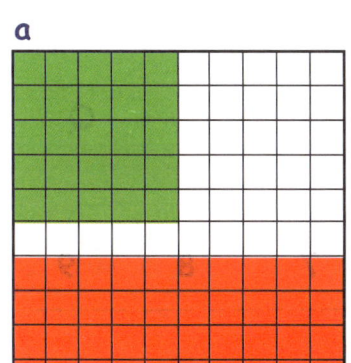

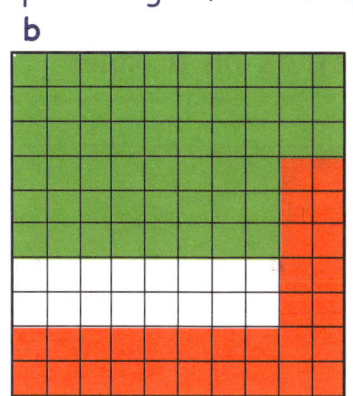

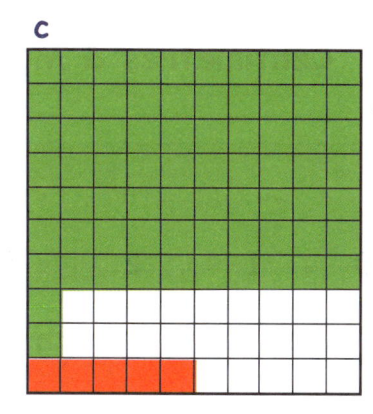

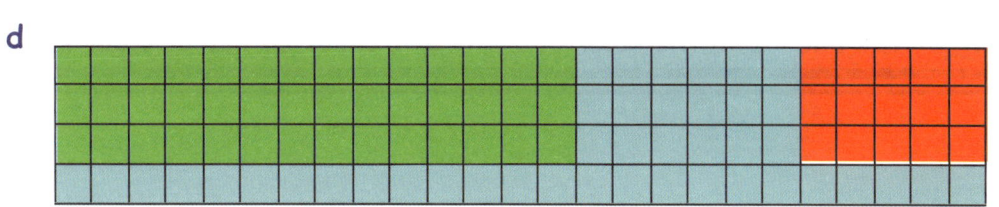

   a   b   c

   d

2. Write each of the following as a **fraction** :-

   a 55%   b 21%   c 80%   d 17%   e 9%   f 1%

3. Write each of the following as a **decimal** :-

   a 41%   b 58%   c 11%   d 8%   e 1%   f 100%

4. Write each of the following as a **fraction** and as a **decimal** :-

   a 18%   b 44%   c 3%   d 10%   e 25%   f 50%

5. Write each **fraction** or **decimal** as a **percentage** :-

   a $\frac{22}{100}$ b 0·67   c $\frac{71}{100}$ d 0·06   e $\frac{7}{100}$ f 0·5

6. Find :-

   a 50% of £80   b 25% of 28 kg   c 10% of 304 cm

7. a Donald lost 25% of his £5 pocket money.

   How much has Donald lost ?

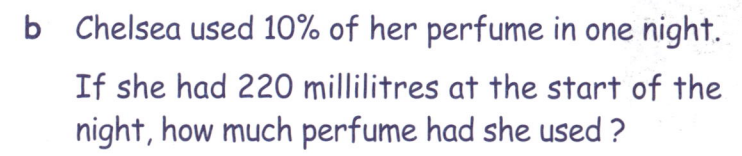

   b Chelsea used 10% of her perfume in one night.

   If she had 220 millilitres at the start of the night, how much perfume had she used ?

Chapter 14

Length & Area

Measuring & Drawing Lengths

Centimetres & Millimetres on a Ruler

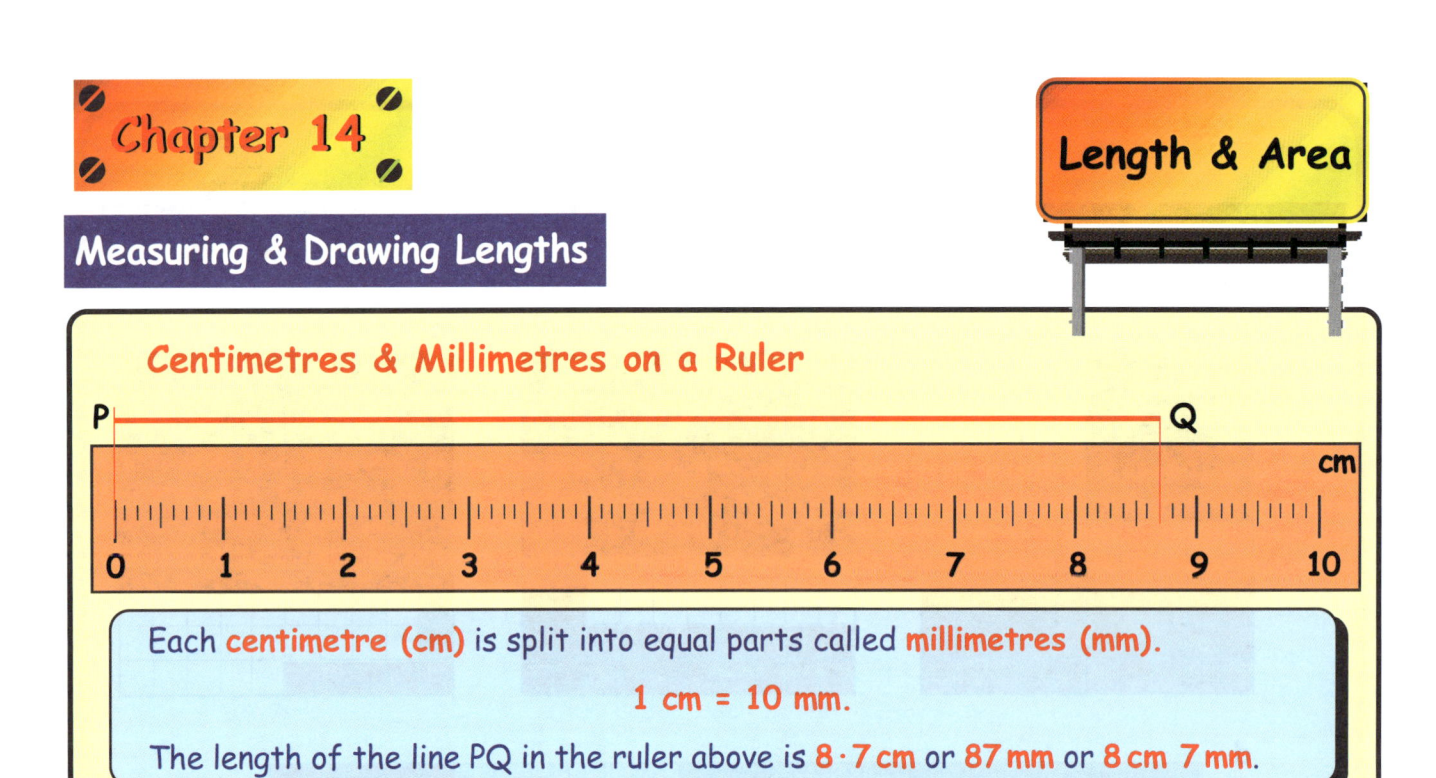

Each **centimetre (cm)** is split into equal parts called **millimetres (mm)**.

1 cm = 10 mm.

The length of the line PQ in the ruler above is **8·7 cm** or **87 mm** or **8 cm 7 mm**.

Exercise 1

1. Use your ruler to measure the length of these lines **in centimetres**. (e.g. 2·4 cm)

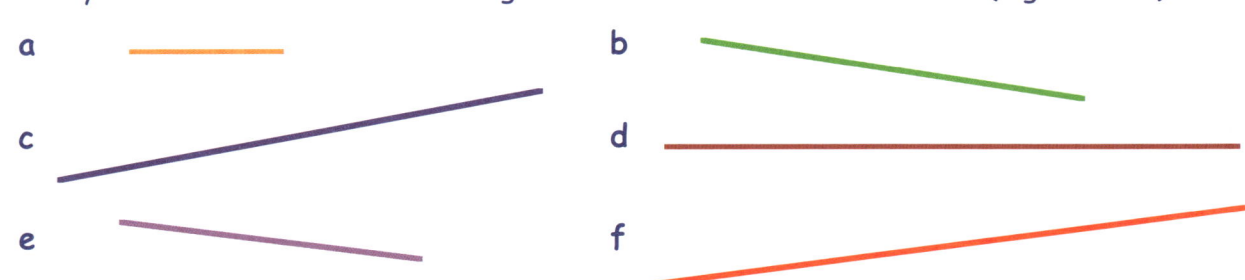

   a
   b
   c
   d
   e
   f

2. Measure each dimension of these toy animals **in millimetres**.

   a
   b
   c
   d
   e

this is Chapter Fourteen   page 148   LENGTH & AREA

3. For the following :-
   (i) Measure each line and write down its length **in millimetres**.
   (ii) List the lines in order of length, longest first.

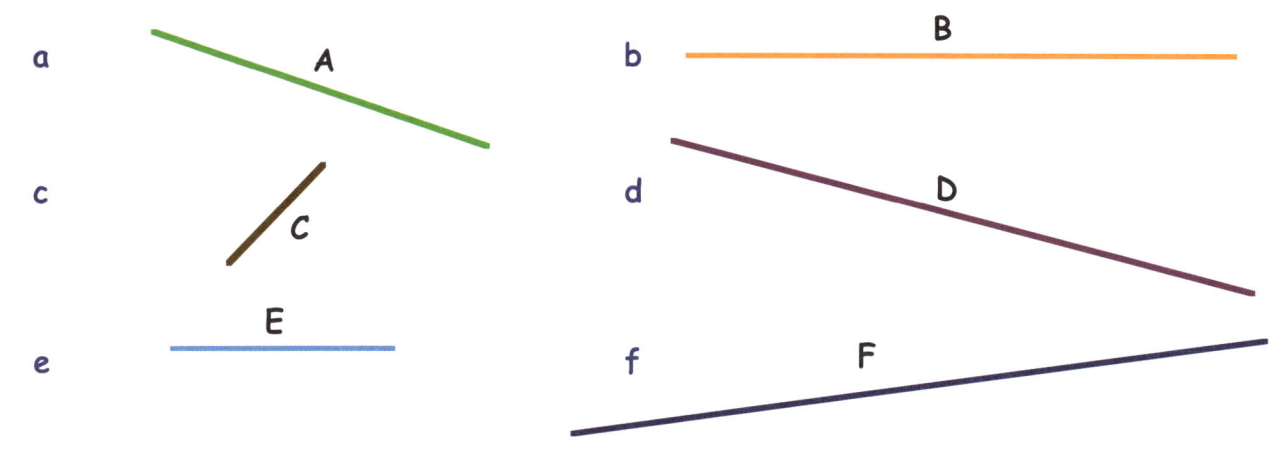

   a   A

   b   B

   c   C

   d   D

   e   E

   f   F

4. a   Measure the four sides of this shape **in centimetres**.

   b   Calculate the difference between the longest and the shortest side.

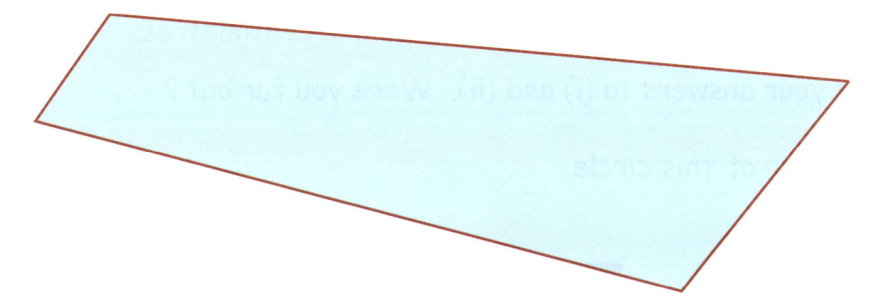

5. Measure the diameters of these circular shapes **in millimetres**.

   a   b    c

   *note - this shape has **3** different sized circles 

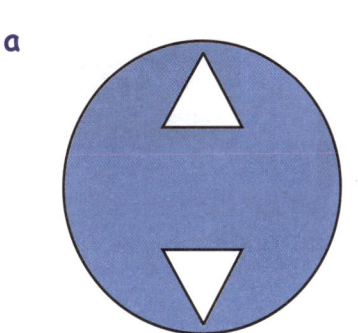

6. How many **millimetres** is the green line shorter than the blue line ?

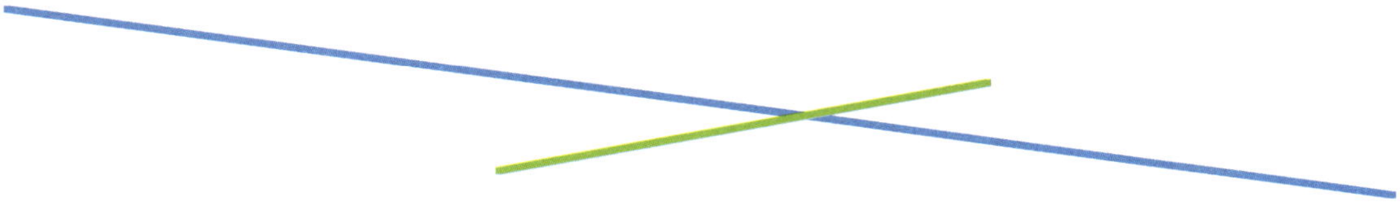

this is Chapter Fourteen   page 149   LENGTH & AREA

7. Measure each line and write down its length in :-
   (i)   millimetres.
   (ii) centimetres.
   (iii) centimetres and millimetres.

   example :- 27 mm = 2·7 cm = 2 cm 7 mm

   a
   b
   c
   d
   e

8. Some children are wearing badges (shown below) because it is their friend's birthday.
   (i)   Write down an estimate of each measurement asked for, in centimetres.
   (ii) Now use your ruler to measure the length, in centimetres.
   (iii) Compare your answers to (i) and (ii). Were you far out ?

   a   The diameter of this circle.
   b   A side of this square.

   c   The length of a diagonal of this rectangle.

9. Use your ruler to **draw** :-
   a   a line of length 25 mm.
   b   a line of length 78 mm.
   c   a line of length 3·5 cm.
   d   a line of length 8·2 cm.
   e   a square of side 45 mm.
   f   a rectangle measuring 4·5 cm by 5·5 cm.

10. Look at your drawings for **e** and **f** in question 9. Measure and write down :-
    a   the length of the 2 diagonals of your square, in millimetres.
        What do you notice ?
    b   the length of the 2 diagonals of your rectangle, in centimetres.
        What do you notice ?

this is Chapter Fourteen   page 150   LENGTH & AREA

Units of Length

There are 4 units of length used in the METRIC system.

kilometre, **millimetre**, **metre**, **centimetre**

The metre — This is the standard unit of length - it is about the distance from the ground to the handle of a door in your house. (1 metre)

The centimetre — This is the metre divided into 100 parts. About the width of your pinky nail.

The millimetre — This is the centimetre divided into 10 parts. About the width of a pin.

The kilometre — This is equal to 1000 metres.

Exercise 2

1. How many :-
   a. metres are there in 1 kilometre ?
   b. centimetres are there in 1 metre ?
   c. millimetres are there in 1 centimetre ?
   d. millimetres are there in 1 metre ?
   e. centimetres are there in 1 kilometre ?
   f. millimetres are there in 1 kilometre ?

2. Since **1 cm = 10 mm**, how many millimetres are there in :-
   a. 6 cm
   b. 2 cm
   c. 15 cm
   d. half a centimetre
   e. 4 cm 2 mm
   f. 8 cm 7 mm
   g. 12 cm 9 mm
   h. 5 cm 5 mm
   i. 1·5 cm
   j. 9·2 cm
   k. 18·9 cm
   l. 21·3 cm ?

3. Since **10 mm = 1 cm**, how many centimetres are equal to :-

   a 40 mm   b 70 mm   c 90 mm   d 130 mm
   e 35 mm   f 49 mm   g 200 mm   h 700 mm
   i 650 mm   j 2000 mm   k 3 mm   l 7 mm ?

4. As **1 m = 100 cm**, how many centimetres are there in :-

   a 3 m   b 9 m   c 14 m   d half a metre
   e 25 m   f 49 m   g 200 m   h quarter of a metre
   i 4 m 50 cm   j 7·05 m   k 0·5 m   l 0·01 m ?

5. Remember, **100 cm = 1 m**. How many metres are there in :-

   a 400 cm   b 700 cm   c 1500 cm   d 4000 cm
   e 440 cm   f 950 cm   g 50 cm   h 25 cm ?

6. **1 km = 1000 m**. Write down how many metres there are in :-

   a 3 km   b 12 km   c 25 km   d half a kilometre
   e $5\frac{1}{2}$ km   f 2 km 750 m   g 9 km 800 m   h 1 km 70 m
   i 5·2 km   j 12·6 km   k 2·25 km   l 0·8 km.

7. **1000 m = 1 km**. Write down how many kilometres there are in :-

   a 5000 m   b 18 000 m   c 300 m   d 7500 m
   e 18 400 m   f 4250 m   g 2150 m   h 6950 m
   i 350 m   j 780 m   k 12 400 m   l 300 000 m.

8. Put these four lengths in order, **smallest** first :-

   6 cm 5 mm   6·2 cm   63 mm   6 cm

9. Put these four lengths in order, **largest** first :-

   8 m 90 cm   8·8 m   870 cm   9 m

10. Jamie measured the length of his sleigh. It was 1200 mm.
    What was its length in :-   (i) centimetres   (ii) metres ?

11. A ball of string is 2500 cm long. How long is this in metres ?

12. The distance round a running track is 400 metres.
    A race consisted of **12 and a half laps** of the track.

    a How long was the race in metres ?
    b How long was it in kilometres ?

this is Chapter Fourteen   page 152   LENGTH & AREA

Problems involving Length

Exercise 3

1. Young Sidney placed some tins of sweets on top of each other.
   The tins were 25 mm, 38 mm, 47 mm and 50 mm in height.

   a   How high did the four tins reach ?

   b   Write this height in centimetres.

2. Ben had a licorice stick 8 cm long. He bit off 25 mm from one end.

   a   Change 8 cm to mm.

   b   Now write down the length of licorice stick which was left (**in mm**).

3. A hot piece of metal was 6·7 cm long. When it cooled its length decreased by 4 mm.

   What length was the cooled piece of metal (**in cm**) ?

4. Alice is making a daisy chain with daisies all 35 mm long.
   She uses 8 daisies in her chain.

   What is the full length of her chain, in **centimetres** ?

5. A pile of six DVD's is stacked in their cases.
   The total thickness of the pile is 15 cm.

   If each of the cases are the same size, find how thick one
   DVD case is, in **millimetres**.

6. Sonya came 2nd in the 100 metre race. A video "close-up" showed that
   she had run 98·5 metres when the winner had crossed the line.

   How many centimetres was Sonya behind the winner ?

7. A coin is 2·4 cm in diameter. I place 100 of these coins in a straight line.

   How far does the line of coins stretch, **in metres** ?

8. Paula is running in the 6 km race.
   She has already covered 4500 metres.

   How many kilometres has Paula still to run ?

9. Professor Jolly is off on holiday.
   320 km by train, 45 km by ferry and 9·2 km by taxi - but now he's lost !

   Before he set off, he had looked up the details of his journey on the
   Internet..... 375 km from home to the holiday hotel !

   How many metres is he now standing from his hotel ?

this is Chapter Fourteen   page 153   LENGTH & AREA

Perimeter

The **Perimeter** of a shape is :-

"the **total** distance around its outside".

Example :-

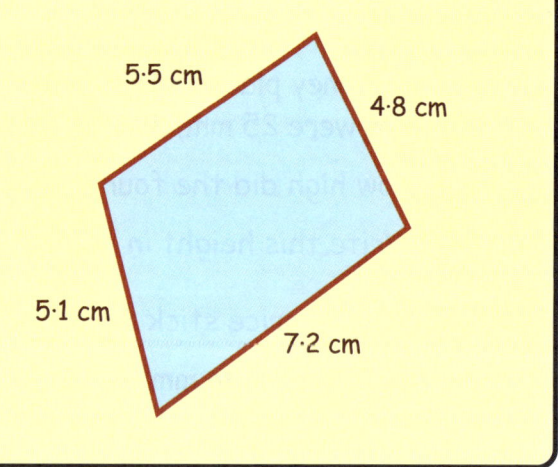

Perimeter = (5·5 + 5·1 + 7·2 + 4·8) cm

= **22·6 cm**

Exercise 4

1. Calculate the perimeter of this triangle.

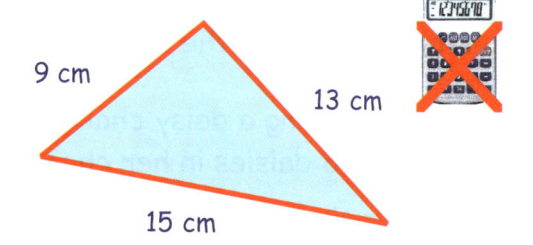

2. Calculate the perimeter of each of the following shapes :-

   a   10 cm, 14 cm, 5 cm, 7 cm

   b   12 mm, 20 mm, 16 mm, 15 mm

   c   3·4 m, 3·8 m, 3 m, 3·2 m, 2·8 m

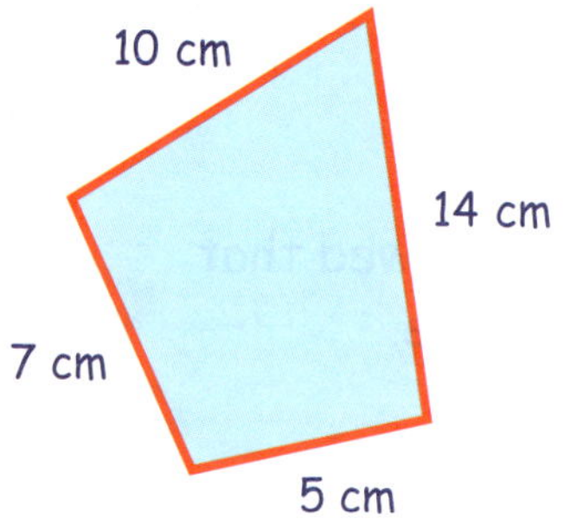

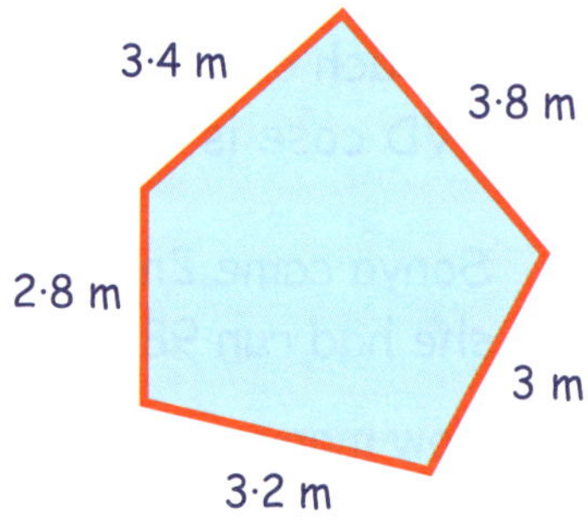

3. Calculate the perimeter of this rectangle.

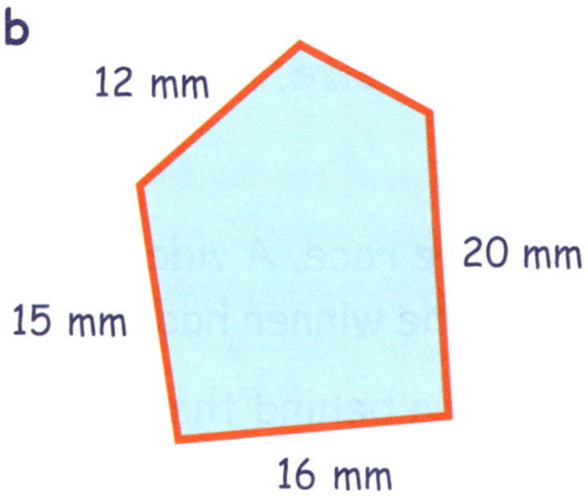

   (note - the answer is <u>NOT</u> 31 cm)

   11 cm, 20 cm

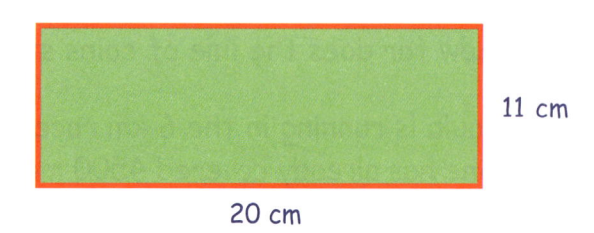

4. Calculate the perimeter of each of these rectangles and squares :-

   a   4 cm, 7 cm

   b   5·5 cm, 2·1 cm

   c   42 mm (square)

   d   8·7 m, 4·4 m

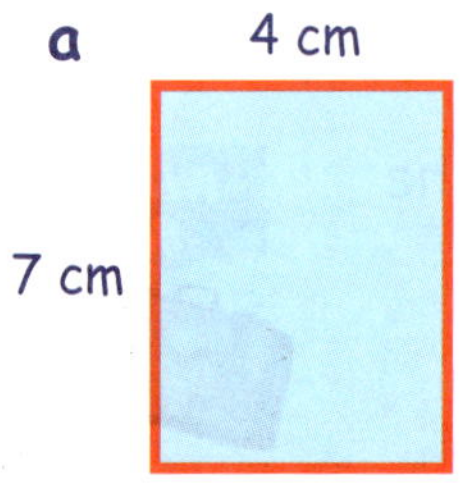

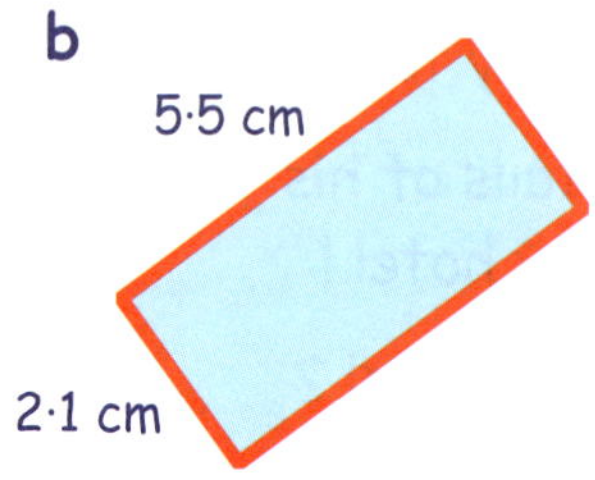

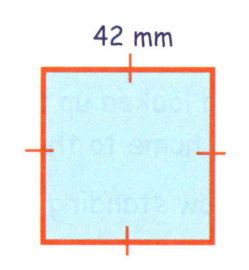

this is Chapter Fourteen   page 154   LENGTH & AREA

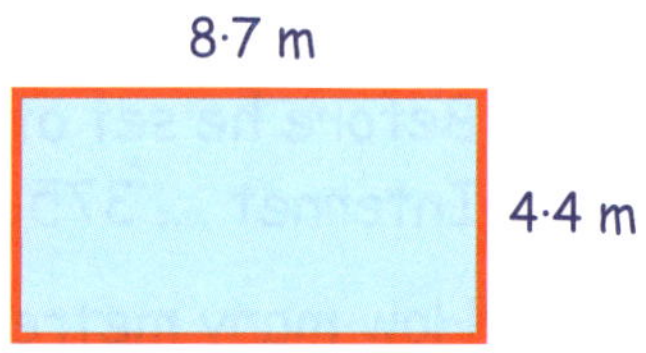

5. This triangle has a perimeter of 68 cm.

Calculate the length of the missing side.
(12 cm + 36 cm + ? cm = 68 cm)

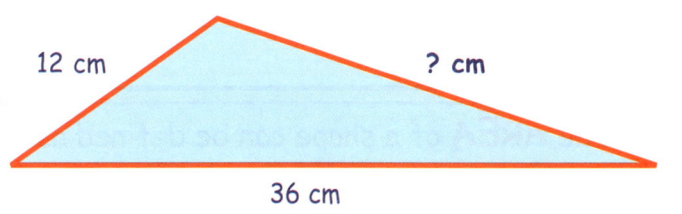

6. Calculate the length of the missing side in these shapes :-

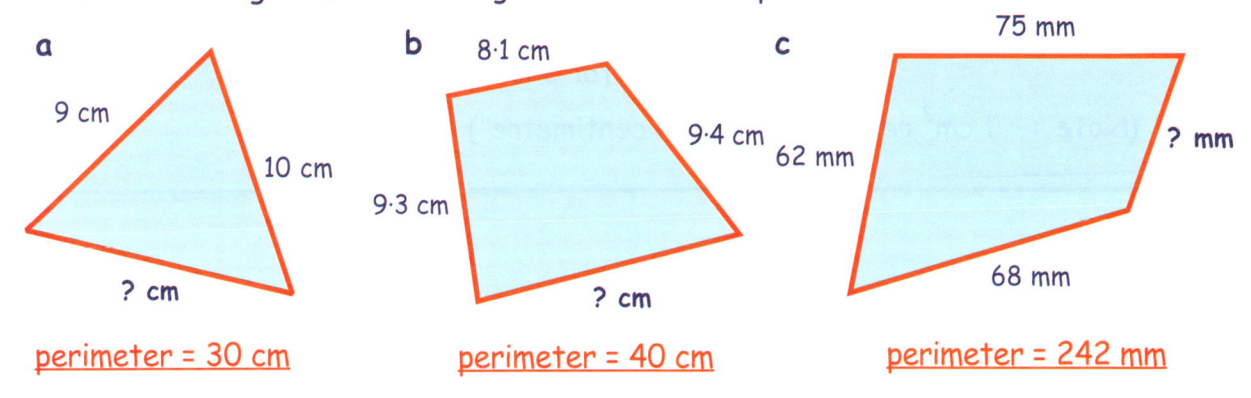

a 9 cm, 10 cm, ? cm — perimeter = 30 cm

b 8·1 cm, 9·4 cm, 9·3 cm, ? cm — perimeter = 40 cm

c 75 mm, ? mm, 68 mm, 62 mm — perimeter = 242 mm

7. Calculate the size of the missing side in the following rectangles :-

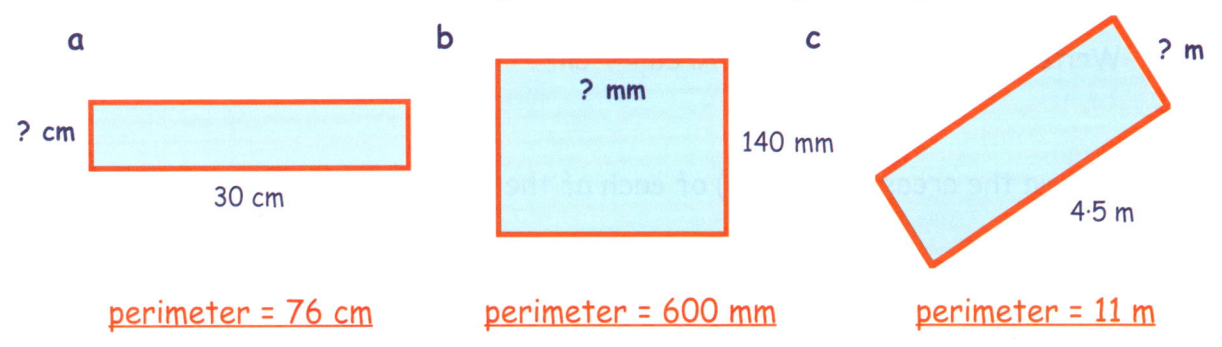

a ? cm, 30 cm — perimeter = 76 cm

b ? mm, 140 mm — perimeter = 600 mm

c ? m, 4·5 m — perimeter = 11 m

8. The diagram shows the floor of Jonathan's playroom.

a Find the perimeter of the floor.

b How much will it cost to surround it with new skirting board costing £3 per metre ?

(The door is 0·7 metres wide).

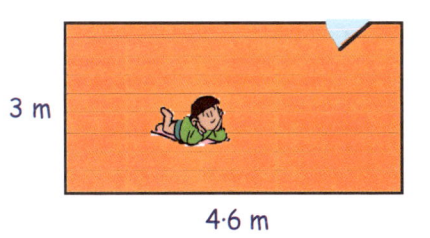

3 m, 4·6 m

9. Farmer Giles has a rectangular field.

He surrounds it with 3 **strands** of barbed wire.

Barbed wire costs 50p per metre.

Calculate the total cost of the wire.

55 m, 80 m

this is Chapter Fourteen   page 155   LENGTH & AREA

Area

The **AREA** of a shape can be defined as :-

"the amount of space it takes up"

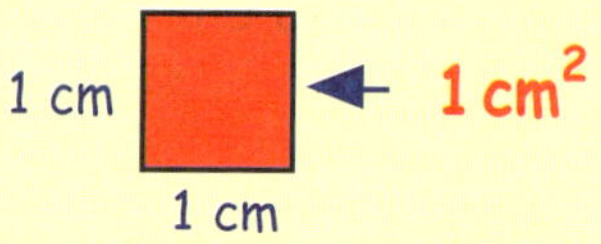

If you think of a box 1 cm by 1 cm, we say it has an area of :- **1 square centimetre**

(or **1 cm²** for short).

(**Note** :- 1 cm² reads as "1 square centimetre")

Exercise 5

1. a How many boxes (1 centimetre by 1 centimetre) are shown here?

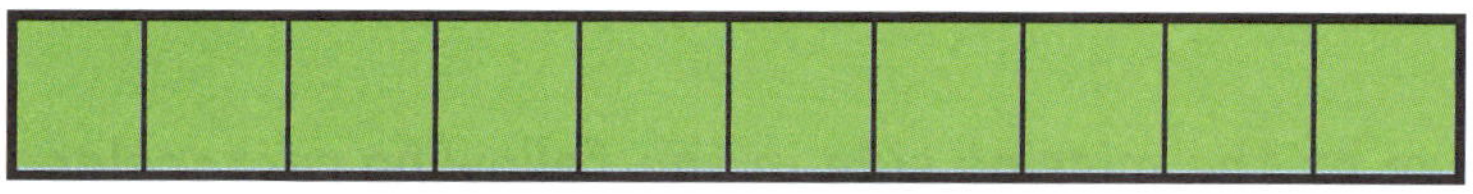

   b Write down the area as :-   Area = ? cm².

2. Write down the areas (using cm²) of each of the following shapes :-

   a   b 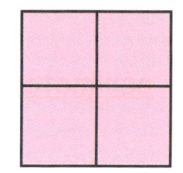   c

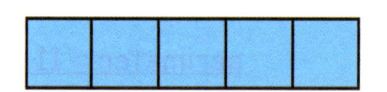

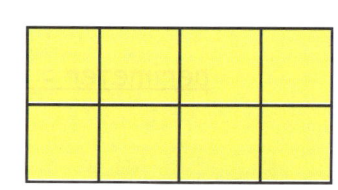

   d 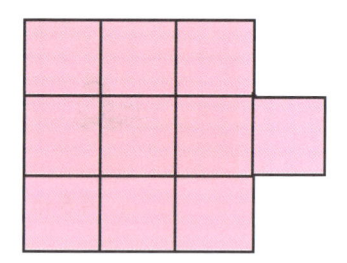   e 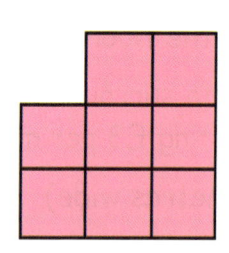   f

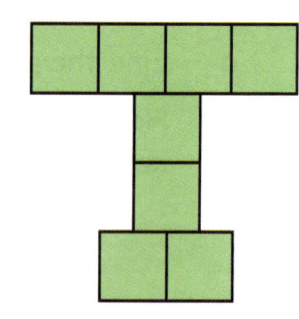

   g 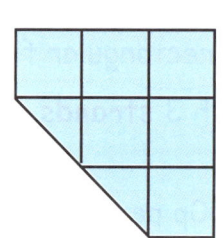   h 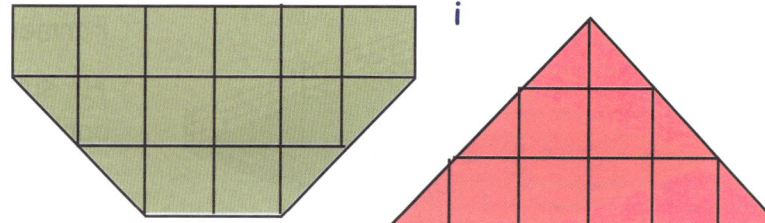   i

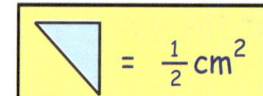

   △ = $\frac{1}{2}$ cm²

this is Chapter Fourteen   LENGTH & AREA

j

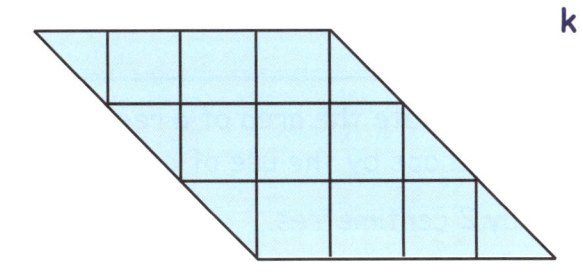

k

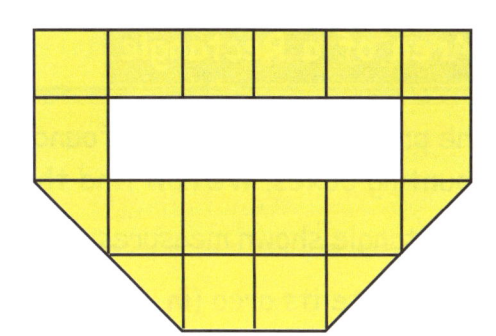

3. Estimate the areas of these shapes as follows :–

> If more than $\frac{1}{2}$ a box is covered —> **count it** as 1 cm^2
> If less than $\frac{1}{2}$ a box is covered —> **do not count it** at all.

a

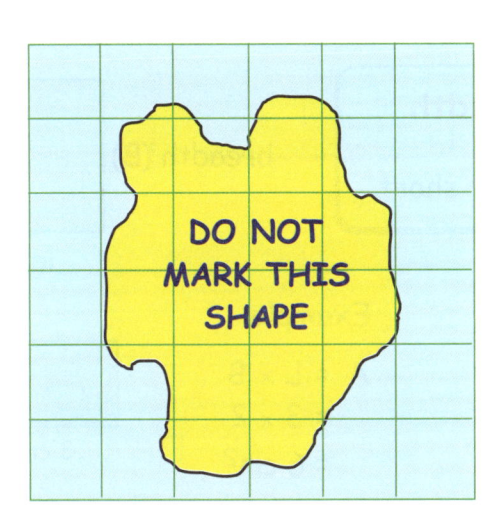

b

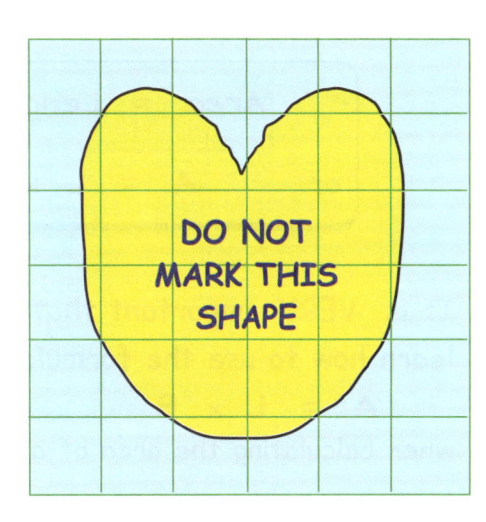

c

d

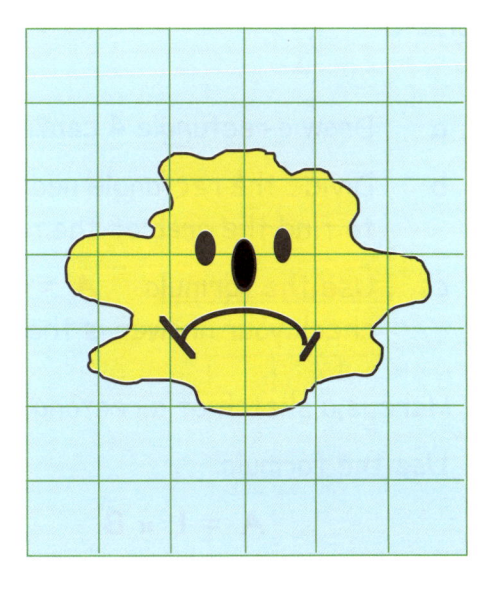

this is Chapter Fourteen   page 157   LENGTH & AREA

The Area of a Rectangle

In the previous exercise, we found out how to calculate the area of a rectangle by counting boxes. We now find the area of this shape by the use of a **FORMULA**.

The rectangle shown measures 4 centimetres by 2 centimetres.

a   Calculate its area (**in cm^2**) by counting all the boxes.

   Do you agree......... 8 boxes, (**cm^2**) ?

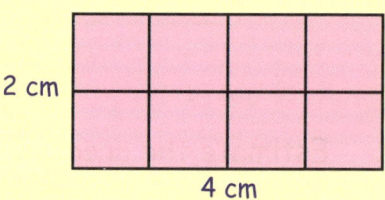

b   Now write down the answer you get when you multiply its length by its breadth :-

   =>   4 cm x 2 cm   (do you get the same answer ?)

Another way to calculate the AREA of a RECTANGLE is as follows :-

> **Area = Length x Breadth**
>
> or   **A = L x B**   for short.

It is VERY important that you learn how to use the formula,

A = L x B

when calculating the area of a rectangle.

Example :-

A = L x B
= 3 x 2
= <u>6 cm^2</u>

Exercise 6

1. a   Draw a rectangle 4 centimetres long by 3 centimetres wide.

   b   Divide the rectangle neatly into 1 cm square boxes and count the boxes to find the area of the rectangle.

   c   Use the formula   **A = L x B**   (with L = 4, B = 3) to calculate the area and check your answer is the same as that obtained in part **b**.

2. Here is a sketch of a rectangle.

   Use the formula

       A = L x B

   to calculate its area (in cm^2).

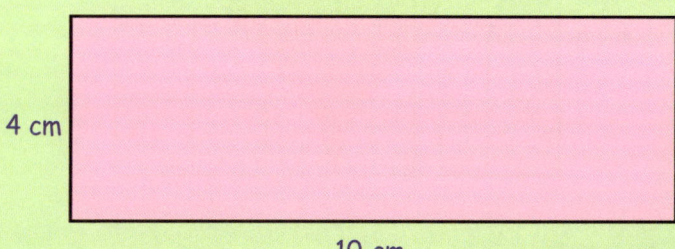

3. Calculate the area of each of the following rectangles.

   (In each case, make a small "sketch" of the rectangle, write down the rule
   A = L × B and calculate the area in cm².)

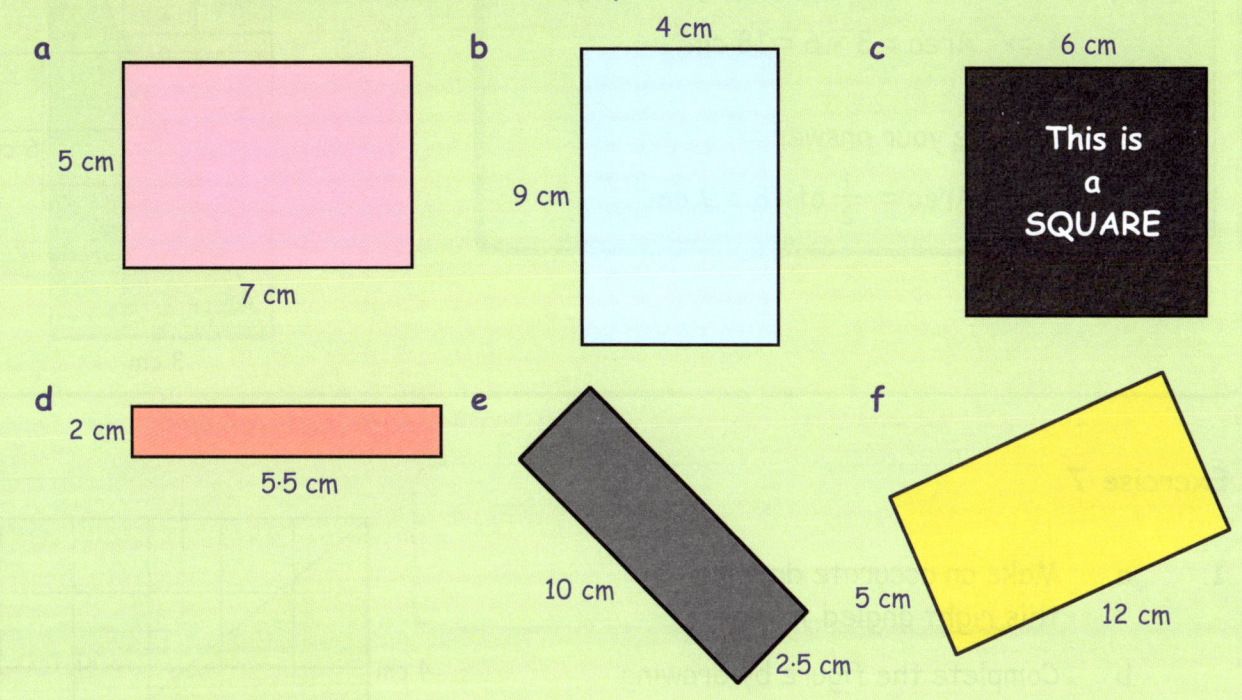

   a 5 cm × 7 cm

   b 4 cm × 9 cm

   c 6 cm × 6 cm (This is a SQUARE)

   d 2 cm × 5·5 cm

   e 10 cm × 2·5 cm

   f 5 cm × 12 cm

4. Larger rectangles such as floors, playgrounds & fields have their areas measured in **square metres** (m²).

   Calculate the area of each of Farmer Giles' 3 fields in m².

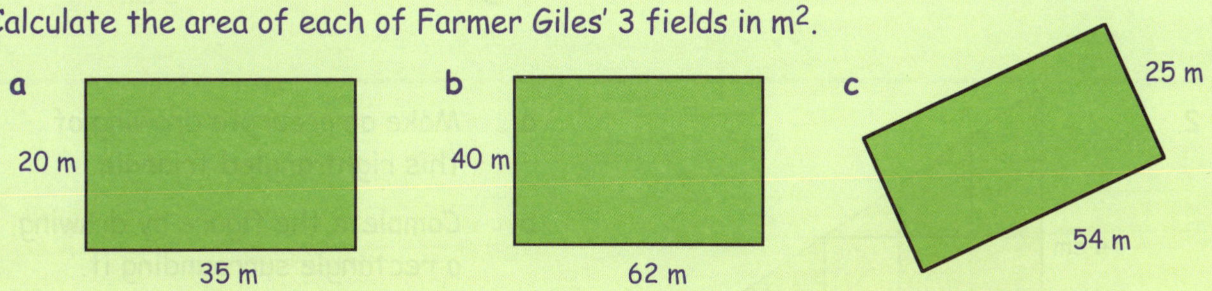

   a 20 m × 35 m

   b 40 m × 62 m

   c 25 m × 54 m

5. This plan shows the ground floor of a bungalow.

   Calculate the area of each of the 6 rooms in m².

   Area (living room) = L × B
   = 5 m × 8 m
   = ... m².

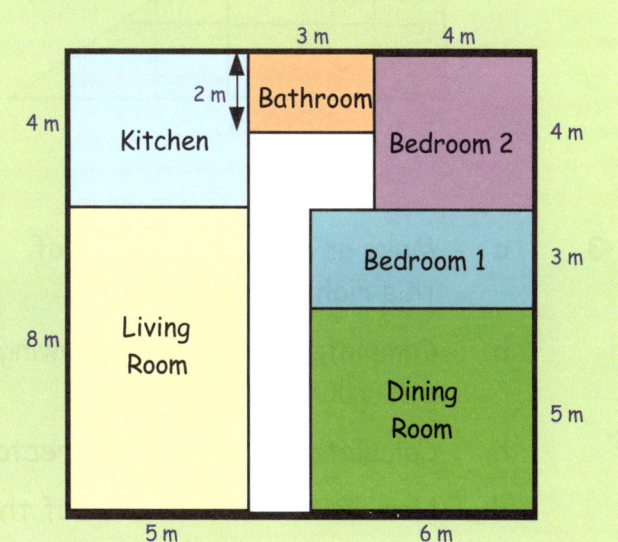

   Kitchen: 4 m, Bathroom: 3 m × 2 m, Bedroom 2: 4 m × 4 m, Bedroom 1: 3 m, Living Room: 8 m × 5 m, Dining Room: 5 m × 6 m

this is Chapter Fourteen   page 159   LENGTH & AREA

The Area of a Right Angled Triangle

To calculate the area of a Right Angled Triangle :-

Step 1 – Look at the surrounding rectangle
=> Area = 3 × 6 = 18 cm^2.

Step 2 – <u>Halve</u> your answer =>
=> Area = $\frac{1}{2}$ of 18 = 9 cm^2.

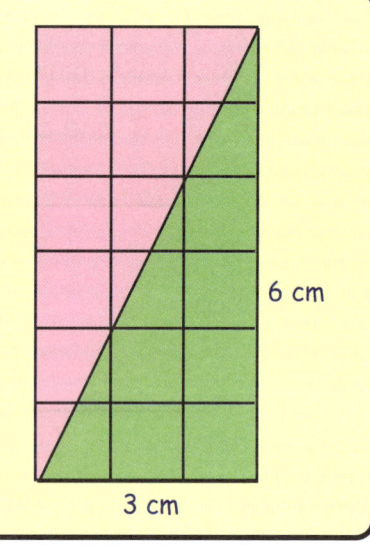

6 cm

3 cm

Exercise 7

1. a   Make an accurate drawing of this right angled triangle.
   b   Complete the figure by drawing a rectangle around it.
   c   Calculate the area of the rectangle.
   d   Now write down the area of the triangle.

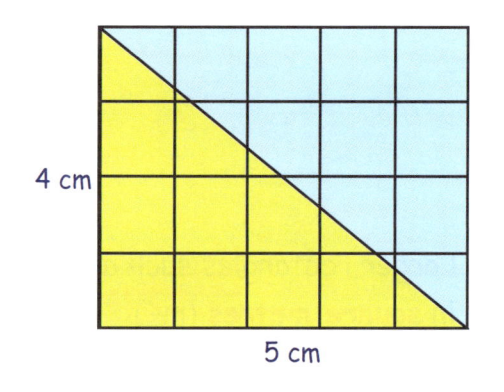

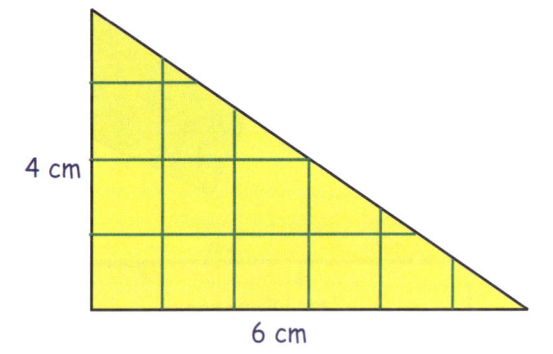

   4 cm
   5 cm

2.
   4 cm
   6 cm

   a   Make an accurate drawing of this right angled triangle.
   b   Complete the figure by drawing a rectangle surrounding it.
   c   Calculate the area of the rectangle.
   d   Write down the area of the triangle.

3. a   Make an accurate drawing of this right angled triangle.
   b   Complete the figure by drawing a surrounding rectangle.
   c   Calculate the area of the rectangle.
   d   Now write down the area of the triangle.

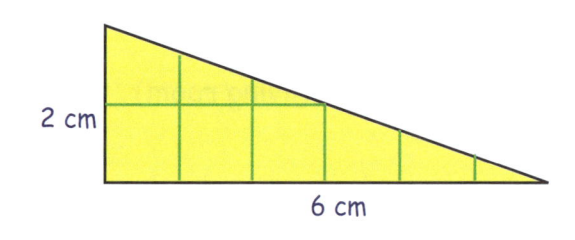

   2 cm
   6 cm

this is Chapter Fourteen   page 160   LENGTH & AREA

4.

5 cm

5 cm

a Make an accurate drawing of this right angled triangle.

b Complete the figure by drawing the surrounding square.

c Calculate the area of the square.

d Now write down the area of the triangle.

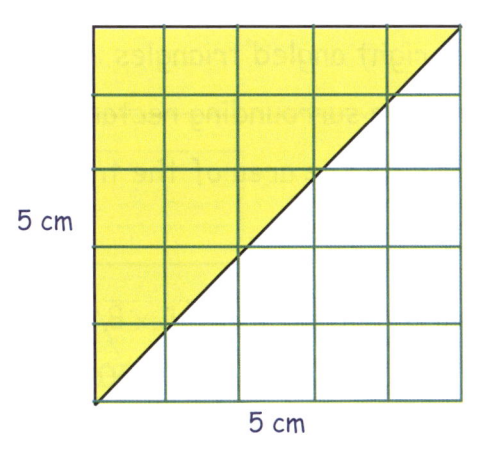

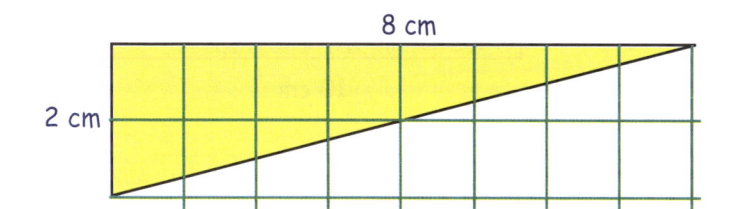

5. In the same way, find the area of this triangle.

8 cm

2 cm

6. Try to imagine a rectangle around each of these right angled triangles and calculate the area of each triangle.

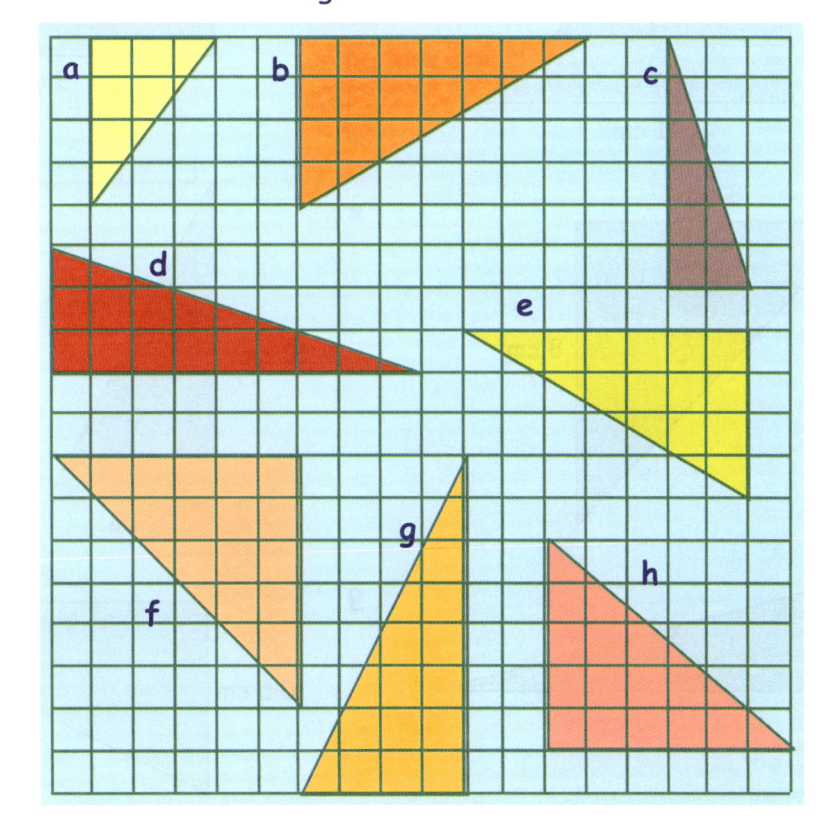

7. Find the total area of each shape :-

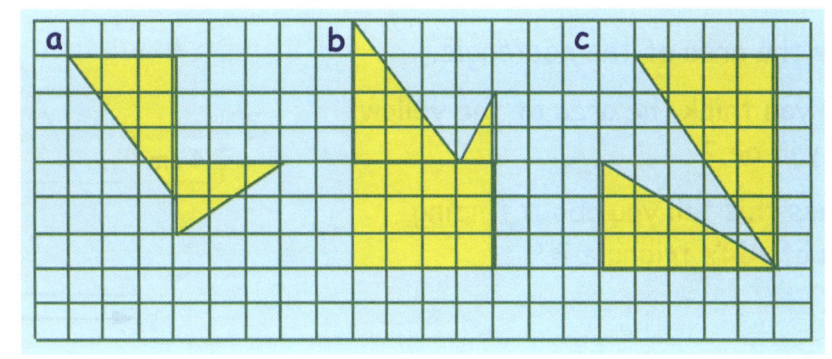

this is Chapter Fourteen   page 161   LENGTH & AREA

8. Use **1 cm squared paper** to draw the following right angled triangles :–

   (i) Make an accurate drawing   **(ii)** Draw the surrounding rectangle.
   (iii) Find the area of the rectangle.   **(iv)** Calculate the area of the triangle

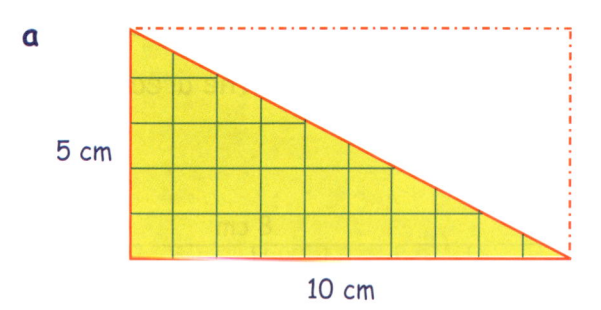

a   5 cm, 10 cm

Area (rectangle) = L × B = 10 × 5
                            = 50 cm²

Area (triangle) = $\frac{1}{2}$ of 50 = ? cm²

b   10 cm, 11 cm

c   4 cm, 9 cm

d   8 cm, 8 cm

e   12 cm, 3 cm

f   1·5 cm, 8 cm

g   20 cm, 10·5 cm

---

9. This triangle is **not** right angled !

   a   Calculate the area of the rectangle.

   b   What do you think the area of the yellow triangle will be ?

   c   What does this tell you about finding the area of ANY triangle ?

4 cm, 5 cm

this is Chapter Fourteen   page 162   LENGTH & AREA

Topic in a Nutshell

1. With your ruler, measure the length of these lines, in centimetres.

    a   b

2. Write down the lengths of the following lines in :-

    (i) millimetres   (ii) centimetres   (iii) centimetres and millimetres.

    a   b

3. Use your ruler to draw a line 105 millimetres long.

4. Change :-

    a   4 m to cm   b   20 cm to mm   c   2·3 km to m   d   7000 m to km

    e   250 cm to m   f   80 mm to cm   g   4500 m to km   h   4 m 30 cm to cm

5. Danny saws 40 cm off a piece of a 2 metre garden bench.
   What length of wood (in cm) remains ?

6. Calculate the perimeter of this shape :-

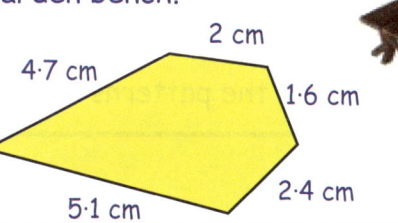

    4·7 cm, 2 cm, 1·6 cm, 2·4 cm, 5·1 cm

7. Find the areas of the figures shown below.
   Each small square stands for 1 cm² in area.

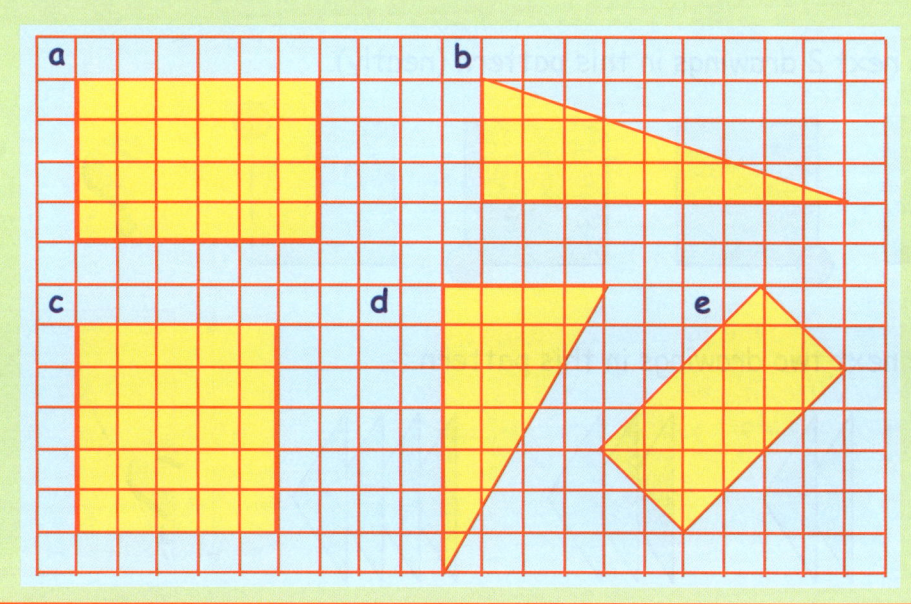

   a   b   c   d   e

this is Chapter Fourteen   page 163   LENGTH & AREA

Chapter 15

Patterns

Revision Work

Basic "Patterns":-

Mathematicians like to look for rules for patterns in drawings and sets of numbers. This helps them decide how to continue the pattern or the set of numbers.

Examples :-   **A Drawing Pattern -**

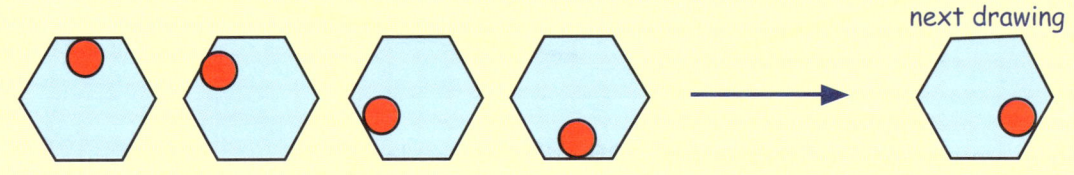

next drawing

A Letter Pattern :-

A,   C,   E,   G,   I,   ……… →   next letter
K

A Number Pattern :-

7,   10,   13,   16,   19,   ……… →   next number
22

Can you explain how the patterns are formed in the above 3 examples?

Exercise 1

1. Look at the 3 examples above. Draw, or write down, the next "**bit**" of the pattern.

2. Show the next 2 drawings in this pattern (neatly).

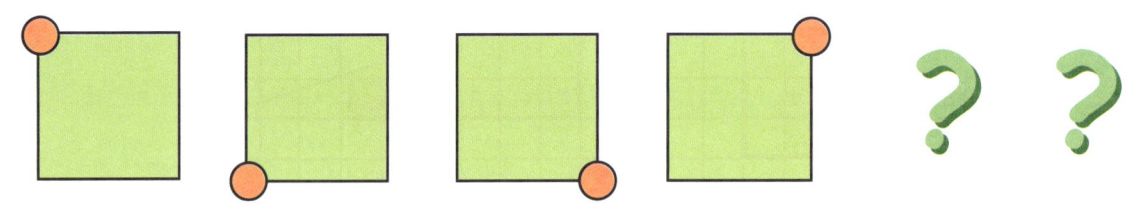

3. Show the next two drawings in this pattern :-

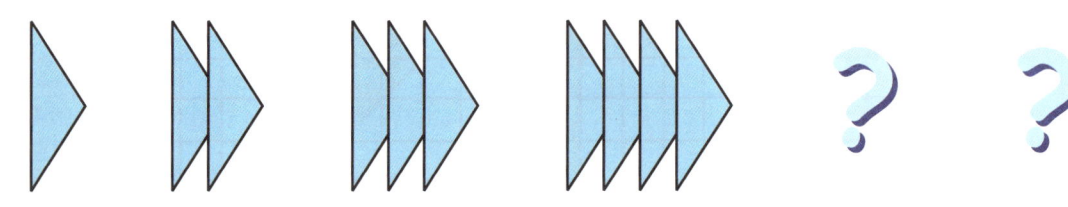

4. **a** Draw these 3 patterns on squared paper.

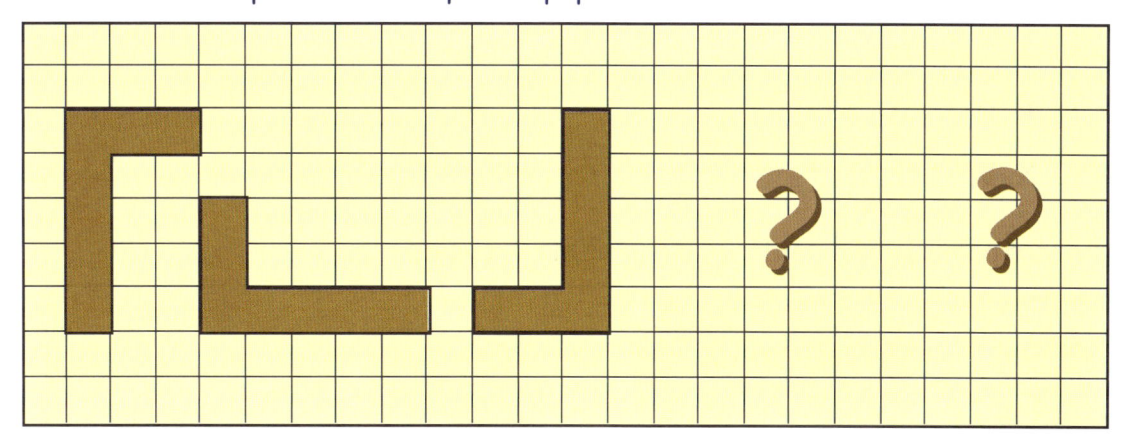

b Now show the next two drawings in the pattern.

5. **a** Copy the four drawings below.

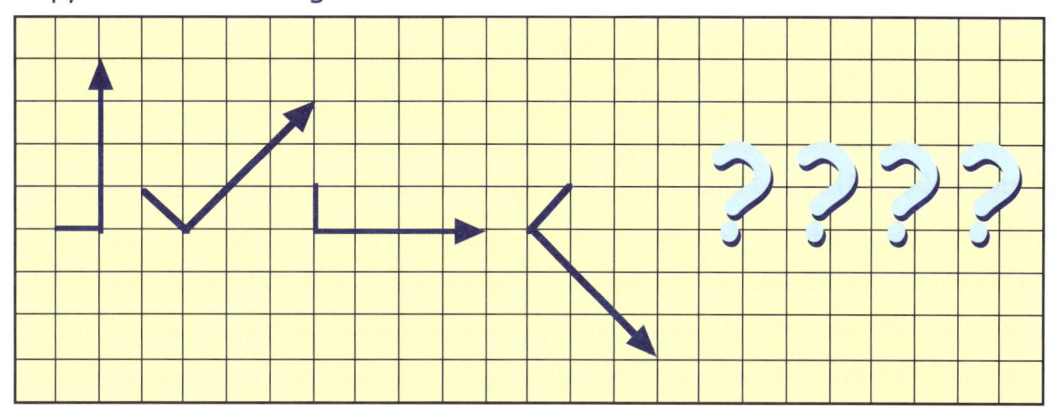

b Show the next 4 drawings which follow the pattern above.

6. This is a more complicated pattern. Draw the next two patterns.
(*Trace the hexagon to help you*).

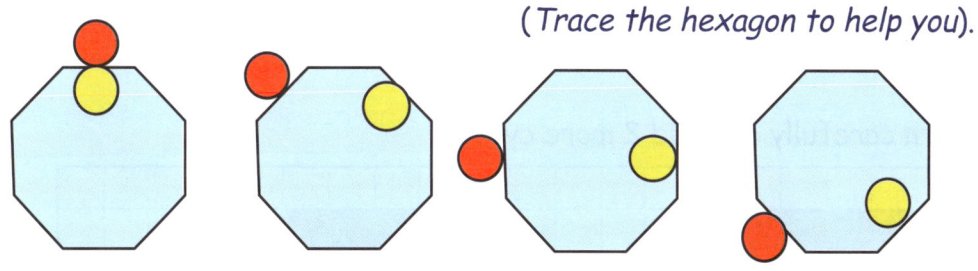

7. **a** Draw the next 2 designs for this pattern :-

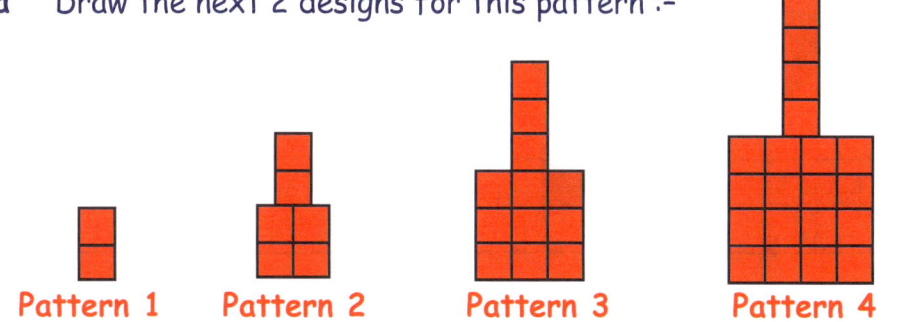

Pattern 1   Pattern 2   Pattern 3   Pattern 4

b How many small squares are there in pattern   (i) 1 (ii) 2 (iii) 3 (iv) 4 ?

c How many small squares will there be in pattern (i) 5 (ii) 6 (iii) 7 (iv) 8 ?

this is Chapter Fifteen   PATTERNS

8. Copy each pattern of letters and find the next letter in the pattern.
   a B, D, F, H, J, ...
   b A, D, G, J, M, ...
   c Q, P, O, N, M, ...
   d a, e, i, o, ...
   e Z, X, V, T, ...
   f B, C, D, F, G, H, ...

9. Copy this pattern and continue it for 2 more **cycles**.

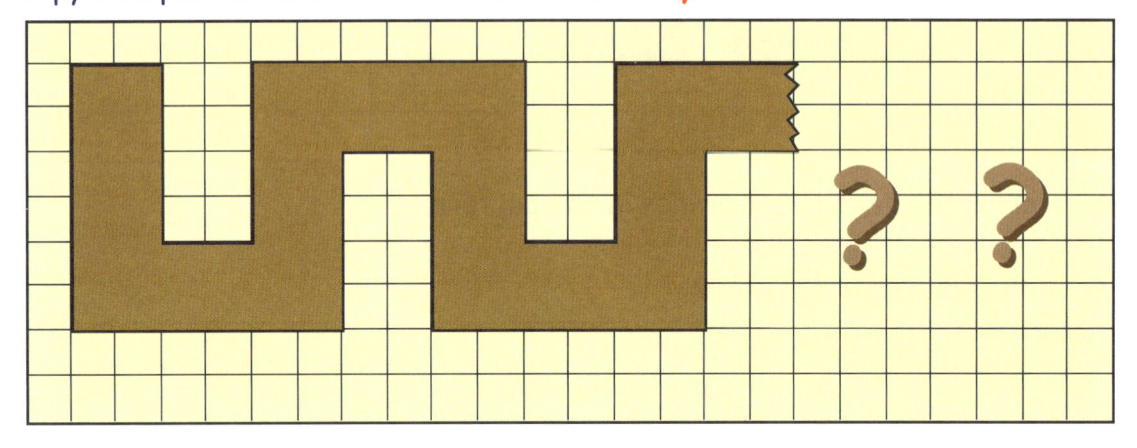

10. **Difficult** — Copy this pattern carefully and add 2 more cycles.

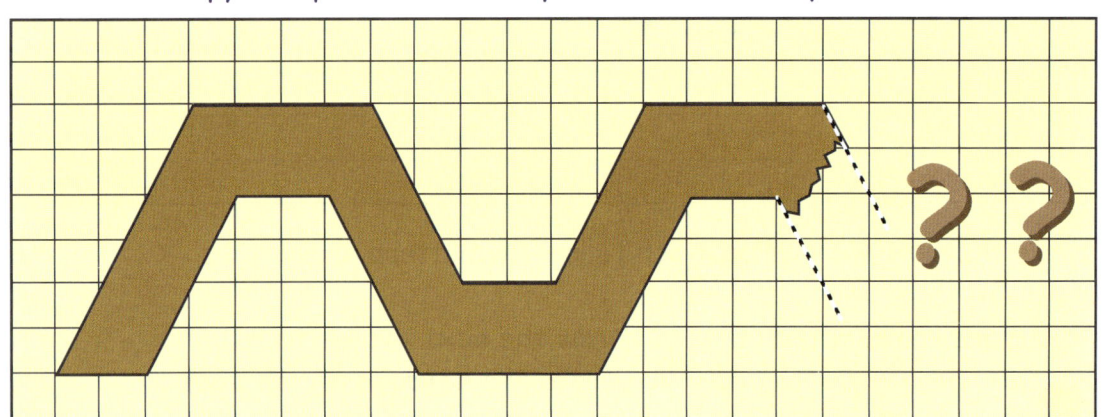

11. Copy this pattern carefully and add 2 more cycles.

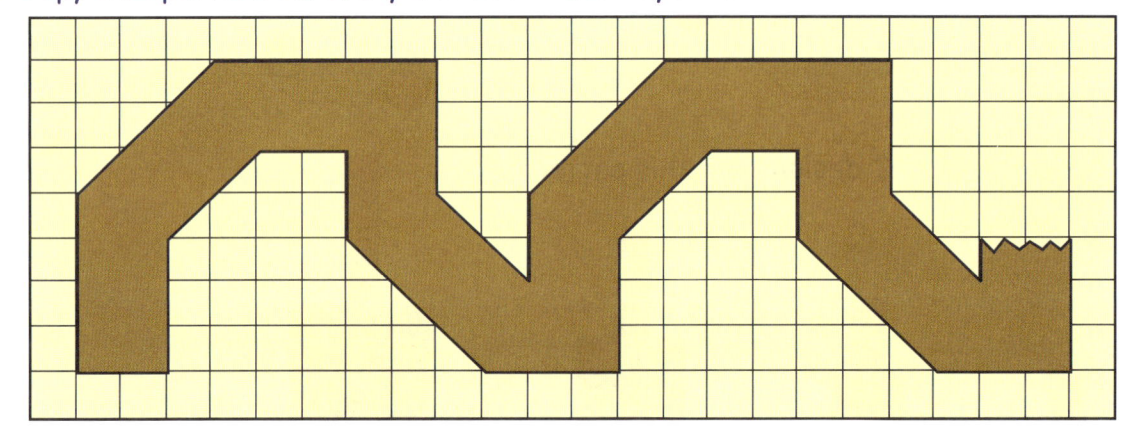

12. Patterns like the one shown in Question 9 often occur in wallpaper. The patterns repeat themselves.

    Design and colour a neat pattern which repeats itself **4** or **5** times.

Patterns with numbers – Sequences (description)

Example 1 :- 3, 6, 9, 12, ... – this is the 3 times table, starting at 3.

Example 2 :- 5, 7, 9, 11, 13, ... – starts at 5 and rises by 2 each time.

Example 3 :- 50, 46, 42, 38, 34, ... – starts at 50 and drops by 4 each time.

Exercise 2

1. Very carefully, describe the following pattern of numbers :-

    8, 12, 16, 20, 24, ...

    Copy :-   this is the "...." times table, starting with the number "....".

2. Describe each of the following sequences using sentences like the one shown in the examples at the top of the page.

    a   5, 10, 15, 20, 25, ...   b   7, 14, 21, 28, 35, ...

    c   9, 12, 15, 18, 21, ...   d   50, 60, 70, 80, 90, ...

    e   24, 32, 40, 48, ...   f   36, 32, 28, 24, 20, ...

3. a   Look at the pattern in Question **2a** :- 5, 10, 15, 20, 25.
      Write down the next 3 numbers in this pattern.

    b   Write down the next **3 terms** in the pattern shown in Question **2b**.

    c   Write down the next **3 terms** in the pattern shown in Question **2c**.

    d   Write down the next **3 terms** in the pattern shown in Question **2d**.

    e   Write down the next **3 terms** in the pattern shown in Question **2e**.

    f   Write down the next **3 terms** in the pattern shown in Question **2f**.

4. Describe the following sequence of numbers :-

    7, 10, 13, 16, 19, 22, ...

    Copy :-   "Begin at the number "...." and go up by "...." each time".

5. Describe each of the following sequences by saying :-

    "Begin at the number "...." and go up (down) by "...." each time".

    a   3, 5, 7, 9, 11, ...   b   5, 8, 11, 14, 17, ...

    c   9, 13, 17, 21, 25, ...   d   3, 13, 23, 33, 43, ...

    e   62, 67, 72, 77, 82, ...   f   6, 6·5, 7, 7·5, 8, ...

    g   3, $4\frac{1}{2}$, 6, $7\frac{1}{2}$, 9, ...   h   30, 26, 22, 18, ...

    i   70, 61, 52, 43, ...   j   2000, 1900, 1800, 1700, ...

6. **a** Look back at the pattern in Question 5a :– 3, 5, 7, 9, 11.
  Write down the next 3 numbers in this pattern.

  b Do the same with the patterns in Questions 5b – j.
  Write down the next **3 terms**.

7. Look at this pattern made with matches.

  1 square   2 squares   3 squares
  4 matches   8 matches   12 matches 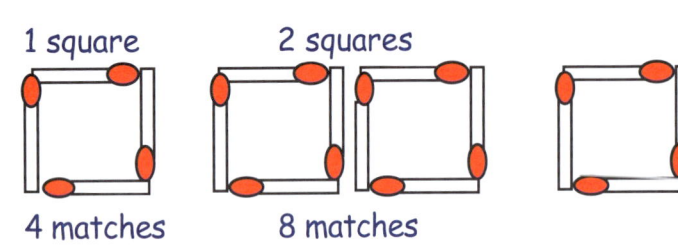 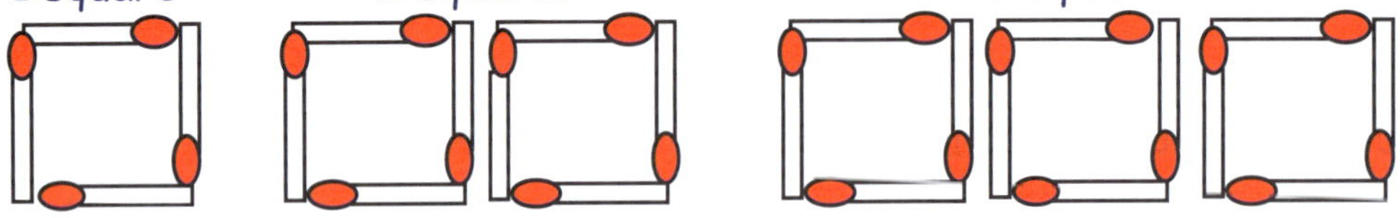

  a Draw the pattern showing the matches needed for 4 squares.

  b The pattern for the number of matches needed is 4, 8, 12, 16.
  Copy this sequence and fill in the next 3 numbers.

  c Copy the following and complete :–

  "Start with 4 matches for 1 square and add on ... matches for each extra square".

  d How many matches are needed for 10 squares ?

8. Mrs Jones makes gingerbread men.

  1 gingerbread man   2 gingerbread men   3 gingerbread men
  (5 smarties)   (10 smarties)   (.... smarties)

  a How many smarties are needed for 4 gingerbread men ?

  b Copy the pattern 5, 10, 15 and write down the next 3 terms.

  c Copy the following and complete :–

  "Start with "...." smarties for 1 gingerbread man and add on
  "...." smarties for each extra gingerbread man.

  d How many smarties are needed for 9 gingerbread men ?

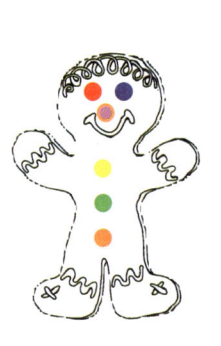

  e If an extra smartie was used on his nose, how many smarties
  would be needed for :–

   (i)   2 gingerbread men   (ii)   3 gingerbread men

   (iii) 6 gingerbread men   (iv) 10 gingerbread men ?

9. A special pattern – **The Fibonacci Sequence**.   Fibonacci

   Look at this sequence :-   1, 1, 2, 3, 5, 8, ...

   The pattern can be described as follows :-

   "Start with any 2 numbers (1 and 1 in the above example).
   "the 3rd number is formed by adding the 1st and 2nd numbers (2 = 1 + 1).
   "the 4th number is formed by adding the 2nd and 3rd numbers (3 = 1 + 2).
   "the 5th number is formed by adding the 3rd and 4th numbers (5 = 2 + 3).

   a   Find the 6th number = 4th number + 5th number.
   b   Find the 7th number = 5th number + 6th number.
   c   What is the 8th Fibonacci number ?
   d   Copy the pattern and find the first 12 Fibonacci numbers :-
       1, 1, 2, 3, 5, 8, ...

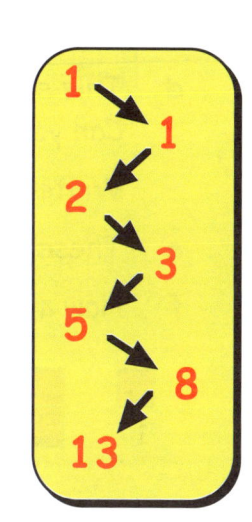

10. Form your own Fibonacci sequence.
    a   Start with any 2 numbers.
    b   The 3rd number = 1st number + 2nd number.
    c   The 4th number = 2nd number + 3rd number.
    d   Carry on with your pattern to produce the first 10 terms in the sequence.

11. **A new pattern**.

    Look at this set of numbers :-   2, 6, 12, 20, 30, 42, ...

    a   It is difficult to see what the next number is. Can you ?
    b   Can you see that   2 = (1 × 2), 6 = (2 × 3), 12 = (3 × 4).
        Write 20 = (4 × ...), 30 = (5 × ...), 42 = (... × ...).
    c   Find the 7th number in the pattern.
    d   Find the first 10 numbers in the sequence.

12. Another new pattern.

    A boy was creating a
    pattern using building blocks.

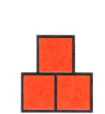

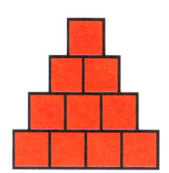

    a   Draw the 4 patterns of blocks neatly and draw the next 2 patterns (**5 and 6**).
    b   Look at this pattern in the table.

        Can you see the connection ?

        Write down the next
        pattern in the same way.

        1 = 1
        3 = 1 + 2
        6 = 1 + 2 + 3
        10 = 1 + 2 + 3 + 4

    c   Write down the 6th, 7th and 8th patterns in a similar way.

13. Look at this pattern :-

1, (1 + 3), (1 + 3 + 5), (1 + 3 + 5 + 7), (1 + 3 + 5 + 7 + 9), ...

a What do you call numbers like :-

(i) 2, 4, 6, 8, 10, 12, ...   (ii) 1, 3, 5, 7, 9, 11, ... ?

b The pattern **1, (1 + 3), (1 + 3 + 5), ..** is made up by adding odd numbers together. Write the next 4 terms in the pattern.

c Write down the **actual values** of each term :-
1 = 1, (1 + 3) = 4, (1 + 3 + 5) = 9, ...

d This set of numbers   1, 4, 9, 16, ... is a special set.
Can you see that :-   1 = (1 × 1),   4 = (2 × 2),   9 = (3 × 3), ...

Write the other numbers like this   16 = (... × ...), 25 = (... × ...), ...

e These numbers have a special name. Do you know what it is ?

f How many small squares are there in each of these squares ?

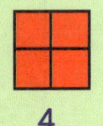

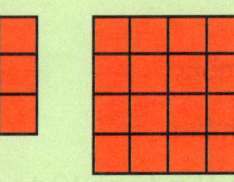

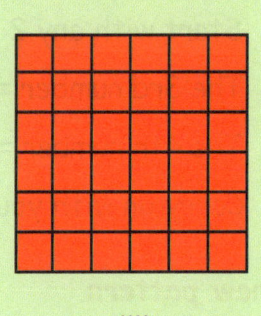

1
4
....
....
....
....

Can you now see why these numbers 1, 4, 9, 16, ... are called **square numbers** ?

14. **A Puzzle** :-

a How many squares are there in this figure ?   (not **4**)

b How many squares are there in this figure ?   (not **9** and not **10**)

c How many squares are there in each of these figures ?

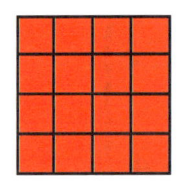

(i)   (ii)

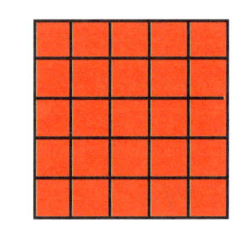

d Try to find how many squares are in a chess board.

Topic in a Nutshell

1. a Neatly, copy the first 3 drawings in this pattern.

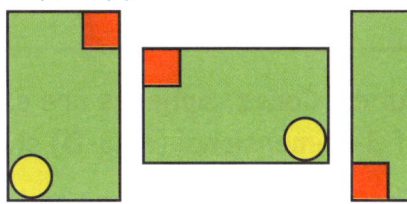

   b Draw the 4th pattern.

2. a Very carefully, describe the following pattern :– 12, 18, 24, 30, 36, ...

   b Write the next 3 terms in the pattern.

3. a Describe this pattern in a similar way :– 80, 76, 72, 68, ...

   b Write the next 3 numbers in the pattern.

4. Describe each of the following pattern of numbers carefully **and** write down the next 3 numbers each time :–

   a 10, 14, 18, 22, 26, ...   b 1, 17, 33, 49, 65, ...

   c 51, 46, 41, 36, ...   d 5·3, 7·0, 8·7, 10·4, 12·1, ...

5. Find the next 4 letters in this pattern. (think carefully !!)

   A, B, C, D, E, H, I, J, K, L, ...

6. A boy is building a pattern with rectangular wooden building bricks.

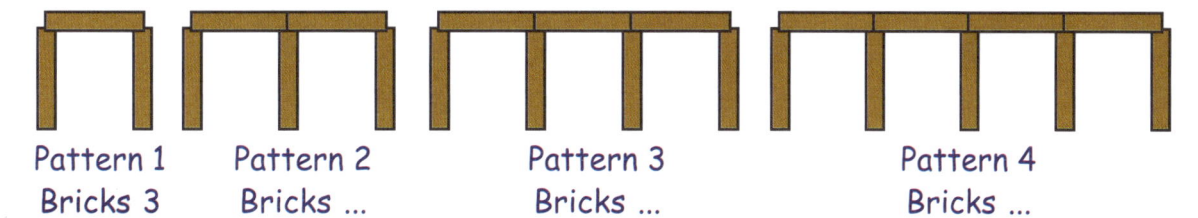

   Pattern 1   Pattern 2   Pattern 3   Pattern 4
   Bricks 3   Bricks ...   Bricks ...   Bricks ...

   a Draw (**neatly**) pattern number 5 and count the number of bricks.

   b Copy and complete this table :–

Pattern no.	1	2	3	4	5	6
Bricks needed	3	...	...	...	...	...

   c Describe carefully how the pattern is formed.

   d Use the description to find how many bricks are needed for pattern 10.

Chapter 16

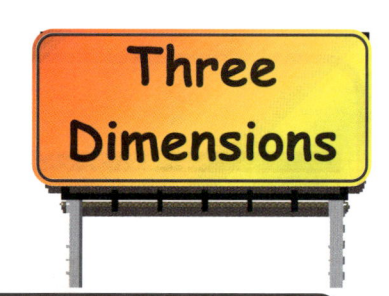

Three Dimensions

Squares, **Triangles**, **Circles** are examples of **2-Dimensional** (or 2-D) shapes.

They can be drawn on a flat surface like your jotter.

Cubes, **Cones**, **Spheres** are examples of **3-Dimensional** (or 3-D) shapes.

They are **SOLID** shapes and can only be **roughly** sketched on a flat surface.

Exercise 1

1. Name the following mathematical shapes :-

   a    b 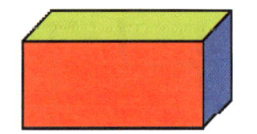   c 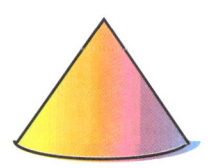   d

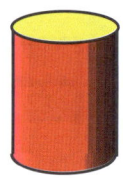

   e    f 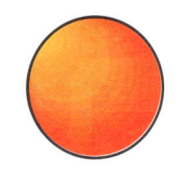   g

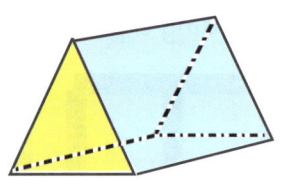

2. Name the following 3-dimensional (mathematical) shapes :-

   a    b    c    d (JUPITER)

   e    f    g    h

this is Chapter Sixteen   page 172   THREE DIMENSIONS

3. Look at this 3-dimensional shape — the **CUBE**.

   a   How many **faces** does it have ?

   b   What shape is each of its faces ?

   c   How many **vertices** (corners) does it have ?

   d   How many **edges** does it have ?

   e   Look at the edge, AB.
       Is the edge AB lying "**horizontal**" or "**vertical**" ?
       (find out what horizontal and vertical mean).

   f   DC is **parallel** to AB [runs in the same direction].

   (i)   Use 2 letters to name another side which is parallel to AB.
   (ii) Name a 4th side which is parallel to AB.

   g   Name 3 sides which are parallel to side BC.

   h   Name 3 sides which are parallel to side AP. (Is AP vertical or horizontal ?)

   i   Make a list of approximately 6 objects in school or at home that are cubes.

4. The **CUBOID**.

   a   How many **faces** does it have ?

   b   What shape is each face ?

   c   How many **vertices** does it have ?

   d   How many **edges** does it have ?

   e   Name 3 edges parallel to edge EF.

   f   Name 3 edges parallel to edge ER.

   g   Name the other set of 4 parallel edges.

   h   Make a list of approximately 6 objects in school or at home that are cuboids.

5. The **SQUARE BASED PYRAMID**.

   a   How many **faces** does it have ?

   b   Copy and complete :–

       "The shape has 1 face which is a s.............
       and 4 faces which are t...........".

   c   How many **vertices** does it have ?

   d   How many **edges** does it have ?

   e   Make a list of about 3 or 4 objects
       in school or elsewhere that are in the shape
       of square based pyramids.

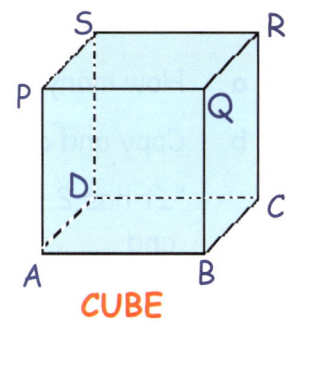

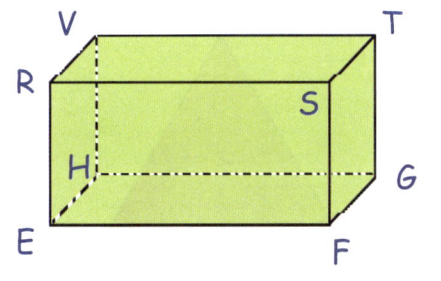

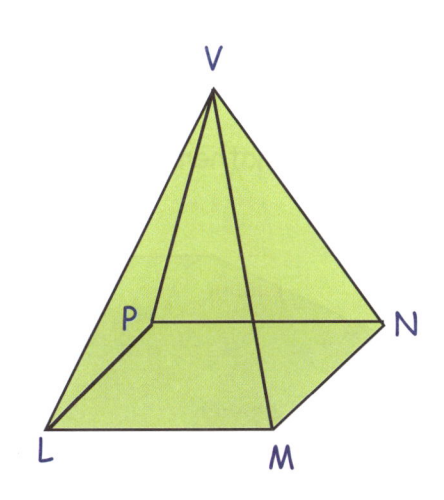

6. The **TRIANGULAR PRISM**.

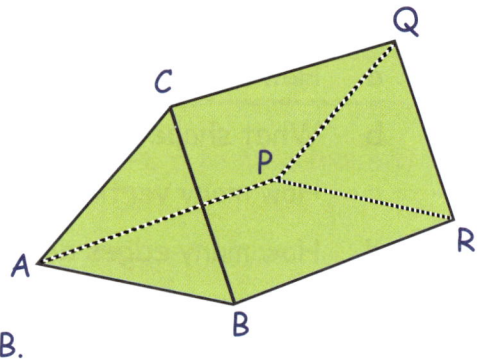

   a How many **faces** does it have ?

   b Copy and complete :-

   "It has 2 faces which are ....
   and .... faces which are ....".

   c How many vertices does it have ?

   d Name another edge (**use 2 letters**) parallel to AB.

   e Name 2 edges parallel to CQ.

   f How many edges does it have altogether ?

   g Make a list of about 2 or 3 objects in school or elsewhere that are in the shape of triangular prisms.

The **SPHERE** has only **one** face (or surface) and it is **curved**.

7. In a similar way, describe the faces (or surfaces) of :-

   a CONE

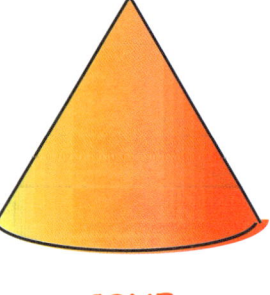

   b CYLINDER

8. Write down the special name for this shape ?

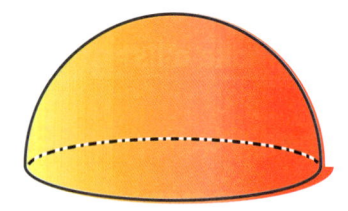

9. Which mathematical shapes can you see here :-

   a

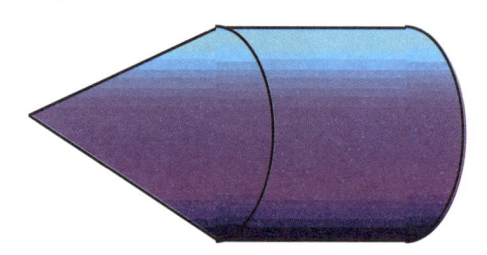

   b

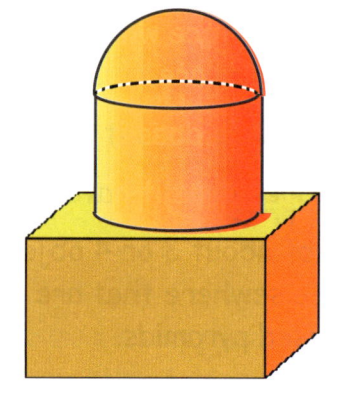

this is Chapter Sixteen   page 174   THREE DIMENSIONS

Some Practical Work — Making Skeletons

The **skeleton** of a 3-D Shape consists of the "**bones**" of the shape.

It is the "**wire frame**" that shows the outline of a shape.

Can you see that, to make the skeleton of this cuboid, we would need 12 straws?

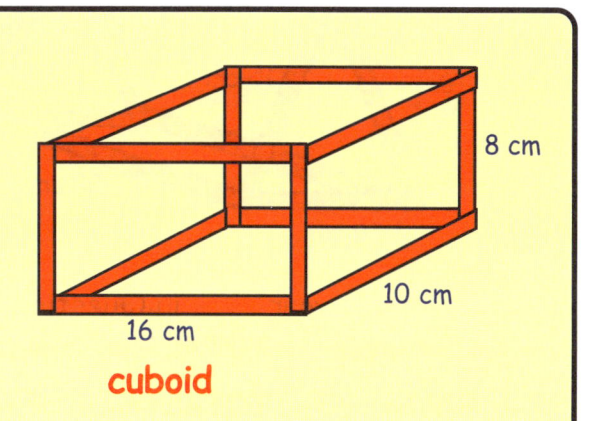

Four pieces measuring 16 cm.
Four pieces measuring 10 cm.
Four pieces measuring 8 cm.

Total length of straw = (4 × 16) + (4 × 10) + (4 × 8)
= 64 + 40 + 32
= 136 cm.

cuboid

Exercise 2

For this exercise, you are going to need lots of pieces of **A4 plain paper** rolled into tubes, **scissors** and **sellotape**. (*You may wish to work in groups*).

1. a Roll up some of your paper, sellotape them and cut them so you have :-

   four pieces of 16 cm, four pieces of 10 cm and four pieces each 8 cm.

   b Use sellotape or blue tack to join the corners. Display the **best** skeleton cuboids.

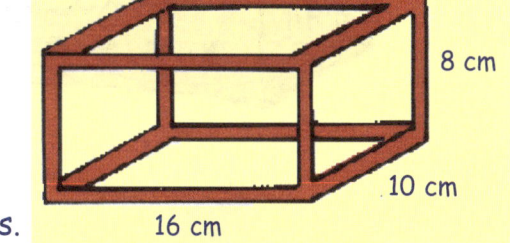

2. Make skeleton models of each of the following shapes as neatly as possible. (You may wish to work in groups – see your teacher).

   a Cube (10 cm)

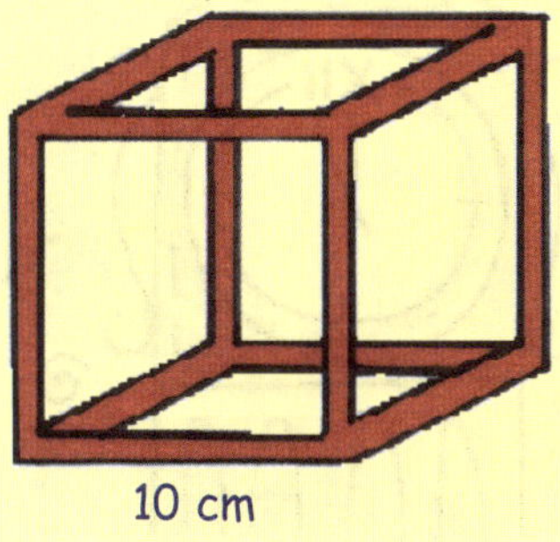

   b Square Based Pyramid (15 cm, 15 cm, 18 cm)

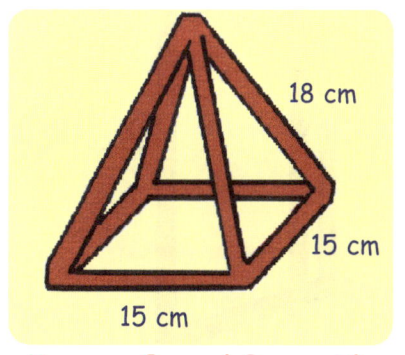

this is Chapter Sixteen   page 175   THREE DIMENSIONS

c

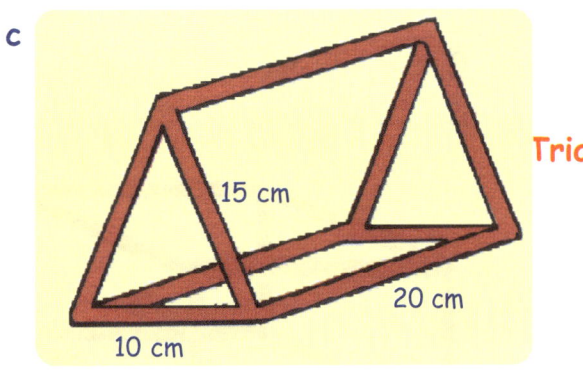

15 cm
10 cm
20 cm

Triangular Prism

3. **a** Look at your **cube** in Question 2a.
What is the **TOTAL** length of straw needed to make this cube?

   b What is the **TOTAL** length of straw needed to make the **square based pyramid** in Question 2b?

   c What is the **TOTAL** length of straw needed to make the **triangular prism** in Question 2c?

4. Use your straws to make this model barn-house.

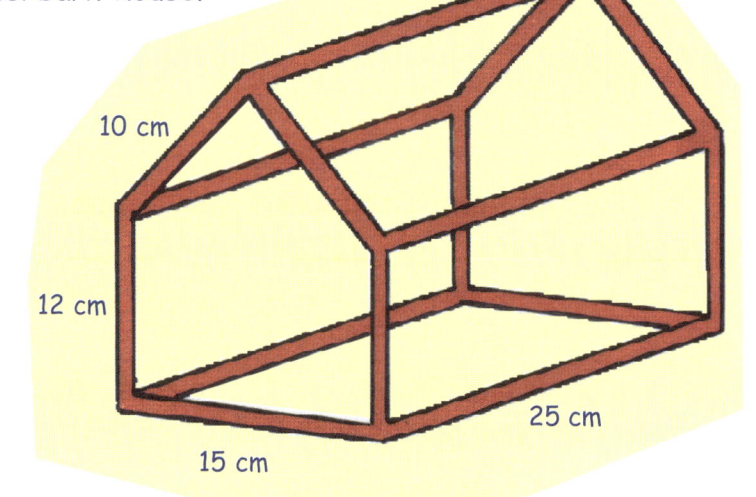

10 cm
12 cm
15 cm
25 cm

5. 15 cm   15 cm

Make a model of this clock tower.

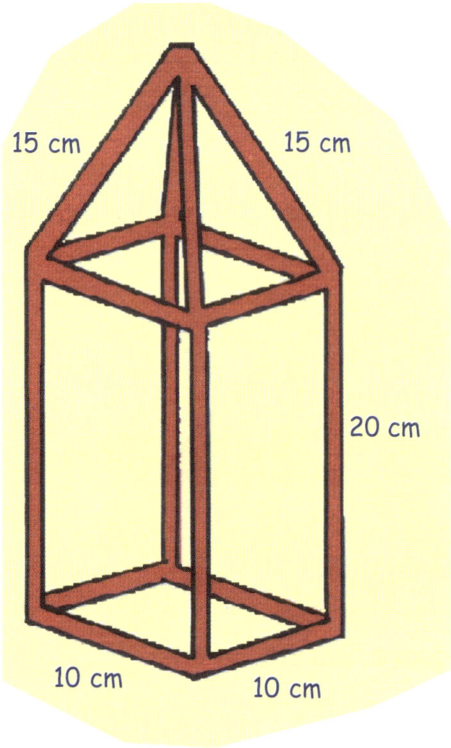

20 cm
10 cm   10 cm

this is Chapter Sixteen   page 176   THREE DIMENSIONS

Nets of Cubes and Cuboids

A cardboard box is made from a flat 2D-Shape which folds to make the box.

This is called the **NET** of the cuboid.

BOX

3 cm
4 cm
6 cm

NET

6 cm
4 cm
3 cm
3 cm
4 cm
3 cm
3 cm

Exercise 3

1. Shown opposite is the net of this box.

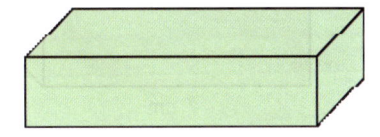

   Make a sketch of the box and fill in the dimensions (**length**, **breadth** and **height**) of the box using the net to help.

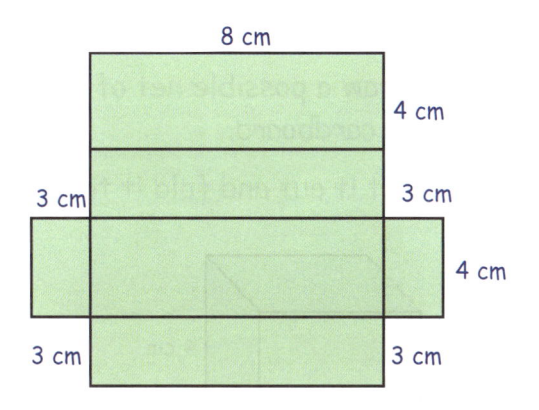

   8 cm
   4 cm
   3 cm
   3 cm
   4 cm
   3 cm
   3 cm

2. Make sketches of the boxes corresponding to these nets and fill in the dimensions :–

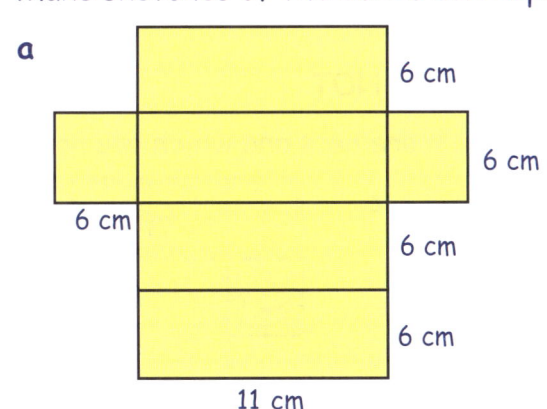

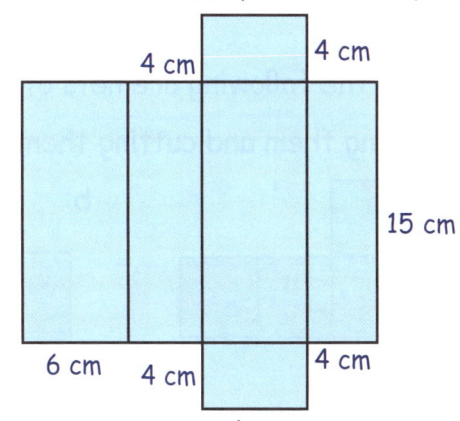

   a
   6 cm
   6 cm
   6 cm
   6 cm
   6 cm
   11 cm

   b
   4 cm   4 cm
   6 cm   4 cm   4 cm
   15 cm
   6 cm

3. **Part** of the net of this cuboid is shown opposite.

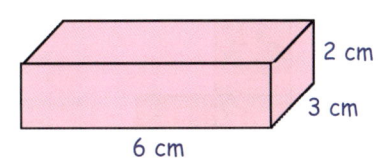

   6 cm
   2 cm
   3 cm

   2 cm 3 cm 2 cm
   6 cm

   a   Make a neat full size copy of this **NET**.
   b   Complete the net showing all the faces.

4. **Part** of the net of this cuboid is shown below.

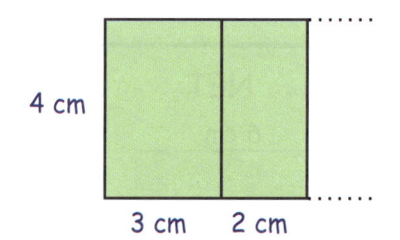

4 cm

3 cm   2 cm

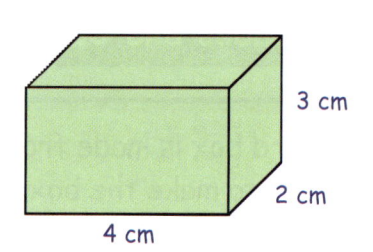

3 cm

2 cm

4 cm

Copy and complete the net showing all **6** faces.

5. Shown below are 2 faces of the net of a **cube**.

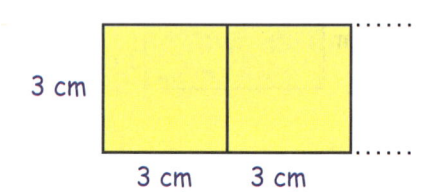

3 cm

3 cm   3 cm

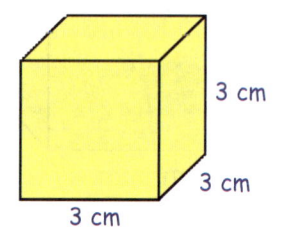

3 cm

3 cm

3 cm

Copy and complete the net of the cube.

6. **a** Draw a possible net of this **cuboid** on cardboard.

  b Cut it out and fold it to form the cuboid.

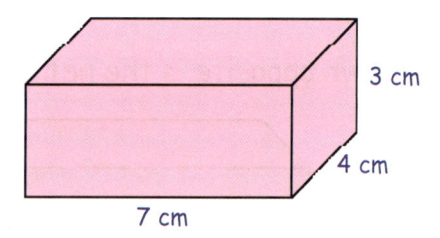

3 cm

4 cm

7 cm

7.

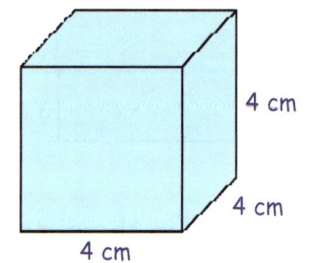

4 cm

4 cm

4 cm

Make a net of this **cube**, cut it out and **sellotape** it to make the cube.

8. Some of the following are nets of cubes, and some are **NOT**.

By drawing them and cutting them out, decide which are nets and which are not.

a

b

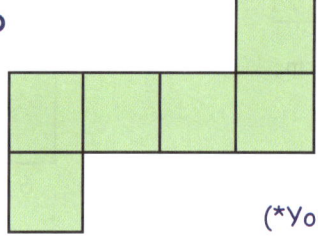

c

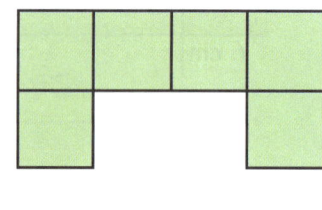

(*You may wish to make your nets larger)

d

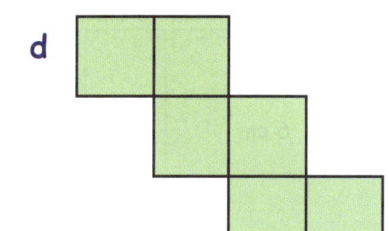

e

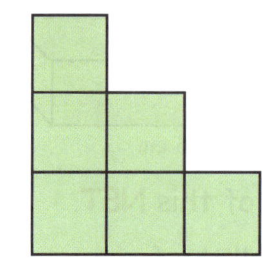

f

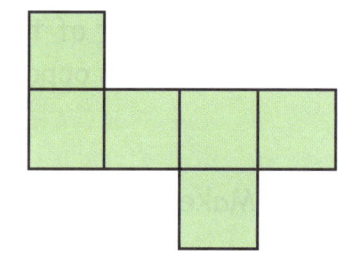

this is Chapter Sixteen   page 178   THREE DIMENSIONS

Topic in a Nutshell

1. Name the two 3-dimensional shapes in this figure.

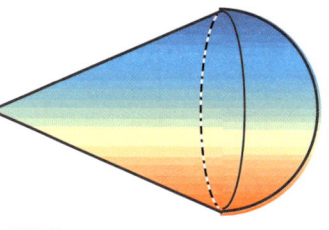

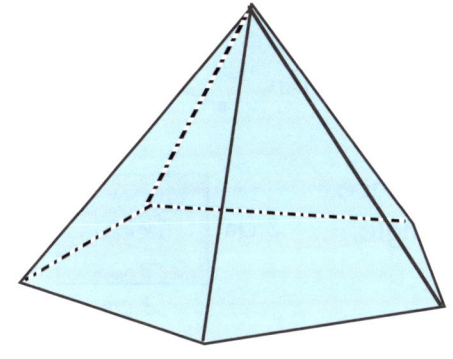

2. This shape is called a **PENTAGONAL** based **PYRAMID**.

   a How many vertices does it have?

   b How many edges does it have?

   c Copy and complete this sentence :-

   "The Pyramid consists of .... faces, one of them being a .... and the others are ....s".

3. This figure represents the **skeleton** of a small doll's house.

   a Name, using 2 letters, an edge running parallel to BC.

   b Name 3 edges the same size as RC.

   c Is the edge SD vertical, horizontal or neither?

   d Is the edge XP vertical, horizontal or neither?

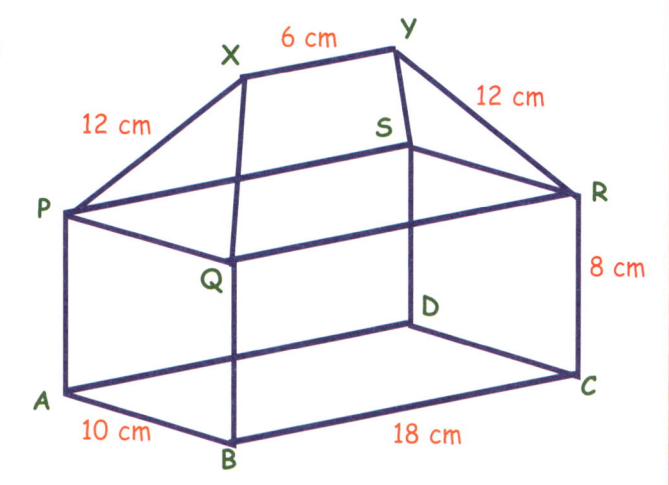

   e Calculate the **total** length of straws needed to make the skeleton.

4. Shown is the net of a cuboid.

   Sketch the cuboid below and fill in its length, breadth and height.

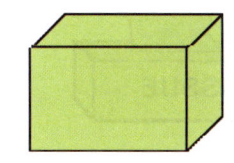

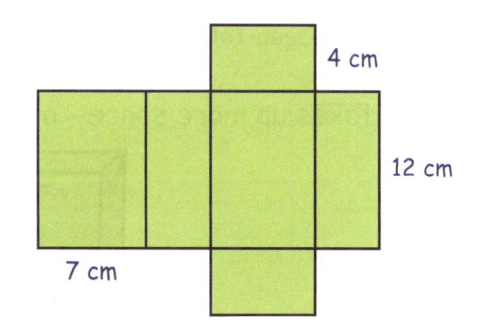

5. Draw an **accurate** net of this cuboid.

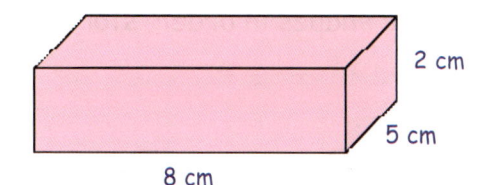

this is Chapter Sixteen   page 179   THREE DIMENSIONS

Chapter 17

Volume

What is "Volume"?

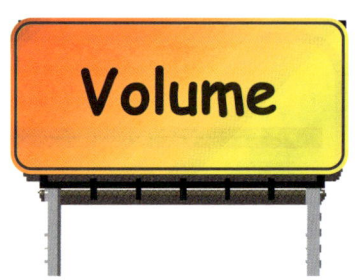

Length, Area and Volume

Length - is a direct measurement from one point to another.
It is often given in mm, cm, metres or km.

Area - is a measurement of a "covering" of a surface.
For example :- a rectangle, circle, triangle.
It is often given in mm², cm², m² or km².

Volume - is a measurement of the space enclosed by a shape.
For example :- a can, a box, a basin, ...
It is often given in mm³, cm³, m³, km³, millilitres or litres.

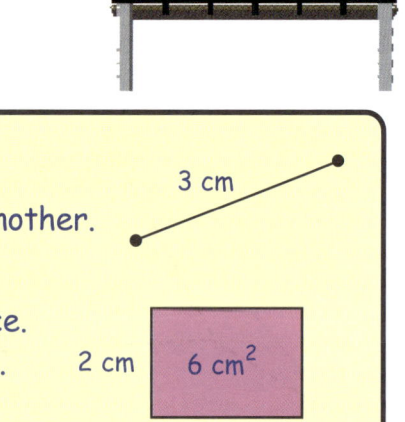

Exercise 1

1. Which of these holds more water when full?

    Bath    Wash-hand Basin

2. Put these shapes in order, starting with the one which holds the **least**.

    Deep-fat Frier    Egg Cup    Mug of Tea

3. Which takes up more space - a packet of breakfast cereal or a box of tissues?

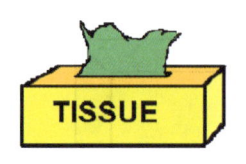

4. Put these shapes in order, starting with the one which takes up the **most** space.

    Truck    Motor Bike    Car 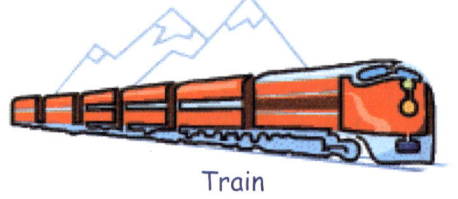   Train

5. Shown below is a recipe for fresh-creme strawberry scones for a party.

Party Surprise
Fresh-Creme Strawberry Scones

20 Strawberries
Half Cup Water
2 Heaped Tablespoons Butter
Cup Milk
4 Teaspoons Sugar
1 Teaspoon Salt
4 Cups Self-raising Flour

The above ingredients makes a batch of 20 scones.

Use the list of ingredients to answer the following questions :-

a How much sugar is used ?

b Which piece of cutlery is used to measure out the butter ?

c What does the recipe use **less** of - water or milk ?

d The amount shown above will make 20 scones.
If I only want to make 10 scones, how much flour will I need to use ?

e If I only had one teaspoonful of sugar left in the house but still wanted to make a few scones, according to the recipe - how many could I make ?

f One bottle of milk holds exactly four cupfuls.
What **fraction** of a bottle was used in the above recipe ?

6. Mick and Elsie make punch in a bowl for their Christmas party.
The bowl holds **30** glasses of punch.
At the party, guests drink **20** glasses of punch.

What **fraction** of the punch is left after the party ?

7. A large tin of condensed soup holds 6 ladlefuls.
4 ladlefuls of water also has to be added before the soup is made.

The Waddell family, consisting of Mr & Mrs Waddell and their 2 children, have a ladleful each on the Monday **and** on the Tuesday.

How much soup is left for Wednesday ?

8. David has to take 2 spoonfuls of cough mixture 4 times per day.
The cough bottle holds 40 spoonfuls of medicine.

How many days will the bottle last David ?

2 spoonfuls
4 times per day

this is Chapter Seventeen   page 181   VOLUME

Litres and Millilitres

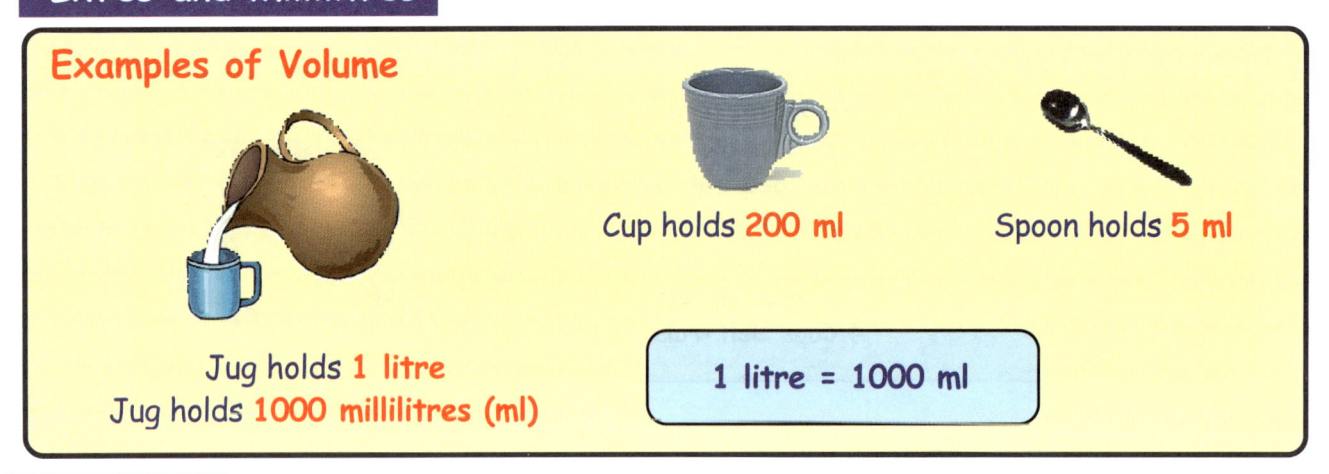

Examples of Volume

Jug holds **1 litre**
Jug holds **1000 millilitres (ml)**

Cup holds **200 ml**

Spoon holds **5 ml**

1 litre = 1000 ml

Exercise 2

1. a   Sadie's mum gives her 30 ml of medicine. 
        How many spoonfuls is this?
   b   An elephant gets an injection of 800 ml of medicine.
        How many cupfuls is this? 
   c   How many spoonfuls does one cup hold?
   d   How many cupfuls does the jug hold?
   e   Jeremy makes 4 jugs of lemonade. How many cups can he fill?

2. What is the volume of juice, in millilitres, in each bottle?

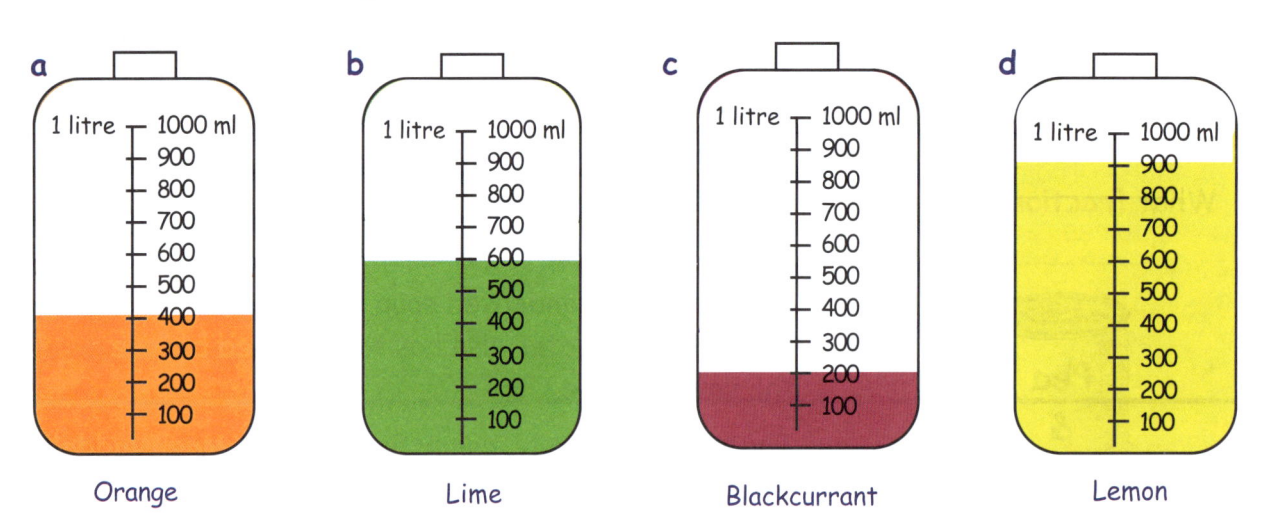

   a Orange
   b Lime
   c Blackcurrant
   d Lemon

3. a   Which bottles contain over **half** a litre?
   b   Which flavour has less than **one quarter** of a litre in its bottle?
   c   How many millilitres of lemon are needed to make it up to 1 litre?
   d   How much more lime is there than blackcurrant?

this is Chapter Seventeen   page 182   VOLUME

4. a   Look at this beaker with yellow bath salts. 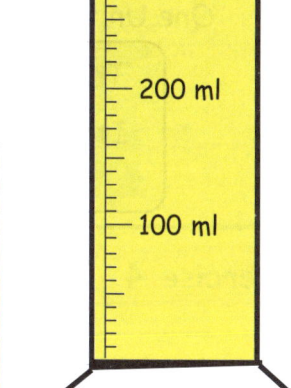 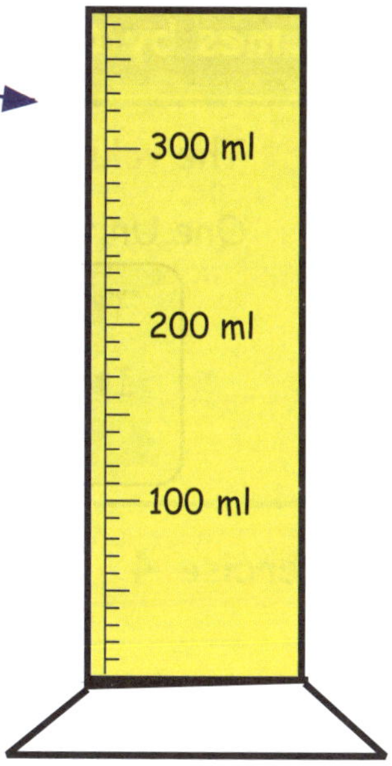

    (i) How many ml does each **small interval** represent ?

    (ii) How many ml of yellow bath salts are in the beaker ?

    b   Give the volume (in ml) of the three coloured bath salt containers shown below.

    (i) (ii) 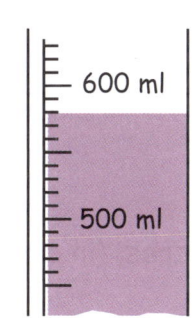 (iii)

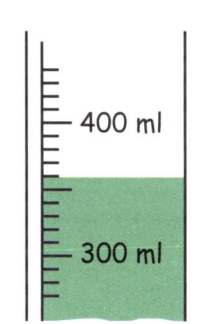

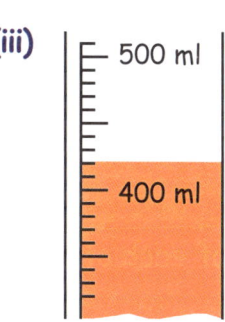

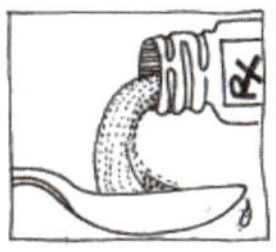

5. Write these volumes **to the nearest 100 ml** :-

    a   b 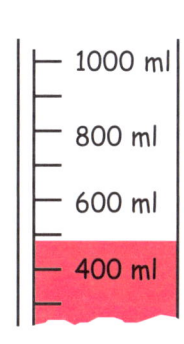   c 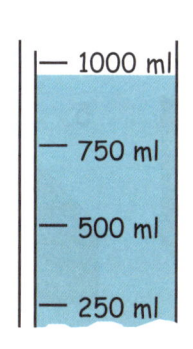   d

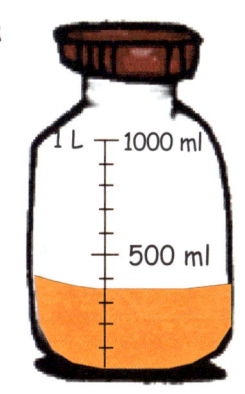

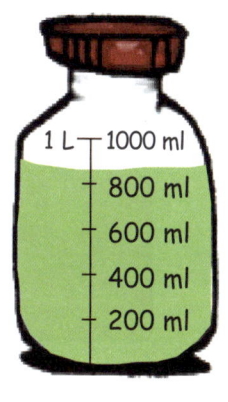

Litres and Millilitres.

To change from one to the other we **multiply** or **divide** by **1000**.

litres —> (× 1000) —> millilitres   millilitres —> (÷ 1000) —> litres

Examples :-

5·5 l —> (× 1000) = 5500 ml   2750 ml —> (÷ 1000) = 2·75 l

Exercise 3

1. Change the following number of litres to millilitres :-

    a 3 litres   b 9 litres   c 15 litres   d 20 litres

    e 1·5 litres   f 6·8 litres   g 7·4 litres   h 5·25 litres

2. Change from millilitres to litres :-

    a 4000 ml   b 7000 ml   c 12 000 ml   d 25 000 ml

    e 7500 ml   f 8200 ml   g 40 000 ml   h 2850 ml

this is Chapter Seventeen   page 183   VOLUME

Volumes by Counting Cubes

The **volume** of a solid is simply the "**amount of space**" it takes up.

One Unit of volume is the "**cubic centimetre**".

The small cube shown measures 1 cm by 1 cm by 1 cm.
It has a volume of **1 cubic centimetre**.
or for short :- 1 cm^3

$1 \text{ cm}^3 \rightarrow$ (1 cm by 1 cm by 1 cm)

Exercise 4

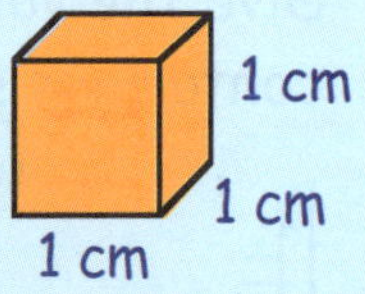

State the volume of each of the following shapes, (in cm^3).

1. 
2. 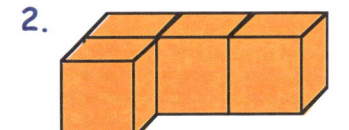
3. 
4. 
5. 
6. 
7. 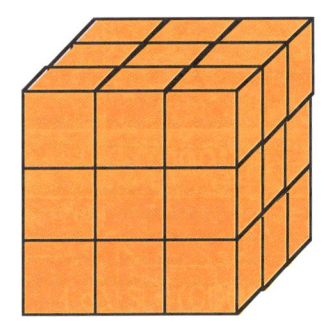
8. 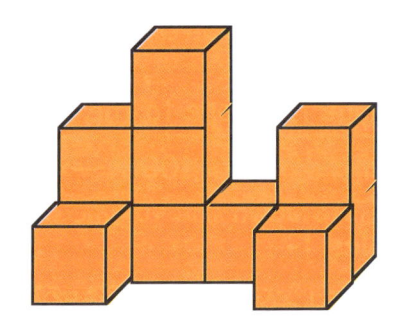
9. 
10.

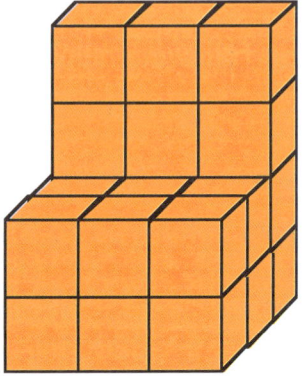

this is Chapter Seventeen   page 184   VOLUME

Topic in a Nutshell

1. Put these shapes in order, starting with the one which has the least volume.

   a Tent   b Champions Trophy   c Sauce Bottle

2. Baby has to have 2 spoonfuls of syrup mixture 5 times per day.

   The bottle holds 140 spoonfuls of syrup.

   How many **weeks** will the bottle last Baby ?

3. A bottle holds 750 ml of liquid, a mug holds 150 ml and a spoon holds only 3 ml.

   a John's mum gives him 15 ml of cod liver oil.
      How many spoonfuls is this ?

   b How many spoonfuls does the mug hold ?

   c How many mugfuls does the bottle hold ?

   d Jeremy makes 3 bottles of limeade. How many cups can he fill ?

4. What is the volume of liquid, (in millilitres), in this bottle of anti-freeze ?

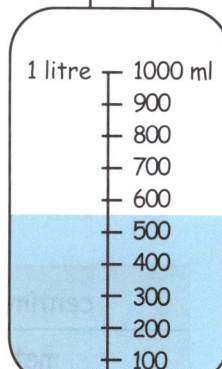

5. Write down the volume of each shape, in cm^3.

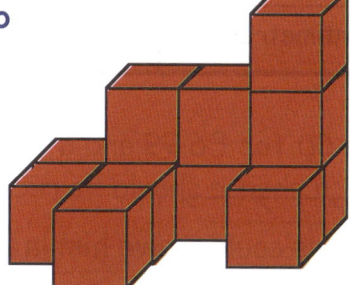

   a   b

6. Change,

   a to millilitres :-   (i) 7 litres   (ii) 27 litres   (iii) 3·5 litres.

   b to litres :-   (i) 6000 ml   (ii) 80 000 ml   (iii) 500 ml.

Chapter 18

Revision

This set of questions revises every topic of Level D.

1. Put in order, **largest first** :-

    20 105, 19 000, 20 009, 19 780, 21 000, 19 099.

2. Write the following **in figures** :-

    a   twenty one thousand and sixty.   b   sixty five thousand four hundred.

3. Write the following **in words** :-

    a   24 080   b   80 302   c   7005   d   89 057.

4. What does the **8** in the number 48 076 represent ?

5. a   What is the number that is 200 **up from** 78 900 ?

    b   What number is 1000 **down from** 140 000 ?

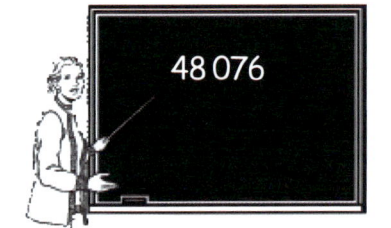

6. Find the missing values here :-

    a $\frac{4}{5} = \frac{?}{30}$ b $\frac{24}{32} = \frac{?}{4}$ c $\frac{14}{20} = \frac{?}{30}$.

7. Write down $11 + \frac{7}{10} + \frac{2}{100}$ as a decimal.

8. Change the following to decimals :-   a   37%   b   82%   c   7%.

9. Copy this table and complete it :-

centimetres	513 cm	.....	.....
metres	.....	4·2 m	.....
metres & centimetres	.....	.....	6 m 9 cm

10. a   I sold a CD for £6·99 and a video for £11·29 to a customer. How much change should he receive from £20 ?

    b   What coins could I give him in his change ?

11. Do the following (**mentally**) :-

    a   64 + 36   b   97 – 35   c   58 + 68   d   91 – 77

    e   320 + 540   f   770 – 330   g   67 + 99   h   330 – 190.

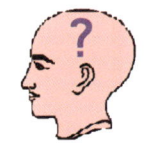

12. Do the following (set down and show your working) :-

    a   5749 + 678

    b   48·78 − 26·92

    c   6000 − 251

    d   10 − 6·72.

13. Do the following (**mentally**) :-

    a   15 × 8
    b   75 ÷ 3
    c   360 ÷ 6
    d   420 × 3.

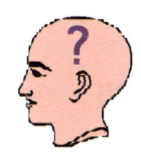

14. Do the following (**mentally**) :-

    a   37 × 10
    b   100 × 520
    c   603 × 100
    d   10 × 0·81

    e   43·7 ÷ 10
    f   100 × 0·032
    g   970 ÷ 100
    h   5·9 × 100.

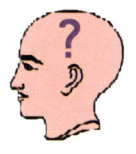

15. Find the following (set down and show your working) :-

    a   6·03 × 7
    b   21·35 × 9
    c   37·28 ÷ 8
    d   1·19 ÷ 7.

16. Round to the nearest **10** :-

    a   83
    b   699
    c   6045
    d   23·74.

17. Round to the nearest **100** :-

    a   648
    b   3663
    c   23 677
    d   9978.

18. Do the following, (**no calculator**) :-

    a $\frac{1}{6}$ of 42
    b $\frac{1}{3}$ of 180
    c $\frac{1}{8}$ of 2400
    d $\frac{1}{10}$ of 9500.

19. Do the following, (**no calculator**) :-

    a $\frac{2}{3}$ of 60
    b $\frac{3}{5}$ of 150
    c $\frac{5}{8}$ of 4000
    d $\frac{5}{6}$ of 120.

20. **Remember** – 30% means $\frac{30}{100}$. Find the following :-

    a   30% of 2000
    b   20% of 700
    c   40% of 6000
    d   70% of 200.

21. What are the **next three terms** in each of the following sequences of numbers ?

    a   1, 3, 5, 7, ...
    b   9, 12, 15, 18, ...
    c   800, 400, 200, ...

    d   3, 6, 12, 24, ...
    e   7, 10, 13, 16, ...
    f   70, 66, 62, 58, ...

22. Can you see the pattern here ?

    2, 4, 6, 10, 16, 26, 42, 68, ..., ..., ..., ...

Find the next **four** terms.

23. If you know the length and the breadth of a rectangle, describe "in words" what you do to calculate its **perimeter**.

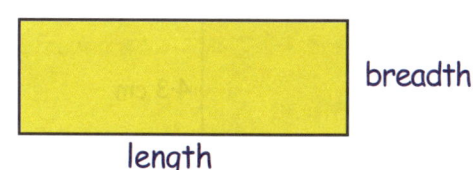

24. **a** Measure this line in **millimetres**.

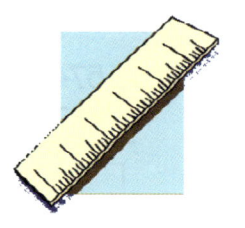

b Write its length in **two** other ways.

25. Say which of the following is the best **approximation** :– 
- **a** an apple's weight – {5 g, 100 g, 750 g, 2 kg}
- **b** height of a door. – {60 cm, 120 cm, 200 cm, 4·1 m}
- **c** volume of water in a teaspoon. – {5 ml, 50 ml, 200 ml, 1·5 litres}

26. Change the following 24 hour times into **am/pm** form :–
- **a** 0735
- **b** 1350
- **c** 2058
- **d** 0045

27. Change these times to **24 hour** format :–
- **a** 4·55 am
- **b** 10 to 6 at night
- **c** 20 to midnight
- **d** 3·20 in the afternoon
- **e** $\frac{1}{4}$ past midnight
- **f** 12·45 pm

28. **a** A city bus tour begins at 11·30 am and lasts for 1 hour 40 minutes.

At what time will the tour finish ?

b An astronomy lecture began at 7·45 pm and finished at 10·05 pm.

For how long did the lecture last ?

29. Calculate the perimeter of the following shapes :–

a square, 11·5 cm

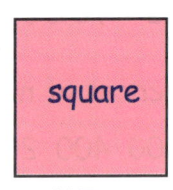

b 15 cm, 35 cm

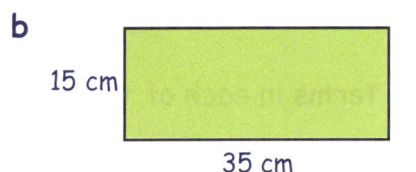

c 6·2 cm, 8·8 cm

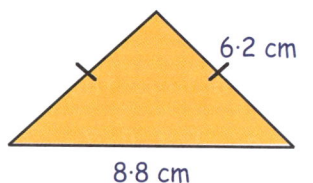

d 4·3 cm, 4·3 cm, 4·3 cm

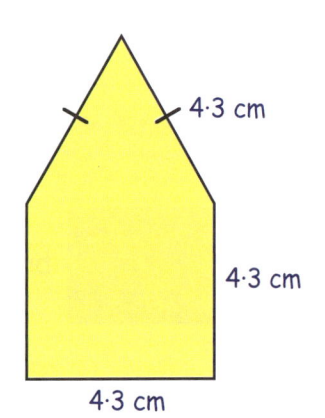

e 3 cm, 11 cm, 15 cm, 6 cm, 4 cm, 9 cm

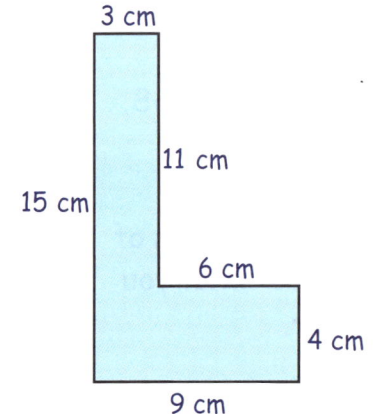

f 12 cm, 5 cm, 3 cm, 7 cm   * (hard)

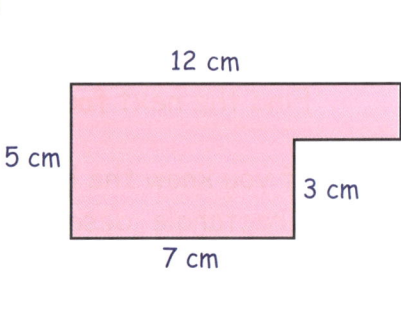

this is Chapter Eighteen   page 188   REVISION

30. Each box in the following figures represents 1 square centimetre (1 cm²).
Write down the area of each shape (**in cm²**).

a 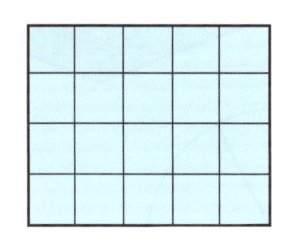   b 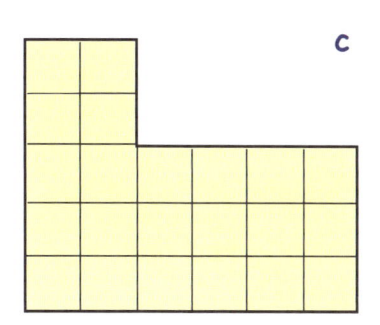   c

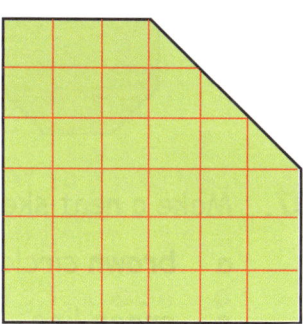

31. a Draw this right angled triangle accurately on squared paper. (*Each box is 1 cm by 1 cm*).

b Calculate the area of the surrounding **rectangle**.

c Write down the area of the **right angled triangle**.

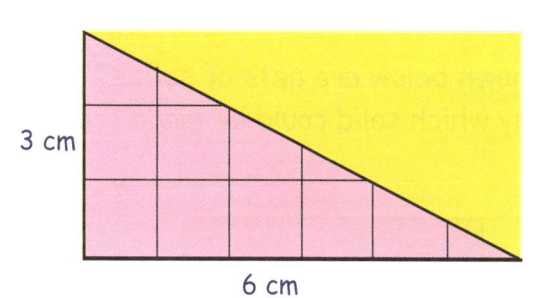

3 cm

6 cm

32. Calculate the area of each of the following right angled triangles.
(*You may like to draw them first*).

a 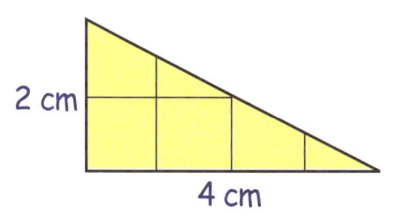   2 cm   4 cm

b   5 cm   4 cm

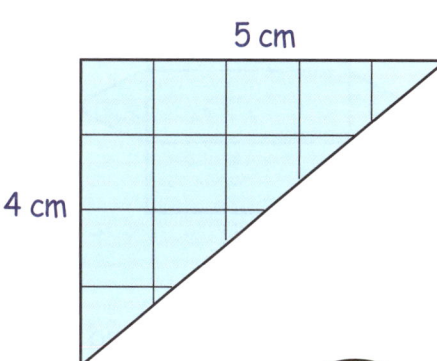

33. Name the following shapes :-

a   b 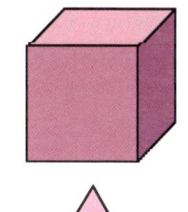   c

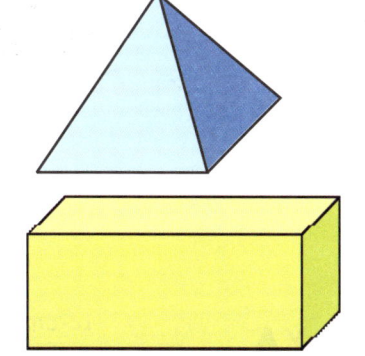

d   e 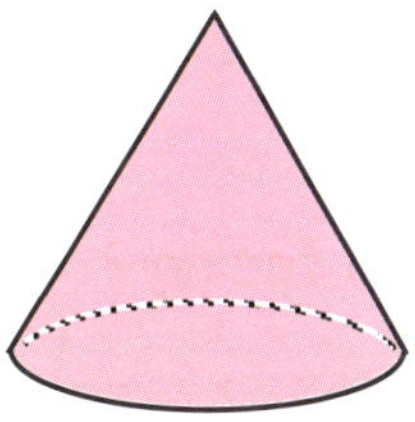   f

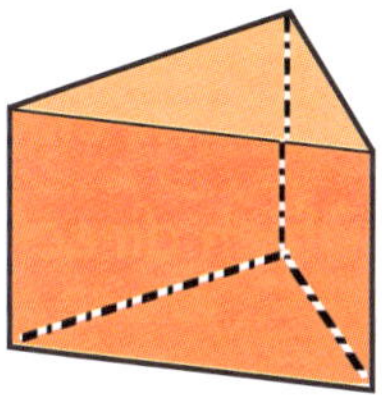

34. How many **edges** has a :-

a cuboid   b square based pyramid   c triangular prism ?

35. How many **vertices** has a :-

a cuboid   b triangular prism   c square based pyramid ?

this is Chapter Eighteen   page 189   REVISION

36. Name the following shapes :–

a 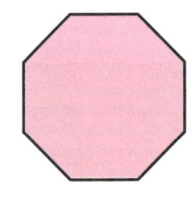   b 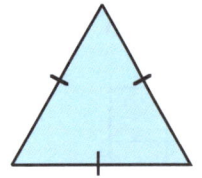   c

37. Make a neat sketch of this circle. Name the :–

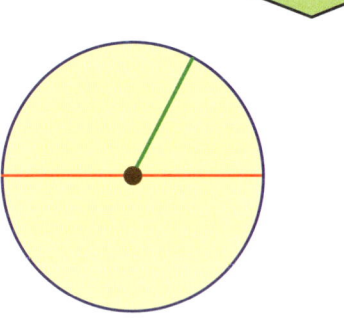

a **brown** circle   b **red** line

c **green** line   d **blue** line.

38. Shown below are nets of solids.
Say which solid could be made from each :–

a 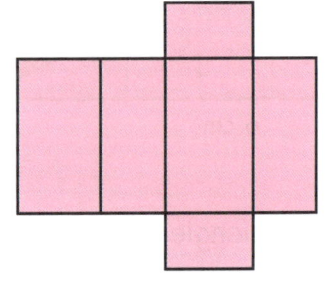   b 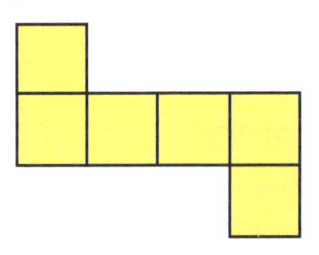   c

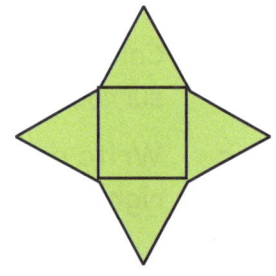

d 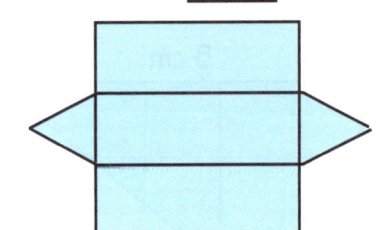   e

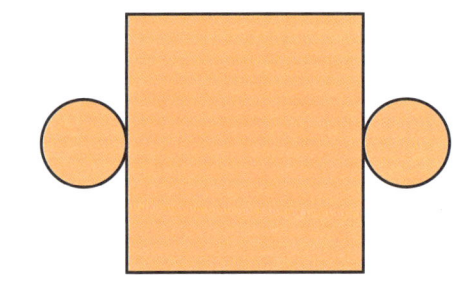

39. Copy this compass rose and fill in the other **6** directions.

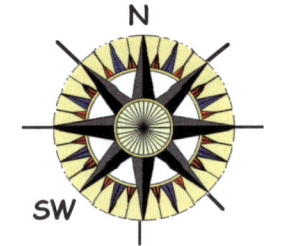

40. A scout was walking South West. He then turned through an angle of 90° anti-clockwise.

In which direction was he then facing ?

41. Write down the coordinates of the three points, P, Q and R in the coordinate diagram shown opposite.

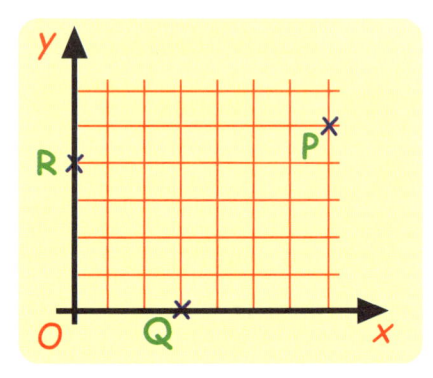

42. How many lines of symmetry do the following shapes have?

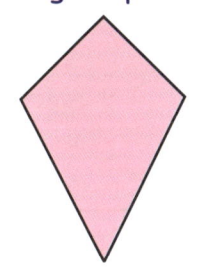

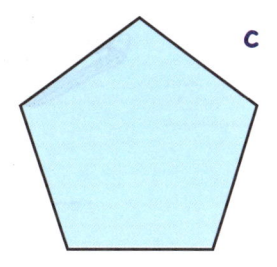

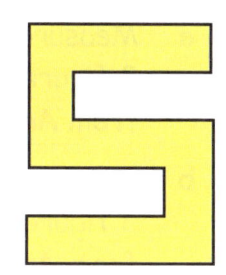

a   b   c   d

43. Copy this figure carefully onto squared paper.

Complete the figure such that the green line is a line of symmetry.

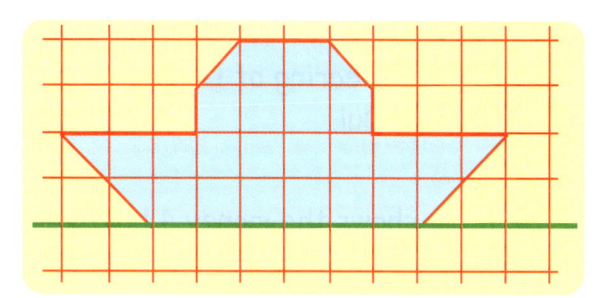

44. Copy this figure carefully and find the other half such that the red line is a line of symmetry.

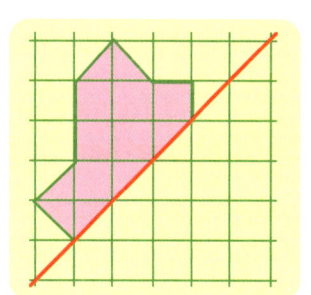

45. Use a **protractor** to measure the following two angles :-

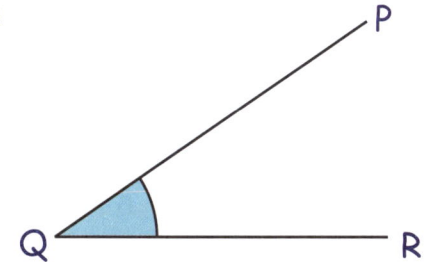

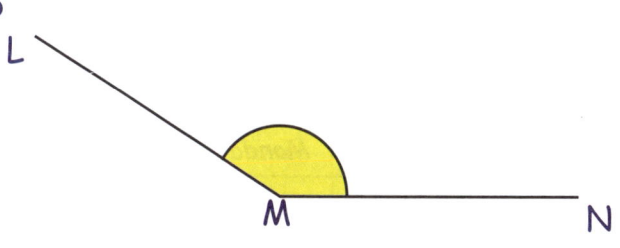

a   b

46. What **type** of angle is each of the following (acute, obtuse, ...)

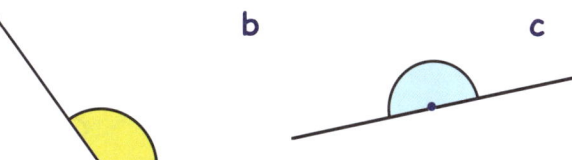

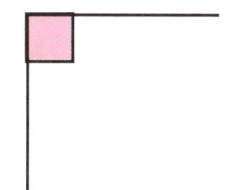

a   b   c   d

47. a   Draw a line PQ = 8 centimetres.

  b   Use a protractor to show –RPQ = 65°.

48. Use a protractor to draw the following angles. (Label them with the given letters).

  a   –ATG = 47°   b   –REN = 136°.

this is Chapter Eighteen   page 191   REVISION

49. Shown are a group of islands, **Ardlui**, **Bromley**, **Cruiker** and **Dopley**.

   a   Measure and write down the 3 figure bearing of **Bromley** from **Ardlui**.

   b   Measure and write down the 3 figure bearing of **Cruiker** from **Ardlui**.

   c   Measure and write down the 3 figure bearing of **Dopley** from **Ardlui**.

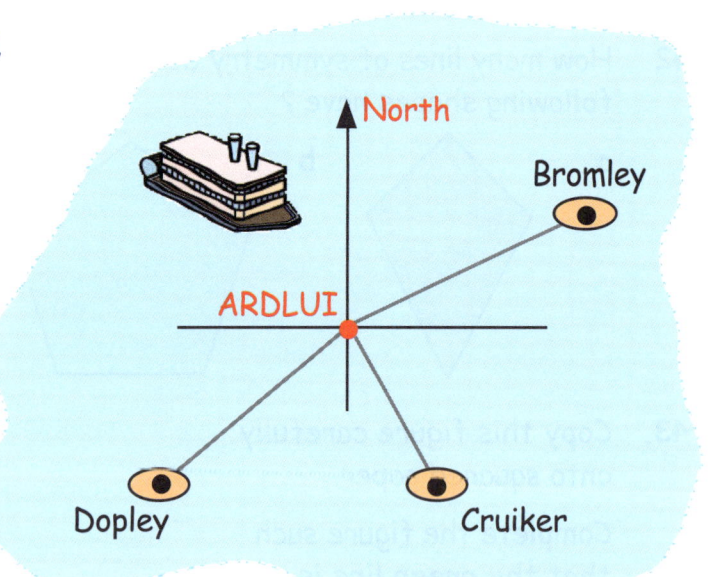

50. The table shows the money 4 boys earned by picking potatoes for Farmer Giles.

   a   How much did Terry earn on the Thursday?

   b   How much did farmer Giles pay the boys **altogether** on Tuesday?

   c   One boy hurt his back and had to rest for a day. Which boy and on which day?

   d   Who earned the most money for his week's work?

Name	Mon	Tue	Wed	Thu	Fri
Billy	£8	£7	£10	£3	£12
Sean	£14	£6	–	£3	£9
Terry	£6	£6	£6	£5	£9
Alex	£14	£11	£7	£4	£2

51. A group of children were asked which day of the week they were born on. The results of the survey are shown below.

Sunday	Monday	Tuesday	Wed'day	Thursday	Friday	Saturday
20	13	17	10	15	8	5

Draw a neat labelled **bar graph** to represent the above results.

52. The **pie chart** shows which radio station a group of 12 year old pupils listened to most often.

   a   What **fraction** of the 12 year olds listened to Beat 106?

   b   If 200 of the 12 year old pupils took part in the survey, **how many** of them listened to :-

   (i)   Clyde 1?   (ii)   Classic FM?

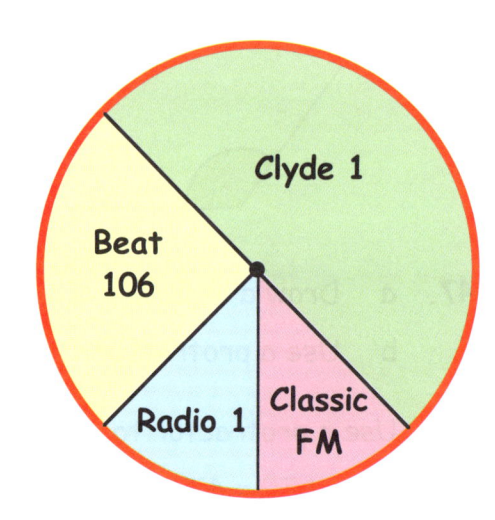

answers to LEVEL D

Answers to Chapter 0

1. a. six thousand eight hundred and twenty
   b. nine thousand and eighty two
   c. five thousand and seven
   d. nine thousand eight hundred and ninety eight
2. a. 7265   b. 9807   c. 6050
3. 6100, 6010, 6001, 5995, 5989, 5898, 5099
4. a. tens   b. hundreds
   c. thousands   d. units
5. a. 6420   b. 4950
6. $\frac{1}{2} = \frac{2}{4}$
7. a. $\frac{6}{8}$ b. $\frac{4}{5}$ c. $\frac{2}{3}$
8. 3·27
9. £16·80
10. a. £4·18   b. £6·08
11. a. £2·57   b. 4 coins
    c. £2, 50p, 5p, 2p
12. a. 14   b. 43   c. 107   d. 148
    e. 280   f. 410   g. 16   h. 45
    i. 123   j. 330   k. 360   l. 830
13. a. 461   b. 442   c. 552   d. 634
14. a. 21   b. 32   c. 42   d. 18
    e. 36   f. 72   g. 56   h. 48
    i. 35   j. 63   k. 54   l. 70
15. a. 70   b. 90   c. 180   d. 710
    e. 1200 f. 3170 g. 5000 h. 7090
16. a. 85   b. 196   c. 552   d. 312
17. a. 60   b. 290   c. 790   d. 500
    e. 80   f. 120   g. 170   h. 40
18. 330 + 150 = 480
19. a. 21   b. 8   c. 15   d. 32
20. a. 15,18,21   b. 25,30,35   c. 32,24,16
    d. 19,23,27   e. 32,38,44   f. 38,35,32
21. a. 6   b. 15   c. 7   d. − 6
22. a. 1000 b. 3000 c. 250   d. 1500
23. 1·75 1 ($1\frac{3}{4}$)
24. a. 15 cm²   b. 10 cm²
25. 2 m
26. 10 cm
27. a. 9   b. 32   c. 35   d. 260
28. a. 25 to 4 in the morning
    b. 20 to 9 at night
    c. quarter to 1 in the morning
29. a. 2 hrs   b. 20 mins   c. 30 mins   d. 45 mins
30. a. 15.01.68   b. 22.11.99   c. 07.08.02
31. a 5th July   b. 26th November
32. a. cube   b. cuboid   c. cone
    d. (square based) pyramid
    e. cylinder   f. sphere
33. a. square   b. triangle
    c. circle   d. rectangle
34. See diagram
35. Turn right outside the bank, take 3rd left then 2nd right and it is at the end of the road
36. a.   b.   c.
37. a.   b.
38. 90°
39. a. obtuse   b. right   c. acute
40. 130°
41.

Fruit	Tally	Number
apple	++++ I	6
orange	++++	5
banana	++++ IIII	9
pear	III	3
grapes	II	2
		25

42. a. 2   b. 4   c. 1·57 m
    d. brown hair, blue eyes, 1·38 m tall
43. see bar graph

Answers to Chapter 1

Ex 1
1. a. thousands   b. hundreds
   c. tens   d. units
2. a. thousands   b. tens
   c. units   d. hundreds
3. a. three thousand eight hundred and seventy
   b. nine thousand and fifty one
   c. twelve thousand and forty five
   d. twenty thousand and forty
   e. one hundred and twenty thousand four hundred and twenty seven
   f. eight hundred thousand three hundred and fifty
   g. seven hundred and two thousand and fifty
   h. nine hundred and nine thousand and ninety
4. a. 910   b. 20,050   c. 60,006
   d. 100,001 e. 909,000   f. 111,011
   g. 1,000,000
5. a. 399,401,406,451,460,499,501,510,603
   b. 7999,8045,8054,8100,8109,8199,8200,9001
6. a. 770   b. 1080   c. 880   d. 5090
   e. 999   f. 7700   g. 8000   h. 1250
   i. 1200   j. 4330   k. 3100   l. 6100
7. A = 67   B = 89   C = 102   D = 18
   E = 32   F = 120   G = 230   H = 400
   I = 520 J = 3500 K = 4750 L = 3000
   M = 9000 N = 7000 O = 11500 P = 8550
   Q = 8625 R = 5400 S = 6300 T = 345
   U = 357 V = 372   W = 1530 X = 1610
   Z = 1690
8. a. 28°C   b. 15°C   c. 72°C   d. 80°C
9. A = 850 B = 990   C = 1120 D = 9250
   E = 9550 F = 1000 G = 1250 H = 4500
   I = 7500 J = 4480 K = 4660 L = 350
   M = 374 N = 404   O = 4300 P = 5000
   Q = 5900
10. a. 145   b. 1300   c. 5400   d. 2100
    e. 4800 f. 6090
11. a. 1350 b. 200
12. 8900 km
13. £500,000

Ex 2
1. a. 93   b. 111   c. 64   d. 95
   e. 120   f. 133   g. 202   h. 139
   i. 450   j. 910   k. 900   l. 1710
   m. 7700 n. 5000 o. 5600 p. 9400
2. a. 13   b. 25   c. 19   d. 13
   e. 35   f. 19   g. 63   h. 151
   i. 70   j. 270   k. 180   l. 130
   m. 1250 n. 2600 o. 2800 p. 7100
3. a. 1220 b. 1140 c. 7250 d. 2730
   e. 8900 f. 8800 g. 5100 h. 7110
4. a. 131   b. £233   c. i) £1750   ii) £170
   d. 1200 e. £610   f. 1800
   g. i) 5590   ii) 690

Ex 3
1. a. 539   b. 826   c. 762   d. 1110
   e. 660   f. 6687 g. 7023 h. 886
   i. 237   j. 9110 k. 4499 l. 2791
   m. 6851 n. 9011 o. 1898 p. 5704
   q. 7101 r. 2109 s. 9912 t. 2109
2. a. i) 8358   ii) 386   b. 1017   c. £7880
   d. 1232   e. £4100   f. 2524

Puzzle 1 :   a. 6 7 2   b. 8 1 6
                   1 5 9   3 5 7
                   8 3 4   4 9 2

Puzzle 2 :   Fill 4 litre jug and pour all into 5 litre jug.
                Fill 4 litre jug again and pour into 5 litre jug until 5 litre jug is full.
                This leaves 3 litres in 4 litre jug.

Ex 4
1. a. 220   b. 120   c. 170   d. 340
   e. 1760 f. 4060 g. 7550 h. 1300
   i. 4500 j. 1010 k. 1400 l. 14720
   m. 15070 n. 23000 o. 45000 p. 60000
2. a. 2300 b. 7600 c. 13700 d. 14000
   e. 29000 f. 70600 g. 30900 h. 34000
   i. 70000 j. 45000 k. 501000 l. 800000

3. a. 17000 b. 21000   c. 3600   d. 31000
   e. 8000   f. 450000 g. 10000 h. 200000
4. a. 1600   b. 4000   c. 16500 d. 80000
5. a. 300   b. 7200   c. 10700 d. 20000
6. a. 70   b. 500   c. 3010   d. 70000

Ex 5
1. a. 24   b. 92   c. 77   d. 321
   e. 140   f. 380   g. 400   h. 220
   i. 6000 j. 9900 k. 1000 l. 10550
   m. 8850 n. 6500 o. 7000 p. 12000
2. a. 4   b. 25   c. 71   d. 390
   e. 900   f. 355   g. 2050 h. 10000
3. a. 70   b. 200   c. 540   d. 350
   e. 35   f. 100   g. 10   h. 1
4. a. 7   b. 90   c. 120   d. 1000
5. a. 70   b. 120   c. 1600 d. 10000
6. a. 7   b. 6000 c. 5   d. 80

Puzzle 3 :   1,000,000 mm
Puzzle 4 :   a. 17   b. 3
Puzzle 5 :   105 km WEST

Ex 6
1. a. 102   b. 108   c. 441   d. 176
   e. 1008 f. 1470 g. 1040 h. 1728
   i. 5008 j. 25333 k. 72036 l. 73104
2. a. 536   b. 588   c. 558   d. 145
   e. 984   f. 1554 g. 5672 h. 2958
   i. 9848 j. 11110 k. 13769 l. 81603
3. a. £144 b. £144 c. 540   d. 1302
   e. i) 768   ii) 2304
   f. i) 340   ii) 552   iii) 1806

Ex 7
1. a. 5   b. 185   c. 124   d. 65
   e. 1081 f. 2252 g. 1252 h. 996
2. a. 12   b. 236   c. 155   d. 89
   e. 104   f. 1263 g. 2177 h. 2187
   i. 133   j. 1207 k. 607   l. 689
   m. 1134 n. 317   o. 988   p. 1258
3. a. 78   b. 423   c. £379 d. 129
   e. i) 337   ii) 1014
4. a. 1   b. 4   c. 2   d. 3
   e. 1   f. 3   g. 6   h. 4
   i. 4   j. 3   k. 3   l. 1
5. a. 16   b. 7
6. a. 104   b. 3   c. 520

Ex 8
1. a. 420   b. 930   c. 480   d. 1920
   e. 500   f. 3090 g. 3000 h. 2400
   i. 5600 j. 6090 k. 12260 l. 36900
2. a. 13640 b. 43380 c. 45810 d. 19460
   e. 14400 f. 64610 g. 9960 h. 25280
   i. 25020
3. a. 50800   b. 80700   c. 83200
   d. 418000   e. 369000   f. 521400
   g. 648900   h. 789600   i. 510300
   j. 899100

Ex 9
1. a. 80   b. 30   c. 90   d. 60
   e. 10   f. 210   g. 370   h. 780
   i. 20   j. 410   k. 850   l. 600
   m. 1870 n. 2610 o. 8730 p. 4000
2. a. 600   b. 1000 c. 400   d. 300
   e. 300   f. 500   g. 1600 h. 3100
   i. 8800 j. 6500 k. 6100 l. 9000
   m. 12200 n. 16900 o. 19900 p. 10000
3. a. 8750 b. 8800
4. a. 9960 b. 10000
5. a. 29950 b. 30000

Ex 10
1. a. 60   b. 80   c. 70   d. 90
   e. 110   f. 130   g. 150   h. 150
   i. 140   j. 230   k. 240   l. 360
   m. 670   n. 440   o. 700   p. 900
2. a. 290   b. £500   c. 180 cm
3. a. 40   b. 60   c. 200   d. 300
   e. 400   f. 300   g. 100   h. 740
4. a. 100   b. 800   c. 960   d. 1100
   e. 90   f. 630   g. 3000 h. 30000

Ex 11
1. a. 211   b. 394   c. 669   d. 1411
   e. 5716 f. 5832 g. 14137 h. 8746
   i. 68   j. 53   k. 2410 l. 1869

m. 1246   n. 1677   o. 26928   p. 18096
q. 103   r. 136   s. 607   t. 640

2. a. 474 km   b. 351 m   c. £37
   d. 5820 m   e. 1068 g   f. £378
   g. i) 109 cm   ii) 8066 cm²

Answers to Chapter 2

Ex 1
1. Check shapes
2. Check shapes
3. a. b. c. d. (none for c)
   e. f. g. h.
   i. j. k. l. (none for o)
   m. n. o. p.
4. Check shapes
5. 4 lines of symmetry
6. a. b. c. 3 lines of symmetry
7. i) a, f, i, o and q
   ii)
   a. 0   b. 2   c. 2   d. 5
   e. 2   f. 0   g. 8   h. 3
   i. 0   j. 5   k. 1   l. 2
   m. 1   n. 2   o. 0   p. 12
   q. 0   r. 8   s. 12 t. 3

Ex 2
1. a. b.
2. a. b. c.
3. a. b. c.
4. a. b. c.
5. a. b. c.

Answers to Chapter 3

Ex 1
1. a. 0·3   b. 0·9   c. 1·2   d. 3·3
   e. 5·6   f. 0·6
2. a   b   c
   d
3. a. 0·2   b. 0·7   c. 2·2   d. 3·5
   e. 0·9   f. 3·8
4. 0·7
5. a. 0·43   b. 0·29   c. 0·75
6. a. 2·31   b. 3·14
7. a. b.
   c. d.
8. a. tenths   b. hundredths
9. a. tens   b. units
   c. tenths   d. hundredths
10. 0·09, 0·17, 0·95, 1·04, 1·16, 1·61
11. a. 1·3   b. 2·3   c. 3·8   d. 0·17
    e. 1·16 f. 1·3
12. a. 0·2   b. 0·8   c. 2·7   d. 2·5
    e. 1·25 f. 0·45
13. a. 1·45 m   b. 1·95 m   c. 37·5 kg

Ex 2
1. a. 2·5 m   b. 3·9 m   c. 2·2 m
2. a. 8·4   b. 11·4   c. 22·8   d. 3·9
   e. 1·5   f. 4·5
3. a. 2·3   b. 1·5   c. 3·2   d. 5·2
   e. 8·6
4. a. 0·25 cm   b. 0·37 cm
5. a. 1·35   b. 3·66   c. 5·35   d. 9·29
   e. 1·24   f. 3·78   g. 4·45   h. 6·05
   i. 1·27   j. 5·37   k. 3·84   l. 9·32
   m. 1·44   n. 6·75   o. 1·28   p. 10·05
6. A = 7·5   B = 8·4   C = 9·8   D = 10·4
   E = 11·5 F = 12·3

Ex 3
1. a. 4   b. 7   c. 4   d. 1
   e. 10   f. 15   g. 9   h. 8
   i. 41   j. 100
2. a. 7   b. 4   c. 8   d. 2
   e. 5   f. 1   g. 11   h. 24
   i. 59
3. a. £4   b. £6   c. £3   d. £9
   e. £13 f. £15 g. £17 h. £19
   i. £0   j. £1   k. £1   l. £101
4. a. 7 cm b. 9 cm c. 10 cm d. 2 cm
   e. 3 cm f. 7 cm g. 15 cm h. 21 cm
   i. 25 cm j. 34 cm k. 42 cm l. 69 cm
5. a. 2   b. 4   c. 7   d. 9
   e. 5   f. 8   g. 12   h. 12
   i. 26   j. 1   k. 28   l. 32
6. a. 8   b. 8   c. 5   d. 4
   e. 5   f. 10   g. 2   h. 13
   i. 24   j. 1   k. 1   l. 1
   m. £881 n. 17 cm o. 2 l
7. a. 5   b. 1   c. 2   d. 10

Ex 4
1. a. 7·9   b. 8·8   c. 11   d. 11·3
   e. 0·59 f. 0·79 g. 1·27 h. 1·29
   i. 9·54 j. 9·55 k. 7·92 l. 8·15
   m. 0·3   n. 7·4   o. 9·1   p. 3
   q. 4·9   r. 5·8   s. 6·25 t. 4·68

6. a. A B C D E J K L M
      Q T U V W Y 3 4 7
   b. H I 8
   c. F G N P R S Z 1 2 5 6 9
10. See Diagram

2. a. 20·9 cm   b. 30 cm   c. 23·7 cm
3. a 7·1 kg   b. 0·4 miles c. £19·90
   d. 11·2 km

4. a. 7·1   b. 26·2   c. 70·5   d. 101·7
   e. 8·78   f. 7·49   g. 9·63   h. 14·29
   i. 7·11   j. 26·34 k. 31·01 l. 57·03
   m. 6·2   n. 22·2   o. 46·7   p. 7·25
   q. 1·27   r. 4·22   s. 3·07   t. 8·42
   u. 2·07   v. 3·71   w. 2·58   x. 1·89
5. a. £7·69   b. £60·81 c. £47·73
   d. £15·81 e. £37·65 f. £78·64
   g. £3·21   h. £3·61   i. £0·04
   j. £34·30 k. £67·51 l. £20·63
6. £33·75   7. £1·85   8. 6·6
9. 50·5 kg   10. 1·95 miles
11. 0·38 cm   12. £9·96
13. a 117·31 kg   b. 8·15 kg
14. a. i) 1·78 m   ii) 3·06 m   b. 1·28 m
15. a. i) £13·93 ii) £37·14   iii) £73·44
    b. £7·38

Answers to Chapter 4

Ex 1
1. a. 0700   b. before (0945)
   c. 1600   d. after (2235)
2. a. 0840   b. 0145   c. 0600   d. 1520
   e. 1425   f. 2100   g. 0635   h. 2050
   i. 0405   j. 0958   k. 1200   l. 0005
   m. 1205   n. 2332   o. 0152   p. 2240
   q. 2344   r. 0000
3. a. 6 am   b. before (10·45 am)
   c. 5 pm   d. after (6·50 pm)
4. a. 3·30 am   b. 11·50 am   c. 9·20 am
   d. 3·45 am   e. 5·40 pm   f. 10·25 pm
   g. 2·40 am   h. 6·45 pm   i. 9·20 pm
   j. 6·12 pm   k. noon   l. 6·50 pm
   m. 3·45 am   n. 3·25 pm   o. 11·45 pm
   p. 9·05 pm   q. 12·40 am   r. 5·05 am
5. 2250 and 0635
6. 8·15 pm and 5·55 am

Ex 2
1. a. 3h   b. 3h 30m   c. 5h 30m
   d. 4h 10m e. 20m   f. 5h 35m
   g. 2h 25m h. 1h 15m   i. 1h 25m
   j. 3h 10m
2. A = 6 pm   B = 3·55 pm   C = 11 pm
   D = 10·30 am E = 1·15 am
3. 3 hrs 15 mins
4. 3 hrs 43 mins
5. a. i) 1h 10m   ii) 45m   iii) 6h 50m
   b. i) 1·25pm   ii) 2·10 pm
6. 10 hrs 25 mins
7. 10 hrs 35 mins
8. a. 1h 35m   b. 1155   c. 10
9. julie by 5 mins

Ex 3
1. a. 24   b. 19   c. 54
   d. 2m 16s e. 5m 9s   f. 23m
2. 3 mins 15 secs
3. a. 1m 40s b. 2m 33s c. 3m 50s
4. a. 1h 35m b. 4h 25m c. 8h 20m
5. a. 9m 55s b. 5m 20s c. 13m 40s
   d. 3m 5s   e. 4m 50s f. 2m 50s
6. 9 mins 20 secs
7. 1 hr 30 mins
8. a. 3m 25·4s b. 5m 17·1s c. 9m 4·8s
   d. 6m 0·9s   e. 45·2s
9. a. 6h 15m 20·5s   b. 7h 38m 10·2s
   c. 5h 59m 0·6s
10. 1 min 14·3 secs
11. a. BILL   b. 1·7 secs
12. a. 3·9 secs   b. 3m 14·5s
13. 2 mins 30 secs

Answers to Chapter 5

Ex 1
1.
| 12 | 13 | 14 | 15 | 16 | 17 |
| 4 | 6 | 7 | 3 | 2 | 2 |

2. a.
| D | T | F | R | S |
| 2 | 3 | 7 | 1 | 3 |

b. 3   c. football d. 6   e. 16

3. a.

38	39	40	41	42	43	44
1	2	4	9	5	0	3

b. 4   c. 8

4. a.

S1	S2	S3	S4	S5	S6
5	1	3	2	4	6

b. S6   c. S2 (only one once)
5. a. i) 4   ii) 6   iii) 9   iv) 3   v) 5
   b. 27
6. a. i) 8   ii) 20 iii) 12 iv) 11 v) 6
   b. 14
7. a. i) 6   ii) 8   iii) 9   iv) 11
   b. P7   c. 36
8. a. i) 20 ii) 2   iii) 18 iv) 22
   b. 90   c. girls (low football)
9. a. i) 20 ii) 12 iii) 19 iv) 29 v) 44
   b. hot dogs   c. 10   d. 124
10. See bar graph
11. See bar graph
12. a. A - 5   B - 10   C - 12   D - 21   E - 12
    b. See bar graph

Ex 2
1. a. i) 120 cm   ii) 130 cm   iii) 135 cm
   b. 16   c. 8   d. 122 - 123 cm
2. a. i) 150   ii) 225   iii) 300
      iv) 225   v) 275   vi) 325
   b. 9 am
   c. approx 8·15 am, 10·30 am and 12·30 pm
   d. 8 am to 9 am
   e. people starting work/school etc.
3. a. 600
   b. i) 200   ii) 1400   iii) 300
   c. 200
   d. i) May to June   ii) Sept to Oct
   e. 5000
   f. Summer - warmer (more sales)
      Winter - colder (less sales)
4. a. i) 28   ii) 29
   b. Tues & Wed   c. Thu
   d. Wed (most sales)
5. a. i) Cars R Us   ii) Best Cars
      iii) Cars R Us   iv) Same
   b. i) Cars 400 - Best 200
      ii) Cars 300 - Best 350
      iii) Cars 250 - Best 450
   c. Best Cars
6. See line graph
7. See line graph
8. See line graph

Ex 3
1. a. Fish
   b. Cat, dog, mouse, fish
2. a. Cola
   b. Cola, orange, water, irn-bru, lemon
3. a. $\frac{2}{10}$ b. $\frac{3}{10}$
4. a. i) $\frac{4}{10}$ ii) $\frac{2}{10}$ iii) $\frac{3}{10}$ iv) $\frac{1}{10}$
   b. Indian, Italian, Chinese, french
5. a. 2   b. 4   c. 8
6. a. 20   b. 15   c. 10   d. 5
7. a. $\frac{1}{20}$
   b. i) $\frac{9}{20}$ ii) $\frac{5}{20}$ iii) $\frac{4}{20}$ iv) $\frac{2}{20}$
   c. 5
   d. i) 45   ii) 25   iii) 20   iv) 10
8. See pie chart showing :-
   maths – $\frac{10}{20}$ english – $\frac{4}{20}$ french – $\frac{1}{20}$
   science – $\frac{3}{20}$ history – $\frac{2}{20}$

Ex 4
1. a. i) 12   ii) 7   iii) 5   iv) 24
   b. i) 27   ii) 12   iii) 53
   c. 29
2. a. i) 5   ii) 4   iii) 3   iv) 1
   b. i) french   ii) music

Answers Level D

iii) P.E.   iv) R.E.
c. i) Mon 1, Tue 2, Wed 4 & 5, Fri 4
   ii) Mon 2, Tue 5, Thu 2, Fri 2
   iii) Wed 1, Fri 3
   iv) Mon 5

3. a. i) £24   ii) £30   iii) £35   iv) £40
   b. small standard
4. a. i) £217   ii) £311   iii) £399   iv) £350
   b. Sun Hotel for 2 weeks
   c. i) £434   ii) £598

5. a. £149   b. £279   c. £358   d. £408
   e. £665
6. a. i) £5·50   ii) £12·50
      iii) £8·50   iv) £8·50
   b. 11 - 20 kg and between 5 - 10 km

Answers to Chapter 6

Ex 1
1. a. 37   b. 45   c. 45·2   d. 72·1
   e. 127·8   f. 9·4   g. 30·08   h. 0·147
2. a. 596   b. 874   c. 205   d. 260
   e. 547   f. 268   g. 5·89   h. 0·68
3. a. 11·6 kg   b. 116 kg
4. a. 414   b. 2760   c. 90   d. 0·3
5. a. 900   b. 9   c. 99   d. 0·9
6. £23·60   7. £50080

Ex 2
1. a. 1·42   b. 3·59   c. 0·784   d. 24·75
   e. 2·382   f. 47·827   g. 5·702   h. 4·6
   i. 0·8   j. 0·034   k. 0·02   l. 0·0047
2. a. 4·884   b. 4·1712   c. 0·158   d. 0·4204
   e. 4·7   f. 0·09   g. 0·056   h. 0·006
3. a. 0·427 g   b. £708·03   c. £2·52
4. a. 6   b. 8·03   c. 42·7   d. 0·06
5. a. 3·03   b. 45·1   c. 0·65   d. 0·07
6. £0·35

Ex 3
1 a. 32   b. 30   c. 48   d. 28
   e. 40   f. 27   g. 35   h. 48
   i. 54   j. 45   k. 54   l. 45
   m. 63   n. 36   o. 42   p. 100
   q. 42   r. 56   s. 40   t. 72
   u. 72   v. 49   w. 81   x. 63
2. a. 9·8   b. 17·4   c. 61·2   d. 461·5
   e. 250·2   f. 228·2   g. 292·8   h. 474·3
   i. 34·09   j. 39·12   k. 183·2   l. 30·96
   m. 17·01   n. 41·3   o. 460·6   p. 61·56
3. a. 6·8   b. 8·1   c. 34·4   d. 17·1
   e. 32   f. 74·4   g. 22·19   h. 16·98
   i. 45·92   j. 34·9   k. 277·8   l. 248·4
4. a. £25·92   b. £43·68   c. 21·33 cm
   d. 49·74 cm   e. 180·6 m²   f. £14·10
   g. £63·40   h. 139·2 m   i. 56·22 cm
   j. 43·96 cm   k. 15·4 kg

Ex 4
1. a. 4   b. 5   c. 6   d. 7
   e. 8   f. 3   g. 7   h. 8
   i. 6   j. 9   k. 9   l. 5
   m. 9   n. 4   o. 7   p. 8
   q. 6   r. 8   s. 5   t. 8
   u. 9   v. 7   w. 9   x. 7
2. a. 4·2   b. 3·2   c. 1·7   d. 1·3
   e. 2·3   f. 6·3   g. 6·7   h. 4·2
   i. 3·68   j. 2·45   k. 1·89   l. 1·95
   m. 0·26   n. 1·39   o. 1·23   p. 1·06
   q. 0·37   r. 1·22   s. 1·22   t. 1·09
   u. 6·8   v. 1·87   w. 1·27   x. 0·1
3. a. 4·7   b. 2·4   c. 1·9   d. 1·09
   e. 3·4   f. 10·6   g. 11·3   h. 7·81
   i. 1·19   j. 0·13   k. 1·08   l. 1·97
   m. 3·69   n. 2·75   o. 2·09   p. 10·3
   q. 0·37   r. 1·22   s. 1·22   t. 1·09
   u. 6·8   v. 1·87   w. 1·27   x. 0·1
4. a. 0·29 kg   b. £6·86
   c. i) 12·9   ii) £1·41
   iv) 1·26   v) 11·5   vi) 0·19
   d. 4·38 cm   e. £2·73   f. £0·89
   g. £0·78   h. 22·5 mins   i. £0·57
   j. 0·3 l

Ex 5
1. £43·84   2. 4·5 mins
3. Dougal by £3·01
4. £14·28   5. £5·46
6. No (1·9 m short)

7. £0·84   8. £15·70
9. No (£0·59 short)
10. £8·24   11. £0·98   12. 7·8 l

13. £3·55
14. a. £29·30   b. £12·27   c. £5·21
15. 7 adults 5 children
16. 30·9 secs

Answers to Chapter 7

Ex 1
1. a. 3   b. 8   c. 5
2. a. 14   b. 0   c. 12   d. 8
   e. 9   f. 10   g. 9   h. 0
   i. 11   j. 29   k. 3   l. 9
   m. 7   n. 8   o. 7   p. 0
   q. 18   r. 40   s. 2   t. 9
   u. 3
3. a. +   b. –   c. x   d. ÷
   e. –   f. x or ÷   g. +   h. ÷
   i. +   j. –   k. ÷   l. x
4. 24, 16, 80 and 5
5. 2,2,6,8,9,15,16,20,28,32,36,60,72,142,146,
   288
6. a. 7   b. 7   c. 8   d. 9
   e. 18   f. 8
7. Cake A by 1
8. a. 12 cm   b. 8 cm
   c. 20 cm   d. 12 cm
9. a. 13 + * = 22   b. 9p
10. a. 16 – * = 5   b. 5 x * = 100
       * = 11   * = 20
    c. $\frac{*}{4}$ = 7   d. 47 + * = 56
       * = 28   * = 9
    e. * x 4 = 160   f. 42 ÷ * = 6
       * = 40   * = 7
    g. * – 8 = 39
       * = 47

Ex 2
1. a. 7   b. 3   c. 12   d. 0
   e. 7   f. 10   g. 12   h. 5
   i. 11   j. 6   k. 7   l. 6
   m. 2   n. 22   o. 45   p. 24
   q. 16   r. 6
2. a. 8   b. 14   c. 5   d. 21
   e. 0   f. 30   g. 7   h. 6
   i. 3   j. 18   k. 5   l. 9
3. a. x + 4 = 11   b. y + 9 = 20
      x = 7   y = 11
   c. 2 x t = 18   d. 4 x n = 32
      t = 9   n = 8
   e. 3 x p = 150   f. f + 30 = 50
      p = 50   f = 20
4. 13 + S = 29
   S = 16
5. m ÷ 4 = 300
   m = 1200 g
6. 4 x t = 240
   t = 60
7. W – 250 = 1230
   W = 1480 ml
8. 3 x d = 36
   d = 12
9. 18 + a = 42
   a = 24
10. C ÷ 3 = 13
    C = 39

Ex 3
1. a. i) 14   ii) 20   iii) 100   iv) 2·4   v) 0
   b. i) 3   ii) 15   iii) 2500   iv) 3·2   v) 4·5
2. a. i) 18   ii) 13   iii) 11   iv) 36   v) 17·5
   b. i) 14   ii) 11   iii) 39   iv) 0·5   v) 6300
3. a. 20
   b. i) 2   ii) 8   iii) 26
   c. i) 15   ii) 9   iii) 27
4. a. 1 —> 8p   b. 8
      2 —> 16p
      3 —> 24p
      4 —> 32p
      5 —> 40p
      6 —> 48p
   c. IN —> x 8 —> OUT
   d. 80p

page 196

5. a. people   1 2 3 4 5 6
    tea bags   2 3 4 5 6 7
   b. add 1
   c. IN —> + 1 —> OUT

6. a. side   1 2 3 4 5 6
      perimeter 3 6 9 12 15 18
   b. <u>times</u> the length of the side by <u>3</u>
   c. IN —> x 3 —> OUT
   d. 30 cm
7. a. side   1 2 3 4 5 6
      perimeter 5 10 15 20 25 30
   b. IN —> x 5 —> OUT
   c. 80

8. a. 21
   b. i) 13   ii) 17   iii) 41   iv) 1   v) 3
9. a. i) 15   ii) 18
   b. i) 23   ii) 26
   c. No
10. a. 20   b. 4   c. 8   d. 24
    e. 4   f. 4$\frac{1}{2}$
11. 5
12. a. Players 1 2 3 4 5 6
       People   3 5 7 9 11 13
    b. IN —> x 2 —> +1 —> OUT
    c. 23
13. a. Days   1   2   3   4   5   6
       Cost   £10 £14 £18 £22 £26 £30
    b. IN —> x 4 —> +6 —> OUT
    c. £46

Answers to Chapter 8
Ex 1
1. a. right   b. obtuse   c. acute
   d. obtuse   e. acute   f. straight
   g. acute   h. reflex
2. a. right   b. obtuse   c. acute
   d. obtuse   e. acute   f. obtuse
   g. acute   h. acute
3. a. acute   b. obtuse   c. right
   d. acute
4. see diagram
5. a. 88°, 17°, 60°, 31°
   b. 110°, 176°, 91°, 169°
   c. 180°   d. 90°   e. 210°, 335°

Ex 2
1. a. ∠TAP   b. ∠VPL   c. ∠ISB
   d. ∠YXZ   e. ∠HJK   f. ∠POD
   g. ∠XTC   h. ∠UVK
2. a. ∠BCG(right)   b. ∠HTR(acute)
   c. ∠EBO(obtuse)   d. ∠CBS(reflex)
   e. ∠POY(acute)   f. ∠SWT(straight)
   g. ∠BUT(acute)   h. ∠ITN(obtuse)
3. a. ∠TYP, ∠MVT, ∠RVS
   b. ∠PTY, ∠MTV, ∠RSV
   c. ∠TPY, ∠VMT, ∠SRV
4. a. b. c. Check diagram
   d. Both angles are the same size

Ex 3
1. a. ∠ACB = 70°   b. ∠DFE = 160°
   c. ∠GHI = 90°   d. ∠KLJ = 65°
   e. ∠MON = 115°   f. ∠QRP = 95°
   g. ∠UST = 100°   h. ∠VWX = 65°
   i. ∠YAZ = 120°
2. a. 60°   b. 30°   c. 110°   d. 140°
   e. 50°   f. 160°
3. a. 28°   b. 111° c. 115°   d. 40°
   e. 137° f. 109° g. 12°   h. 175°
   i. 75°   j. 45°   k. 43°   l. 110°
   (accept answers 2° either side of above)

Ex 4
1. Check all diagrams

Ex 5
1. a. 60°   b. 20°   c. 45°   d. 65°
   e. 15°   f. 47°   g. 150° h. 40°
   i. 90°   j. 130° k. 55°   l. 145°
   m. 110° n. 130° o. 190°
2. a. 153° b. 46°   c. 13°   d. 104°
   e. 91°   f. 28°   g. 132° h. 90°
   i. 238°

Ex 6
1. a. p = 40°, q = 140°, r = 40°, s = 140°
   b. equal   c. equal
2. a. e = 80°, f = 100°, g = 80°, h = 100°
   b. i) equal   ii) equal
3. equal

4. a. 40°   b. 93°   c. 90°   d. 149°
   e. 100° f. 163°
5. a. 142° b. 142° c. 38°
6. a.   b.
   (diagrams)
   c.   d.
   e.   f.

Ex 7
1. equal   2. equal   3. equal
4. a. 76°   b. 52°   c. 68°
5. a.   b.
   (diagrams)
   c.   d.
6. equal   7. equal   8. equal
9. a. 25°   b. 76°   c. 122°
10. a.   b.
    (diagrams)
    c.   d.
    e.

Ex 8
1. Check drawing
2. a. 90°   b. 90°   c. 90°   d. 270°
   e. 45°   f. 135° g. 180° h. 135°
   i. 135° j. 135°
3. a. South   b. NE   c. SW
   d. i) 135° ii) 135° iii) 225° iv) 315°
   e. North   f. North   g. 270°   h. NE
4. a. i) N   ii) E   iii) SE   iv) S
   b. i) N   ii) W   iii) S   iv) SW
   c. W —> NE —> SE —> SW   d. East

Ex 9
1. a. 040°   b. 090°   c. 320°   d. 050°
   e. 099°   f. 010°   g. 180°   h. 240°
   i. 070°   j. 005°   k. 105°   l. 310°
2. a. 045°   b. 098°   c. 122°   d. 053°
   e. 112°   f. 030°   g. 047°   h. 240°
   (all ± 2°)

3. a. 090°   b. 270°   c. 045°   d. 000°
4. a. 315°   b. 250°   c. 340°   d. 181°
5. a. 247°   b. 320°   c. 340°   d. 146°
6. Barton 032°   Carton 072°
   Darton 097°   Earton 150°
   Feeton 195°   Geeton 252°
   Heaton 282°   Jayton 320°

7. See diagrams
8. See diagrams
9. 250°

Answers to Chapter 9
Ex 1
1. a. 10   b. 35   c. 30   d. 60
   e. 35   f. 35

2. a. 4   b. 6   c. 12   d. 12
   e. 12   f. 14
3. £10, £5, 50p, 20p, 10p
4. a. £7·31   b. various
5. a. £6·73   b. various

Ex 2
1. a. £3·79   b. £5·67   c. £4·81
   d. £7·56   e. £18·22 f. £18·41
   g. £18·91 h. £19·52 i. £4·11
   j. £2·36   k. £3·09   l. £1·37
   m. £12·17 n £16·15   o. £5·36
   p. £10·90 q. £14·40 r. £6·51
   s. £15·93 t. £9·99   u. £13·58
   v. £12·55 w. £20   x. £0·75
2. a. £7·79   b. £5·31   c. £15·03
   d. £10·88 e. £13·42 f. £4·83
   g. £19·98 h. £8·02   i. £19·90
   j. £11·01 k. £19·93 l. £17·69
3. a. £2·50   b. £6·45   c. £5·04
   d. £17   e. £17·30 f. £18·28
   g. £18·57 h. £19·94 i. £18·84
   j. £16·45 k. £12·32 l. £18·54
4. a. £1·30   b. £3·21   c. £2·12
   d. £1·10   e. £1·01   f. £2
   g. £1·02   h. £1·03   i. £8·18
   j. £5·37   k. £1·83   l. £3·79
   m. £0·24   n £2·52   o. £2·45
   p. £0·06
5. a. £17·14 b. £9·68   c. £12·51
   d. £5·82   e. £4·54   f. £15·24
   g. £0·77   h. £2·69   i. £19·02
   j. £1·57   k. £0·09   l. £20·65
6. a. £20·90 b. £24·30 c. £40·50
   d. £61·35 e. £35·75 f. £53·45
   g. £44·88 h. £85·08 i. £66·77
   j. £83·64 k. £41·10 l. £48·99
   m. £84·14 n £85·15   o. £59·30
   p. £73·75 q. £104·80 r. £100
7. a. £8·30   b. £13·70 c. £20
   d. £27·80 e. £17·20 f. £39
   g. £11·01 h. £15·37 i. £30·81
   j. £20·77 k. £16·90 l. £22·89
   m. £5·77   n £14·92   o. £29·32
   p. £1·08   q. £9·69   r. £51·03
8. a. £30·50 b. £58·96 c. £52·05
   d. £138·57 e. £62·20 f. £84·72
   g. £63·75 h. £99·80 i. £56·70
   j. £88·68 k. £44·59 l. £94·15
   m. £61·12 n £99·12   o. £95·22
   p. £99·63 q. £29·90 r. £283·00
9. a. £45·25 b. £32·69 c. £24·57
   d. £29·94 e. £22·49 f. £19·99
   g. £16·45 h. £19·09 i. £14·68
   j. £13·26 k. £14·23 l. £6·41
   m. £11·28 n £9·86   o. £5·17
   p. £10·58 q. £1·54   r. £7·29

Ex 3
1. a. £4·23   b. £4·27   c. £7·48
   d. £14·77   e. £11·12
2. a. £13·72   b £0·28
3. a. £17·15   b. £1·50
4. a. £13·20   b. £9·95   c. £3·25
5. a. Joe £18·66,   Jan £20·12,
      Dawn £20·29,   Dave £17·84
   b. Dawn (most)   Dave (least)
   c. £0·17
   d. Family (£38·80)   Others (£5·85)
6. £3·14
7. a. £17·77   b. £2·23

8. 6 pack = £3·28 each
   4 pack = £3·29 each (6 pack cheaper)

9. a. 5·70   b. 2·70   c. 3·20
      6·30   2·25   12·90
      7·50   0·70   3·52
      £19·50 **£5·65** **£19·62**
   d. 8·67
      8·96
      1·17
      £18·80

10. £7·38
11. a. £3·89   b. £7·45
12. 500g box   £1·33/100g   cheaper
    300g box   £1·48/100g
13. £2·30   14. £17·08   15. £4·38
16. £4·79   17. £5·18   18. £3·43
19. £15·60

Answers to Chapter 10

Ex 1

1. a. square   b. rectangle   c. triangle
   d. circle   e. kite   f. rhombus
   g. parallelogram
2. a. hexagon & rectangle
   b. kite & triangle
   c. triangle   d. rhombus   e. circle
   f. rectangle   g. square
   h. rectangle & parallelogram
3. a. see diagram b. pentagon
   c. 5   d. 5
4. a. 6   b. see diagram
   c. hexagon
5. a. see diagram
   b. i) heptagon   ii) octagon
      iii) nonagon   iv) decagon
6. a. square   b. right
   c. see diagram d. 2
7. a. see diagram b. 5
8. a. see diagram b. 9
9. i) 14   ii) 20   iii) 27   iv) 35
10. a. 1 square 4 triangles
    b. 5 squares
    c. 1 rectangle 2 squares
    d. 1 square 1 circle
    e. 1 pentagon 2 squares
    f. 4 hexagons
    g. 1 rectangle 4 triangles
    h. 1 octagon 8 squares
    i. 1 hexagon 6 triangles (and a star)
11. See designs

Ex 2

1. a. see diagram   b. scalene
2. a. see diagram   b. isosceles
3. a. see diagram   c. equilateral
4. a. isosceles   b. equilateral
   c. isosceles   d. scalene
   e. equilateral   f. isosceles
   g. isosceles   h. scalene
5. a. 35 cm   b. 28 cm   c. 33 cm
   d. 24 cm   e. 7·8 cm   f. 305 mm
   g. 12·9 cm   h. 24 m   i. 59 cm
6. a. 9 cm   b. 15 cm   c. 15 cm
   d. 10 cm   e. 10 cm   f. 9 cm

Ex 3

1. a. obtuse   b. right   c. acute
   d. acute   e. obtuse   f. acute
2. a. ΔGET   b. ΔFLK   c. ΔMIQ
   d. ΔRDL   e. ΔPHN   f. ΔVJS
3. ΔDGM right angled scalene
4. ΔXTP acute angled isosceles
5. a. ΔGMW right angled isosceles
   b. ΔRFD acute angled scalene
   c. ΔHSE acute angled equilateral
   d. ΔCZN obtuse angled scalene
   e. ΔSBJ right angled scalene
   f. ΔQVN obtuse angled isosceles

Ex 4

---

1. 2. 3. 4.   Check diagrams
5. Check diagrams (trapezium)
6. 7. 8. 9.   Check diagrams

Ex 5

1. Check diagram
2. 8 cm   3. 46 mm
4. a. 7 cm   b. 3·5 cm
5. a. Check diagram   b. 12 cm
6. length 42 cm, breadth 14 cm
7. a. 5 cm   b. 2·5 cm
8. a. 6 cm   b. 3 cm   c. 8 cm
9. – 11. Check diagrams

Ex 6

Check all diagrams

Answers to Chapter 11

Ex 1

1. a. $\frac{1}{2}$ b. $\frac{2}{3}$ c. $\frac{1}{3}$ d. $\frac{5}{8}$
   e. $\frac{5}{6}$ f. $\frac{9}{12}$ g. $\frac{1}{6}$ h. $\frac{3}{4}$
   i. $\frac{3}{5}$ j. $\frac{3}{8}$ k. $\frac{4}{5}$ l. $\frac{5}{6}$
   m. $\frac{7}{8}$ n. $\frac{7}{12}$ o. $\frac{5}{8}$

2. a. $\frac{1}{2}$ b. $\frac{1}{3}$ c. $\frac{2}{3}$ d. $\frac{3}{8}$
   e. $\frac{1}{6}$ f. $\frac{3}{12}$ g. $\frac{5}{6}$ h. $\frac{1}{4}$
   i. $\frac{2}{5}$ j. $\frac{5}{8}$ k. $\frac{1}{6}$ l. $\frac{1}{6}$
   m. $\frac{1}{8}$ n. $\frac{5}{12}$ o. $\frac{3}{8}$

3. a. $\frac{4}{15}$ b. $\frac{1}{15}$ c. $\frac{7}{15}$ d. $\frac{1}{15}$

4. check diagrams

Ex 2

1. a. $\frac{3}{6}$ b. $\frac{3}{9}$ c. $\frac{9}{15} = \frac{3}{5}$
2. a. $\frac{2}{8}$ b. $\frac{3}{12}$
3. a. $\frac{6}{8}$ b. $\frac{9}{12}$ c. various
4. a. $\frac{3}{6}$ b. $\frac{9}{15}$ c. $\frac{12}{21}$ d. $\frac{9}{24}$
   e. $\frac{21}{30}$ f. $\frac{39}{60}$
5. a. $\frac{4}{8}$ b. $\frac{12}{20}$ c. $\frac{16}{28}$ d. $\frac{12}{32}$
   e. $\frac{28}{40}$ f. $\frac{52}{80}$
6. various
7. a. $\frac{1}{2}$ b. $\frac{1}{3}$ c. $\frac{4}{5}$ d. $\frac{5}{9}$
   e. $\frac{3}{11}$ f. $\frac{9}{10}$
8. a. $\frac{1}{3}$ b. $\frac{2}{5}$ c. $\frac{3}{7}$ d. $\frac{6}{7}$
   e. $\frac{8}{11}$ f. $\frac{6}{15}$
9. a. $\frac{3}{4}$ b. $\frac{2}{3}$ c. $\frac{1}{6}$ d. $\frac{1}{3}$
   e. $\frac{1}{3}$ f. $\frac{1}{3}$ g. $\frac{5}{9}$ h. $\frac{1}{3}$
   i. $\frac{2}{5}$ j. $\frac{2}{7}$ k. $\frac{3}{11}$ l. $\frac{8}{9}$
   m. $\frac{1}{2}$ n. $\frac{1}{20}$ o. $\frac{1}{3}$ p. $\frac{4}{7}$
   q. $\frac{1}{3}$ r. $\frac{11}{16}$

Ex 3

1. a. 4   b. 4   c. 3   d. 8
   e. 9   f. 9   g. 12   h. 12
   i. 13   j. 20   k. 3   l. $3\frac{1}{2}$
2. a. 7   b. 6   c. 5   d. 8
   e. 14   f. 11   g. 4   h. 100
   i. 30
3. a. 20   b. 5   c. 6   d. 10
   e. i) 6   ii) 42
   f. i) 10   ii) 20
4. a. 9   b. i) 5   ii) 30
5. a. 8   b. 6   c. 4   d. 3

---

e. 3   f. 18

Ex 4

1. a. 14   b. 24   c. 16   d. 21
   e. 36   f. 14   g. 22   h. 35
   i. 28   j. 56   k. 108   l. 40
   m. 4   n. 27
2. a. 24   b. 18

Answers to Chapter 12

Ex 1

1. a. C(1, 2)   b. B(2, 5)   c. S(3, 3)
   d. F(4, 0)   e. V(5, 4)
2. A(2, 7)   B(10, 4)   C(4, 0)
   D(5, 4)   E(0, 9)   F(8, 2)
   G(4, 9)   H(1, 3)   I(8, 8)
3. a. i) T   ii) P   iii) M   iv) M
   b. i) (1, 8) ii) (5, 7) iii) (1, 5) iv) (9, 0)
   c. i) KNML
      ii) K(1, 8) N(1, 5) M(8, 5) L(8, 8)
4. see diagram   d. square
5.

hexagon

Ex 2

1. a. F (tree)   b. B (shoe)
   c. 5   d. 1
   e. E (present) f. D (pumpkin)
   g. C (turkey)
   h. C(0, 3) A(5, 3)
   i. E(2, 2) G(2, 4)
   j. F to A
2. a. (4, 7)   b. P   c. T   d. L
   e. K(0, 7) Q(4, 7) N(10, 7)
   f. K(0, 7)   g. W(8, 8)
   h. vertical
3. a. b.   c. (3, 3)

4. a. b.   c. (3, 3)

5. a. b.

   c.   d.

   e.

Ex 3

1 to 5

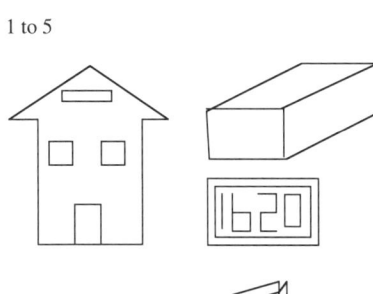

Answers to Chapter 13

Ex 1
1. a. Green 50%   b. Green 80%
      Red 30%   Red 20%
   c. Green 31%   d. Green 42%
      Red 7%   Red 36%
   e. Green 62%   f. Green 56%
      Red 29%   Red 2%
2. a. Green 48%   b. 100%
      Red 34%
      Blue 18%
3. a. i) 15% ii) 54%
   b. 31% c. 100 – (54 + 15)
4. a. $\frac{23}{100}$ b. $\frac{49}{100}$ c. $\frac{60}{100}$ d. $\frac{14}{100}$
   e. $\frac{99}{100}$ f. $\frac{17}{100}$ g. $\frac{66}{100}$ h. $\frac{8}{100}$
   i. $\frac{3}{100}$ j. $\frac{4}{100}$ k. $\frac{1}{100}$ l. $\frac{100}{100}$ (1)
5. a. 0·31 b. 0·59 c. 0·77 d. 0·11
   e. 0·18 f. 0·99 g. 0·09 h. 0·08
   i. 0·03 j. 0·04 k. 0·01 l. 1·0
6. a. $\frac{12}{100}$ (0·12)   b. $\frac{33}{100}$ (0·33)
   c. $\frac{50}{100}$ (0·50)   d. $\frac{25}{100}$ (0·25)
   e. $\frac{10}{100}$ (0·10)   f. $\frac{19}{100}$ (0·19)
   g. $\frac{68}{100}$ (0·68)   h. $\frac{40}{100}$ (0·40)
   i. $\frac{13}{100}$ (0·13)   j. $\frac{2}{100}$ (0·02)
   k. $\frac{5}{100}$ (0·05)   l. $\frac{6}{100}$ (0·06)
   m. $\frac{1}{100}$ (0·01)   n. $\frac{3}{100}$ (0·03)
   o. $\frac{100}{100}$ (1·0)
7. a. 19% b. 79% c. 8% d. 89%
   e. 41% f. 8% g. 62% h. 1%
   i. 1% j. 93% k. 50% l. 5%

Ex 2
1. a. 0·28 = 28%
   b. 8 ÷ 10 = 0·8 = 80%
   c. 3 ÷ 5 = 0·6 = 60%
   d. 18 ÷ 40 = 0·45 = 45%
2. a. 0·2 = 20%   b. 0·15 = 15%
   c. 0·8 = 80%   d. 0·28 = 28%
   e. 0·58 = 58%   f. 0·1 = 10%
3. a. 20% b. 20% c. 60% d. 20%
   e. 30% f. 4%
4. 75%
5. a. English 75% French 80% History 78%
   b. French   c. English

Ex 3

1. a. £30   b. 6p   c. 9 cm
2. a. £13   b. 28 km   c. 62 mm   d. $2
   e. 12 ml f. 200 m   g. 60 m   h. 20 ml
   i. 10 cm j. £450   k. 80 mm   l. 16 p
   m. £7·50 n. £2·50   o. £1·30
3. a. £15   b. 20 kg   c. 9 kg
4. a. £1·20 b. £10·80

Answers to Chapter 14

Ex 1
1. a. 2·1 cm   b. 5·3 cm   c. 6·8 cm
   d. 7·9 cm   e. 4·2 cm   f. 8·7 cm
2. a. 38 mm   b. 30 mm   c. 69 mm
   d. 21 mm   e. 62 mm
3. i) A 49 mm B 76 mm C 19 mm
      D 83 mm E 31 mm F 96 mm
   ii) F, D, B, A, E, C
4. a. 10·2 cm, 1·8 cm, 9·2 cm, 3·6 cm
   b. 8·4 cm
5. a. 38 mm   b. 16 mm
   c. 49 mm, 17 mm, 10 mm
6. 98 mm
7. a. i) 59 mm ii) 5·9 cm iii) 5 cm 9 mm
   b. i) 79 mm ii) 7·9 cm iii) 7 cm 9 mm
   c. i) 35 mm ii) 3·5 cm iii) 3 cm 5 mm
   d. i) 80 mm ii) 8·0 cm iii) 8 cm 0 mm
   e. i) 157 mm ii) 15·7 cm iii) 15 cm 7 mm
8. a. 3·4 cm   b. 3·6 cm   c. 7 cm
9. Check diagrams
10. a. equal   b. equal

Ex 2
1. a. 1000   b. 100   c. 10
   d. 1000   e. 100000   f. 1000000
2. a. 60   b. 20   c. 150   d. 5
   e. 42   f. 87   g. 129   h. 55
   i. 15   j. 92   k. 189   l. 213
3. a. 4   b. 7   c. 9   d. 13
   e. 3·5 f. 4·9 g. 20 h. 70
   i. 65 j. 200 k. 0·3 l. 0·7
4. a. 300   b. 900   c. 1400   d. 50
   e. 2500 f. 4900 g. 20000 h. 25
   i. 450 j. 705 k. 50 l. 1
5. a. 4   b. 7   c. 15   d. 40
   e. 4·4 f. 9·5 g. 0·5 h. 0·25
6. a. 3000   b. 12000   c. 25000
   d. 500   e. 5500   f. 2750
   g. 9800   h. 1070   i. 5200
   j. 12600   k. 2250   l. 800
7. a. 5   b. 18   c. 0·3   d. 7·5
   e. 18·4 f. 4·25 g. 2·15 h. 6·95
   i. 0·35 j. 0·78 k. 12·4 l. 300
8. 6 cm, 6·2 cm, 63 mm, 6cm 5 mm
9. 9 m, 8m 90 cm, 8·8 m, 870 cm
10. i) 120 cm   ii) 1·2 m
11. 25 m
12. a. 5000 m   b. 5 kl

Ex 3
1. a. 160 mm   b. 16 cm
2. a. 80 mm   b. 55 mm
3. 6·3 cm   4. 28 cm   5. 25 mm
6. 150 cm   7. 2·4 m   8. 1·5 km
9. 800 m

Ex 4
1. 37 cm
2. a. 36 cm   b. 63 mm   c. 16·2 m
3. 62 cm
4. a. 22 cm   b. 15·2 cm   c. 168 mm
   d. 26·2 m
5. 20 cm
6. a. 11 cm   b. 13·2 cm   c. 37 mm
7. a. 8 cm   b. 160 mm   c. 1 m
8. a. 15·2 m   b. £43·50
9. £405

Ex 5
1. a. 10 boxes   b. 10 cm²

2. a. 5 cm²   b. 4 cm²   c. 8 cm²
   d. 10 cm² e. 8 cm²   f. 8 cm²
   g. 7 cm²   h. 14 cm² i. 9 cm²
   j. 12 cm² k. 16 cm²
3. a. 14 cm²   b. 15 cm²   c. 14-15 cm²
   d. 10 cm²

Ex 6
1. 12 cm²
2. 40 cm²
3. a. 35 cm²   b. 36 cm²   c. 36 cm²
   d. 11 cm²   e. 25 cm²   f. 60 cm²
4. a. 700 m²   b. 2480 m²   c. 1350 m²
5. Kitchen   20 m²
   Bathroom   6 m²
   Bedroom 1   18 m²
   Bedroom 2   16 m²
   Living Room 40 m²
   Dining Room 30 m²

Ex 7
1. a/b. Check diagram c. 20 cm²   d. 10 cm²
2. a/b. Check diagram c. 24 cm²   d. 12 cm²
3. a/b. Check diagram c. 12 cm²   d. 6 cm²
4. a/b. Check diagram c. 25 cm²   d. 12·5 cm²
5. 8 cm²
6. a. 6 cm²   b. 14 cm²   c. 6 cm²
   d. $13\frac{1}{2}$ cm²   e. 14 cm²   f. 18 cm²
   g. 16 cm²   h. 15 cm²
7. a. 9 cm²   b. 19 cm²   c. $19\frac{1}{2}$ cm²
8. a. 25 cm²   b. 55 cm²   c. 18 cm²
   d. 32 cm²   e. 18 cm²   f. 6 cm²
   g. 105 cm²
9. a. 20 cm²   b. 10 cm²
   c. A = $\frac{1}{2}$ x l x b

Answers to Chapter 15

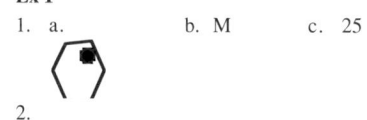

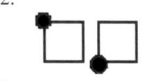

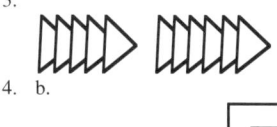

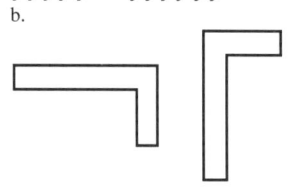

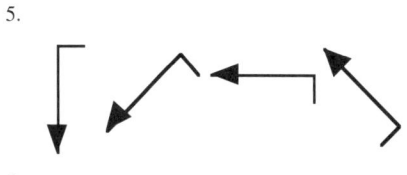

Ex 1
1. a.   b. M   c. 25

7. a. Check patterns
   b. i) 2 ii) 6 iii) 12 iv) 20
   c. i) 30 ii) 42 iii) 56 iv) 72
8. a. L   b. P   c. L   d. U

e. R   f. J
9./10./11.   Check diagrams

Ex 2
1. 4 times table starting with no. 8
2. a. 5 times table
    b. 7 times table
    c. 3 times table starting with no. 9
    d. 10 times table starting with no. 50
    e. 8 times table starting with no. 24
    f. starts at 36 and drops 4 each time

3. a. 30, 35, 40   b. 42, 49, 56
    c. 24, 27, 30   d. 100, 110, 120
    e. 56, 64, 72   f. 16, 12, 8
4. 7 go up by 3
5. a. begin at 3   go up by 2
    b. begin at 5   go up by 3
    c. begin at 9   go up by 4
    d. begin at 3   go up by 10
    e. begin at 62   go up by 5
    f. begin at 6   go up by 0·5
    g. begin at 3   go up by $1\frac{1}{2}$
    h. begin at 30   go down by 4
    i. begin at 70   go down by 9
    j. begin at 2000   go down by 100
6. a. 13, 15, 17
    b. 20, 23, 26
        29, 33, 37
        53, 63, 73
        87, 92, 97
        8·5, 9, 9·5
        $10\frac{1}{2}$, 12, $13\frac{1}{2}$
        14, 10, 6
        34, 25, 16
        1600, 1500, 1400
7. a. Check diagram
    b. 20, 24, 28   c. 4   d. 40
8. a. 20   b. 20, 25, 30   c. 5, 5
    d. 45
    e. i) 12   ii) 18   iii) 36   iv) 60
9. a. 8   b. 13   c. 21
    d. 1, 1, 2, 3, 5, 8, 13, 21, 34, 55, 89, 144
10. Check sequence
11. a 56
    b. 20 = (4 x 5), 30 = (5 x 6), 42 = (6 x 7)
    c. 56 = (7 x 8)
    d. 2, 6, 12, 20, 30, 42, 56, 72, 90, 110
12. Check diagrams
    b. 15 = 1 + 2 + 3 + 4 + 5
    c. 21 = 1 + 2 + 3 + 4 + 5 + 6
        28 = 1 + 2 + 3 + 4 + 5 + 6 + 7
        36 = 1 + 2 + 3 + 4 + 5 + 6 + 7 + 8
13. a. i) even   ii) odd
    b. (1 + 3 + 5 + 7) (1 + 3 + 5 + 7 + 9)
        (1 + 3 + 5 + 7 + 9 + 11)
        (1 + 3 + 5 + 7 + 9 + 11 + 13)
    c. 1, 4, 9, 16, 25, 36, 49
    d. 16 = (4 x 4)   25 = (5 x 5)
        36 = (6 x 6)   49 = (7 x 7)
    e. Square numbers
    f. 1, 4, 9, 16, 25, 36
14. a. 5   b. 14   c. i) 30   ii) 55
    d. 204

Answers to Chapter 16

Ex 1
1. a. cube   b. cuboid
    c. cone   d. cylinder
    e. squared based pyramid
    f. sphere   g. triangular prism
2. a. cone   b. cylinder
    c. triangular prism d. sphere
    e. squared based pyramid
    f. cubes   g. sphere
    h. cuboid
3. a. 6   b. square
    c. 8   d. 12
    e. horizontal
    f. i)ii) PQorSR
    g. AD, PS, QR
    h. BQ, CR, DS (vertical
    i. Check list
4. a. 6   b. rectangles (and squares)
    c. 8   d. 12   e. HG, VT, RS

    f. FS, GT, HV   g. EH, FG, ST, RV
    h. Check list
5. a. 5   b. 1 square 4 triangles
    c. 5   d. 8   e. Check list
6. a. 5   b. 2 triangles 3 rectangles
    c. 6   d. PR   e. AP, BR
    f. 9   g. Check list
7. a. 2 faces, 1 curved, 1 circle
    b. 3 faces, 1 curved, 2 circles
8. Hemisphere
9. a. cone, cylinder
    b. hemisphere, cylinder, cuboid

Ex 2
1./2. Check models
3. a. 120 cm   b. 132 cm   c. 140 cm
4./5. Check models

Ex 3
1.-7. Check diagrams
8. a) b) d) f) are nets

Answers to Chapter 17

Ex 1
1. bath
2. egg cup, mug, frier
3. cereal
4. train, truck, car, bike
5. a. 4 teaspoons   b. tablespoon
    c. water   d. 2 cups
    e. 5 scones   f. $\frac{1}{4}$
6. $\frac{10}{30}$ ($\frac{1}{3}$)   7. 2   8. 5 days

Ex 2
1. a. 6   b. 4   c. 40   d. 5
    e. 20
2. a. 400 ml   b. 600 ml   c. 200 ml
    d. 900 ml
3. a. lime, lemon   b. blackcurrant
    c. 100 ml   d. 400 ml
4. a. i) 10 ml   ii) 380 ml
    b. i) 360 ml   ii) 580 ml   iii) 420 ml
5. a. 400 ml   b. 500 ml   c. 1000 ml
    d. 900 ml

Ex 3
1. a. 3000 ml   b. 9000 ml   c. 15000 ml
    d. 20000 ml   e. 1500 ml   f. 6800 ml
    g. 7400 ml   h. 5250 ml
2. a. 4 l b. 7 l c. 12 l d. 25 l
    e. 7·5 l f. 8·2 l g. 40 l h. 2·85 l

Ex 4
1. 4 cm³   2. 4 cm³   3. 9 cm³
4. 18 cm³   5. 12 cm³   6. 6 cm³
7. 27 cm³   8. 10 cm³   9. 41 cm³
10. 24 cm³

Answers to Chapter 18

1. 21000, 20105, 20009, 19780, 19099, 19000
2. a. 21060   b. 65400
3. a. Twenty four thousand and eighty
    b. Eighty thousand three hundred and two
    c. Seven thousand and five
    d. Eighty nine thousand and fifty seven
4. thousand
5. a. 79100   b. 139,000
6. a. 24   b. 3   c. 21
7. 11·72
8. a. 0·37   b. 0·82   c. 0·07
9. cm   513 cm   420 cm   609 cm
    m   5·13 m   4·2 m   6·09 m
    m & cm 5 m 13 cm 4 m 20 cm 6 m 9 cm
10. a. £1·72   b. Check list
11. a. 100   b. 62   c. 126   d. 14
    e. 860   f. 440   g. 166   h. 140
12. a. 6427 b. 21·86 c. 5749 d. 3·28
13. a. 120   b. 25   c. 60   d. 12
14. a. 370   b. 52000 c. 60300 d. 8·1
    e. 4·37 f. 3·2   g. 9·7   h. 590
15. a. 42·21 b. 192·15 c. 4·66 d. 0·17
16. a. 80   b. 700   c. 6050 d. 20

17. a. 600   b. 3700   c. 23700 d. 10000
18. a. 7   b. 60   c. 300   d. 950
19. a. 40   b. 90   c. 2500   d. 100
20. a. 600   b. 140   c. 2400   d. 140
21. a. 9, 11, 13   b. 21, 24, 27
    c. 100, 50, 25   d. 48, 96, 192
    e. 19, 22, 25   f. 54, 50, 46
22. 110, 178, 288, 466
23. 2 x ($l + b$)
24. a. 118 mm   b. 11·8 cm
    c. 11 cm 8 mm
25. a. 100 g   b. 200 cm   c. 5 ml
26. a. 7·35 am   b. 1·50 pm   c. 8·58 pm
    d. 12·45 am
27. a. 0455   b. 1750   c. 2340
    d. 1520   e. 0015   f. 1245
28. a. 1·10 pm   b. 2 hrs 20 mins
29. a. 46 cm   b. 100 cm   c. 21·2 cm
    d. 21·5 cm   e. 48 cm   f. 34 cm
30. a. 20 cm²   b. 22 cm²   c. 31·5 cm²
31. a. Check diagram
    b. 18 cm²   c. 9 cm²
32. a. 4 cm²   b. 10 cm²
33. a. square based pyramid   b. cube
    c. sphere   d. cuboid
    e. cone   f. triangular prism
34. a. 12   b. 8   c. 9
35. a. 8   b. 6   c. 5
36. a. octagon   b. equilateral triangle
    c. rhombus
37. a. centre   b. diameter
    c. radius   d. circumference
38. a. cuboid   b. cube
    c. square based pyramid
    d. triangular prism   e. cylinder
39. See drawing
40. SE

41. P(7, 5) Q(3, 0) R(0, 4)
42. a. 1   b. 5   c. 2   d. 0
43.   44.

45. a. 34°   b. 148°
46. a. obtuse   b. straight   c. acute
    d. right
47. Check diagram
48. Check diagram
49. a. 064°   b. 150°   c. 230°
50. a. £5   b. £30
    c. Sean (Wed)   d. Billy (£40)
51. Check bar graph
52. a. $\frac{1}{4}$ b. i) 100   ii) 25